The Political Economy of Environmental Policy

NEW HORIZONS IN ENVIRONMENTAL ECONOMICS

General Editors: Wallace E. Oates, *Professor of Economics, University of Maryland, USA* and Henk Folmer, *Professor of Economics, Wageningen Agricultural University, The Netherlands and Professor of Environmental Economics, Tilburg University, The Netherlands*

This important series is designed to make a significant contribution to the development of the principles and practices of environmental economics. It includes both theoretical and empirical work. International in scope, it addresses issues of current and future concern in both East and West and in developed and developing countries.

The main purpose of the series is to create a forum for the publication of high quality work and to show how economic analysis can make a contribution to understanding and resolving the environmental problems confronting the world in the twenty-first century.

Recent titles in the series include:

The Political Economy of Environmental Policy

A Public Choice Approach to Market Instruments

Bouwe R. Dijkstra

Postdoctoral Researcher,
Department of Economics, Faculty of Law,
University of Groningen, The Netherlands

NEW HORIZONS IN ENVIRONMENTAL ECONOMICS

Edward Elgar
Cheltenham, UK ● Northampton, MA, USA

Published by
Edward Elgar Publishing Limited
Glensanda House
Montpellier Parade
Cheltenham
Glos GL50 1UA
UK

Edward Elgar Publishing, Inc.
6 Market Street
Northampton
Massachusetts 01060
USA

A catalogue record for this book
is available from the British Library

ISBN 1 85898 964 7

Printed and bound in Great Britain by Bookcraft (Bath) Ltd.

Contents

List of Figures

List of Tables

Foreword

This is the streamlined version of my PhD thesis 'The Political Economy of Instrument Choice in Environmental Policy'. The largest cuts have been made in Chapters 5, 6 and 10. I would like to thank the people of Edward Elgar for their excellent assistance in preparing the manuscript.

The defining moment of my PhD research must have been in July 1994, when we had dinner at Hotel Engiadina in Silvaplana, Switzerland. Heinrich Ursprung was talking about how he auctioned 20 DM to his students: 'Everyone has to pay the amount they bid to me. Whoever pays the most, will get the 20 DM.' Arye Hillman said: 'The equilibrium is clearly a mixed strategy.' And I thought: 'What would I do?' and: 'What in the world is a mixed strategy?' In the meantime, I have found the answer to the second question.

The Silvaplana workshop aroused my interest in rent seeking. It marks one of the more idiosyncratic twists in my research, for which my promotor Andries Nentjes gave me every room. I want to thank him for that, as well as for his tireless efforts to make sense of my findings. My interest in rent seeking led me to Casper de Vries, from whose insistence on clarity, depth and rigour this thesis has greatly benefited.

The survey of Dutch interest groups (Chapter 5) is definitely something I could not have done on my own. Jan de Vries, Dick van Namen and Karin Wittebrood have been very helpful in setting up the survey. Many thanks are due to the participants, listed in Table 5.1, especially to those who granted me an interview. They have answered a lot of questions, some of which did not make much sense to them. Moreover, they kindly agreed to the elaborate quotations from their answers under their own names.

The NAKE (Netherlands Network of Economics) offered great opportunities for learning more and meeting other PhD students. The course 'Behavioral models of government decision making' by Frans van Winden has been especially helpful for my research. Furthermore, in the framework of NAKE, Jan Potters and Pieter Ruys provided me with useful comments on my research plan.

In the 'miscellaneous' category, I thank Rob Dellink for trying to incorporate instruments of environmental policy into a general equilibrium model of the Dutch economy. Randolph Sloof had a good look at an earlier piece of mine on cooperation in rent seeking contests, which was still pretty much misguided.

Georg von Wangenheim played the same role for the two-stage rent seeking game.

Finally, the largest group, both in terms of persons and contacts, is of course the Department of Economics and Public Finance at the Faculty of Law. I am not making a distinction here between (former) PhD students (Jan-Tjeerd Boom, Anton Duizendstraal, Mirjam Koster, Roelof de Jong, Rob van der Laan, Frans de Vries and Edwin Woerdman), other general economists (Pierre Eijgelshoven and ZhongXiang Zhang), business economists (Wout Hendriksen, Han Scholten and Teo Tuinstra) and secretaries (Christina Huisman). They have all been very interested in what I was doing. Some of them even found out what it was. They have been inspiring colleagues and pleasant company to have seminars, coffee, lunch and card and laser games with.

Groningen, September 1998

1. Introduction

1. THE PROBLEM

When the government wants to reduce the polluting emissions of firms, it can do so in several ways, i.e. with several instruments. These instruments of environmental policy are usually divided into three main classes, according to the three ways in which a government can influence an agent's behaviour (e.g. Turner and Opschoor, 1994):

- with direct regulation, also known as 'command-and-control', the government changes the set of options open to agents. The government can restrict, or even forbid, certain actions and prescribe other actions. This is the traditional approach to environmental policy. Instruments of direct regulation are, for example, licences for a certain amount of emissions, maximum emissions to input (or output) ratios, mandatory use of specific abatement equipment and bans on the use of specified inputs;
- with market instruments, or economic instruments, the government changes the costs and/or benefits relevant to agents. These instruments indirectly result in environmentally friendly behaviour, because they make such behaviour in a firm's own (financial) interest. Examples of market instruments are emissions charges[1] (first proposed by Pigou, 1920) and tradable emission permits (first proposed by Dales, 1968). Tradable emission permits can be grandfathered (i.e. distributed for free among incumbent firms) or auctioned. Emissions charges and an auction of tradable permits are also called financial instruments;
- with suasive instruments, the government changes the priorities and significance agents attach to the environment. This class of instruments works even more indirectly than market instruments, because firms are supposed to reduce emissions of their own accord. Examples of suasive instruments are education, information extension, training, pressure and negotiation. One could say that covenants, or voluntary agreements, are a suasive instrument. However, when industry makes a commitment to a certain action (however weak this commitment is), a covenant also has elements of direct regulation.

In our subsequent treatment of instruments, we shall largely disregard suasive instruments, because it seems that government cannot rely on suasion alone to reduce industry emissions.

With economic analysis we can compare the performance of market instruments and direct regulation on social welfare or efficiency: with which instrument can the environmental goal be reached at the lowest social cost? On the criterion of efficiency, market instruments perform better than direct regulation. The efficiency advantages of market instruments can be divided into the following three classes:[2]

- static efficiency: the available emission room is distributed efficiently across the firms. Emission reduction measures are taken there, where they are least costly.

  With emissions charges, static efficiency is realized because firms reduce emissions up to the point where it is more profitable to pay the charge. In other words, their marginal cost of emission reduction (the cost of the last unit of emission reduction) will equal the charge rate. Because the charge rate is equal for all firms, the marginal emission reduction cost will be equal for all firms. Thus, there is no alternative distribution of emissions across firms that would decrease aggregate costs for all firms: emissions charges are statically efficient.

  With tradable emission permits, static efficiency is realized because firms with high emission reduction costs can buy permits from firms with low emission reduction costs. Firms with high emission reduction costs will reduce their emissions less than firms with low emission reduction costs, to the point where their marginal emission reduction costs are equal to each other and to the permit price.

  Static efficiency can in principle be achieved with direct regulation as well. But then the government would have to find out and implement the efficient distribution of the emission room. It would have to collect a great deal of information about abatement technologies and their cost. Furthermore, firms may be reluctant to report this information sincerely. Thus, the government had better leave the efficient distribution of the emission room to the market, instead of trying to find it itself;

- productive efficiency: with market instruments, the size of the firms and the number of firms is optimal. With direct regulation, firms could be too large or too small, and the number of firms is too large. There are too many firms with direct regulation, because firms do not have to pay for their residual emissions. In order to reach the optimal number of firms and production quantity per firm, the input of the environment should be treated in the same way as other inputs like capital and labour;

- dynamic efficiency: with direct regulation, firms have no incentive to reduce their emissions beyond the level that environmental policy prescribes. With market instruments, firms have a permanent incentive to further reduce their emissions. When they decrease emissions, they have to pay less emissions charges (in case emissions charges are applied), or they can sell emission permits (in case of tradable emission permits). This permanent incentive to further reduce emissions will prompt firms to do R&D for new and superior ways of emission reduction, i.e. to innovate. These innovations will reduce the cost of emission reduction in the future. This property of market instruments to offer more incentives to innovate than direct regulation, is called dynamic efficiency.

Because economists believe market instruments are efficient for society as a whole, they would like to see them applied in environmental policy. Presuming a tendency for society to adopt the efficient solution to a particular problem,[3] one might expect that economists would only have to present their case. According to this line of reasoning, once the relevant actors understand the case for market instruments, they will be implemented.

However, this is not the way it works. Market instruments are only rarely applied in environmental policy. And when they are applied, it is often in a different way than economists recommend.[4] This discrepancy between economists' recommendations and policy reality is the theme of this book. The question we seek to answer is thus: 'Why are market instruments not more widely applied in environmental policy, although economists believe they are efficient?'

2.   THE APPROACH

As we shall see in Chapter 2, one can think of many reasons why market instruments are not applied in reality, although economists think they are efficient. Perhaps political actors do not understand the workings of, and the case for, market instruments. Perhaps market instruments are not as efficient as economists claim, because their assumptions are not realistic. Alternatively, market instruments may be efficient in a narrow economic sense, but this does not necessarily make them the best instrument overall. Economic models only model part of reality, and the part they leave out may be relevant in this context. For instance, in a model that demonstrates the efficiency advantages of market instruments it is assumed that there is full employment. Thus, when in reality there is involuntary unemployment instead of full employment, and more workers are laid off in the polluting industry with market instruments than with direct regulation, these costs are ignored in the model.

In our own analysis, however, we shall assume that market instruments are efficient, or welfare-maximizing. That is, we assume that somehow we can quantify and aggregate all advantages and disadvantages of market instruments compared to direct regulation, and that on aggregate the advantages of market instruments are larger than the disadvantages. This assumption may be more plausible for some areas of environmental policy than for others. If it is, then our analysis is only applicable to those situations where the advantages of market instruments can be expected to outweigh their disadvantages. We feel that even in this subset of environmental policy, the application of market instruments is still far from universal.

Taking for granted that market instruments are welfare-maximizing for society as a whole, we will try to explain the political choice for direct regulation by a public choice, or political economy, argument. According to this argument, there are powerful interest groups that prefer direct regulation to market instruments. These interest groups are so powerful, that they can block the introduction of market instruments.

We can cast the political economy argument in terms of weighing the advantages and disadvantages of market instruments. When we want to assess whether a market instrument or direct regulation is better for society as a whole, we have to bring all the advantages and disadvantages of market instruments under one common denominator, which we have called 'welfare'. In other words, we have to assign weights to all advantages and disadvantages. As we said above, we are looking at situations where the result of this weighing is that market instruments perform better than direct regulation. When in this case the political decision is to apply direct regulation, we can say that apparently a politician, or the political process, weighs the advantages and disadvantages in a different way than we did. The advantages of market instruments are given a relatively low weight, and/or the disadvantages of market instruments are given a relatively high weight. This is because the politician (or the political process) pays more attention to the people, or interest groups, that are against market instrument than to those in favour of market instruments. Of course, this is only a way of looking at the discrepancy between a researcher's finding that market instruments are more efficient than direct regulation and the political decision to apply direct regulation. It is not an explanation of this discrepancy. The question remains why a politician would weigh the disadvantages of market instruments more heavily, and their advantages less heavily, than a researcher would. This is the question we shall address in this book.

To recapitulate: we want to know why market instruments are seldom applied in environmental policy, although they are efficient. We will try to find an answer in political economy. This means that we will analyse instrument choice as a political decision, influenced by interest groups. We can then split our original question into the following two research questions:

1. What are the preferences of the relevant interest groups for environmental policy instruments?
2. Given the preferences of everyone affected by instrument choice, and given that market instruments are efficient, why does the political process so often

result in the choice of direct regulation?

With respect to the first question, we note that in our political economy approach, the existence of an interest group that is in favour of direct regulation is a necessary condition for the political process to result in the choice of direct regulation. If there were no interest group in favour of direct regulation, direct regulation would not be chosen. But it is not a sufficient condition. By assumption, market instruments result in higher welfare for society as a whole. This implies that there must be people in favour of market instruments. For the political process to result in the choice of direct regulation, the proponents of direct regulation must somehow be more influential than the proponents of market instruments. In other words: the political process, or the politicians, weigh(s) the interests of the proponents of direct regulation more heavily than the interests of the proponents of market instruments. Our second research question asks how that can occur.

Looking at the literature on these two research questions, we see that the first question has received most attention. There are many stories about the objections of the interest groups of shareholders and workers in a polluting industry, environmentalists and the environmental bureaucracy against market instruments. As well as bringing these issues together in this book, we shall also expand upon them in two main directions. The one direction is a rigorous derivation of the preferences of shareholders and workers from an industry model. Such a derivation has been lacking in the literature until now. For this task, we shall also make use of another strand of literature, which assesses the effects of different environmental policy instruments without making the link to shareholders' and workers' preferences. The other extension is a survey among Dutch interest groups about their preferences for environmental policy instruments.

There is less literature on our second research question. When writing about the political choice for direct regulation, most authors only point at the interest groups that are in favour of direct regulation, i.e. they only go into our first research question. But as we said above, the existence of interest groups that are in favour of direct regulation is a necessary but not a sufficient condition for direct regulation to be the political choice.

So how was the step from interest groups that prefer direct regulation to the political choice for direct regulation made in the literature until now? We can distinguish three approaches. Some authors do not make this step at all, or do not pretend to offer a solid logical ground for it, restricting themselves to our first research question. Other authors imply that the interest groups' objections to market instruments that they describe have not been taken into proper account yet by those (mainly economists) who claim that market instruments are welfare-maximizing. Thus, they say, market instruments may not be welfare-maximizing at all.[5] When market instruments are not welfare-maximizing, the task of explaining the political choice for direct regulation instead of market instruments becomes a lot easier. However, we have chosen not to take this 'easy way out'. We will try to explain the choice for direct regulation, although market instruments are welfare-maximizing. The assumption that market instruments are welfare-maximizing makes the question why they are not chosen more difficult to answer, but also more interesting. Indeed, the assumption has not been based on a careful consideration of whether the advantages of market instruments really outweigh their disadvantages,[6] but it was made primarily to make our second research question more challenging.

In the third approach to our second research question, the political decision-making process plays a role. Some authors argue that next to interests, arguments also count in the political process, and the case for market instruments has some argumentative weaknesses. Others assume, implicitly or explicitly, that the gains from market instruments relative to direct regulation are spread over large groups, so that each 'winner' only has a small stake in market instruments, and the losses from market instruments are concentrated in small groups, so that each 'loser' has a large stake in direct regulation. It is a well-known result of political economy, at least since Olson (1965), that a small group with high per capita stakes will have more influence on the political decision than a large group with small per capita stakes.

For our own treatment of the second research question we shall mainly use rent seeking analysis. Rent seeking analysis has been applied to other areas of environmental policy (Heyes, 1997; Hurley and Shogren, 1997), but not to instrument choice in environmental policy. We will make some original contributions to rent seeking analysis, especially in Chapters 9 and 10. Although these contributions are inspired by and applied to instrument choice in environmental policy, they are also relevant for other applications.

3.   THE BOOK

Chapter 2 reviews the existing literature on our initial question: 'Why are market instruments hardly ever applied in environmental policy, although economists believe they are welfare-maximizing?' We first review the arguments that economists might be wrong and market instruments are not really welfare-maximizing. Then we move on to the literature on our second research question: 'Given the preferences of everyone involved, and given that market instruments are welfare-maximizing, why are they hardly ever applied in environmental policy?' The literature on our first research question, about the preferences of interest groups, will be discussed along with our own theoretical elaboration in Chapters 3 and 4.

In Chapters 3 to 6, we address the first research question. In Chapters 3 and 4, we discuss the literature and expand it theoretically. We derive the effects of different environmental policy instruments from a partial equilibrium model of a polluting industry in Chapter 3. These effects, and more particularly the effects of the instruments on profits, employment and product price, will be of great interest to the interest groups of shareholders, workers and consumers, respectively. In Chapter 4 we discuss the less formal and more verbal accounts of the preferences of the polluting industry, and the preferences of environmentalists and the environmental bureaucracy.

The empirical examination of the preferences of interest groups is found in Chapters 5 and 6. Chapter 5 is the report of our survey among Dutch interest groups (industry organizations, trade unions, environmental organizations and environmental bureaucracy) about their preferences for and ideas about environmental policy instruments. In Chapter 6 we discuss market instruments in practice. After a brief review of the application of market instruments across the world, we look at the discussions and the political decisions about market instruments and the application of market instruments in the Netherlands. Chapter 6 is an empirical approach to both of our research questions. We will see for which instruments the interest groups lobbied, and how politicians responded to that.

Chapters 7 to 11 are exclusively devoted to our second research question. In Chapter 7 we present two models of interest group influence on political decisions. The first is the institutional model of a democracy with proportional representation where parties, taking the preferences of interest groups into account, form a government coalition. The other model of interest group influence, introduced in Chapter 7, is the rent seeking contest. In a rent seeking contest, the interest groups (called rent-seeking agents) do their best to increase the probability that the decision maker will select their favourite instrument. We shall see that the rent seeking model needs to be expanded considerably in order to apply it to instrument choice in environmental policy. These expansions will be undertaken in Chapters 8 to 10.

Rent seeking analysis commonly assumes that the interests of the rent-seeking agents are completely opposed to each other. But with respect to instrument choice, agents' interests can run (partly) parallel. For instance, two interest groups both prefer instrument A to instrument B. In Chapter 8 we analyse the rent seeking contest in case all agents act on their own (i.e. noncooperatively), although they have common interests. In Chapter 9 we analyse cooperation between agents who prefer the same instrument. We discuss cooperation in the form of support, which is a new cooperation concept for rent seeking analysis. With support, one agent pays a fraction of another agent's rent seeking efforts. In Chapter 10 we address another typical feature of instrument choice in environmental policy, namely that the political issue is not only which instrument to use, but also what to do with the revenues of financial instruments. This combination of two rent seeking contests has not been studied before.

With all our extensions of the rent seeking model, we ask the question: 'Can this model explain why the alternative with the highest aggregate valuation (which is the market instrument in environmental policy) has a low, or even zero, probability of being implemented?' We shall see that in all these setups, there are circumstances under which this can happen.

In Chapter 11 we shall assess the institutional model and the rent seeking model of interest group influence on political decisions from two angles. We shall see what representatives from Dutch interest groups have to say about their influence on environmental policy and identify directions for future research.

We conclude with Chapter 12.

NOTES

1. In environmental policy, charges (alternatively called taxes, levies, duties or fees) can have several functions (e.g. EEA, 1996): covering the cost of specific environmental programmes, raising revenue for general (non-specified) purposes and reducing pollution. When we speak about emissions charges or environmental taxes in this book, we have the last mentioned function in mind. Thus, we are talking about regulatory charges, meant to decrease emissions by making them costly. However, we will also pay attention to what is done with the charge revenue.
2. Static and dynamic efficiency are always named in a comparison between market instruments and direct regulation, e.g. in Tietenberg (1985) and Baumol and Oates (1988). Productive efficiency, introduced by Spulber (1985), is hardly ever mentioned in introductory texts. We name it here for completeness' sake and because it appears in our industry model in Chapter 3.
3. Of course, one may find that this presumption does not hold in reality, and that many policies (not only instrument choice in environmental policy) are inefficient according to economic theory.
4. For market instruments in practice, see Opschoor et al. (1994) and our Chapter 6.
5. Some authors also imply that the attempt to bring all advantages and disadvantages of market instruments under the same heading is futile.
6. However, we are confident that this is a realistic assumption for a considerable subset of environmental problems. Our confidence is derived a.o. from the studies on cost savings with tradable permits, reviewed in Klaassen (1996).

2. The Positive Literature on Instrument Choice

1. INTRODUCTION

In this chapter we review the positive literature on instrument choice.[1] This literature addresses the question of which instrument is chosen in reality, instead of which instrument should be chosen. The latter is the domain of the normative literature on instrument choice.

In Chapter 1 we have seen that economists have demonstrated the advantages, or even the superiority, of market instruments above direct regulation. The general idea is that the same environmental quality can be obtained at lower cost with market instruments: market instruments are more efficient.

Thus, the message of this normative literature on instrument choice is: market instruments should be applied. But in reality, the application of market instruments in environmental policy is very limited. The positive literature on instrument choice has emerged to address this difference between recommendations and reality. It seeks to answer the question which also lies at the heart of this book (see Chapter 1): why are market instruments not more widely applied in environmental policy, although economists claim they are more efficient? Here we shall review the different answers the literature has offered to this question. Most of the literature reviewed here specifically addresses environmental policy, but part of it deals with efficient instruments in other policy areas or in general.

Section 2 contains the practical considerations. We review the arguments that economists have demonstrated the advantages of market instruments in a highly theoretical setting, ignoring the real world problems of implementing them, and contrasting problem-free working market instruments to the most unfavourable forms of direct regulation. Thus, section 2 reviews the literature claiming that the advantages of market instruments should not be overstated or are absent.

In the rest of the literature, the advantages of market instruments are taken for granted. This part of the literature seeks to address the question: 'Why are market instruments not more widely applied in environmental policy, although they are more efficient?'

The literature reviewed in section 3 focuses on the 'message' that an instrument confers. The approach to the environmental problem implicit in market instruments differs from the approach implicit in direct regulation. Politicians may be reluctant to adopt this different approach.

Section 4 reviews the literature on distributional issues. Market instruments may yield a higher aggregate welfare level than direct regulation, but there are also groups that have a higher welfare with direct regulation. If these groups are somehow politically more powerful than the groups that gain from market instruments, market instruments will not be accepted.

In the literature reviewed in section 4, the political decision making process is a black box. The literature reviewed in section 5 looks inside this black box to find elements that favour direct regulation.

In section 6 we look at two instances where the policy makers favoured an inefficient over a more efficient policy. However, market instruments are also applied in environmental policy, albeit on a modest scale. The experience with market instruments will be reviewed in Chapter 6.

In section 7 the positive literature on instrument choice is evaluated. Furthermore we shall see how the analysis in this volume fits into and can be expected to contribute to the literature.

2.   PRACTICAL CONSIDERATIONS

Under this heading, we look at a number of reasons why the theoretical welfare superiority of market instruments in environmental policy does not apply in practice.[2] Reason 1 applies primarily to tradable permits. Reasons 2 and 3 apply to charges. The other reasons apply both to charges and tradable permits.

1. Market imperfections
The welfare superiority of market instruments in economic theory is always demonstrated in a model with perfect competition in all relevant markets: the tradable permit market, the factor market and the product markets. If we change the assumptions of the model, making them more realistic, market instruments may no longer be welfare-maximizing. We can call this a 'second best' argument (Lipsey and Lancaster, 1956):[3] if all (potential) markets work well, market instruments are welfare-maximizing. But if there are other imperfections (other than that environmental damage is not fully taken into account), then direct regulation can become the welfare-maximizing instrument.[4]

However, we should also take into account that to implement the kind of direct regulation that is welfare-superior to market instruments, the government would need a lot of information on the production and abatement cost of firms and on market conditions (Sartzetakis, 1997). When the government does not have this kind of information, market instruments may still be the 'best bet'.

Let us now see what can go wrong with imperfectly competitive markets. We will look first at the implications of a noncompetitive tradable permit market.

In order for a system of tradable permits to result in a cost-effective reduction of emissions, there has to be a well-functioning market for tradable permits. This means that there should be enough suppliers and demanders so that the actors know the permit price and take it as given. When the market does not function well, there are a number of problems:[5]

- firms that wish to buy or sell permits may not be able to find a trading partner, or have to incur high search costs (Stavins, 1995). Furthermore, the trade may take place at the 'wrong' price;
- firms with a dominant position on the permit market may manipulate the permit price to their own advantage (Hahn, 1984; Tietenberg, 1985). When product markets are not perfectly competitive either, firms with market power in the permit market may also raise the permit price to reduce their competitors' market shares (Sartzetakis, 1993) or even to drive or keep competitors out of business.

But even when the tradable emission permit market itself is perfectly competitive, or a uniform charge rate is applied, market instruments may result in lower welfare than direct regulation. This is because other markets may not be competitive. For instance, when there is Cournot competition instead of perfect competition on the product market, direct regulation may be welfare-maximizing (Besanko, 1987).

The source of another problem is that the welfare-maximizing emissions charge rate for a non-competitive industry is lower than for a competitive industry (Buchanan, 1969). This becomes a problem when, for instance, a monopolist has to trade emission permits with firms from a competitive industry. Then the monopolist will have less emission permits and produce less than what is socially optimal (Hung and Sartzetakis, 1997).

The labour market may also work imperfectly in reality. The assumption that labour markets work perfectly, and therefore everyone can work as much as he wants to, is especially important for partial equilibrium models. With a perfect labour market, it is no problem that in some industries, employment decreases as a result of environmental policy. The workers that are laid off in one industry can immediately go to work in another industry. In a partial equilibrium model, these workers simply 'disappear' out of the framework that is studied. In a general equilibrium model, there may be an indirect repercussion via a lower wage rate.

In reality, there is involuntary unemployment. Workers who are laid off from one industry cannot immediately go to work in another industry. In the period that they are unemployed, they do not contribute to the economy. They receive unemployment benefits, the revenues for which are raised by distorting taxes. The workers also incur costs when they get a job in another industry (immediately or eventually), because the skills that were specific to the industry where they worked become useless.

The way employment is treated in the model is important, because employment in a polluting industry is lower with market instruments than with direct regulation, as we shall see in Chapter 3. Thus, whereas market instruments are welfare-maximizing in a model with full employment, they may not be welfare-maximizing in a model with involuntary unemployment.

2. The uncertain relation between the charge rate and emissions

An emissions charge indirectly determines the emissions. Industry reacts to the charge by cutting back emissions because it is cheaper to abate than to pay the charge. But usually, the government does not know in advance the exact relation between the charge rate and industry emissions.

Baumol and Oates (1971) propose that the government sets the charge in a process of trial-and-error: when emissions are below (above) the policy target, the charge is adjusted downward (upward). However, the government cannot simply adjust the charge rate overnight. Furthermore, adjustment of the charge rate is costly when investment in pollution control is irreversible. When firms have made a large investment in abatement equipment as a reaction to a high charge rate, and then the charge rate is decreased, their investment becomes less valuable. As a result, firms might postpone their investment in abatement equipment and pollution control in the adjustment period will be more expensive.[6]

Another problem is that there may be large environmental damage when the emissions are above the target. Emissions may be above the target either in the process of trial and error or because marginal abatement costs are higher than the government had estimated. The phenomenon that environmental damage rises disproportionately when emissions rise slightly, is known as the threshold effect. Threshold effects occur when the emissions exceed a certain critical level, beyond which there is irreparable damage to the ecosystem, species become extinct, etc.

The last argument to be brought under this heading is that when the government has enough information to set the appropriate charge rate, it may also be able to apply direct regulation. To determine the appropriate charge rate, the government must know which measures the polluters will take as a reaction to the charge. But then the government can also prescribe these measures.

3. The 'emergency' problem

Charges are inappropriate when unexpected events necessitate a quick reduction in emissions. One can think of extreme weather conditions or large emissions from a factory due to an accident. Charges are inappropriate because it takes time for the government to change the charge rate and for the firms to react to the higher charge rate. Baumol and Oates (1988: 198–206) argue that direct regulation is needed in case of emergencies, whereas according to Tietenberg (1985: 149–51) emergencies can be handled with tradable permits.

4. The pollutant should be banned

Market instruments are inappropriate when the government wants to ban a certain pollutant. Tradable permits cannot be used, because there will be no permits. The government could levy a prohibitive charge, but (as we have seen under reason 2) there is a risk that the charge rate is set too low, so that there will be emissions after all.

5. The danger of hot spots

The environmental damage of some pollutants depends on where they are emitted. These pollutants are called non-uniformly mixed (Tietenberg, 1985). When the government does not take this property into proper account in the design of market instruments, there will be hot spots: places where the pollution exceeds the target level. To avoid hot spots, the government could set a very high uniform charge rate or issue a limited number of tradable emission permits, so that the target will be met everywhere. But this will result in relatively low total emissions and high abatement costs. With charges, the other solution is to differentiate the charge rate by location. This will complicate the system considerably. Furthermore, differentiating charge rates per source may not be permitted by fiscal legislation.

For tradable permits, there are a number of alternative solutions (Baumol and Oates, 1988: 181–188):

- subdivide the area into zones and allow trades within, but not between, zones. The problems are the determination of the number of permits per zone, the loss in cost-effectivity because trades between zones are prohibited, and the 'thinness' of zone markets (see reason 1);
- issue ambient permits instead of emission permits. Ambient permits give the right to cause a certain amount of pollution at a specific receptor point. The problems are the complexity of the system, the 'thinness' of markets and the possibility of hot spots at non-receptor points;
- a pollution offset system. In this system, a permit transaction is allowed as long as it does not result in a violation of the environmental quality standard at any receptor point. Thus, official permission is necessary for every permit transaction. This system seems to be the most promising.

6. Market instruments are new

Government regulation, in environmental policy as well as in other policy areas, mainly consists of direct regulation. Thus, civil servants and the firms subject to regulation have experience with direct regulation. They may know that it does not work perfectly, but at least they know how it works. When a market instrument is put in place, the civil service and the firms have to get used to it. There will be adjustment costs to the introduction of market instruments.

The cost of adjusting to market instruments will be lower when environmental policy has evolved to a certain level of maturity (Nentjes, 1991). National or regional emission targets should be in place, emission sources should be known and registered, emissions have to be monitored and sanctions should be applied in case of non-compliance. These conditions should also be met for direct regulation to be really effective, but even more so for tradable permits.

To illustrate the above points, we present two reasons that are often given to explain why it was relatively easy to introduce the market instrument of tradable permits in the US. These are that the political culture is very 'market-minded', and direct regulation was based on quantitative emission limits for individual sources (OECD, 1997).

There will also be costs *before* market instruments are implemented. Because these instruments are new, costly research is necessary before they can be considered as a serious alternative. Research is necessary to find out the experience in other countries and other fields with these instruments, how to implement market instruments, the advantages over the existing approach, possible unwelcome side-effects, the compatibility with the existing legal framework, etc. Once it becomes clear that market instruments are considered as a serious alternative, their proponents will start lobbying for market instruments, and their opponents will start lobbying against them (Leidy and Hoekman, 1996).

Taking into account the adjustment cost, the cost of research, the cost of lobbying and the possibility that in the end, market instruments will not be implemented at all, a policy maker may decide not to consider market instruments seriously in the first place. The lower the advantages the policy maker expects from the market instruments before specific research takes place, the more likely the decision not to consider them at all becomes.

7. Monitoring and enforcement may be more problematic for market instruments[7]
With charges, the size of the charge bill depends on the firm's emissions. Thus, emissions must be measured precisely. With tradable permits, the government must keep track of the permit trades so that it can compare a firm's emissions to its permit holding. With direct regulation, monitoring will be easier. This is especially true for technical standards, where the authorities only have to check whether the prescribed equipment has been installed.[8] De Savornin Lohman (1994a) asserts that monitoring with an emission standard will be more demanding, but still the authorities only have to determine whether the standard is met or not. However, a more sophisticated sanction system also requires information about the size of a violation. The more emissions exceed the standard, the more severe should be the sanction (Russell, 1979).

Another problem is that direct controls can, and do to a large extent, rely on voluntary compliance. This is not true for a charge, because without a tax collector, nobody pays taxes.

8. The limited scope of economic models

Economic models only model part of reality. But some disadvantages of market instruments may manifest themselves outside the scope of economic models (Kelman, 1981; see also Chapter 4, section 4.2 of this book).

For instance, economic models typically assume that people only derive utility from consumption. But people may also derive utility from things that are not so easily expressed (or that economic models do not express) in terms of consumption. For instance, environmentalists may fear that the use of market instruments will decrease the public or the politicians' interest in environmental protection.

Furthermore, economic models only look at the interaction between people on markets. But there are also non-market interactions, that may in fact be more efficient. However, the introduction of market instruments threatens to undermine these non-market interactions.

9. The design of direct regulation and market instruments in reality

Under this heading, we shall first argue that the efficiency disadvantages of direct regulation are not as large as sometimes argued, because the design of direct regulation can be more sophisticated than it is sometimes given credit for. Then we shall see that the efficiency of market instruments may be disappointing in reality, because they are not applied in the way that economists recommend.

Some of the disadvantages of direct regulation *vis-à-vis* market instruments can be, and are, overcome by the design of more sophisticated forms of direct regulation. When presenting the advantages of market instruments, one should not make a caricature of direct regulation as completely rigid and insensitive to differences between polluters. In reality, there are forms of direct regulation that allow firms to find the most efficient way to reduce emissions. When applying direct regulation, the government does try to take cost differences between firms into account. One way to make direct regulation more flexible is by drawing up a covenant. With a covenant, an industry can commit to a certain reduction in emissions. The reduction by each firm is decided by the industry itself.

The above discussion pertains to the alleged static efficiency of market instruments. With respect to dynamic efficiency, direct regulation can also stimulate innovation. This is possible with so-called 'technology-forcing standards', or 'progressive standard-setting'. These are standards for a future date that mandate a stricter emission reduction than is feasible with the presently known technologies. Thus, firms can only comply with these standards when new technologies will be invented. In this way, innovation is stimulated.

On the other side of the equation, the design of market instruments in practice differs from the design found in economic textbooks. These differences undermine the theoretical effectiveness and efficiency of market instruments. Charges are set too low to reach the desired emission reduction, and rebates and exemptions compromise the effectiveness of the charge. When a tradable emission permit system is set up, there will be restrictions upon trade (Hahn and Noll, 1990).

One reason why the design of market instruments differs from theoretical prescriptions is that it is too costly to abolish the existing system of direct regulation (see our reason 6). Thus, market instruments are introduced as an addition to existing direct regulation. Another reason is that there is a large political resistance against implementing market instruments in the theoretically correct way, as we shall see in the rest of this volume.

3.   ARGUMENTS AND ETHICS

The arguments reviewed in this section follow Majone's (1989) and Kelman's (1981) interpretation of policy making as a process of mutual persuasion. Policy makers, and perhaps also the general public, must be convinced that it is a good idea to apply market instruments in environmental policy. Thus, they must understand the case for market instruments. But even if they do, they may have objections to market instruments, that economists usually do not address.

Bohm and Russell (1985: 437–9) present a list of eight reasons why politicians prefer direct regulation to market instruments in environmental policy. We can bring their reasons 2 and 7 under the heading of 'Arguments and ethics'. Reason 2 is that politicians do not understand the economist's case for market instruments.[9] This can be substantiated with the results of a survey in the USA from 1978 (Kelman, 1981, 1983), where two out of nine congressional environmental committee staffers correctly presented the efficiency argument for charges. In the whole sample of 63 congressional staffers, environmentalists and industry representatives, 16% spontaneously cited the efficiency argument for charges. The other 84% could not make the efficiency argument when presented with the statement that some people think that an environmental goal can be reached at lower cost with charges.

Bohm and Russell (1985) go on to say that if politicians do understand the argument, they think they will not be able to make the public understand it. Reason 7 is an elaboration of this point. Regulation has the aura of being a 'no-nonsense' instrument, adequate for the control of serious environmental problems. In contrast, charges have often been viewed as an imperfect obstacle to continued environmental degradation and even as a 'licence to pollute'.

De Savornin Lohman (1994a) expands upon this argument. He exposes the argumentative weaknesses of the case for charges versus direct regulation.

Direct regulation states the environmental objective in physical terms, whereas the charge is a monetary mechanism. With direct regulation, environmental benefits stand out cleary, but the economic repercussions of the environmental policy are not immediately apparent. The politician arguing in favour of direct regulation can try to avoid talking about the economic repercussions or even declare them of a 'lower order'. The politician assumes the role of the knight fighting for the Good (the environment) against the evil polluters. With a charge, environmental policy is directly linked to the economic repercussions. The argument that environmental policy is of a 'higher order' can no longer be sustained.

The implication of this difference is twofold:

1. The economic and distributional effects of charges will be determined in the highly visible political arena, and the economic and distributional effects of direct regulation will be determined in the less visible administrative arena. We shall return to this matter in sections 4.3.3 and 5.
2. A charge condones polluting behaviour: 'It is okay if you pollute, as long as you pay for it'.[10] The moral indictment of polluters, implicit or explicit in direct regulation, may strengthen the electorate's environmental awareness and increase voluntary compliance (Kelman, 1981).

Frey (1992), while criticizing other explanations, also points out the different impact on ethics as an advantage of direct regulation. Charges destroy environmental ethics, while direct regulation may strengthen them. This may not make a difference to the sector where either instrument is applied, but it may make a difference in other sectors. When charges are applied in one sector, environmental ethics are reduced everywhere. People will not voluntarily act in an environmentally friendly way anymore. They will not act more environmentally friendly than what the government commands, and will reduce voluntary compliance.

One can say that according to Frey (1992), introducing market instruments in one sector has negative external effects: it destroys environmental ethics in other sectors. Kelman (1981) points out these negative external effects in a wider sense. Society relies on a mixture of altruism and self-interest. Introducing the market into environmental policy means that the realm of self-interest increases at the expense of altruism. This would be a problem already if the pre-existing mixture of self-interest and altruism was socially optimal. But when the realm of self-interest is increased in one part of society, people may start acting more out of self-interest in other parts as well.

The plight of a politician arguing in favour of charges (or an auction of tradable permits) becomes even worse if he does not intend to earmark the revenues for environmental purposes. Then he comes up against the following arguments (De Savornin Lohman, 1994a: 129):

– 'The revenue of the charge should be spent on improving the environment – if not, it is a mere pretence for shaking money out of people's pockets.'

The first part of the argument can be countered by reason, which is not so easily done for the second part. This second part emanates from a distrust in

government intentions, which may be justified.
- 'The charge rate is arbitrary, as it is not based on the need to cover objective, identifiable costs.' The risk of a debate on the technical issue of the appropriate charge rate is indeed present.

When assessing the validity of the arguments put forward in this section, it is worth noting that the direct empirical evidence is rather weak. There is only the 1978 survey by Kelman (1981), that may be outdated. In particular the argument that policy makers do not know or do not understand how market instruments work, seems to have lost its relevance. In the US, tradable permits are applied, and in some Scandinavian countries, emissions charges are applied.[11] In most other OECD countries, the government has ordered studies about market instruments. More generally, increased knowledge about the workings of market instruments will lower policy makers' resistance based on 'gut feelings'.

However, some of the arguments about why politicians are reluctant to accept market instruments may be valid. But for an economist it is difficult to judge or expand upon the arguments.

4.   DISTRIBUTIONAL EFFECTS

4.1   Introduction

In this section we shall look at the distributional effects of environmental policy instruments. The idea is that whereas aggregate benefits are higher for market instruments, some groups are better off with direct regulation. It may be that the interests of these groups are weighted more heavily in the political process.

In section 4.2 we shall look at the analysis of interest group influence in economics. In section 4.3 we shall discuss the applications of this theory to instrument choice in environmental policy.

4.2   Interest Group Influence

Economic theory has identified the conditions under which the market mechanism produces efficient outcomes. If these conditions are not met, there is a market failure. Normative economic theory states that when there are market failures, there is a case for government intervention. For a long time, economists did not bother to ask the question whether actual government policy was intended to, and did, remedy these market failures. Perhaps they even adhered to the public interest theory (Posner, 1974), that the normative economic theory is not only a prescription for, but also a description of, actual government behaviour.[12,13]

This changed with the introduction of the economic theory of regulation, initiated by Stigler (1971: 3), who stated: 'as a rule, regulation is acquired by the industry and is designed and operated primarily for its benefits'. The theory has been further developed by Posner (1974), Peltzman (1976) and Becker (1983, 1985). These other authors recognize that there are also other interest groups besides industry that can influence government policy.

The basic insight in the economic theory of regulation and subsequent theories is due to Olson (1965), who states that a small group of agents with high per capita stakes will wield more influence than a large group of agents with small per capita stakes. The reason is that the former kind of group is easiest to organize. As a result, government policy that favours small groups, the members of which will enjoy high per capita gains, at the expense of large groups, the members of which will sustain small per capita losses. This government policy may well result in a reduction of total welfare, contrary to normative economic theory.

For an overview of the current approaches to interest group influence in economic research, I draw on Potters and Van Winden (1996), who distinguish four approaches to interest group influence. The counterpart of this paper is Potters and Sloof (1996) which gives a survey of the empirical literature.

The first approach to interest group influence uses an *influence function* that determines the supply of government policy beneficial to an interest group as a result of the influence exerted by this and other interest groups. This approach is used in the rent seeking literature, where the supply is the part of the rent that the interest group will receive, or the probability that an interest group will receive the whole rent. It is also used in Becker (1983, 1985), where the supply is the subsidy or tax that the interest group receives or pays. While the rent seeking literature mainly concentrates on the total rent seeking effort, Becker is interested in the effect of deadweight cost on the tax-subsidy distribution.

The second approach uses a *vote function and campaign contributions*. There are two versions of this approach. The first is that an interest group contributes to a party's campaign to elicit a favourable policy position. The second is that an interest group contributes to the campaign of the party with a favourable policy position to increase this party's expected number of votes.

The third approach assumes that the government maximizes a *composite utility function*, which is composed of the utilities of the interest groups and (possibly) general welfare. The weights attached to the interest groups' utilities can be determined in several ways. One can take a cooperative solution concept, an interest function approach or a probabilistic voting model.

The fourth approach models *games with asymmetric information*. In these games, an interest group knows something about the state of the world that the political decision maker does not know. The interest group can then decide to send a message to the decision maker, which may induce the decision maker to change his beliefs about the state of the world and his decision on which action to take.

Let us now assess these approaches, specifically looking at the applicability to instrument choice in environmental policy. The first approach seems appropriate. Instrument choice will be determined by the government, influenced by interest groups. The issue is of such minor importance to the general electorate, that the direct reaction of the voters to instrument choice can be neglected.[14] Thus, the influence function, that focuses solely on interest groups, is a useful tool. However, we have to recognize the drawbacks mentioned in Potters and Van Winden (1996). These are first, that it is not clear which activities by interest groups influence the government, and secondly, why the government should react to interest group pressure.

With respect to the second approach, we must distinguish between the two variants. When an interest group makes a campaign contribution to a party to elicit a favourable policy position, this can be seen as a specification of the means by which interest groups influence political parties. Therefore, as Potters and Van Winden (1996) have noted, this approach is closely related to the first approach of the influence function.

The other variant is that an interest group makes a contribution to the campaign of the party that promises to implement a favourable policy. This variant seems inappropriate for instrument choice in environmental policy, because it is only a minor part of government policy. It seems unlikely that interest groups would support a particular party or politician just because they propose a favourable environmental policy instrument. Of course, instrument choice can play a part in a policy platform that makes a party or a politician attractive to an interest group. But when taking this route, we would have to consider the connection of instrument choice with other policy items, which would complicate matters considerably.

The third approach is interesting, in as far as the composite utility function is derived from the interest function. But then it does not add much to the first approach. The other derivations seem less appropriate. Instrument choice in environmental policy is too unimportant for interest groups to mobilize the votes they control. The cooperative derivation includes some strong assumptions, especially on an interest group's ability to commit to and follow a 'destructive' course of action if the government does not heed its interest.

The attraction of the fourth approach is that it specifies what interest groups do to influence the decision and why these efforts influence the decision. Furthermore, the idea that an interest group knows more about its own situation than the government does, is realistic. However, there is the technical problem that the analysis typically identifies multiple equilibria. A more fundamental problem is that an interest group can influence the policy maker's beliefs about the *size* of its stake in the decision, but not the *weight* the policy maker attaches to this stake. Next to these general problems, it is dubious whether the model of asymmetric information can be used to explain why market instruments are hardly ever applied in environmental policy, although they are welfare-maximizing. If the government wants to maximize aggregate welfare and it knows that market instruments maximize welfare, it will always choose market instruments. In order for the model of asymmetric information to explain why direct regulation is chosen, the assumptions have to be modified in one of the following ways:

- the government does not know that market instruments are welfare-maximizing. This is inconsistent with the fact that the model builder does know that they are;
- although market instruments are expected to maximize welfare, they are not always welfare-maximizing. This would require adjusting our research question;
- the government does not maximize aggregate welfare, but only takes into account the welfare of some specific groups. Then the explanation of the choice for direct regulation lies outside the realm of the model, because the model does not explain why the government favours one group over another;
- although market instruments maximize aggregate welfare, there is an interest group that manages to convince the government that the introduction of market instruments would cost votes. Again, the explanation lies outside the realm of the model.

4.3   Distributional Effects of Environmental Policy Instruments

4.3.1 Introduction
In this section we shall discuss the literature on the distributional effects of environmental policy instruments. A necessary condition for the distributional effects to matter for the political decision is that at least one group in society is against market instruments. However, in this section we shall not discuss what interest groups could possibly have against market instruments. The literature on shareholders' and workers' resistance against market instruments, derived from a partial equilibrium model, will be discussed in Chapter 3, section 2.3. The verbal accounts of industry, environmentalists' and bureaucrats' preferences are discussed in Chapter 4.

In this section we shall take for granted that some groups are against market instruments. However, we do note that the mere fact that there are groups opposed to market instruments does not explain their absence. There may also be groups in favour of market instruments. Indeed, if it is assumed that market instruments yield higher overall welfare, there must be groups in favour of market instruments. The point to be made is that somehow, the groups that lose from the introduction of market instruments have more political influence than the groups that gain. In this section we shall review the literature that makes this point.

In section 4.3.2 we review the literature on the pattern of distribution. There the argument is that there are small groups with large per capita losses from market instruments and large groups with small per capita gains. In section 4.3.3 we look at the arguments that the losses from market instruments are more certain or more visible than the gains and that with market instruments, politicians have less control over the distribution of gains and losses than with direct regulation. In section 4.3.4 we see why the larger size of the distributional effects (losses as well as gains) with market instruments compared to direct regulation could be a problem. We discuss the literature in section 4.3.5.

4.3.2 Pattern of distribution

The pattern of distribution across groups may work against market instruments. This explanation is given by Buchanan and Tullock (1975). According to Buchanan and Tullock, whose model is extensively discussed in Dijkstra (1994), the polluting industry prefers direct regulation to an emissions charge, because direct regulation yields higher profits (or lower losses). On the other hand, the emissions charge yields government revenue. Buchanan and Tullock (1975) assume that every citizen can expect to benefit from this government revenue. Thus, the polluting industry, a small group with high per capita stakes, is in favour of direct regulation. The rest of the population, a large group with low per capita stakes, is in favour of emissions charges. As we have seen in section 4.2, the polluting industry is likely to have its way.

A similar argument is given by Svendsen (1998: 37) who gives three reasons why, in the case of CO_2 taxation with complete refunding, the potential losers (the capital-intensive firms) will be more influential than the potential winners (the labour-intensive firms). One reason[15] is that the capital-intensive firms are usually larger and more likely to have a small number advantage when organizing and lobbying in the political arena. A major firm might also lobby on its own.

There is also the pattern of distribution in time. In Bohm and Russell's (1985) list of reasons why market instruments are not applied, reason 5 is that charges may first result in higher prices than regulation, and later in lower prices. For politicians with a short time horizon, this is a disadvantage of charges.

Hahn (1990) models the decision problem of a regulator. His utility function is composed of the polluting industry's and the environmentalists' interest. Thus, this is an example of a composite utility function, the third approach distinguished by Potters and Van Winden (1996). The industry is in favour of a lenient and market-oriented environmental policy. The environmentalists are in favour of a strict environmental policy and against market orientation. In this model, an increase in industry influence will lead to an increase in emissions and/or an increase in market orientation in environmental policy.

In Becker's (1983) model, the political success of more efficient instruments depends on whether the instrument is a tax or a subsidy. In his model, there are two interest groups. The government can impose taxes on one group and subsidize the other group with the revenues. Due to deadweight costs, tax revenues are below the utility loss of the taxed group, and the utility gain of the subsidized group is below subsidy expenditures. The size of the redistribution is determined by the political pressure from the groups to increase their subsidy and to reduce their tax, respectively.

A more efficient tax instrument will decrease the deadweight loss between the utility loss of the taxed group and the tax revenues. As a result, the taxed group will reduce its pressure for lower taxes, and both the taxed group and the subsidized group are better off. Or, as Becker (1983) puts it in his Proposition 4: competition among pressure groups favours efficient methods of taxation.

With a more efficient subsidy instrument, the result is ambiguous. The subsidized group is obviously better off, but it is unclear what happens to the taxed group.

4.3.3 Uncertainties and controllability

In general, it is assumed that the distributional effects of charges are clearer than those of direct regulation, as we have seen in section 3. There is also a connection with the pattern of distribution: when economic subjects are slightly better off with market instruments, they will probably not be aware of it. As a result, the groups that will lose from environmental policy will oppose charges more vehemently than direct regulation..

This reason is put forward by Svendsen (1998: 37) in the case of CO_2 taxation with complete refunding, benefiting labour-intensive firms:

> if the state is to use taxation, then it should clearly identify winners first and mobilize their support by refunding revenue as financial transfers and not as complicated subsidies. However, the actual design might not have a clear-cut and simple refund system. As such, losses for losers might be evident and transparent, whereas potential winners might not be easily identifiable, e.g. potential winners would first have to apply for earmarked subsidies.

In Eichenberger and Serna (1996), uncertainty plays a subtler role. They assume that voters are able to make an unbiased estimate of the utility they will derive from a policy proposal. However, their estimates are affected by random errors. Thus, an individual's estimate of his own utility can be described with a probability function. The expected value of the individual's estimate of his utility equals the true value μ of his utility. The variance of the estimate declines when the individual receives more ('good') information.

Eichenberger and Serna (1996) offer an explanation for the occurrence of inefficient policy instruments, based on their model.[16] Suppose that there are two proposals to do something about an environmental problem, e.g. for an urban road transport policy to restrain commuter traffic. The one proposal is based on pricing P, and the other on regulation R. Relative to the status quo SQ, both proposals will make some people lose (e.g. commuters and people working in the car industry) and other people win (e.g. the inhabitants of the city, and people who do not use a car). Eichenberger and Serna assume that the people who lose (win) from P relative to SQ also lose (win) from R relative to SQ.

The winners will win more with P than with R. Thus, the expected value of the estimated utility from P is higher: $\mu_P > \mu_R$. But it seems plausible that (for the non-economists among the winners) there will be more uncertainty about the gains from P than about the gains from R. As a result, a considerable number of winners think that they will actually lose from P. Thus, almost all the winners will vote for R against SQ, but a considerable number of winners will vote for SQ against P.

The losers will lose more with R than with P: $\mu_P > \mu_R$. But it seems plausible that there will be more uncertainty about the losses from R than about the losses from P. With pricing, a loser's cost is simply the price he has to pay to use his car, whereas in the regulation case his costs are much more difficult to estimate; they depend, for instance, on the possibilities to evade the regulations. As a result, a considerable number of losers think that they will actually gain from R. Thus, almost all the losers will vote for SQ against P, but a considerable number of losers will vote for R against SQ.

Combining the votes from winners and losers, we see that regulation R has a better chance against the status quo SQ than pricing P has. However, there is an opportunity for P to 'get in through the back door'. Suppose that first the vote is between SQ and R. Then R is likely to win. After R has been introduced, there is a vote between R and P. Now, P is likely to win, because for both groups (originally losers and winners) $\mu_P > \mu_R$, so that the expected number of votes for P is higher. Once P is introduced, people will experience how P works, and the estimates of their utility with P will become more accurate. All the winners will see that they are indeed better off with P than with SQ. This makes it unlikely that SQ will beat P, as was the case originally.

We can conclude that: 'Sophisticated efficient policy proposals which originally do not command a majority may be introduced through apparently inefficient transitional steps' (Eichenberger and Serna, 1996: 149).

Another consideration to be brought under this heading is that with direct regulation, politicians have more control over the allocation of emissions across firms, industries and regions (Hahn and Noll, 1990). Furthermore, for a tradable permit system to work well, the emission cap has to be specified for a long period (say 15 years) in advance. Politicians have to 'tie their hands', giving up the opportunity to lower the cap when environmental concern rises, or economic activity declines, and to raise the cap when economic activity rises, or stimulating the economy is seen as more urgent than protecting the environment.

As we have seen in section 4.2, the basic idea of the economic theory of regulation is that the political process favours politically powerful interest groups at the expense of less powerful and unorganized groups. Politicians prefer to allocate emissions according to the political strength of the various groups of polluters, instead of according to how emissions can be reduced most efficiently.

Thus, they sacrifice effiency (that can be brought about by market instruments) for political acceptability (Zeckhauser, 1981). The influential groups will have a lower (marginal) cost of complying with environmental policy. With an efficient environmental policy, all groups would have the same marginal costs.

4.3.4 Size of distributional effects

De Savornin Lohman (1994b) notes that, as polluters (probably) face a heavier financial burden with financial instruments, these involve a more radical redistribution than direct regulation. This is a disadvantage for financial instruments, if the political process exhibits 'distributional inertia', i.e. if it favours small redistributions to large ones.

De Savornin Lohman quotes Rolph (1983) and Welch (1983) as empirical evidence of this phenomenon. In fact, Welch attributes this distributional inertia to the political strength of the group involved and lack of knowledge of market instruments. Thus, Welch does not see distributional inertia as an independent reason. Rolph (1983), however, asserts that US regulatory programs that confer property rights sacrifice efficiency to maintain the economic status quo. But there is no evidence that they intend these programs to shift wealth from a weaker to a stronger group. Rolph does not address the question of what other reason policy-makers have to maintain the economic status quo.

Svendsen (1998: 37) makes the point that the political process weighs losses more heavily than gains of the same magnitude:

> potential losing firms in an arguably competitive industry may claim that they are in normal profit equilibrium and that further taxation will have damaging effects. Because they cannot pass on the costs of CO_2 reduction to consumers by raising product prices, taxation will lead to lost jobs. Even if both winners and losers have the starting point of normal return or zero profit, and even if winners can offset the loss in jobs by creating new jobs, winners are in a less critical situation. In contrast to the losers, the winners are not forced out of business and will therefore have lesser gains in utility terms.

Theoretical underpinnings of distributional inertia can be found in Becker (1983) and Grossman and Helpman (1994). Becker argues that redistribution is accompanied by progressively increasing deadweight costs, i.e. the difference between what the losers pay and the winners receive. These deadweight costs are a barrier to redistribution in the first place (a result that Becker calls 'the tyranny of the status quo') and serve to limit redistribution, if it takes place. Grossman and Helpman derive a rationale for applying inefficient instruments in trade policy. They suggest (p. 849) that their model can also be applied to environmental regulation.

In Grossman and Helpman (1994), the government maximizes the weighted average of general welfare and the welfare of interest groups that make campaign contributions. These campaign contributions reflect the increase in interest group welfare owing to a favourable trade policy. Thus, this model is a combination of the second and the third approach to modelling interest group influence as discussed in section 4.2.

With trade policy, the government effectively determines the domestic price vector **p**. All interest groups i submit a contribution schedule $C_i(\mathbf{p})$, that shows how much they will contribute when the government implements a certain price vector **p**. Each interest group consists of the owners of a production factor that is specific to one industry. Thus, an interest group's contribution will be rising in the price of its 'own' product and declining in the prices of all other products.

Grossman and Helpman (1994) derive four conditions that the equilibrium contribution schedules and price vector should satisfy. The third and fourth conditions are relevant here.

The third condition is that the price vector must maximize the sum of welfare for a lobby i and the government, given the contribution schedules of other lobbies. Therefore a differentiable contribution schedule should be locally truthful, i.e. around the equilibrium a change in the lobby's gross welfare induces the same change in its contribution. One can extend this notion of truthfulness to a truthful contribution schedule C_i^T, which is always in a lobby's best response set:

$$C_i^T = \max\ [0,\ W_i(p) - B_i]$$

Here $W_i(\mathbf{p})$ is the welfare of the lobby, gross of contributions. When the lobby's gross welfare $W_i(\mathbf{p})$ is less than B_i, the lobby does not make a contribution. When the lobby's welfare $W_i(\mathbf{p})$ exceeds B_i, the campaign contribution consists of the difference $W_i(\mathbf{p}) - B_i$. A lobby sets its B_i such that the government is indifferent between a policy that induces a contribution from the lobby and a policy that ignores the lobby. This is the fourth condition for a political equilibrium.

Lobbies will be against less distorting redistribution policies (e.g. production subsidies instead of import taxes) if their interests are opposed to each other. With less distorting policies, the level of welfare that the government and the other lobbies together can achieve when one lobby is ignored, is higher. Thus, a lobby has to lower its B_i.

Aidt (1998), Emeny et al. (1997) and Fredriksson (1997) apply Grossman and Helpman's (1994) model to environmental policy. They all copy the assumption of the small open economy, i.e. the country cannot influence the world prices. Aidt studies the political equilibrium with and without an environmentalist lobby, where the instrument is an emissions charge. Fredriksson studies the instruments of an emissions charge and an abatement subsidy. Emeny et al. discuss environmental policy in the form of an industry emission ceiling in a federation of states, where capital is mobile across states.

The papers also differ in their treatment of environmentalists: how they make a living, whether they are the only ones who are hurt by pollution or the only ones who do something about it, and how the environmental lobby works. Aidt (1998) assumes that every consumer's utility is declining in domestic emissions. In his first model, there are only industry lobby groups, which also take into account the adverse effect of pollution on their members' welfare. In his second model, the environmentalist lobby, consisting of part of the population, only cares about pollution, and the industry lobby groups only care about profits. Emeny et al. (1997) assume that workers and capital owners do not suffer from pollution. The people that are hurt by pollution, i.e. the environmentalists, do not receive income from work or capital. Instead, their income is exogenously determined. Fredriksson (1997) assumes that some consumers (i.e. the environmentalists) are, and others are not, adversely affected by pollution. The environmentalist lobby maximizes its members' aggregate payoff, taking into account the effect of environmental policy on its members' income from capital and the redistribution of environmental tax revenues.

4.3.5 Discussion

As we already said in section 4.3.1, the mere fact that there are groups opposed to market instruments does not explain their absence. Particularly if one wants to maintain the assumption that market instruments yield higher overall welfare, one must also pay attention to the groups that gain from the introduction of market instruments. The authors that do this, usually assume that the gains from market instruments will be dispersed among large groups, so that it is difficult for these groups to organize and exert pressure. Another argument, that can be related to the previous one, is that people do not even know, or are uncertain, about their gains from market instruments.

The idea of dispersed benefits from market instruments can be criticized for two reasons. First, the small group of the shareholders in the polluting industry benefits a lot from grandfathering of tradable permits, as we shall see in Chapter 3. Second, interest groups may try to obtain large parts of the revenue of financial instruments, possibly by way of earmarking them for environmental cleanup. Hahn (1990) is the only one who takes this into account in a theoretical model.

It is questionable whether the implications of Becker's (1983) model with respect to efficient instruments and distributive inertia, as discussed here, are relevant for environmental policy. Environmental policy is usually associated with increasing overall welfare, whereas Becker has derived the results we discussed here from a model where government policy decreases overall welfare.

The relevance of Eichenberger and Serna's (1996) contribution in its present from is dubious, because it relies on voting. Typically, voters choose between different platforms, of which instrument choice only constitutes a minor part.

The idea that direct regulation allows a policy maker more control, or discretion, over the outcome, as articulated by Hahn and Noll (1990), looks like a straightforward application of the idea that interest groups influence government policy. However, two caveats are in order. First, when a financial instrument is used, the government will also have susbtantial control by deciding how to spend the revenues of this instrument. Second, interest groups may be against government discretion, because then they must compete with each other for the benefits of this discretion. The latter argument is employed by Grossman and Helpman (1994) and also appears in our Chapter 10.

The reasons Hahn and Noll (1990) and Grossman and Helpman (1994) provide for the absence of efficient instruments, are opposed to each other in the following sense. Hahn and Noll argue that direct regulation enables the government to hand out 'presents' to specific groups. According to Grossman and Helpman, the size of the 'presents' is larger with market instruments, forcing interest groups to pay more to the government. Therefore interest groups do not like market instruments. The difference in these views can be traced back to the assumptions about how a market instrument is applied. Hahn and Noll assume there will be a market (or a uniform tax rate) across groups, so that the allocation of the emissions across the interest groups is not up to the government. In Grossman and Helpman's model, the government can decide on the tax rate for each interest group separately.

Let us now look more closely at Grossman and Helpman's (1994) argument, made in a model of trade policy. The problem with their argument is that they do not model the political decision about which instruments to consider. The government and the interest groups have opposed interests in this decision. The government would like to apply efficient instruments if it could, whereas the interest groups would like to keep the government from considering these efficient instruments (Dixit et al., 1997). We have seen that a number of authors have applied Grossman and Helpman's model to environmental policy. But in these applications as well, the decision of which instruments to consider still takes place before the decisions considered in such a model.

Thus, Grossman and Helpman (1994) offer a suggestion about why efficient instruments are not applied in trade policy. It remains to be seen whether this suggestion can be made more solid and whether it can also be applied to environmental policy. The theoretical foundations for distributional inertia are still weak, but the phenomenon does seem to play a role in practice.

5.   THE STRUCTURE OF GOVERNMENT DECISION MAKING

In this section, we review an approach that is not mentioned in Potters and Van Winden (1996). This approach takes explicit account of the *structure of government decision making*. Examples of this approach are McCubbins and Page (1986) and Spiller (1990). Most of these studies are strongly US-oriented in that they assume (as opposed to, for example, the Dutch system) a relatively weak party affiliation, a strong Parliament relative to the executive branch of government and a district system of elections. In these models, an individual Parliament member's voting behaviour is assumed to further her chances of being reelected. Campos (1989) and De Savornin Lohman (1994a,b) apply this approach to instrument choice.

Campos' (1989) model combines two decisions by Congress: instrument choice and the level of regulation (e.g. the strictness of environmental policy). Both decisions influence the payoff to all kinds of groups in society. Every Congress member votes in the interests of his own constituency, which is only a subset of the whole of society. Congress treats the decisions in two rounds: first the instrument is chosen, and then the level of regulation. This level of regulation will be the preferred level of the median representative. Thus, in the first round, a representative chooses the instrument that yields the highest benefits for himself at the preferred level of the median representative. The resulting combination of the level and the instrument of regulation need not be efficient. The instrument need not be efficient, because first, some interests (particularly concentrated interests) may be better represented in Congress than others. Secondly, the number of Congress members in favour of an instrument is decisive, and not the size in the difference in payoff between one instrument and the other.

The structure of government decision making also figures in the notion of 'arenas', already referred to in section 3. The term is introduced by De Savornin Lohman (1994a,b), but it is also implicit in arguments by others. The key idea is that the more detailed impacts of a charge are determined in different policy arenas than those of direct regulation.

According to Bohm and Russell's (1985) first reason of why market instruments are not more widely applied, economists hardly have access to the arena where the administrative groundwork for environmental policy takes place. According to Kneese and Schultze (1975), lawyers are more influential in this arena, and lawyers prefer direct regulation.

As we have already seen in section 3, De Savornin Lohman (1994a) points out that the details of applying the instrument are determined in the political arena for charges and in the administrative arena for direct regulation. Because the political arena is more visible, the groups that lose from the introduction of a charge will see that they lose and oppose the charge. With direct regulation, people may not even know that they will lose (Bohm and Russell, 1985, reason 5).

Also, it is sometimes argued that the design and the implementation of direct regulation leave more room for influence from the polluters (Bohm and Russell, 1985, reasons 8b and 8c). In the administrative arena, the polluters can obtain special benefits (like more time to comply to the regulations, or stricter standards for new firms) without drawing attention from the public. This matter will be further discussed in Chapter 4, section 2. Assuming that the polluters will fight the charge proposal in the visible political arena and direct regulation in the less visible administrative arena, we have found another reason why politicians favour direct regulation. With less resistance from the polluters in the political arena, it is easier to get direct regulation accepted. The politician will count and present acceptance in the political arena as his success. That direct regulation will be less successful in the administrative arena, is something a politician does not know, tries to conceal, or regards or presents as 'beyond his control'.

Another aspect of the 'arena' notion is the fact that the application of a charge is the competence of the Department of Finance, or in the case of the US, a finance committee[17] (De Savornin Lohman, 1994b). The finance committee is primarily interested in the revenues of a charge, and not in its incentive effect. The incentive effect is usually seen as an unwanted byproduct of a revenue-raising tax (De Clercq, 1996). The environmental committee will be unwilling to share its authority with the finance committee, because the latter is less committed to protecting the environment, and because in general, committees do not like to share their authority (Anderson et al., 1977: 154).

The uncertain revenue of a charge is a disadvantage from the budgetary view of the Department of Finance (Bohm and Russell, 1985, reason 3). Next to this, the charge may have other drawbacks when evaluated from other fields. For example, a charge adds more to inflation (Bohm and Russell, 1985, reason 4).

We can conclude that opening up the 'black box' of government has yielded some interesting considerations. A model with no regard for the processes within the government may yield erroneous conclusions. However, most of the present literature is strongly US-oriented, assuming a district system of voting and weak party discipline. In Chapter 7, I will present a model that is more applicable to Europe.

6.   INSTANCES OF INEFFICIENT GOVERNMENT POLICY

Most of the literature reviewed in this chapter was aimed at explaining the minor importance of market instruments in environmental policy in general. Sometimes, a specific instance of instrument choice is analysed. An advantage of such a case study is that it sheds more light on why direct regulation (or more generally: an inefficient policy) was chosen. When trying to explain the absence of market instruments in general, one is tempted to list many factors: 'Maybe this is playing a role, maybe that is playing a role...', etc.

Here, two cases will be highlighted. The first concerns the choice of an inefficient over an efficient environmental policy (where both policies can be characterized as direct regulation), and the second concerns the choice of direct regulation over a market instrument.

A striking example of the political inclination towards inefficient environmental policy is the legislation with respect to SO_2 emissions in the 1977 amendments to the Clean Air Act in the USA (Ackerman and Hassler, 1981; Crandall, 1983; Daly and Mayor, 1986). The initial idea was to reduce SO_2 emissions from electric utilities. However, a tightening of the standard, formulated in pounds of SO_2 per unit of electricity produced, would induce many utilities to shift from eastern high-sulphur coal to western low-sulphur coal. Instead of tightening the existing standard, the new regulation required the utilities to remove a certain percentage of sulphur before emission. Thus, utilities could keep using high-sulphur coal, although it would have been more efficient to switch to low-sulphur coal.

According to Daly and Mayor (1986), the inefficient regulation was due to the successful lobby of eastern miners and trade unions. According to Crandall (1983), this explanation alone is not sufficient. He points out that as a result of the regulation, electricity rates will rise faster in the West than in the East. This will slow down industry relocation from the East to the West.

Hahn (1988, 1990) gives another example of inefficient government policy, in which the motives of visibility, controllability and distribution are combined. The state of Wisconsin had generated a surplus of emission rights for CFCs. As instruments to allocate this surplus, the state considered a fee reflecting the marginal cost of a permit and a market in permits. In the end, a regulatory strategy was chosen, based on first-come, first-served, with only a nominal fee for the permits.

Hahn's first explanation for this choice is that 'first-come first-served' results in visible job creation, whereas the costs are not readily apparent to the population at large. The instrument is designed to help accommodate 'blockbuster' projects which would bring large numbers of jobs to a depressed economic region. The costs are, that the emission rights will not be distributed in an efficient way.

Market instruments, on the other hand, have highly visible costs and far less visible and diffuse benefits. The costs fall directly on industry in terms of tax expenditures or expenditures for permits. Job creation is less visible, because firms do not have to consult a government agency, and there is no explicit need to justify the use of these rights on the basis of employment impacts. Moreover, job creation will be spread across a lot of firms, each hiring a few extra workers.

Next to this, Hahn (1988) also points out that concern about the social acceptability of using market approaches to control pollution may have played a role. He refers to Kelman (1981), whose arguments appeared in section 3 of this chapter, and will appear again in Chapter 4, section 4.

7.   CONCLUSION AND OWN APPROACH

This chapter has presented an overview of the answers to be found in the literature to the question: 'Why are market instruments not more widely applied in environmental policy, although economists think they are efficient?' Here we shall appraise the answers given and lay out the approach followed in this volume.

In section 2 we looked at why market instruments may not be all that efficient in reality. These arguments should be taken seriously. One cannot simply apply market instruments to any environmental problem and then expect everything to work smoothly. This is especially true for the application of the simpler forms of market instruments, like a uniform emissions charge or tradable emission permits.

However, in the rest of this volume I will assume that there are efficiency advantages to market instruments. This may be because the problems mentioned in section 2 are not relevant for the specific environmental problem that the market instruments are applied to, or because these problems are not important enough to completely wipe out the efficiency advantages of market instruments.

Thus, instead of examining the question: 'Why are market instruments not more widely applied in environmental policy, although economists think they are efficient?', we shall examine the question: 'Why are market instruments not more widely applied in environmental policy, although they are efficient?' This second formulation of the question prompts us to find the reason for the impopularity of market instruments in the political process. When we begin our answer to the first question with: 'First of all, market instruments are not really that efficient', then it becomes a lot easier to explain why they are not selected in the political process. It is a challenge to find out why market instruments are not selected in the political process, although they are efficient. That is the primary reason why we take the efficiency of market instruments for granted, and not because we think market instruments are efficient.

In section 3 we looked at why it may be difficult, or even impossible, to convince policy makers that it is a good idea to apply market instruments in environmental policy. While acknowledging the possible relevance of some of the arguments, we shall not develop them further in this book.

In section 4 the distributional effects of environmental policy instruments were analysed. The distributional effects are important when government policy is influenced by interest groups. Therefore, the analysis of interest group influence in economics was discussed in section 4.2. We have concluded that the approach of the interest function was most suitable for instrument choice in environmental policy. This approach focuses on interest group activities. Policy makers and voters do not play an active role. The former can be seen as a drawback, the latter as appropriate.

In this volume, we shall take one model from the interest function approach and develop it further. This is the rent seeking model. The model will be introduced in Chapter 7, section 3, and developed in Chapters 8 to 10.

When discussing the distributive effects of environmental policy instruments, many authors point out that there are groups that lose from the introduction of market instruments. However, this is an incomplete argument for their absence. The winners should also be taken into account. When this is done, it is mostly assumed that the benefits from market instruments are widely dispersed. But this assumption may not be valid. Our rent seeking model will take into account the gains from market instruments, and the possibility that they are concentrated.

In section 5 we reviewed the literature that examines decision making within the government. We concluded this is a useful approach. However, most of the literature is US-oriented and not directly applicable to a system with elections based on proportional representation. In Chapter 7, section 2, we present a model based on proportional representation, an electoral system which is applied in many European countries.

NOTES

1. Keohane et al. (1998) also present a survey. They emphasize the choice of the politician and the role and preferences of interest groups.
2. These considerations are discussed a.o. in Baumol and Oates (1988), De Savornin Lohman (1994a), Majone (1989), Bohm and Russell (1985) and Russell (1979).
3. In the sense that market instruments are only efficient under specific assumptions that may not apply in reality, all practical considerations discussed in this section are 'second best' considerations.
4. This argument may also work the other way around, i.e. other imperfections can strengthen the case for market instruments. The issue that has received most attention in this context is the 'double dividend'. The idea is that the revenues of financial instruments of environmental policy are used to reduce the distortionary taxes on labour. The conclusion in the literature is that the double dividend is certainly a reason to prefer financial instruments to other instruments (Goulder et al., 1998). However, in general, the double dividend is not so strong that financial instruments are preferable for non-environmental reasons alone (Goulder, 1995).
5. See Koster (1996) for a survey.
6. Ermoliev et al. (1996) suggest that the government operates a 'virtual' system of charges, which can also be used for non-uniformly mixed pollutants (see our reason 5): the government announces a set of charge rates, firms announce their emission levels, the government adjusts the charge rates, etc. until the environmental targets are realized.
7. We have already alluded to this in our sixth reason.
8. Russell (1979) argues there is more to monitoring a technology standard than this.
9. Blinder (1987: 147) also raises this point.
10. We will further elaborate this argument, also put forward by De Clercq (1996), in our discussion of environmentalists' preferences in Chapter 4, section 4.2.
11. See Chapter 6, section 2.
12. One may wonder whether the public interest theory is a caricature of economists' ideas of regulation and an easy target for those opposed to it. 'Economists make a ritualistic practice of kicking around the "public interest" model of regulatory origin before settling down to serious analysis of the subject' (Fiorina, 1982: 43).
13. Wittman (1995) is a contemporary advocate of the public interest theory.
14. Hamilton (1997) shows that this is true for US Congressional votes on instruments for the Superfund.
15. We will discuss the other two reasons in the appropriate sections.
16. Eichenberger and Serna (1996: 145) themselves already indicate that their discussion 'crucially hinges on the debatable assumptions made about the capabilities of losers and winners to understand the consequences of different policy measures.' However, they do not see this as a drawback, but as an illustration of how political decisions can be improved, but also manipulated, by supplying information.
17. In the following, I will use the term 'committee', because we are concerned here with the motivations of politicians. A committee consists of politicians, whereas a Department consists of bureaucrats (and a Minister). The argument also applies to bureaucrats, but the motivations of bureaucrats will be discussed later (in Chapter 4, section 3).

3. Effects of Instruments in an Industry Model

1. INTRODUCTION

This is the first of four chapters in which we discuss our first research question: what are the preferences of interest groups for environmental policy instruments? In order to establish interest group preferences for instruments, we must first know the interest groups' criteria. For example: shareholders rank the instruments according to profits. When we know the interest groups' criteria, we can then determine the instruments' performance on these criteria: is instrument A better for profits than instrument B? Combining interest groups' criteria with the instruments' performance on these criteria, we obtain the ranking of instruments for each group.

In this chapter, the approach to interest group preferences is quite theoretical. In a partial equilibrium model of a polluting industry with perfect competition, we assess the performance of several instruments on the criteria of profits, product price and employment. These are the criteria for the interest groups of shareholders, consumers and workers, respectively.

We shall examine the effects of the following instruments:

- direct regulation in the form of:
    * performance standards, alternatively called standards: a maximum ratio of emissions to output;[1]
    * firm bubbles, alternatively called bubbles: a ceiling to the total emissions of a firm;
- market instruments in the form of:
    * emissions charges: a charge per unit of emission;
    * tradable emission permits: permits for a unit of emission.
    The permits can be either auctioned or grandfathered (i.e. distributed for free among the existing firms).

Emissions charges and an auction of tradable permits are also called financial instruments. We shall use this terminology for the instruments throughout the chapter, including our review of the literature.

Another concept we have to define at the beginning of this chapter is the concept of profits. Shareholders are interested in profits, and more precisely in accounting profits. These have to be distinguished from economic profits. Accounting profits are the profits that figure in the firm's financial accounts, which we assume will all accrue to the shareholders. Economic profits are the difference between a firm's revenue and its cost of *all* inputs. For the present analysis, it is important that two cost components are part of accounting profits, but not of economic profits. One component is the normal (or market) return on the shareholders' capital. The other component is the value of the grandfathered permits. There will be a market for these permits, with a permit price. The permit price reflects the accounting profit that a firm can make on one grandfathered permit. The value of the grandfathered permits is not a part of economic profits, because it represents a cost to the firm: the cost of being allowed to emit. One can say that the firm pays this cost to the shareholders. Thus, the shareholders are interested in the value of grandfathered permits, although this is not a part of economic profits.

This chapter is organized as follows. In section 2, we review the literature on the effects of environmental policy instruments in models of the firm, the industry and the economy. Special attention is paid to the literature about the performance of instruments on the criteria of interest groups. In section 3, we shall present our own analysis. This analysis is meant to be more firmly based and more comprehensive than the literature until now. The concluding section 4 gives a summary of the preference rankings that have been derived.

2. OVERVIEW OF THE LITERATURE

2.1 Introduction

When constructing an industry model to determine interest group preferences for environmental policy instruments, we can draw on two strands of literature. One strand, reviewed in section 2.2, is aimed at determining the effects of instruments on variables like output, product price, input usage, etc. The authors do not explicitly connect these effects to the preferences of interest groups. However, this part of the literature is interesting because it has achieved a greater degree of sophistication than the second part.

The other strand of literature, reviewed in section 2.3, is concerned with the effects of environmental policy on variables that interest groups find important. For instance, the shareholders in the polluting industry are interested in profits, and the workers are interested in employment. In section 2.4 we shall see what we can conclude from both strands of the literature and which questions still remain to be examined.

2.2   The Effects of Environmental Policy Instruments

2.2.1 Overview

In this section, we shall first review the theoretical research into the effects of environmental policy instruments, and then the empirical research. The theoretical studies all yield similar results, namely that given the level of industry emissions:

-   market instruments result in less production than performance standards;
-   in the short run, firm bubbles yield the same production level as market instruments;
-   profits are higher for firm bubbles than for performance standards.

Despite the agreement between authors, it is not clear whether these outcomes are generally true. This is because with the exception of Spulber (1985, 1989), the analyses are based on limiting assumptions, a.o. that the number of firms is fixed.

Hochman and Zilberman (1978) employ a perfect competition model with the emissions to output ratio and the input–output ratio fixed per production unit, but different across firms. In this model, environmental policy results in retiring the most pollution-intensive production units. Hochman and Zilberman (1978) show that charges are welfare-maximizing and that they result in a lower output level than performance standards.

Harford and Karp (1983) note that, given output and pollution per firm, input usage will be the same for a cost-minimizing firm under performance standards and firm bubbles.

Besanko (1987) uses a model of Cournot competition with a fixed number of firms to show that with firm bubbles, production is lower and profits are higher than with design standards, that specify the level of the pollution abatement input. Emissions charges have the same effect on production as firm bubbles. In this model, the instruments cannot be ranked on welfare grounds.

Helfand (1991) employs a model of one firm that faces a constant product price to show that with firm bubbles, production is lower and profits are higher than with performance standards. Helfand (1993) extends the Hochman and Zilberman (1978) model, so that input use and pollution are not necessarily linear with output. She finds that product price and profits are lower with performance standards than with firm bubbles. It depends on the parameter values which instrument is welfare-maximizing.

Spulber (1985, 1989) offers the most general discussion. Because we extend upon his analysis, we treat his contribution more extensively, in section 2.2.2.

Another contribution that deserves special mention is Kohn's (1998), for his specific functional forms of production and emission functions and his numerical simulations. We will discuss this in section 2.2.3.

Empirical studies on the effects of instruments have recently been reviewed in

EEA (1996) and OECD (1997), and before that in Opschoor et al. (1994). Most empirical studies are *ex ante* studies: they investigate what will happen when market instruments are applied.

Since the mid-1970s, research has been done into the cost savings that can be achieved with tradable permits (see Tietenberg (1985) and Klaassen (1996) for reviews). Some studies assume that the cost-effective solution will result with market instruments, others take into account the fact that emissions trading will typically be bilateral and sequential, so that the cost-effective solution will not be reached.

More recently, there have been many studies using macroeconomic or general equilibrium models to assess the effects of charges, mostly energy charges. The interest in this issue was aroused, directly or indirectly, by government plans to levy such charges. These studies typically compare the economy with the charge to the economy without the charge, i.e. the economic impacts are to be attributed to the use of the charge *and* to a stricter environmental policy.[2]

Ex post studies have been few in number. EEA (1996) and OECD (1997) argue for more studies of this kind. OECD (1997) features an extensive discussion on how *ex post* studies should be conducted.

The general results from empirical studies are:

- environmental taxation tends to have a slightly regressive impact on income distribution;
- the effects on the economy as a whole are small, but the impact on specific sectors and regions can be negative;
- the 'double dividend' effect (increasing employment because labour taxes can be reduced with the revenues of environmental taxes) is small;
- the scarce *ex post* studies suggest that economic instruments are effective and efficient, at least there is no evidence to support the opposite.

We can conclude that the empirical studies do not offer much insight in the comparison we are mainly interested in. This is the comparison between different instruments, given the strictness of environmental policy, on variables like output, product price, employment and profits.

2.2.2 Spulber (1985, 1989)

Spulber (1985, 1989) compares a number of instruments in a partial equilibrium model with perfect competition. He uses more general cost and production functions than the authors reviewed in section 2.2.1, so that his results are more widely applicable. Furthermore, he also considers the effects of instruments in the long run, with free entry and exit of firms. In the analysis of the authors reviewed so far, the number of firms is fixed.

Let us first look at Spulber's specifications of the production and cost function.

He assumes there are fixed costs to production, that also persist in the long run.

Spulber (1985) uses the production function $q = f(x_1, ..., x_m)$, where q is the output quantity, and $x_1, ..., x_m$ are the respective input quantities, and the function f is twice differentiable, increasing and concave. A firm's emissions E are given by $E = h(x_1, ..., x_m)$, where h is convex and differentiable.

Spulber (1989) uses the cost function instead of the production function as the basis for his analysis. He uses the following cost function:

$$C(q,E) = K + V(q,E)$$

where $K > 0$ is the fixed cost and V is twice differentiable and convex in (q,E) and increasing in q.

Now we come to Spulber's results. Spulber (1985) shows that emissions charges and tradable emission permits are welfare maximizing in the long run, i.e. with free entry and exit of firms, given a limit on total industry emissions.[3] In this context, welfare is the sum of consumer surplus, government revenue and profits.

A firm bubble does not yield the optimal solution in the long run (Spulber, 1985, 1989). This is because with bubbles, the firm does not have to pay for the permission to emit. This result had not been stated formally before Spulber (1985).

To meet the industry emission limit in the long run, the emission ceiling per firm should be below the optimal emission level per firm. If the government sets the emission ceiling equal to the optimum, there will be excessive entry, and industry emissions will exceed the target level.

Spulber (1985) proves these propositions with production and emission functions that are more specific than the ones we presented above. He uses a two-input production function $q = f(x_1, x_2)$, where polluting emissions E are generated by the use of one input: $E = h(x_2)$.

Spulber (1989) also proves that output per firm will be below the optimal level, and uses a different proof. Here he uses the cost function we presented above, but again, he needs an additional assumption. We shall further treat this subject in Appendix A, section A.5, where we shall see that this additional assumption is in fact quite dubious.

Spulber (1989) also considers subsidies, but does not add to Baumol and Oates (1988) in this respect. Furthermore, Spulber (1989) considers technological standards. He models this as follows. Emissions E depend on the output level q and the abatement technology x: $E = h(q,x)$. With a technological standard, the government prescribes a certain value of x. Technological standards do not yield the optimal solution either.

Spulber (1985, 1989) devotes considerable attention to the output charge. This analysis can be seen as a reaction to Carlton and Loury (1980, 1986) who assert that a Pigouvian tax does not always yield the optimal result in the long run. This is due to two specific assumptions:

- the tax is levied on output instead of on emissions (Carlton and Loury, 1980);
- the pollution damage as a function of emissions per firm E and the number of firms n is specified as $D(n,E)$, instead of as $D(nE)$ (Carlton and Loury, 1980, 1986).

The problem is that the tax is not levied on the item that gives rise to the problem. When the government wants to reduce emissions, it should tax emissions, and not output. The specification $D(n,E)$ for the damage function is somewhat strange. The only way in which the number of firms could have an independent effect on pollution damage would be in a spatial model. But even then, it would be hard to specify the relation. Anyway, if pollution damage cannot be written as $D(nE)$, one unit of emission differs from another because it occurs somewhere else. Then a uniform emission tax is indeed not optimal: the tax should vary with respect to location.

Kohn (1998: 81–84) presents a model in which the number of firms does have an independent effect on pollution. He assumes the firms are evenly spread across a plain, such that every firm is in the centre of a square and all squares have the same size. He further assumes that every firm only pollutes its 'own' square and pollution does not depend on the location within the square. There are two major problems with this model. First, it is very strange that the area that a firm pollutes depends upon the location of other firms. Secondly, the firms have no incentive to spread evenly across the plain. Firms would only do so in a spatial model of competition (e.g. Greenhut et al., 1987). Alternatively, the government could force the firms to spread by zoning restrictions or induce them to spread by a regionally differentiated charge. Kohn (1998), however, asserts that a combination of a uniform emissions charge and a lump-sum tax or subsidy is optimal.

Now we turn to Spulber's (1985, 1989) own analysis. In the short run, given the number of firms, an output charge is only optimal if there is a fixed relation between output and emissions.[4] In that case, abatement is not possible: a certain amount of output is always produced with the same amount of emissions. When abatement is possible, an output charge will not bring about the optimal solution. In general, it will be optimal to reduce emissions partly by reducing output and partly by abatement. But an output charge does not give any incentive to abate. Thus, the reduction in emissions will be achieved completely by a reduction in output.

In the long run, the condition for output charges to be optimal is even stricter: emissions must be proportional to output. Only in that case is there a fixed relation between *industry* output and industry emissions. Contrary to Carlton and Loury's (1980) assertion, this result does not change when an entry fee is added to the output charge.

2.2.3 Kohn (1998)

Kohn (1998) consolidates the author's articles in which the environment is incorporated in the microeconomic theory of the firm. He focuses on computable numerical models, long-run analysis in which the number of firms is endogenous, Pigouvian taxation and general equilibrium models. The author hardly compares different instruments, except to note that abatement subsidies cannot be optimal. What makes Kohn interesting for our purposes is his treatment of a firm's production and emission. We shall briefly discuss this point here and comment on his method in section 3.3.2.

For the production function of a firm, Kohn (1998) uses a Cobb-Douglas variant, adapted from Henderson and Quandt (1958):

$$Y = aL^u K^v - bL^{u+1} K^{v+1} \qquad u + v = 1 \qquad u^2 + v^2 < 1$$

where Y is production, L is labour and K is capital. This production function has a number of 'neoclassical' properties. For instance, returns to scale are first increasing and then decreasing.

Kohn (1998) first discusses the case where abatement is not possible, but the emissions to output ratio may vary with the scale of the firm. Emissions can then be reduced by reducing the output of the polluting firm and adjusting the number of firms. An efficient combination of these two methods is achieved by an emissions charge. Later, Kohn also discusses other ways of reducing emission and pollution damage: recycling pollutive output, exposure avoidance, reducing the use of a pollutive input, switching to a cleaner production process and end-of-pipe abatement.

We shall look more closely at the latter three methods, which involve the behaviour of the polluting firm only. Kohn (1998: 94–100) presents a model in which the reduction of a polluting input and the switch to a cleaner production process are combined. He assumes there are two ways of producing a good: one with a polluting input and one without it. When environmental policy is lenient, firms can comply by reducing their use of the polluting input. Beyond a certain point, firms start switching to the clean production process.

For end-of-pipe abatement, Kohn (1998) uses a function introduced by Harford (1989). Harford (1989) assumes that the fraction B of gross emissions G abated is:

$$B(L_a, K_a, G) = \frac{L_a^\gamma K_a^\gamma}{L_a^\gamma K_a^\gamma + \sigma G^\theta}$$

where $L_a (K_a)$ is the amount of labour (capital) used in abatement. In Appendix A, section A.2.1, we show that with this abatement function, marginal cost of abatement is positive for $B = 0$. This implies that when the emissions charge is low, a firm will not abate, but reduce its output instead.

Kohn (1998) recognizes the problem of a threshold value of marginal abatement cost in his Chapter 14 about the optimal combination of abatement and avoidance. He presents a model in which the emissions of the one sector reduce the output of the other sector. However, this other sector can take measures to avoid the adverse effects of pollution. Then the problem with Harford's (1989) abatement function is the following. Suppose that, starting from the *laissez-faire* equilibrium, the emissions charge is raised until it equals marginal pollution damage. The adjustment process may end at a point in which there is avoidance but no abatement, whereas it is optimal to have abatement and no avoidance.

2.3 Preferences Derived from Partial Equilibrium Models

2.3.1 Buchanan and Tullock (1975)

Buchanan and Tullock (1975) were the first to argue that the real world dominance of direct controls over market-oriented instruments could be explained by the preferences of interest groups. They show that profits in the polluting industry are higher (or losses lower) for direct regulation than for an emissions tax. Thus, the polluting industry, that will be very influential in the decision making process, prefers direct regulation. The political economy part of their argument has been discussed in Chapter 2, section 4.3.2. Here we shall look at how Buchanan and Tullock derive the preferences of the polluting industry.[5]

In Buchanan and Tullock's (1975) model, the industry is perfectly competitive, consisting of a large number of identical firms. In the initial situation, without pollution control, there is long-run equilibrium. Then the government decides to reduce industry emissions. Buchanan and Tullock assume that emissions are linear in the output level: there is no technology available to reduce pollution per unit of output. The only way to reduce pollution is by reducing output.

Two instruments to reduce output are compared: an output charge versus direct regulation in the form of non-tradable output quotas per firm. In the short run, a firm's losses will be lower with direct regulation than with an output charge, because with an output charge the firm has to pay for its output. There may even be a short-run profit with direct regulation. In the long run, there will be no profits with an output charge. There may be long-run profits with direct regulation, if it discriminates against new firms. Thus the polluting industry, interested in profits, prefers direct regulation to charges.

2.3.2 Dewees (1983)

Buchanan and Tullock's (1975) analysis suffers from the weakness that the case they analyse is rather exceptional: pollution can only be reduced by curtailing output. In the real world, however, pollution control technologies are available and economically feasible.

Dewees (1983) takes this crucial fact into account. He starts from the assumption that emissions can be reduced by taking measures that decrease emissions per unit of output. Compared with Buchanan and Tullock (1975), Dewees also broadens the analysis in that tradable emission permits (that can be auctioned or grandfathered) are included in the instrument set. Next to that, environmentalists' preferences are discussed. Dewees refines the analysis by sub-dividing the industry interest group into shareholders and workers. He discusses the consequences of environmental policy for these two groups when capital is malleable, or mobile (capital can be transferred from one firm or industry to another without capital loss), and when capital is non-malleable, or immobile (it is productive only in its present use). Shareholders are interested in profits, workers incur costs when they have to shift to another firm within the industry, and even more when they have to shift to another industry. Labour costs are assumed to be a fixed percentage of long-run operating costs.

Dewees assumes that the policy measure to be taken is aimed at a reduction of emissions per unit of output to a certain level. This implies that industry emissions can vary among instruments: the instrument that results in higher industry output will also result in higher industry emissions.

In the main analysis, Dewees assumes a unitary demand elasticity. The instruments considered are: an emissions charge per unit of emission, tradable emission permits (that can be auctioned or grandfathered) and direct regulation in the form a performance standard.

Dewees discusses three cases:

A.   costs and policies are identical for incumbent firms and new firms;
B.   costs are identical for incumbent firms and new firms, but standards are stricter for new firms;
C.   costs are lower for new firms, but policies are identical for incumbent firms and new firms.

Here we shall only consider case A. In the initial situation, without pollution control, there is long-run equilibrium. In Dewees' model, output is produced by capital and labour, and pollution is a byproduct.[6] Pollution per unit of output can only be reduced by tail-end treatment. The capital–labour ratio of these abatement activities is constant and equal to the constant long-run capital–labour ratio in production. Dewees assumes the average cost (AC) curve is U-shaped. He further assumes that with environmental policy, the minimum of the AC curve will occur at the same, or at a higher, production level. This means that the efficient size of a firm (i.e. the production level at which AC is at its minimum) does not decrease with environmental policy. In his figures and mathematical expressions, he assumes the minimum will occur at the same production level, i.e. the AC curve rises vertically as a result of environmental policy.

Although Dewees distinguishes between malleable and non-malleable capital, this distinction is not always apparent in his discussion. For instance, in his analysis and figures, Dewees mistakenly uses the same cost functions and cost curves for malleable and non-malleable capital. This is wrong, because with malleable capital, any quantity of output q is produced with the *optimal* amount of capital for that particular q, and with non-malleable capital, any q is produced with the *same* amount of capital. Thus, with non-malleable capital, production costs will exceed those with malleable capital, except in one point: at the minimum of the respective AC curves.

Let us first look at the effects of instruments with malleable capital: capital can be shifted to other industries without cost. There will never be any loss for shareholders. Should the yield on capital in this particular industry be lower than in other industries, the shareholders simply move their capital to other industries. With grandfathering, they even enjoy a gain, because the firm will make an accounting profit than can be ascribed to the permits initially grandfathered. The amount that the firm has to pay to the government with emissions charges and a tradable permit auction accrues to the shareholders with grandfathering. Thus with malleable capital, shareholders prefer grandfathering to the other instruments and to no environmental policy, and are indifferent between all other instruments and no environmental policy.

Industry employment is the same with the standard as in the initial situation. This is due to two assumptions. First, the demand function is unitary elastic, so that the amount consumers spend on the product is independent of the product price. Secondly, the capital–labour ratio is constant and equal in the output and abatement department of the firm, so that a fixed part of operating costs goes to labour. Since with standards all of the firm's revenues go to capital and labour, the wage sum will be the same with standards and with no environmental policy. And because the wage rate is the same, industry employment will be the same.

However, employment does shift between firms within the industry. Environmental policy raises the industry's costs, so that product price must rise and the quantity produced by the industry must decline. Due to the assumption that the firm's efficient size does not decrease with environmental policy, the number of firms will decline. The employees of the firms that leave the industry can find a job with the firms that stay in the industry. The firms that stay in the industry need more workers, because they have to abate their pollution.

With market instruments, the consumers still spend the same amount of money on the product, because demand is unitary elastic. But not all of the firms' revenue is a reward for capital and labour. Part of it goes to the government (with emissions charges and a tradable permit auction) or to the shareholders (with grandfathering). Thus, the wage sum with market instruments will be lower than with standards, and industry employment will be lower. Compared with the initial

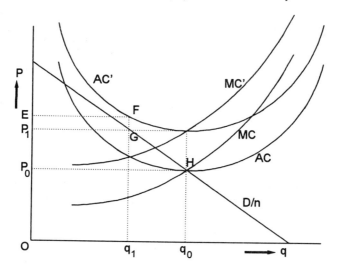

Figure 3.1 Short-run losses

situation, industry employment will decline.

Thus, with malleable capital, workers prefer standards to market instruments, and are indifferent between market instruments. Workers will be against environmental policy, because it always results in firms leaving the industry, the employees of which will have to find a new job.

The product price will be higher for market instruments than for standards, because with market instruments firms must pay for their residual emissions. Thus, production will be lower with market instruments. Because all instruments result in the same emission to output ratio, market instruments result in lower emissions. Thus, environmentalists will prefer market instruments.

Now we turn to the analysis for non-malleable capital: capital cannot be moved to another industry, because it is productive in its present use only. Because of Dewees' assumption that the efficient firm size does not decline with environmental policy, there will always be an economic loss with all instruments of environmental policy. This is illustrated in Figure 3.1. Here, D/n is the demand curve for the industry, divided by the number of firms.[7] AC and MC are the average and marginal cost curves without environmental policy. The initial equilibrium is at H, where each firm produces q_0 and product price is P_0. Due to environmental policy, the cost curves rise to AC' and MC'. In Figure 3.1, they rise vertically. In the new short-run equilibrium, each firm produces q_1 and product price is P_1. The firm's loss is $EFGP_1$.

The shareholders receive a lower return on their capital than what can be earned elsewhere. The shareholders accept this loss, because they cannot move the industry's non-malleable production capital to a more productive use.

According to Dewees, accounting losses are higher for financial instruments than for standards, because average and marginal costs are higher for market instruments. The reason Dewees gives for this is that with market instruments, firms must also pay for their residual emissions. We shall shortly come back to this latter assertion, but we note that higher average and marginal costs are not sufficient conditions for an instrument to result in higher losses. The additional condition needed is that the efficient scale of the firm with market instruments should not be too far below the efficient scale with standards. Dewees himself does not mention this condition.

Obviously, accounting losses will be higher for financial instruments than for grandfathering, because economic losses are equal.[8] The only difference is that with financial instruments, firms have to pay the government for their residual emissions. According to Dewees, grandfathering might result in lower accounting losses than standards, but it is unlikely that the value of the rights exceeds the economic loss.

Thus, with non-malleable capital, shareholders will be most opposed to financial instruments. They will also oppose standards. They will probably oppose grandfathering as well.

With respect to industry employment L with standards and non-malleable capital, Dewees writes: 'Total employment was unchanged in the malleable capital case above. Here capital bears more of the losses, so L should increase...' (p. 58). Dewees' reasoning seems to be: with environmental policy and non-malleable capital, there is a loss. A firm's production costs exceed its revenues. Without environmental policy, a firm's production costs equal its revenues. With environmental policy, a firm's revenues are the same as without environmental policy, because demand is unitary elastic. Therefore, total costs are higher with environmental policy. Since a fixed part of total costs is for labour, employment is higher with environmental policy. However, the final part of this reasoning is wrong. With non-malleable capital, the capital–labour ratio is not independent of the quantity produced. The amount of capital used in production is the same, regardless of the quantity produced. With environmental policy, the firm would like to reduce its production capital along with the quantity produced, but capital is non-malleable: it cannot be put to any other use. Thus, the amount of production capital remains the same, and the number of workers in production is reduced relatively drastically. Meanwhile, the firm attracts abatement capital and abatement workers. The capital–labour ratio in abatement equals the long-run capital–labour ratio in production, so that with non-malleable capital, the overall capital–labour ratio rises as a result of environmental policy. It is unclear whether employment rises.

Dewees does not offer a discussion of employment in the case of non-malleable capital with market instruments. Presumably this is because he applies the above argument to market instruments as well.[9] In his table, he writes that there will be 'No drop' in employment with any instrument. Thus, with non-malleable capital, the workers are indifferent between any instrument of environmental policy and no environmental policy, because their own firm will still be able to employ every one of them.

Dewees states that with non-malleable capital as well, product price will be higher with market instruments than with standards. The explanation, that is supposed to be valid for malleable as well as for non-malleable capital, is that with market instruments, firms must also pay for their residual emissions. Thus, average and marginal costs will be higher with market instruments, resulting in a higher product price. This explanation can be accepted for the case of malleable capital, because the product price has to cover all costs. But with non-malleable capital, the product price is at the intersection of the demand curve and marginal costs, and there can be losses. According to Dewees, marginal costs will be higher for market instruments than for standards, because with market instruments firms must also pay for their residual emissions. But while this is a reason for *average* cost to be higher with market instruments, it does not apply to *marginal* cost. In fact, as we shall see in section 3.2.1, short-run marginal cost at the intersection with the demand curve will be equal for the financial instruments and the direct regulation instrument of firm bubbles.

According to Dewees, product price is higher, and thus production lower, with market instruments than with standards. Because all instruments result in the same emission to output ratio, market instruments result in lower emissions. Thus, environmentalists will prefer market instruments with malleable as well as with non-malleable capital.

We conclude that the intentions of Dewees (1983) were good. He wanted to consider the effects of tradable permits and performance standards, which had not been done before. He noted that within the polluting industry, the preferences of shareholders and workers should be distinguished. He wanted to take into account that, contrary to Buchanan and Tullock's (1975) assumption, emissions per unit of output can be reduced. Finally, he treated the option of a difference in policies and in costs between incumbent firms and new firms.

On the downside, we note that his assumption that the government goal is to reduce emissions per unit of output to a certain level, is a bit eccentric. This makes it difficult to compare his results with other analyses that take reduction of total emissions as the government goal. But the most important criticism of Dewees is that at a number of points, his analysis is incomplete, obscure and wrong.

2.3.3 Leidy and Hoekman (1994)

Leidy and Hoekman (1994) expand upon Buchanan and Tullock's (1975) model in a different way. They analyse what happens if the polluting industry is exposed to foreign competition, so that the country imports part of its consumption of the

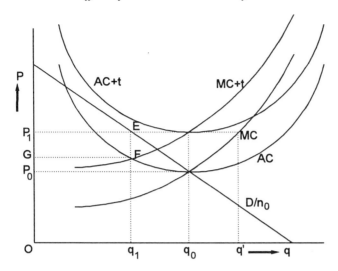

Figure 3.2 Long-run equilibrium

product. As in Buchanan and Tullock (1975), pollution can only be reduced by reducing output.

Leidy and Hoekman's contribution consists of three elements. The first is the introduction of foreign competition in Buchanan and Tullock's analysis. Because foreign competition does not change the qualitative results of Buchanan and Tullock (1975), we do not present this analysis here. Furthermore, Leidy and Hoekman discuss the indirect effect of international competition on industry preferences. We shall present their arguments on this point in Chapter 4, section 2.2. Finally, Leidy and Hoekman (1994) make some remarks about the preferences of workers and environmentalists, that can also be appreciated without reference to international trade. These latter remarks will be discussed here within Buchanan and Tullock's (1975) framework, i.e. the industry is not exposed to foreign competition.

Figure 3.2 illustrates the long-run equilibrium of the case that Leidy and Hoekman (1994) discuss most extensively. Suppose the government wishes to reduce industry output from Q_0 to Q_1. In the initial situation there are n_0 firms in the industry. The industry demand curve divided by the number of firms n_0 is drawn as D/n_0 in Figure 3.2. In the initial situation, AC and MC are the cost curves. Each firm produces q_0, and $Q_0 = n_0 q_0$. Product price is P_0. Direct regulation consists of giving each of these n_0 firms a nontradable production quota $q_1 = Q_1/n_0$. Leidy and Hoekman (1994) assume that this quota will enable firms to sustain a long-run profit. In Figure 3.2 this profit is $P_1 EFG$. With a tax t, cost curves rise vertically with t to MC+t and AC+t. In the long run, some firms will leave the industry. This is because production per firm with a tax is still q_0, since the efficient scale of a firm is not affected by the tax. For total industry output to fall to Q_1, some firms must leave the industry.

Now we move to interest group preferences. Workers will prefer direct regulation to emissions charges for three reasons. First, industry employment will be higher with direct regulation, since the output is produced inefficiently in the long run. In Figure 3.2, average production costs are OG with direct regulation and OP_0 with an emissions charge. Secondly, the workers hope to capture part of the firms' excess profit. And thirdly, layoffs (if any) under direct regulation will occur at all firms, while with emissions charges only the workers of the firms that leave the industry lose their job. The former option will be seen as more equitable. The exit of firms will also have regional implications, that regional labour officials would like to avoid. Moreover, if part of the workers of a firm will be fired, these will mostly be the younger workers. They can find a new job relatively easily. When a complete firm leaves the industry, everyone loses his job, including the older employees, who will not find a new job so easily.

Leidy and Hoekman (1994) argue that environmentalists will also prefer direct regulation, although firms have an incentive to produce more than their quota. In Figure 3.2, they would like to produce q' instead of q_1, because at q' their profit is maximized given the product price P_1.[10] This means that a firm's output must be monitored to keep it from producing more than q_1. Assuming perfect enforcement, however, the environmental goal will be reached with certainty by direct regulation. With emissions charges, the producers will increase production above Q_1 when there is economic growth or factor prices decline. Moreover, with direct regulation it is easier to require firms to clean up past environmental degradation, since no firms will leave the industry, and they have supernormal profits.

The government can use the revenues from an emissions charge to make this alternative more attractive, but there are two caveats. First, when the revenues are directed to the producers, they might be competed away by entry. Secondly, the revenues can be directed to the environmentalists, but the producers might also offer the environmentalists part of their profits under direct regulation.

We can conclude that Leidy and Hoekman (1994) offer some interesting thoughts on the preferences of workers and environmentalists. We can also conclude that taking into account international trade does not affect the interest groups' preferences, as derived from the analysis of the model. However, international trade can influence the industry's preferences in an indirect way, as we shall discuss in Chapter 4, section 2.2.

2.3.4 Dijkstra and Nentjes (1998)

Dijkstra and Nentjes (1998) set out to construct a post-Keynesian industry model that is more realistic than the other models considered here. The differences with the other models are:

- firms differ in their production and abatement costs;
- firms set their price at average variable cost plus a given and constant markup.

Dijkstra and Nentjes (1998) consider the market instruments of an emissions charge and tradable emission permits that are either grandfathered or auctioned, and direct regulation in the form of a firm bubble and a performance standard. They model this performance standard as a maximum emissions to output ratio, but also remark that a standard in reality often contains more detailed prescriptions. This means there are efficiency gains for a firm when moving from a standard to a firm bubble. However, Dijkstra and Nentjes do not explicitly model these efficiency gains.

Dijkstra and Nentjes (1998) present a model with two monopolists who can abate their emissions by end-of-pipe equipment. Production and abatement costs differ between the two firms. When determining the employment effects, Dijkstra and Nentjes only look at employment in production. They justify this by arguing that abatement is quite capital-intensive and does not require much labour.

They conclude that shareholders will probably prefer grandfathering to bubbles, and bubbles to financial instruments. However, if demand is very elastic, shareholders would prefer bubbles to grandfathering. If there are large differences between the firms' abatement costs, the efficiency gains from market instruments are large. In that case, shareholders would prefer financial instruments to bubbles.

Workers prefer bubbles to market instruments when the efficiency gains from market instruments are low. When the efficiency gains are high, they prefer market instruments.

2.4 Conclusion

In this conclusion, we summarize the results of the literature reviewed in sections 2.2 and 2.3, and look at the methods by which these results were obtained. The results from the literature on the effects of environmental policy instruments are that, given the level of industry emissions:

- in the short run, market instruments result in less production than performance standards;
- in the short run, firm bubbles yield the same production level as market instruments;
- profits are higher for firm bubbles than for performance standards;
- in the long run, market instruments are welfare-maximizing, and instruments of direct regulation are not;
- in the long run, there are more firms with bubbles than with market instruments, and production per firm is lower with bubbles than with market instruments.

It is more problematic to state the general conclusions from the literature reviewed in section 2.3. The contributions to this literature, on the preferences of interest groups derived from industry models, differ widely in their initial assumptions. Dewees (1983) assumes the government goal is a certain emissions to output ratio, whereas the others assume the government goal is a certain level of industry emissions. Dijkstra and Nentjes (1998) employ a post-Keynesian model, whereas the other authors employ a neoclassical model.

Another obstacle to drawing conclusions is the combination of limiting assumptions and the lack of rigorous derivation of results in the literature reviewed. This combination casts doubts on the general applicability of the results. With this in mind, we can draw the following tentative conclusions:

- shareholders' favourite instrument is grandfathering. Their least favourite instruments are the financial instruments;
- workers prefer standards to market instruments, and are indifferent between market instruments.

Now we shall look at the methods used in the literature. From our review of the literature on effects of environmental policy instruments in section 2.2, we can conclude that Spulber (1985, 1989) represents the frontier, because he uses the most general cost and production functions and he also analyses the long run. The literature on interest groups' preferences, reviewed in section 2.3, has not yet reached the same level of formalization. The authors mainly use graphical and verbal expositions, instead of mathematical analysis, and introduce simplifying assumptions. Buchanan and Tullock (1975) as well as Leidy and Hoekman (1994) assume a fixed emissions to output ratio. Dewees (1983) assumes the firm's efficient scale is nondecreasing in the strictness of environmental policy. Dijkstra and Nentjes (1998) do not use any particular simplifying assumptions, but this in turn makes it difficult to arrerive at a definite preference ranking.

Thus, from the first strand of literature, we shall borrow the analytical tools to examine the question from the second strand of literature: what are the preferences of the interest groups in the polluting industry for instruments of environmental policy?

3.   THE PARTIAL EQUILIBRIUM MODEL

3.1   Introduction

3.1.1 General introduction
In this section, I will present a general analysis of the effects of environmental policy instruments in a partial equilibrium model of perfect competition. The

discussion of the effects will ultimately result, in section 3.6, in a derivation of the preferences of the interest groups in the polluting industry: the consumers, the shareholders and the workers.

We shall examine the effects of the following instruments:

- direct regulation in the form of:
  * performance standards, or standards: a maximum ratio of emissions to output;
  * firm bubbles, or bubbles: a ceiling to the total emissions of a firm;
- market instruments in the form of:
  * emissions charges: a charge per unit of emission;
  * tradable emission permits: permits for a unit of emission.
    These permits can be either auctioned or grandfathered.

In section 3.1.2 we shall discuss covenants and see how they fit into this taxonomy.

We assume that before environmental policy is introduced, the industry is in long-run equilibrium without any government intervention. The level of allowed industry emissions is taken as given, both in the short run and the long run. We assume the government has the knowledge to apply the instruments in such a way that the desired reduction in industry emissions is reached.

We distinguish a short-run and a long-run response to environmental regulation. In the short run, the number of firms is given, but production per firm is variable. In the long run, firms can enter and leave the industry at no cost, so that economic profit is zero in equilibrium.

The cost function we employ, also called operating cost function, has the general form $C(q,E)$, where q is production and E is emissions per firm. Although the short-run cost function will differ from the long-run cost function, we shall use the same notation for both. For the moment, we only give the signs of the first derivatives:

- $C_q > 0$: cost rises when production rises;
- $C_E < 0$ with environmental policy: cost rises when emissions decline.

Other properties of the cost function are derived in Appendix A and discussed in section 3.3.

By choosing perfect competition as our market model, we eliminate two differences between market instruments and direct regulation, which we discussed in Chapter 1. First, the static efficiency advantage of market instruments is eliminated, because all firms are equal. Secondly, the dynamic efficiency advantage is eliminated, because we abstract from technological progress. However, we shall see in section 3.5 that market instruments do have the productive efficiency advantage we also mentioned in Chapter 1. Thus, market instruments are welfare-maximizing in our model.

There are two reasons for examining the effects of instruments in a partial equilibrium model of perfect competition. First, this model is a 'basic' case that has not been completely examined yet. One can think of a lot of different models in which to study the effects of instruments:

- with heterogeneous firms;
- with imperfect competition;
- with more than one market, or even a general equilibrium model.

The effects of instruments in all these models can be split analytically into two terms. The first is the 'competitive' effect, that corresponds to the effect in a partial equilibrium model of perfect competition. The second is the 'other' effect, that stems from the difference between the model studied and the perfect competition model. Thus, before one can model and understand the effects of instruments in any other model, one should first understand the effects in a partial equilibrium model of perfect competition.

Secondly, we have decided in Chapter 2 that we were going to look at situations where market instruments are welfare-maximizing. In order to be consistent, we should then derive the effects of instruments and the preferences of interest groups from a model in which market instruments are welfare-maximizing. This is the case with the partial equilibrium model of perfect competition, as we shall see in section 3.5.

The improvements and extensions we offer to the literature reviewed in section 2 are:

- the use of the most general cost function and of rigorous analysis;
- a complete overview of the effects of the instruments in the short run and the long run, including interest groups' preferences;
- the derivation of consumers' preferences.

The rest of this section is organized as follows. In section 3.2 we give the equilibrium conditions for the short run and the long run. In section 3.3 we discuss the properties of the cost function. These properties are derived in Appendix A. In section 3.4 we compare the effects of the instruments on product price, production per firm, number of firms and emissions per firm. In section 3.5 the welfare effects are analysed. In section 3.6 we derive the preferences of the consumers, the shareholders and the workers.

3.1.2 Covenants
Voluntary agreements, or covenants, are not explicitly analysed in our model.

Compared with direct regulation, the instrument of covenants gives industry a larger say in how to attain the environmental targets.[11] Covenants are most widely applied in the Netherlands. In this section we shall first discuss covenants in general, and then we shall see how they fit into our model.

With covenants, the government typically makes an agreement about emission reduction with a number of, or all, firms in an industry, most often via the industry organization. The firms then have to find a way of distributing the emission reductions among themselves. Finally, each firm has to find a way to achieve the emission reduction it has taken upon itself.

The advantages of covenants to direct regulation are first, that they promote efficiency. Firms can decide how to reduce their own emissions, and to a certain extent also how to distribute the industry emission reduction among themselves. This will result in lower abatement costs than the alternative where the government determines by how much and how firms should reduce emissions.

The second advantage of covenants is that industry is more involved in, and will feel more responsible for, environmental policy, because more decisions are left to the firms themselves. This more positive attitude toward environmental policy can be expected to result in a higher acceptability of environmental policy and a better environmental performance.

The disadvantage of covenants is their questionable environmental effectiveness. We can distinguish two kinds of covenants. The first kind of covenant specifies the industry's effort: 'We will try to achieve a 30% emission reduction'. The second kind specifies the result: 'We will achieve a 30% emission reduction'. It is very uncertain in how much emission reduction the first kind of covenant will eventually result, but the expected value will be below 30%. The second kind of covenant gives more certainty, but there can still be a problem. The government signs a covenant with a number of firms, but the individual firms have to reduce their emissions. If total emissions exceed the emissions agreed upon in the covenant, who is held responsible? Firms may expect they can get away with an emission level that is higher than the level compatible with the total emission level from the covenant. Then industry emissions will exceed the emission level agreed upon in the covenant.

How do covenants fit into our model and our taxonomy of instruments? It is clear that covenants are not market instruments, because there is no charge to be paid, and there are no tradable permits. However, it is unclear how the emission reductions from the covenant are actually distributed among firms. In fact, a tradable emission permit system may develop out of a covenant (Koutstaal, 1992). But it seems most appropriate to consider covenants as an instrument of direct regulation.

Let us now consider the differences between covenants and the instruments of direct regulation from our model. There may be a difference with respect to compliance. As we have seen, firms may expect they can get away with a high emission level under a covenant. On the other hand, firms may be more motivated to comply with covenants than with the other forms of direct regulation. We have completely abstracted from this issue by assuming perfect compliance with all instruments.

A covenant specifying industry effort should be treated carefully. We wish to compare instruments with the same effect on expected industry emissions. Thus, a covenant stipulating: 'We will try to reduce emissions by 30%' should be compared to, for instance, firm bubbles resulting in less emission reduction, say 20%. However, it will be difficult to obtain a value for the expected emission reduction from a covenant specifying industry effort.

Finally, let us discuss the efficiency of covenants. Covenants give a firm the freedom of how to achieve its emission reduction. This concurs with our specification of direct regulation: firms are only given an emission ceiling or an emissions to output ratio, and they can determine themselves how to achieve this. Furthermore, covenants also take into account differences in abatement costs between firms. Firms with low abatement costs will have to abate more than firms with high abatement costs. This might even result in an efficient distribution of emissions across the firms, a result for which the government would otherwise need a lot of information (which it probably does not have) or market instruments.

In our model, we abstract from cost differences between firms, because we assume all firms are equal. Thus there is no difference in this respect between covenants and the instruments of direct regulation we consider.

To look at it in another way, we have assumed that with direct regulation the available emission room is distributed efficiently across firms. This assumption is problematic for the more traditional forms of direct regulation, because then we must assume the government has the information and the authority to achieve the efficient distribution. In fact, it becomes more credible when we consider covenants, where the distribution of the emission room is left to the firms.

To conclude on a positive note, we have seen that covenants can easily be incorporated in our partial equilibrium model. To conclude on a negative note, the model is not very appropriate for the study of the differences between covenants and other instruments of direct regulation.

Thus, within the class of direct regulation, we shall not distinguish between imposed instruments and voluntary agreements. We shall distinguish between regulation specifying the level of emissions per firm, and regulation specifying the allowed emissions to output ratio. All four combinations of imposed instruments or voluntary agreements, and firm bubbles or standards, are found in practice.

3.2 Equilibrium Conditions

3.2.1 Short run
In the short run, the number of firms is given. Profits and losses can occur. Profits

do not immediately induce entry, because it takes time to enter an industry (build a factory, etc.). Losses do not immediately induce exit, because the incumbent firms have already invested in capital goods. To shift these capital goods to other uses entails costs. We assume losses are not so high that firms will want to leave the industry in the short run.

In the short run, the number of firms n is equal for all instruments. Since industry emissions are taken as given, emissions per firm E must be equal for all instruments to keep industry emissions equal. With firm bubbles, the government simply restricts emissions per firm to E. With tradable permits the government issues permits allowing industry emissions of nE. With emissions charges, the government has to set the charge at the level at which the firm chooses to emit E. With standards, the government has to set the emissions to output ratio at the level at which the firm chooses to emit E.

Thus, there are two variables in the short run: product price P and production per firm q. The value of these variables is determined by two equations. The one is the inverse demand function $P = P(nq)$. The other is the supply function, determined by the first order condition for profit maximization. These first order conditions also apply to the long-run equilibrium.

We shall now determine the first order conditions. The intuition behind these conditions and their implications are discussed in section 3.4.2.

With firm bubbles, the firm maximizes revenues minus operating cost with a restriction of E' on its emission level:

$$\max \ Pq - C(q,E) - \lambda(E - E')$$

With an emissions charge of t, the firm maximizes revenues minus operating cost minus the charge bill:

$$\max \ Pq - C(q,E) - tE$$

With tradable permits, the firm maximizes revenues minus operating cost minus the cost of permits (with E_0 the amount of permits initially received for free and t' the permit price):

$$\max \ Pq - C(q,E) - t'(E - E_0)$$

We see that, with firm bubbles as well as with the market instruments of emissions charges and tradable permits, the first order conditions are the same:

$$P - C_q(q,E) = 0 \qquad\qquad (3.1^m), (3.1^b)^{12}$$
$$\lambda = t = t' = -C_E(q,E)$$

The product price equals the marginal cost of producing output, keeping emissions constant. The marginal cost of emission reduction equals the price of emission, either in the form of an emissions charge, a permit price or the shadow price with a bubble.

With standards, the result is different. The firm maximizes profit under the restriction that the emissions to output ratio does not exceed the allowed maximum e:

$$\max \ Pq \ - \ C(q,E) \ - \ \lambda(E \ - \ eq)$$

The first order condition is:

$$P \ - \ C_q(q,E) \ - \ eC_E(q,E) \ = \ 0 \qquad\qquad (3.1^s)^{13}$$

3.2.2 Long run

In the long run, the number of firms is variable. The equilibrium number of firms will be such that the remaining firms make zero economic profit.

In the long run, there are four equations for every instrument, which determine the equilibrium values of the product price P, production per firm q, emissions per firm E and the number of firms n:[14]

$$P \ = \ C_q \qquad\qquad (3.1^b),\ (3.1^m) \qquad P \ = \ C_q \ + \ \frac{E}{q}C_E \qquad (3.1^s)$$

$$Pq \ = \ C(q,E) \ - \ EC_E \qquad (3.2^m) \qquad Pq \ = \ C(q,E) \qquad (3.2^b),\ (3.2^s)$$

$$nE \ = \ L \qquad\qquad\qquad\qquad\qquad\qquad\qquad\qquad\qquad (3.3)$$

$$P \ = \ P(nq) \qquad P'(nq) \ < \ 0 \qquad\qquad\qquad\qquad\qquad (3.4)$$

Equations (3.1) are the profit maximization conditions, that have already been derived in section 3.2.1. Equations (3.2) are the zero (economic) profit conditions. With direct regulation, firms should cover their operating cost $C(q,E)$. With market instruments, there is an extra cost component $-EC_E$:[15] the cost of the right to emit E. With emissions charges and an auction of tradable permits, a firm must pay the government for this right. But with grandfathering as well, the firm must cover $-EC_E$. If a firm would only cover its operating cost, it had better sell its permits and leave the industry. The amount $-EC_E$ is a cost to the firm, and a revenue to its shareholders.

Equation (3.3) states that industry emissions for all instruments equal the government target of L. Equation (3.4) is the inverse market demand function for the product.

3.3   Analysis of the Cost Function

3.3.1 Introduction
In this section, we wish to derive the effects of environmental policy from the general cost function $C(q,E)$. Unlike the previous studies, we try not to impose any properties on this cost function with the purpose of facilitating the analysis. Instead, we derive the properties from specific conditions. Before we discuss these conditions in section 3.3.3, we shall first present the case for an analysis that is more mathematical than the work of most other authors in the field, in section 3.3.2.

3.3.2 The need for a general mathematical analysis
In section 2 we saw that the literature on the effects of instruments (section 2.2) mainly uses mathematical analysis, whereas the literature on preferences (section 2.3) mainly uses graphical analysis and verbal expositions. However, the way in which both approaches are followed leaves something to be desired.

Let us first consider the studies that rely mainly on graphical analysis and verbal exposition. These studies frequently employ simplifying assumptions, such as: the emissions to output ratio is given and constant (Buchanan and Tullock, 1975; Leidy and Hoekman, 1994), or the efficient scale of a firm is nondecreasing in the strictness of environmental policy (Dewees, 1983). The drawback of this approach is that it may be very difficult or even impossible to reproduce the arguments with a more formal approach. Frequently, the results of the not-so-formal model are too outspoken. For instance, Buchanan and Tullock (1975) claim that in their model, direct regulation always results in lower short-run losses than charges. But this is not true (Dijkstra, 1994). The problem with graphical and verbal analysis is that one may not have an *a priori* sense of the effects of environmental policy instruments,[16] for instance whether the minimum of the average cost curve moves left or right as a particular instrument becomes stricter. From the idea that cost curves could be drawn in a lot of ways, one could conclude 'Anything goes' or 'To obtain definite results, let me assume that the cost curves move in a specific way'. However, more formal analysis may reveal that there is less variety in the possible shapes and positions of cost curves than one might suspect, and that specific assumptions cannot be justified.

Furthermore, with verbal and graphical analysis one can simply say: 'Let us assume the average cost curve with instrument X is U-shaped'. With mathematical analysis, one is forced to state the condition under which the average cost curve is U-shaped. This condition may prove useful in another part of the analysis, for instance when comparing product price with instruments X and Y.

The problem with simplifying assumptions is that it is not always clear whether the assumptions were strictly necessary to obtain the results. In other words: would the results also hold under different, less restrictive, assumptions? This problem seems to be less relevant for formal models, because with formal models one can rely more on complicated proofs than on simplifying assumptions.

Another problem that may occur when analysing verbal expositions is that the results do not follow immediately from the assumptions presented. The author invokes other assumptions, or uses ways of reasoning, that are not explicitly stated. These assumptions, or ways of reasoning, may be invalid. This is true for Dewees' argument that environmental policy increases short-run employment.

When constructing a more mathematically-based model, one is forced to make the restrictions explicit. Some authors explicitly introduce simplifying assumptions. For instance, Helfand (1991) assumes that the product price is given and constant, and Helfand (1993) relies on simulation with specific parameter values.

Kohn (1998) uses specific functional forms and numerical values throughout his book. This approach is useful in an early stage of research. One can play around with the model to see how it works. For instance, one may try to find parameter values for which the number of firms rises and parameter values for which the number of firms declines with a certain instrument. If the number of firms can rise and decline, there is no general rule. If one fails to find parameter values for which the number of firms rises, it is worthwhile to search for a general rule. Kohn (1998) provides a useful toolbox for numerical simulations. However, after having gained insight with numerical simulations, one is inclined to proceed to more general models, to see whether the results hold for all parameter values and all admissible functional forms.

A pitfall of working with a general cost function is that the properties of the cost function are not always presented as a simplifying assumption, nor as a result of underlying conditions. This is the case with Spulber's (1989) assumption, which we will discuss in section A.5 of Appendix A. It is important to check (for instance with numerical simulations as in Kohn (1998)) whether an assumption has any unwanted side-effects, apart from the results that it is meant to produce.

3.3.3 Properties of the cost function

Unlike other authors, we will try to derive the properties of the cost function from underlying conditions. The mathematical analysis is in Appendix A. There we show that for the first order conditions (3.1) to be globally applicable, $C_E = 0$ without environmental policy (section A.2.1). We see that the condition $C_{qE} < 0$ is a sufficient condition for $C_E < 0$ to hold (section A.2.2).

In section A.3 we discuss the second order conditions for profit maximization. These second order conditions can be summarized with:

$$C_{xx} = \begin{pmatrix} C_{qq} & C_{Eq} \\ C_{qE} & C_{EE} \end{pmatrix} \quad \text{is positive semidefinite} \qquad (A.7^m)$$

The condition of monotonicity (section A.4) implies that industry emissions are declining in the strictness of the instrument. For charges in the short run and the long run, and for standards in the long run, (A.7^m) is a necessary and sufficient condition for monotonicity. For standards in the short run, and bubbles in the long run, an additional restriction is required:

$$qC_{qq} + EC_{qE} > 0 \qquad (A.8)$$

Despite our good intentions of deriving the properties of the cost function from underlying conditions only, we do find that in the comparative statics analysis and the comparison of instruments, an additional restriction is useful:

$$qC_{qE} + EC_{EE} < 0 \qquad (A.9)$$

In section A.5 this restriction is discussed, along with Spulber's (1989) restriction.

We use the properties of the cost function for two purposes. In section 3.4, we compare the effects of the instruments, given total industry emissions. In section A.6, we perform comparative statics: what happens when we increase the strictness of environmental policy?

In section A.6.1 we find that in the short run, product price is rising in the strictness of standards if (A.9) is satisfied. Product price is always rising in the strictness of the other instruments.

For the long run, treated in section A.6.2, product price is rising and emissions per firm are declining in the strictness of all instruments. The number of firms is declining in the strictness of standards and market instruments. Production per firm is declining in the strictness of standards and market instruments if (A.9) holds. We cannot be sure what happens to the number of firms and production per firm with bubbles.

3.4 Direct Effects of the Instruments

3.4.1 Introduction
In section 3.2 we derived the equilibrium conditions for the short and the long run. But before we could proceed with the comparison of the equilibrium for the different instruments, we first had to derive a number of properties of the cost function. These properties are derived in Appendix A and discussed in section 3.3. So now we can compare the equilibria for the different instruments.

In the following three sections, we shall compare the effects of the instruments, given the strictness of environmental policy, represented by expected industry emissions L. In this section we shall look at the direct effects of the instruments, that is the effects on the variables of the model: product price P, production per firm q, the number of firms n and emission per firm E.

In section 3.4.2 we look at the effects of instruments in the short run. As we have seen before, the number of firms is equal for all instruments in the short run.

Thus, emissions per firm are also equal across instruments. This means that for the short run, we only have to compare product price P and production per firm q for the instruments. And of course, if one instrument has a higher P than the other, it has a lower q.

In section 3.4.3 we consider the effects of instruments in the long run. In the long run, all four variables we are interested in can differ across instruments. In section 3.4.4 we summarize our findings and compare them with other sources.

In sections 3.5 and 3.6 we shall continue our comparison of the instruments given L, but there we shall look at more composite or indirect variables. In section 3.5 we analyse economic welfare, and in section 3.6 the criteria that interest groups find important.

3.4.2 Short run

In section 3.2.1 we have seen that market instruments and firm bubbles have the same first order condition:

$$P = C_q \qquad\qquad (3.1^m), (3.1^b)$$

Thus, market instruments and firm bubbles yield exactly the same production per firm and product price. The reason for this is easily seen when comparing firm bubbles to the market instrument of grandfathering of tradable permits. With both instruments, all firms receive the right to pollute E. The only difference is that with grandfathering, this right is tradable, while with firm bubbles it is not. But since all firms are equal and the number of firms is given, there will be no trade in the short run and firm bubbles are equivalent to grandfathering.

With standards, the first order condition is different:

$$P = C_q + \frac{E}{q} C_E \qquad\qquad (3.1^s)$$

We shall now see what this means for production and product price. Because $C_E < 0$, we see that with standards:

$$P - C_q < 0$$

Since $C_{qq} \geq 0$ (inequality (A.7^b), derived in Appendix A, section A.3), q must be higher and P must be lower under standards than under the other instruments (remember that E must be equal). The reason for this result is that given q and E, the marginal cost of producing an extra q is lower with standards. When firms increase q with standards, they are allowed to increase their emissions as well. When firms increase q with firm bubbles, they have to incur the additional cost of keeping E constant.

Thus, if firm bubbles were replaced by standards, with the emissions to output ratio unchanged, firms would increase production and emission. Therefore, E/q should be lower and q will be higher with standards than with firm bubbles and market instruments.

3.4.3 Long run

Comparing standards to firm bubbles
In section 3.5 we shall see that in the long run, standards yield a higher welfare level than firm bubbles. With both instruments of direct regulation, welfare in the long run only consists of consumers' surplus. The permission to emit is given administratively, and the firms do not have to pay for this permission. Thus, the lower the product price, the higher the consumers' surplus. This means that the finding that standards yield a higher welfare level than bubbles implies:

$$P^s < P^b$$

The intuition behind this is as follows. Consider what would happen if, starting from long-run equilibrium, the system of standards were changed into firm bubbles, keeping emissions per firm constant. This is illustrated in Figure 3.3. D/n is market demand, divided by the number of firms. AC and MC represent average and marginal cost for standards (s) or for bubbles (b). Long-run equilibrium with standards occurs in point A. With bubbles, average cost is lower for $q < q^s$ and higher for $q > q^s$. The reason is that when firms decrease q with bubbles, they are allowed to keep E at the same level. With standards, E must decrease with q. But when firms increase q with bubbles, they must keep E constant. With standards, E is allowed to increase with q. For the same reason, marginal cost is higher for bubbles than for standards. The switch from standards to bubbles yields a short run equilibrium at C. Firms cut back their production. Product price rises and firms make a profit of BCFG. This profit will attract new firms. Allowed emissions per firm will have to be adjusted downward to accommodate the new firms. Profits per firm will decline with the decrease of allowed emissions per firm, until they are back to zero again. In the new long run equilibrium with firm bubbles, there will be more firms than with standards:

$$n^b > n^s$$
$$E^b < E^s$$

As new firms enter, product price will decline again. But it will not decline below the initial P^s, the long run price level with standards.[17]

From $P^b > P^s$ and (3.4) it follows that $n^b q^b < n^s q^s$. Combining this with $n^b > n^s$:

$$q^s > q^b$$

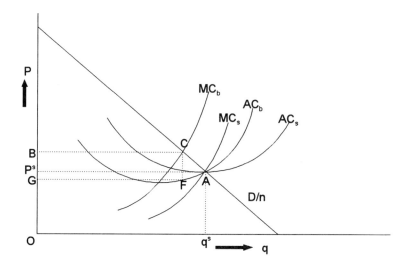

Figure 3.3 The switch from standards to bubbles

Comparing firm bubbles to market instruments
From economic analysis, it follows that:

$$n^m < n^b$$
$$E^m > E^b$$

To see this, consider what would happen if charges were replaced by bubbles. Firms would receive the non-tradable right to emit as much as they did under charges. They would keep producing the same quantity of output, since the first order condition (3.1) is equal for emissions charges and firm bubbles. Then they would make a profit, because they would no longer have to pay the charge bill. The profit will induce entry and consequently the number of firms in long run equilibrium will be higher under standards and emission per firm will have to be lower than they are with market instruments.

Furthermore, we can show that:

$$q^m > q^b$$

This follows from the fact that $q^m \leq q^b$ is impossible. If $q^m \leq q^b$, then $P^m > P^b$, from $n^m < n^b$ and (3.4). According to (3.1), $P^m > P^b$ implies $C_q^m > C_q^b$. But $q^m \leq q^b$ and $E^m > E^b$ imply $C_q^m \leq C_q^b$, since $C_{qq} \geq 0$ and $C_{qE} < 0$.

Finally,

$$P^m \geq P^b$$

To see that $P^m < P^b$ is impossible, we look at:

$$\frac{dC_q}{dq} = C_{qq} + \frac{E}{q}C_{qE}\frac{dE/E}{dq/q} \qquad (3.5)$$

For $P^m < P^b$, the left hand side of the expression should be nonpositive, in view of $q^m > q^b$ and (3.1). But $P^m < P^b$ also means that $E^m/q^m < E^b/q^b$, because of (3.3) and (3.4). Thus, going from q^b and E^b to q^m and E^m:

$$\frac{dE/E}{dq/q} < 1$$

This inequality, together with (A.8) and $C_{qq} \geq 0$, implies that the right hand side of (3.5) will be positive. Thus, we have generated an impossibility, and therefore the only possibility left is $P^m \geq P^b$.

Comparing standards to market instruments
From $P^m \geq P^b$ and $P^b > P^s$ it follows immediately that:

$$P^m > P^s$$
$$E^m/q^m > E^s/q^s$$

From this last inequality we can derive:

$$E^m > E^s$$
$$n^m < n^s$$

This is because with standards as well as with market instruments, we can derive from (3.1) and (3.2) that the cost function satisfies the homogeneity condition:

$$C(q,E) = EC_E + qC_q \qquad (3.6)$$

This means that, when decreasing the allowed industry emissions L from a non-binding level to zero, (q,E) follows the same path both with market instruments and standards, only at a different speed. Since long-run monotonicity for standards (see section A.4.1 of Appendix A) implies that E/q declines when L declines, and $E^m/q^m > E^s/q^s$ given L, (q^s,E^s) is 'ahead of' (q^m,E^m) for any given level of L.

In Appendix A, section A.6.2, we see that $dE/dL \geq 0$ for all instruments. Thus, emissions per firm decline faster with standards as environmental policy is tightened. As a result, emissions per firm are higher for market instruments given

Table 3.1   Effects of instruments

	Short run	Long run
Product price	$P^s < P^m = P^b$	$P^m > P^b > P^s$
Number of firms	$n^s = n^m = n^b$	$n^m < n^s < n^b$
Emission per firm	$E^s = E^m = E^b$	$E^m > E^s > E^b$
Production per firm	$q^s > q^m = q^b$	$q^m > q^s > q^b$

Notes
b = firm bubbles
m = market instruments
s = performance standards

the strictness of environmental policy: $E^m > E^s$.

In order to compare production per firm with standards and market instruments, we have to invoke our additional assumption (A.9), introduced in Appendix A, section A.5. As can be seen in Appendix A, section A.6.2, assumption (A.9) implies $dq/dL \geq 0$ for standards and market instruments. Since, as we have seen, (q^s, E^s) is 'ahead of' (q^m, E^m), (A.9) implies:

$$q^m > q^s$$

3.4.4 Conclusion

The short-run and long-run effects of the instruments are summarized in Table 3.1. We already encountered the results with respect to the short run in our overview of the literature in section 2.2.1, but this is the first time they have been derived from the most general cost function.

With respect to the long run, the differences between firm bubbles and market instruments had already been noted by Buchanan and Tullock (1975) and Spulber (1989). But Buchanan and Tullock assumed a constant emissions to output ratio, which we did not. Spulber needs a very dubious assumption to arrive at the same result. We comment on Spulber's analysis in Appendix A, section A.5.

This is the first time performance standards have been compared with other instruments in the long run, given industry emissions. Thus we cannot compare our results involving standards with other results.

3.5   Welfare

As we saw in section 3.1.1, there are no differences between the instruments with respect to static and dynamic efficiency. However, when we examine the effect of the instruments on the product market, we shall find differences, which we call differences in productive efficiency. Table 3.2 summarizes our findings on productive efficiency, i.e. the effects of the instruments on total welfare. Total welfare consists of consumer surplus, economic profits and government revenue. We will compare the welfare effects of the instruments under the restriction that all instruments yield the same total industry emissions L. In order to find out which instrument maximizes welfare W, i.e. is productively efficient, we maximize the following expression:

$$W = \int_0^{nq} P(y)dy - nC(q,E) - \lambda(nE - L) \qquad (3.7)$$

The first term on the right hand side of (3.7) is the area below the inverse demand curve $P(nq)$. To obtain total welfare, we have to deduct industry cost (which is the second term) from this first term, and we add the constraint that industry emissions do not exceed L.

Bearing in mind that the short-run cost and demand functions differ from their long-run counterparts, (3.7) applies to the short run and the long run. The short-run conditions for welfare maximizing differ from the long-run conditions, because in the short run, n is fixed, while in the long run, n is variable.

Thus, in the short run version of (3.7), E is fixed, since n and L are fixed. The only variable is q, which determines P. Maximizing (3.7) with respect to q gives the following first order condition:

$$nP(nq) - nC_q(q,E) = 0$$

This condition is identical to (3.1^m) and (3.1^b), the first order conditions for profit maximization with market instruments and bubbles. It differs from (3.1^s), the condition for profit maximization with standards. Thus, market instruments and bubbles maximize welfare and are productively efficient in the short run, and standards are not. We have already encountered this result in our review of the literature in section 2.2.1, but here we have derived it, using the most general cost function.

For long-run welfare, we maximize (3.7) with respect to q, n, E and λ respectively:

$$nP(nq) - nC_q(q,E) = 0$$

$$qP(nq) - C(q,E) - \lambda E = 0$$

$$nC_E(q,E) - \lambda n = 0$$

$$nE - L = 0$$

Table 3.2   Welfare ranking of instruments

Short run	Long run	Final rank
1, 2. Market instruments, bubbles	1. Market instruments	1. Market instruments
	2. Standards	2/3. Bubbles or standards
3. Standards	3. Bubbles	

It turns out that the welfare maximum satisfies (3.1^m) and (3.2^m), the profit maximization and zero profit condition for market instruments. Market instruments maximize welfare and are productively efficient in the long run, because the cost $-EC_E$ of polluting the environment is completely covered by the product price. In section 2.2.2, we saw that Spulber (1985) had already derived that market instruments are productively efficient.

Direct regulation cannot maximize long-run welfare, because the zero profit condition of direct regulation is $Pq = C(q,E)$, which deviates from (3.2^m). In other words: direct regulation is not productively efficient. The product price only covers operating costs, but not the cost of the right to emit.

However, one can also compare the welfare impacts of different instruments of direct regulation. To see which form of direct regulation maximizes long run welfare (which now only consists of consumer surplus), we maximize welfare under the additional restriction (3.2^b), (3.2^s) of zero profit under direct regulation:

$$\max \ W = \int_0^{nq} P(y)dy - nC(q,E) - \lambda(nE - L) - \mu\left[qP(nq) - C(q,E)\right]$$

In Appendix B we show that the solution to this maximization problem is identical to (3.1^s), the first order condition for profit maximization with standards. Thus, standards are the welfare-maximizing instrument of direct regulation in the long run. They perform better on welfare in the long run than firm bubbles. This result has not been derived before.

Thus, when comparing different instruments of direct regulation, we find that firm bubbles are welfare-maximizing in the short run, and standards are welfare-maximizing in the long run. Acquainted with this second best property of standards, we are inclined to look for an expression that standards have in common with the first best market instruments. This expression is the homogeneity condition we encountered when comparing standards to market instruments in section 3.4.3:

Table 3.3   Consumers' preferences for instruments

Short run	Long run	Final rank
1. Standards	1. Standards	.1. Standards
2, 3. Bubbles, market instruments	2. Bubbles	2. Bubbles
	3. Market instruments	3. Market instruments

$$C(q,E) = EC_E + qC_q \qquad (3.6)$$

Given industry emissions L, we shall find different values for (q,E) with standards and with market instruments. However, the value for (q,E) that we find with standards for a certain L, say $L = L^s$, is also found with market instruments, but with a different L, say $L = L^m$.

The second best property of performance standards can then be described as follows: with standards, the (q,E) combination is 'right' (in the sense that we also encounter this combination with market instruments), but at the 'wrong' L (in fact, $L^s < L^m$).

3.6   Interest Group Preferences

3.6.1 Introduction
Until now, we have determined the effects of instruments on product price, production per firm, the number of firms and emissions per firm (section 3.4), and on total welfare (section 3.5). But we have not paid any specific attention yet to the variables that interest groups are particularly interested in. This is the ultimate goal of our analysis, to which we now turn. We shall discuss the preferences of the consumers (section 3.6.2), the shareholders (section 3.6.3) and the workers (section 3.6.4).

3.6.2 Consumers
Consumers' preferences are summarized in Table 3.3. Consumers of a specific product are interested in low product prices, for example car drivers prefer low fuel prices. The consumers will prefer the instrument that yields the lowest product price. The lower the product price, the higher consumer surplus will be. Thus, we can derive consumers' preferences from our findings about the product price, summarized in Table 3.1.

In the short run, standards are the consumers' favourite instrument. The consumers are indifferent between all other instruments. In the long run, standards are again the consumers' favourite instrument. Bubbles rank second and market instruments last. Thus, the consumers' overall preference ranking is the same as the ranking on long-run effects.

3.6.3 Shareholders

Shareholders' preferences are summarized in Table 3.4. The shareholders receive a normal rate of return on the capital they invested, plus the economic profit or loss. With grandfathering, they also receive the revenues from the grandfathered permits. Let us first look at short-run profits.

With the financial instruments of a permit auction and emissions charges, as well as with standards, economic profits can be written as:[18]

$$\pi = qC_q + EC_E - C(q,E)$$

Differentiating this partially to q yields:

$$\frac{\partial \pi}{\partial q} = qC_{qq} + EC_{Eq} > 0$$

We derive this inequality in section A.4.2 of Appendix A as (A.8).

We see that given E, profits are higher, the higher q. Thus, profits will always be higher with standards than with the financial instruments, because given E, q is higher with standards.

It is clear that shareholder revenues with firm bubbles and grandfathering will always be higher than with emissions charges and an auction of tradable permits. All of these instruments result in the same level of production. The only difference is that with the financial instruments, firms have to pay the government for the residual emissions, whereas they do not have to pay with grandfathering of permits and firm bubbles. The amount that goes to the government with financial instruments, accrues to the shareholders with grandfathering and bubbles.

To compare profits under firm bubbles and grandfathering with profits under standards, we use the result from section 3.5 that firm bubbles, and market instruments, are the welfare-maximizing instrument in the short run. But we have also shown that consumer surplus is higher with standards (section 3.6.2). With total welfare lower and consumer surplus higher, profits must be lower with standards than with bubbles.

We have assumed that there were no entry and exit costs, so that shareholders are indifferent between their firm's leaving or staying in the industry, and economic profit is zero in the long-run equilibrium. But there is a long-run gain for shareholders with one instrument, namely grandfathering of tradable permits. Shareholders of a firm that leaves the industry will receive the revenues from the sale of the firm's permits. Shareholders of a firm that stays in the industry will

Table 3.4 Shareholders' preferences for instruments

Short run		Long run		Final rank	
1, 2.	Grandfathered permits, bubbles	1.	Grandfathered permits	1.	Grandfathered permits
				2.	Bubbles
3.	Standards	2–5.	Bubbles, standards, permit auction, charges	3.	Standards
4, 5.	Permit auction, charges			4, 5.	Permit auction, charges

demand that the firm make an accounting profit on the grandfathered permits, equal to the permit price. This accounting profit counts as an economic (opportunity) cost to the firm, but as a revenue to its shareholders. Due to this long-run gain, grandfathering rises to the number one position in the final ranking for shareholders, whereas the rest of the ranking is based on short-run profits.

3.6.4 Workers

The preferences of the workers are summarized in Table 3.5. We only look at the workers that are in the industry in the initial situation, where they are all in the same position: given the strictness and the instrument of environmental policy, all workers have an equal chance of having to leave the firm or the industry. We shall identify workers' preferences first and foremost with industry employment.

With respect to a decline in industry employment, we assume that when workers are laid off, they cannot start working somewhere else costlessly. They may incur costs of searching and adjusting for a new job or being unemployed. They may have sector-specific skills that will not be rewarded in a different industry. They may lose seniority positions or incur losses on pension rights.

The traditional welfare measure (3.7) does not take these costs into account. There it is assumed that workers can change employment without cost, in which case they would of course be indifferent between all instruments.

Unlike Dewees (1983), we also take into account that an increase in industry employment will have positive effects for the workers, although these will probably be smaller than a decrease of the same magnitude. The potential benefits from an increase in employment for the workers presently in the industry are:

— the workers in the industry may be altruistic in the sense that they would like to employ those previously unemployed;
— the workers may (transitionally) acquire better working conditions and higher

Table 3.5   Workers' preferences for instruments

Short run	Long run $\|\epsilon\| > 1$	$\|\epsilon\| < 1$	Final rank $\|\epsilon\| > 1$	$\|\epsilon\| < 1$
1. Standards	1. Standards	1. Bubbles	1. Standards	1 or 2. Standards or bubbles
2,3. Bubbles, market instruments	2. Bubbles	2. Standards	2. Bubbles	
	3. Market instruments	3. Market instruments	3. Market instruments	3. Market instruments

wages, because it is difficult to find new employees;
–   in an expanding organization, the 'good' employees are more easily promoted, and the 'not so good' employees are less easily fired.

Let us now compare the employment effects of the instruments. It is easily seen that short-run employment is highest with standards and equal for all other instruments. This is because E is the same for all instruments, while q is higher with standards, and equal for all other instruments.

To compare long-run employment we assume, following Dewees (1983), that the long-run cost function is homothetic, that is: labour costs are a fixed percentage of operating costs. Industry employment is always lowest with market instruments. This is easily seen from Figure 3.4 which illustrates long-run market equilibrium under different instruments. With market instruments price is highest (as can be seen in Table 3.1), and industry output $Q = nq$ is lowest. Total cost consists of operating cost $C(q,E)$ (represented by the area OKJH), plus charges or permit cost (area KNBJ). It has been demonstrated in section 3.5 that market instruments maximize welfare. Therefore the area KABJ must be larger than the consumer surplus under standards (LAE). That is to say, consumer surplus plus charge revenues with market instruments must exceed consumer surplus with direct regulation. Since consumer surplus is lowest with market instruments, average operating cost must also be lowest with market instruments: point K must be below point L in Figure 3.4. In other words, market instruments maximize welfare mainly because they are associated with low cost of production. However, from the point of view of employment, this is their weakness. With total production and average operating cost lowest, total industry cost must be lowest under market instruments. In Figure 3.4, the area OKJH will always be smaller than the areas OLEF (industry cost with standards) and OMDG (industry cost with bubbles), because K will be below L and M, and H will be to the left of G

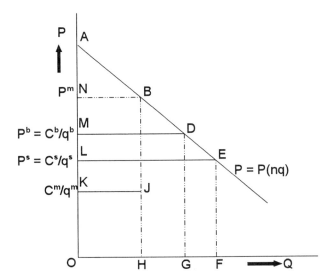

Figure 3.4 Employment in long-run equilibrium

and F.

Since employment is assumed to be a fixed percentage of total operating cost, employment will be lowest under market instruments. The difference between employment with standards and firm bubbles depends on the elasticity of demand. Remember that with bubbles, product price is higher. With inelastic demand ($|\epsilon| < 1$), the amount of money that consumers spend on the product rises with the product price. In that case, bubbles will yield higher industry employment. With elastic demand ($|\epsilon| > 1$), standards will yield higher industry employment.

We can conclude that on the basis of industry employment, workers rank market instruments lowest. With elastic long-run demand, they prefer standards to bubbles. With inelastic demand, it depends on the workers' trade-off of short-run and long-run effects.

A possible refinement is to consider the number of firms in the industry as well. As Dewees (1983) has noted, workers will incur costs when they move from one firm in the industry to another. Leidy and Hoekman (1994) give additional arguments why workers would like as many firms as possible to stay in the industry (see section 2.3.3). Because market instruments score so low on industry employment, it is most interesting to compare firm bubbles and standards on this criterion. In section 3.4.2 we found that the number of firms is higher with firm bubbles than with standards. However, the good performance of bubbles on this criterion may be compromized by the fact that the number of firms may rise. From the comparative statics results in Appendix A, section A.6.2, we see that with standards, the number of firms is decreasing in the strictness of environmental policy. With bubbles, it is unclear what happens to the number of firms in general. But with a lenient environmental policy, the number of firms will rise, because the determinant $|\mathbf{A}_n^b|$ is negative for $C_E = 0$.

If workers have to incur costs when moving from one firm to another within the same industry, as Dewees (1983) assumes, they will not welcome an increase in the number of firms. For example, suppose that initially there are 100 firms in the industry, each with 100 workers. In the long-run equilibrium with environmental policy, there are 95 firms with 110 workers each under standards, and 130 firms with 90 workers each under bubbles. Thus, with standards, 500 workers have to shift from one firm to another, and with bubbles, 1000 workers have to shift from one firm to another.

From this discussion we can conclude that considering what happens to the number of firms is to the advantage of standards over bubbles, if the number of firms rises with bubbles.

4.   CONCLUSION

In this chapter, we have studied short-run and long-run industry response to instruments of environmental policy in a perfectly competitive market, with the purpose of deriving a preference ordering of instruments for consumers, shareholders and workers. The market instruments of tradable emission permits, with grandfathering and auction, and emissions charges were taken into consideration, as well as direct regulation in the form of firm emission bubbles and performance standards specifying the maximum emission to output ratio.

In section 3, we derived the full range of results for the above-mentioned instruments from the most general cost function, given the level of industry emissions. Such a general analysis has not been performed before, as became clear from our review of the literature in section 2.

After having identified the equilibrium conditions in section 3.2, we discussed restrictions on the cost function in section 3.3. Then we studied the differences between the instruments in section 3.4. These differences are summarized in Table 3.1. We discussed the welfare effects in section 3.5 and the preferences of interest groups in section 3.6. The preference orderings of interest groups are summarized in Table 3.6.

In the ranking of shareholders in Table 3.6, derived in section 3.6.3, grandfathering of permits is the most preferred instrument. It maximizes profits in the short run, and is the only instrument that yields extra shareholder revenues in the long run. Firm bubbles come next. On the basis of short-run profits they are preferred to standards, that come in third. Emissions charges and an auction of tradable permits rank lowest.

Table 3.6   Preferences for instruments

Shareholders	Workers $\|\epsilon\| > 1$	$\|\epsilon\| < 1$	Consumers
1. Grandfathered permits	1. Standards	1 or 2. Standards or firm bubbles	1. Standards
2. Firm bubbles	2. Firm bubbles		2. Firm bubbles
3. Standards	3. Market instruments	3. Market instruments	3. Market instruments
4, 5. Permit auction, charges			

Table 3.6 also summarizes workers' preferences, which are based on employment impact as discussed in section 3.6.4. Direct regulation is always preferred to market instruments. When long-run demand for output is elastic, direct regulation in the form of standards offers more employment than bubbles. With inelastic demand, standards might still be the preferred instrument if the workers' rate of time preference is high; if not it is firm bubbles, since they offer highest employment in the long run.

Finally, Table 3.6 presents the impact of environmental policy instruments on product price, which is of interest to consumers (section 3.6.2). It shows that with elastic demand, lower prices and more employment go together. Consumer and worker interests are identical. More generally: workers and consumers will always prefer direct regulation to market instruments.

In section 3.5 and Table 3.2 we have shown that market instruments are welfare-maximizing in this model. When we restrict the choice of instruments to direct regulation, bubbles maximize short-run welfare, and standards maximize long-run welfare.

Comparing our results with the results from the literature collected in section 2.4, we see that we have been able to confirm the previous results with our more general formal approach. Furthermore, we have filled some gaps that existed in the literature so far, especially concerning the analysis of performance standards. The main contribution of this chapter is then that a complete preference ordering of environmental policy instruments has been derived from a cost function that is as general as possible.

Finally, let us consider two limitations to the preference orderings we have derived. First, we have derived the orderings from a very simple theoretical model, with perfect competition and identical firms, only considering one product market.

The assumption of identical firms, which implies that direct regulation results in an optimal distribution of the available emission room across firms, is especially heroic. There is a need for more realistic models as well, like Dijkstra and Nentjes (1998).

Secondly, when deriving the preference orderings we have not taken into account the government revenues from the financial instruments. We have implicitly assumed that the interest groups would not benefit from the spending of the revenues. It is perhaps not so surprising that under this assumption, the interest groups rank the financial instruments so low. When we analyse the political decision-making process, we should (and in our own analysis we will) take these revenues into account. When the interest groups analysed in this chapter benefit from these revenues, financial instruments will rise in their preference ordering. When other interest groups benefit from the revenues, their influence should be taken into account.

APPENDIX A. PROPERTIES OF THE COST FUNCTION

A.1 Introduction

Rather than assume that the cost function $C(q,E)$ satisfies certain restrictions, we shall derive these restrictions from a variety of underlying conditions. In section A.2 we discuss the conditions that $C_E = 0$ without environmental policy, and $C_{qE} = C_{Eq} < 0$. In section A.3 we derive restrictions on the cost function from the second order conditions for profit maximization. Section A.4 does the same for monotonicity: the condition that industry emissions are declining in the strictness of the instrument. In section A.5 we introduce a useful additional assumption. Finally, in section A.6, we perform comparative statics: what happens to product price, production per firm, emissions per firm and the number of firms when the strictness of the instrument increases? The conclusions from this Appendix can be found in section 3.3 of this chapter.

A.2 Restrictions on First and Second Derivatives

A.2.1 The condition $C_E(q_0, f(q_0)) = 0$
In this section we look at the rationale behind the condition $C_E(q_0, f(q_0)) = 0$. The output quantity q_0 is produced in the absence of environmental policy. The function $f(q)$ defines unabated emissions resulting from an output of q.

The effects of $C_E(q_0, f(q_0)) \neq 0$ will be demonstrated with a cost function that satisfies this inequality. We shall derive the cost function for the abatement technology, as introduced by Harford (1989) and used by Kohn (1998). Harford (1989) assumes that the fraction B of gross emissions G abated is:

$$B(L_a, K_a, G) = \frac{L_a^{\gamma} K_a^{\gamma}}{L_a^{\gamma} K_a^{\gamma} + \sigma G^{\theta}} \qquad (A.1)$$

where L_a (K_a) is the amount of labour (capital) used in abatement. It can be shown that the cost function of abatement technology (A.1) satisfies $C_E(q_0, f(q_0)) < 0$. We shall demonstrate this for a simplified version of (A.1):

$$B(L_a) = \frac{L_a}{L_a + \sigma} \qquad (A.1')$$

The residual emission E from the gross emission level $G = f(q)$ is then:

$$E = \frac{\sigma f(q)}{L_a + \sigma} \qquad (A.2)$$

Solving (A.2) for L_a:

$$L_a = \sigma\left(\frac{f(q)}{E} - 1\right)$$

The cost of abatement C_a, given the output level q, the desired level of residual emissions E and the wage rate w is then:

$$C_a(q, E) = wL_a = w\sigma\left(\frac{f(q)}{E} - 1\right) \qquad (A.3)$$

We assume that emissions per unit of output can only be reduced by end-of-pipe abatement in the way just described. The total cost function, of production and abatement, is:

$$C(q, E) = C_p(q) + C_a(q, E) = C_p(q) + w\sigma\left(\frac{f(q)}{E} - 1\right) \qquad (A.4)$$

where $C_p(q)$ is the cost of producing q. Differentiating (A.4) with respect to E:

$$C_E = \frac{-w\sigma f(q)}{E^2}$$

Without abatement, $E = f(q)$, for which we find:

$$C_E(q, f(q)) = \frac{-w\sigma}{f(q)} < 0 \qquad (A.5)$$

This implies that when the firm starts abating, $-C_E$ already has a positive value c. Then the first order condition with emissions charges $t = -C_E$ cannot be satisfied for a value of t below this c. For low values of t, the firm will not abate, but react to the charge by reducing q.[19] The emissions charge has the effect of an output charge. In the same way, emissions quotas (tradable or nontradable) have the effect of output quotas. This effect may persist when environmental policy becomes stricter. The higher the charge rate is, the lower the firm's production and unabated emissions. As (A.5) shows, the marginal cost of emission reduction is declining in unabated emissions. This is because the cost of a relative reduction in emissions is constant. When unabated emissions decline, the cost of a unit decrease in emissions rises. Thus, when the charge rate rises, the marginal cost of emission reduction rises as well. It is unclear whether the charge rate will ever exceed the marginal cost of emission reduction, which is the condition for abatement to occur.

When the firm is confronted with emissions charges and it does not abate, its maximization problem is:

$$\max \; Pq - C_p(q) - tE = Pq - C_p(q) - tf(q)$$

The first order condition is:

$$P = C'_p(q) + tf'(q) \tag{A.6}$$

This condition does not correspond to the first order condition (3.1^m) that we derived in section 3.4.1 for market instruments. In (3.1^m), product price equals the marginal cost of production, keeping E constant. In (A.6), product price equals the marginal cost of production without abatement, allowing E to increase according to $E = f(q)$. Thus, the problem with $C_E(q_0, f(q_0)) \neq 0$ is, that the first order conditions derived in section 3.2.1 $((3.1^b)$ and (3.1^m) in our example) do not apply globally, at least not to a lenient environmental policy. This is a problem in the long run as well as in the short run. For another problem, see Kohn (1998: Ch. 14) and our section 2.2.3.

A.2.2 The condition $C_{qE} = C_{Eq} < 0$
This condition implies:

- $C_{qE} < 0$: when the allowed emissions per firm decline, the marginal cost of production will rise;
- $C_{Eq} < 0$: when the production declines, the marginal cost of reaching E will decline (since $C_E < 0$, C_E will rise).

We shall focus on the first implication here: $C_{qE} < 0$, and on the long-run cost function. In Figure 3.5, $C_q(q, f(q))$ is the marginal cost function without environmental policy. The firm is allowed to make all the emissions $E = f(q)$ that come with whatever q it chooses to produce. $C_q(q, f(q_2))$ is the marginal production cost

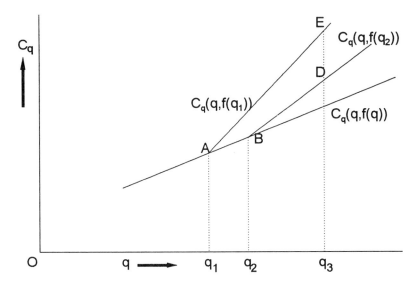

Figure 3.5 The condition $C_{qE} < 0$

function with a restriction of $E = f(q_2)$ on total emissions (i.e. a firm bubble). Beyond q_2, $C_q(q, f(q_2))$ exceeds $C_q(q, f(q))$, since it is costly to reduce emissions.

The condition $C_{qE} < 0$ means that when reducing emissions, for instance from $f(q_2)$ to $f(q_1)$ in Figure 3.5, the marginal production cost C_q will rise: $C_q(q, f(q_1))$ is above $C_q(q \cdot f(q_2))$. C_q must rise because:

1. $C_E < 0$: when we reduce emissions, the total cost $C(q, E)$ of producing a given q rises;
2. $C(q, E)$ is the area below the C_q curve.

In Figure 3.5, the total cost of producing q_3 with emission level $E = f(q_2)$ is the unconstrained cost of producing q_2 plus the area below $C_q(q, f(q_2))$ between q_2 and q_3:

$$C(q_3, f(q_2)) = C(q_2, f(q_2)) + area\ (q_2 BDq_3)$$

The total cost of producing q_3 with emissions $E = f(q_1)$ is the unconstrained cost of producing q_1 plus the area below $C_q(q, f(q_1))$ between q_1 and q_3:

$$C(q_3, f(q_1)) = C(q_1, f(q_1)) + area\ (q_1 AEq_3)$$

From $C_E < 0$ and $f(q_1) < f(q_2)$, it follows that $C(q_3, f(q_1)) > C(q_3, f(q_2))$. This means that the area $q_1 AEq_3$ in Figure 3.5 must be larger than the area $q_1 ABDq_3$.

The way to achieve this is by drawing $C_q(q, f(q_1))$ above $C_q(q, f(q_2))$. In other words: C_q should rise as E declines, or even shorter: $C_{qE} < 0$.

Strictly speaking, $C_{qE} < 0$ does not have to be satisfied globally for $C_E < 0$ to hold. In Figure 3.5, $C_q(q, f(q_1))$ can be below $C_q(q, f(q_2))$ for larger values of q, as long as the area below $C_q(q, f(q_1))$ is larger than the area below $C_q(q, f(q_2))$. But this would complicate matters considerably. Thus, we hold on to $C_{qE} < 0$ as a sufficient condition for $C_E < 0$.

A.3 Second Order Conditions

The second order conditions ensure that the first order conditions define a profit maximum, instead of a profit minimum. The second order conditions derived in this section apply to the short run as well as to the long run.

With market instruments, profit is maximized with respect to q and E, so that the second order condition is:

$$\mathbf{C_{xx}} \equiv \begin{pmatrix} C_{qq} & C_{Eq} \\ C_{qE} & C_{EE} \end{pmatrix} \quad \textit{is positive semidefinite} \qquad (\text{A.7}^m)$$

The fact that $\mathbf{C_{xx}}$ is positive semidefinite has the following implications:

- $C_{qq} \geq 0$;
- $C_{EE} \geq 0$;
- $\mathbf{h C_{xx} h'} \geq 0$ for any vector $\mathbf{h}$;
- the determinant is nonnegative:

$$C_{qq} C_{EE} - C_{Eq} C_{qE} \geq 0 \qquad (\text{A.7})$$

Now we turn to firm bubbles. We differentiate the first order condition

$$P = C_q \qquad (3.1^b)$$

to q, since E is constant:

$$C_{qq} \geq 0 \qquad (\text{A.7}^b)$$

We have just seen that (A.7^m) implies (A.7^b). This means that when the second order condition for market instruments (A.7^m) is satisfied, the second order condition for bubbles (A.7^b) is also satisfied.

For standards, we totally differentiate the first order condition

$$P = C_q + \frac{E}{q} C_E \qquad (3.1^s)$$

to q, with $dE/dq = E/q$:

$$C_{qq} + \frac{E}{q}C_{qE} + \frac{E}{q}C_{Eq} + \left(\frac{E}{q}\right)^2 C_{EE} \geq 0 \qquad (A.7^s)$$

Note that (A.7^m) implies (A.7^s): positive semidefiniteness means that $\mathbf{h}C_{xx}\mathbf{h}' \geq 0$ for any $\mathbf{h}$. If we take $\mathbf{h} = (1\ E/q)$, we get (A.7^s). Thus, when the second order condition for market instruments (A.7^m) is satisfied, the second order condition for standards (A.7^s) is also satisfied. We conclude that when (A.7^m) is satisfied, the second order conditions for all instruments are satisfied.

A.4 Monotonicity

A.4.1 Introduction
The monotonicity condition implies that the strictness of environmental policy is increasing, and thus industry emissions $nE = L$ are decreasing in the strictness I of the instruments. In other words, total industry emissions must decline when we:

— reduce allowed emissions per firm (with firm bubbles);[20]
— reduce the maximum emissions to output ratio (with standards);
— increase the emissions charge rate (with emissions charges).

In Figure 3.6 we have drawn industry emissions L as a function of the strictness I of the instrument. Figure 3.6 shows what can happen if we do not impose the monotonicity condition:

— a certain level of industry emissions might be attainable with several levels of strictness of the instrument (curve 1). Then either we would have to analyse the interaction between entry/exit decisions and the government setting of I, to determine which I will be reached for the long run, or we must assume that the government can make a credible announcement of I (but which I will the government choose?). This would complicate matters considerably;
— industry emissions might even rise above the no-policy level $L(0)$ when the strictness of the instrument is increased, making the function $L(I)$ in fact discontinuous (curve 2);
— there might be several equilibria with different levels of industry emission associated with the same level of strictness of the instrument (curve 3);
— certain industry emission levels might not be attainable (with curve 4: from L_1 to $L(0)$).

A.4.2 Short run
With standards, the monotonicity condition is:

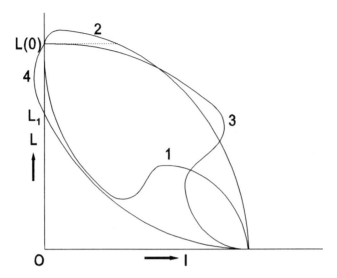

Figure 3.6 Monotonicity

$$\frac{d(E/q)}{dE} = \frac{q - E\,dq^s/dE}{q^2} \geq 0$$

$$\frac{dq}{dE} \leq \frac{q}{E} \tag{A.8^s}$$

We can substitute the value of dq^s/dE from (A.10^s'), derived in section A.6.1:

$$\frac{C_{qE} + C_E/q + C_{EE}E/q}{nP' - C_{qq} - C_{Eq}E/q + C_E E/q^2} \leq \frac{q}{E} \tag{A.8$_s$}$$

Now suppose the denominator on the left hand side (LHS) of (A.8$_s$) were positive. Then (A.8$_s$) implies:

$$C_{qq} + \frac{E}{q}C_{Eq} + \frac{E}{q}C_{qE} + \left(\frac{E}{q}\right)^2 C_{EE} \leq nP' \tag{A.8^{sn}}$$

This inequality cannot be satisfied, since the LHS is nonnegative according to (A.7^s), derived in section A.3, and the RHS is negative. Thus, the denominator on the LHS of (A.8$_s$), which is the RHS of (A.10^s') in section A.6.1, must be negative, so that the inequality sign in (A.8^{sn}) is reversed.

The condition that the denominator on the LHS of (A.8$_s$) be negative combines features of the demand function and the cost function. When we only want a restriction on the cost function, the following is a sufficient condition:

$$qC_{qq} + EC_{qE} > 0 \qquad (A.8)$$

Thus, (A.8) is a sufficient condition for monotonicity with standards in the short run.

With charges, the monotonicity condition is:

$$\frac{dC_E}{dE} = C_{EE} + C_{Eq}\frac{dq}{dE} \geq 0$$

Substituting (A.10^m) from section A.6.1:

$$C_{EE} + \frac{C_{qE}C_{Eq}}{nP' - C_{qq}} \geq 0$$

Multiplying both sides by $(nP' - C_{qq}) < 0$:

$$nP'C_{EE} - [C_{EE}C_{qq} - C_{Eq}C_{qE}] \leq 0$$

The inequality holds because $P' < 0$ and $C_{EE} \geq 0$, and the term in square brackets is nonnegative according to (A.7).

Thus, we do not need an extra condition to ensure monotonicity with emissions charges in the short run. When the second order condition (A.7^m) is satisfied for charges, then there is also monotonicity.

A.4.3 Long run
With market instruments, the monotonicity condition is:

$$\frac{dC_E}{dL} = C_{EE}\frac{dE}{dL} + C_{Eq}\frac{dq}{dL} \geq 0 \qquad (A.8^m)$$

Combining (3.1^m) and (3.2^m):

$$C(q,E) = qC_q + EC_E \qquad (3.6)$$

From (3.6):

$$(qC_{qq} + EC_{Eq})\frac{dq}{dL} = -(qC_{qE} + EC_{EE})\frac{dE}{dL} \qquad (3.6')$$

Substituting this into (A.8^m) yields:

$$\frac{-C_{Eq}(EC_{EE} + qC_{qE})}{qC_{qq} + EC_{Eq}}\frac{dE}{dL} + C_{EE}\frac{dE}{dL} \geq 0$$

Now we substitute the value of dE/dL found with comparative statics (section A.6.2). Since $|\mathbf{A}^m| > 0$ and $-qP' > 0$:

$$C_{Eq}(EC_{EE} + qC_{qE}) + C_{EE}(EC_{Eq} + qC_{qq}) \geq 0$$

This can be rewritten as:

$$-C_{Eq}C_{qE} + C_{EE}C_{qq} \geq 0 \tag{A.7}$$

Inequality (A.7) again requires that the determinant of the $\mathbf{C_{xx}}$ matrix be non-negative. Thus, when the second order condition (A.7^m) is satisfied, there is also monotonicity in the long run for market instruments.

Before deriving the monotonicity condition for standards, we note than condition (3.6), derived for market instruments, also applies to standards: (3.6) is obtained by combining (3.1^s) and (3.2^s). Thus, conditions (3.6) and (3.6') can also be used for standards.[21]

With standards, the monotonicity condition is:

$$\frac{d(E/q)}{dL} = \frac{1}{q}\frac{dE}{dL} - \frac{E}{q^2}\frac{dq}{dL} \geq 0$$

Substituting (3.6'), this becomes:

$$\frac{1}{q}\frac{dE}{dL} + \frac{E(C_{EE} + qC_{qE})}{q^2(qC_{qq} + EC_{Eq})}\frac{dE}{dL} \geq 0$$

Now we substitute the value of dE/dL found with comparative statics in section A.6.2. Since $|\mathbf{A}'| > 0$ and $-P' > 0$:

$$C_{qq} + \frac{E}{q}C_{qE} + \frac{E}{q}C_{Eq} + \left(\frac{E}{q}\right)^2 C_{EE} \geq 0$$

which is identical to the second order condition (A.7^s). Thus, when the second order condition for standards (A.7^s) holds, there is also monotonicity for standards in the long run.

For firm bubbles, the monotonicity condition is:

$$\frac{dE^b}{dL} \geq 0 \tag{A.8^b}$$

In section A.6.2, we see that $|\mathbf{A}_E^b| \geq 0$, because of (A.7^b). Then, dE^b/dL will be nonnegative if $|\mathbf{A}^b| > 0$. We have to impose an extra restriction to make sure that $|\mathbf{A}^b| \geq 0$. Remember that $C_E = 0$ without environmental policy and $C_E < 0$ with environmental policy. Thus, a necessary (for $C_E = 0$) and sufficient (for $C_E \leq 0$) condition for (A.8^b) to hold is:

$$qC_{qq} + EC_{qE} > 0 \qquad (A.8)$$

Thus, we need the extra condition (A.8) to ensure monotonicity in the long run for bubbles.

A.4.4 Conclusion

Requiring monotonicity does not result in a vast increase of the number of restrictions on the cost function. In most cases, the restriction emanating from the second order conditions (A.7^m) is sufficient to ensure monotonicity. Only for standards in the short run, and for bubbles in the long run, an extra condition is needed. In both cases, this is the same condition:

$$qC_{qq} + EC_{qE} > 0 \qquad (A.8)$$

A.5 Additional Restrictions

Additional assumptions about the cost function, not derived from second order conditions or monotonocity, may be called for to determine the signs of certain expressions. We shall discuss our additional assumption and compare it to Spulber's (1989), whose analysis we reviewed in section 2.2.2.

We use the additional assumption

$$qC_{qE} + EC_{EE} < 0 \qquad (A.9)$$

With this assumption, applied to the short-run cost function, product price is rising in the strictness of the standard. Applied to the long-run cost function, production per firm is declining in the strictness of the standard and the strictness of a market instrument. From that we can derive, as we did in section 3.4.3, that long-run production per firm is higher for market instruments, given the strictness of environmental policy.

Another useful feature of (A.9) is, that it implies (A.8) via (A.7^s). Thus, assumption (A.9) is not just added to our assumptions, but it is a strong assumption replacing the weaker assumption (A.8).

Spulber (1989, p. 359) assumes:

$$C_E - qC_{qE} \leq 0 \qquad (A.9a)$$

As a result of this assumption, the efficient scale is nonincreasing in the externality level. The efficient scale q_M is the output level where marginal cost equals average cost: $C_q(q_M, E) = C(q_M, E)/q_M$. Spulber (1989) needs assumption (A.9a) to prove that in the long run, $n^b > n^m$, $E^b < E^m$ and $q^b < q^m$. In section 3.4.3, we have proved these inequalities with economic reasoning and the inequalities $C_{qq} \geq 0$ and $C_{qE} < 0$.

The problem with assumption (A.9a) is that without environmental policy $C_E = 0$, so that (A.9a) implies $C_{qE} \geq 0$. This is the opposite of the condition $C_{qE} < 0$ we derived in section A.2.2. $C_{qE} \geq 0$ implies that when allowed emissions decline, total cost $C(q, E)$ of producing any q declines or remains equal, which is inadmissible.

A.6 Comparative Statics

A.6.1 Short run
In this section we look at what happens to the product price and the produced quantity of the good (which of course move in opposite directions) as the strictness of environmental policy increases from non-binding to prohibitive. Note that in the beginning, with a non-binding (or no) environmental policy, as well as in the end, with a prohibitive environmental policy (if this is feasible), the effects of the instruments are equal. The strictness of environmental policy is defined as total allowed industry emissions. In the short run, with the number of firms given, we can also define it as emissions per firm E.

To see what happens, we take the supply equations (3.1) and the demand equation (3.4):

$$P^b = P^m = C_q(q, E) \qquad (3.1^m)$$

$$P^s = C_q(q, E) + \frac{E}{q} C_E(q, E) \qquad (3.1^s)$$

$$P = P(nq) \qquad (3.4)$$

and differentiate them with respect to the strictness of environmental policy, E:

$$\frac{dP^m}{dE} = C_{qE} + C_{qq} \frac{dq}{dE} \qquad (3.1^{m\prime})$$

$$\frac{dP^s}{dE} = C_{qE} + C_{qq} \frac{dq}{dE} + \frac{d(E/q)}{dE} C_E + \frac{E}{q} C_{EE} + \frac{E}{q} C_{Eq} \frac{dq}{dE} \qquad (3.1^{s\prime})$$

$$\frac{dP}{dE} = \frac{dq}{dE} nP'(nq) \qquad (3.4')$$

Combining $(3.1^{m\prime})$ and $(3.4')$, we see that with market instruments and bubbles:

$$\frac{dP^b}{dE} = \frac{dP^m}{dE} = \frac{C_{qE}}{1 - (C_{qq}/nP')} \qquad \frac{dq^b}{dE} = \frac{dq^m}{dE} = \frac{C_{qE}}{nP' - C_{qq}} \qquad (A.10^m)$$

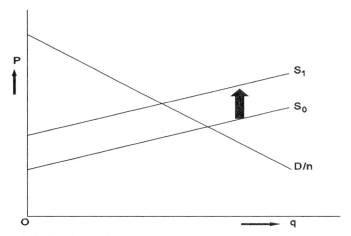

Figure 3.7 Standards, short run

From the second order conditions for profit maximization treated in section A.3, we know that $C_{qq} \geq 0$ (inequality (A.7^b)). Furthermore, the demand function is declining: $P' < 0$. In section A.2.2 we have shown that $C_{qE} < 0$, so that $dP^b/dE = dP^m/dE < 0$ and $dq^b/dE = dq^m/dE > 0$: the stricter environmental policy becomes, the higher will be the product price and the lower will be production per firm.

For standards, combining (3.1^s') and (3.4'):

$$\frac{dq^s}{dE} = \frac{C_{qE} + C_E/q + C_{EE}E/q}{nP' - C_{qq} - C_{Eq}E/q + C_E E/q^2} \qquad (A.10^{s'})$$

The denominator is negative, as we have seen in section A.4.2. The sign of the numerator is ambiguous. We cannot exclude the possibility that, when increasing the strictness of environmental policy from non-binding, the production per firm will first rise. This will happen when the numerator is positive. We do know that production will eventually decline if $E = 0$ can be reached.

To rule out the possibility of rising production and declining product prices, we use the assumption introduced in section A.5:

$$qC_{qE} + EC_{EE} < 0 \qquad (A.9)$$

This is a necessary (for $C_E = 0$) as well as a sufficient (for $C_E \leq 0$) condition for the numerator in (A.10^s') to be positive.

That assumption (A.9) implies $dP^s/dE < 0$ can also be seen with the aid of Figure 3.7, that shows the demand function divided by the number of firms D/n and S_0, the supply function (3.1^s). Note that

$$\frac{\partial P}{\partial E} = C_{qE} + \frac{E}{q}C_{EE} + \frac{C_E}{q}$$

which follows from (3.1$^{s'}$) with $dq/dE = 0$. Thus, assumption (A.9) implies that $\partial P/\partial E < 0$: the supply curve will shift upward from S_0 to S_1 when E declines. Since the supply curve is rising and the demand curve is declining, q will decline and P will rise as environmental policy becomes stricter.

A.6.2 Long run
Now we shall examine the long-run movement of E, q, P and n as the strictness of environmental policy is increased. For every instrument, we have four equations:

$$P = C_q \qquad\qquad (3.1^b), (3.1^m) \qquad P = C_q + \frac{E}{q}C_E \qquad\qquad (3.1^s)$$

$$Pq = C(q,E) - EC_E \qquad (3.2^m) \qquad Pq = C(q,E) \qquad\qquad (3.2^b), (3.2^s)$$

$$nE = L \qquad\qquad\qquad\qquad\qquad\qquad\qquad\qquad\qquad (3.3)$$

$$P = P(nq) \qquad\qquad P'(nq) < 0 \qquad\qquad\qquad\qquad\qquad (3.4)$$

We can differentiate these equations totally with respect to L and put them in a matrix equation $\mathbf{Ax} = \mathbf{b}$ with:

$$A^b = \begin{pmatrix} -1 & C_{qq} & C_{qE} & 0 \\ q & 0 & -C_E & 0 \\ 0 & 0 & n & E \\ -1 & nP' & 0 & qP' \end{pmatrix} \qquad A^m = \begin{pmatrix} -1 & C_{qq} & C_{qE} & 0 \\ q & EC_{Eq} & EC_{EE} & 0 \\ 0 & 0 & n & E \\ -1 & nP' & 0 & qP' \end{pmatrix}$$

$$A^s = \begin{pmatrix} -1 & C_{qq} - \dfrac{E}{q^2}C_E + \dfrac{E}{q}C_{Eq} & C_{qE} + \dfrac{1}{q}C_E + \dfrac{E}{q}C_{EE} & 0 \\ q & \dfrac{E}{q}C_E & -C_E & 0 \\ 0 & 0 & 0 & n & E \\ -1 & nP' & 0 & qP' \end{pmatrix}$$

$$x = \begin{pmatrix} dp/dL \\ dq/dL \\ dE/dL \\ dn/dL \end{pmatrix} \qquad b = \begin{pmatrix} 0 \\ 0 \\ 1 \\ 0 \end{pmatrix}$$

To find the value of an element x_i of the vector $\mathbf{x}$, we apply Cramer's rule. We form the matrix A_i which is A with b as the ith column. The value of x_i is then the determinant of A_i divided by the determinant of A. For example, the value of dP/dL with market instruments is:

$$\frac{dP^m}{dL} = \frac{|A_P^m|}{|A^m|}$$

where A_P^m is A^m with the first column replaced by b.

The determinants of the A-matrices with their signs are:[22]

$$|A^b| = EC_E(nP' - C_{qq}) - nqP'(qC_{qq} + EC_{qE}) > 0 \qquad \text{[A.6]}$$

$$|A_P^b| = -C_E C_{qq} qP' \leq 0 \qquad \text{[A.7}^b\text{]}$$

$$|A_q^b| = qP'(qC_{qE} - C_E)$$

$$|A_E^b| = -q^2 C_{qq} P' \geq 0 \qquad \text{[A.8}^b\text{]}$$

$$|A_n^b| = C_E nP' - C_{qq} C_E - qC_{qE} nP'$$

$$|A^s| = -(q^2 nP' + EC_E)\left(C_{qq} + \frac{E}{q}C_{qE} + \frac{E}{q}C_{Eq} + \left(\frac{E}{q}\right)^2 C_{EE} \right) \geq 0 \qquad \text{[A.7}^s\text{]}$$

$$|A_P^s| = -qP'C_E\left(C_{qq} + \frac{E}{q}C_{qE} + \frac{E}{q}C_{Eq} + \left(\frac{E}{q}\right)^2 C_{EE} \right) \leq 0 \qquad \text{[A.7}^s\text{]}$$

$$|A_q^s| = P'(qC_{qE} + EC_{EE}) > 0 \qquad \text{[A.9]}$$

$$|A_E^s| = -P'(qC_{qq} + EC_{Eq}) > 0 \qquad \text{[A.8]}$$

$$|A_n^s| = C_E nP' - C_E\left(C_{qq} + \frac{E}{q}C_{qE} + \frac{E}{q}C_{Eq} + \left(\frac{E}{q}\right)^2 C_{EE} \right) \geq 0 \qquad \text{[A.7}^s\text{]}$$

$$|A^m| = -nP'\left(C_{qq} + \frac{E}{q}C_{qE} + \frac{E}{q}C_{Eq} + \left(\frac{E}{q}\right)^2 C_{EE} \right) + E^2(C_{qq}C_{EE} - C_{qE}C_{Eq}) \geq 0 \, \text{[A7}^m\text{]}$$

$$|A_P^m| = EqP'(C_{qq}C_{EE} - C_{qE}C_{Eq}) \leq 0 \qquad \text{[A.7]}$$

$$|A_q^m| = qP'(EC_{EE} + qC_{qE}) > 0 \qquad \text{[A.9]}$$

$$|A_E^m| = -qP'(EC_{Eq} + qC_{qq}) > 0 \qquad \text{[A.8]}$$

$$|A_n^m| = -EC_{EE} nP' + E(C_{qq}C_{EE} - C_{qE}C_{Eq}) \geq 0 \qquad \text{[A.7]}$$

APPENDIX B. MAXIMIZING WELFARE IN THE LONG RUN WITH DIRECT REGULATION

In this appendix we derive the condition for welfare maximization with the second-best instruments of direct regulation.

$$\max \ W \ = \ \int_0^{nq} P(y)dy \ - \ nC(q,E) \ - \ \lambda(nE \ - \ L) \ - \ \mu\big[qP(nq) \ - \ C(q,E)\big]$$

Differentiating with respect to n, q, E, λ and μ respectively, we find:

$$qP(nq) \ - \ C(q,E) \ - \ \lambda E \ - \ \mu q^2 p'(nq) \ = \ 0 \tag{B.1}$$

$$nP(nq) \ - \ nC_q(q,E) \ - \ \mu\big(P(nq) \ + \ nqP'(nq) \ - \ C_q(q,E)\big) \ = \ 0 \tag{B.2}$$

$$-nC_E(q,E) \ - \ \lambda n \ + \ \mu C_E(q,E) \ = \ 0 \tag{B.3}$$

$$nE \ = \ L \tag{B.4}$$

$$qP(nq) \ - \ C(q,E) \ = \ 0 \tag{B.5}$$

Solve λ from (B.3):

$$\lambda \ = \ \frac{\mu-n}{n}C_E(q,E)$$

Substitute λ and (B.5) in (B.1) and solve for $1/\mu$:

$$\frac{1}{\mu} \ = \ \frac{1}{n} \ + \ \frac{q^2P'(nq)}{EC_E(q,E)}$$

Divide (B.2) by μ and substitute $1/\mu$:

$$\left(\frac{1}{n} \ + \ \frac{q^2P'(nq)}{EC_E}\right)[nP(nq) \ - \ nC_q] \ - \ P(nq) \ - \ nqP'(nq) \ + \ C_q \ = \ 0$$

$$\frac{q^2P'(nq)}{EC_E}[nP(nq) \ - \ nC_q] \ - \ nqP'(nq) \ = \ 0$$

$$\frac{q}{EC_E}[P(nq) \ - \ C_q] \ = \ 1$$

$$P(nq) \ = \ C_q \ + \ \frac{E}{q}C_E$$

APPENDIX C. SYMBOLS AND EQUATIONS

C.1 Variables

$C(q,E)$ = the firm's cost function
e = maximum emissions to output ratio with performance standards
E = emissions per firm
L = industry emissions
n = number of firms
P = product price
q = production per firm
t = charge rate on emissions

C.2 Instruments

b = firm bubbles
m = market instruments
s = performance standards

C.3 Equations

First and second derivatives

$$C_q > 0 \qquad C_E \leq 0 \qquad C_{qE} = C_{Eq} < 0 \qquad C_{EE} \geq 0$$

$$C_{qq} \geq 0 \tag{A.7^b}$$

3.1 First order conditions

$$P = C_q \tag{3.1^b),(3.1^m}$$

$$P = C_q + \frac{E}{q}C_E \tag{3.1^s}$$

3.2 Zero profit conditions

$$Pq = C(q,E) - EC_E \tag{3.2^m}$$

$$Pq = C(q,E) \tag{3.2^b),(3.2^s}$$

3.3 Restriction on industry emissions

$$nE = L \tag{3.3}$$

3.4   Demand function

$$P = P(nq) \qquad P'(nq) < 0 \tag{3.4}$$

$$\frac{dP}{dE} = \frac{dq}{dE}nP'(nq) \tag{3.4'}$$

3.6   Homogeneity condition

$$C(q,E) = qC_q + EC_E \tag{3.6}$$

A.7   Second order conditions

$$-C_{Eq}C_{qE} + C_{EE}C_{qq} \geq 0 \tag{A.7}$$

$$C_{xx} \equiv \begin{pmatrix} C_{qq} & C_{Eq} \\ C_{qE} & C_{EE} \end{pmatrix} \quad is\ positive\ semidefinite \tag{A.7^m}$$

$$C_{qq} \geq 0 \tag{A.7^b}$$

$$C_{qq} + \frac{E}{q}C_{qE} + \frac{E}{q}C_{Eq} + \left(\frac{E}{q}\right)^2 C_{EE} \geq 0 \tag{A.7^s}$$

A.8   Monotonicity conditions

$$qC_{qq} + EC_{qE} > 0 \tag{A.8}$$

A.9   Additional restriction

$$qC_{qE} + EC_{EE} < 0 \tag{A.9}$$

$$C_E - qC_{qE} \leq 0 \tag{A.9a}$$

A.10 Comparative statics

$$\frac{dP^b}{dE} = \frac{dP^m}{dE} = \frac{C_{qE}}{1 - (C_{qq}/nP')} \tag{A.10^m}$$

$$\frac{dq^s}{dE} = \frac{C_{qE} + C_E/q + C_{EE}E/q}{np' - C_{qq} - C_{Eq}E/q + C_E E/q^2} \tag{A.10$^{s'}$}$$

NOTES

1. In general, standards relate the maximum emission level of a firm to a variable that is positively associated with the activity level of a firm. For instance, standards specify the maximum concentration of polluting substances in smoke or effluent, or in an input (typically fuel) in which they are found. In our model, the most direct way to represent standards is by a maximum emission to output ratio.
2. In Chapter 6, section 3.4, we will discuss the study the Dutch government ordered (Stuurgroep, 1992) in more detail.
3. We will reproduce these welfare results in section 3.5.
4. This condition is more general than Spulber's (1985) own condition that there is only one input.
5. For an extended analysis of Buchanan and Tullock's (1975) model, their treatment of it, the ensuing discussion (Coelho, 1976; Yohe, 1976; Buchanan and Tullock, 1976) and the expansion to tradable permits, see Dijkstra (1994).
6. When pollution is a byproduct, production can also be written as a function of capital, labour, and pollution (as Dewees does), but this does not affect the analysis.
7. The demand curve in Figure 3.1 is linear instead of unitary elastic, but this does not make a difference here.
8. See section 1 for the difference between accounting and economic profits.
9. Following his erroneous argument, there would be a drop in employment with market instrument if the value of the rights exceeded the economic loss (or capital loss, as Dewees calls it). But Dewees himself deems this possibility 'unlikely'.
10. This point was originally made by Buchanan and Tullock (1975).
11. For an evaluation of covenants, see OECD (1995) and Van de Peppel (1995).
12. The superscript 'm' is used for market instruments. The superscript 'b' is used for firm bubbles.
13. The superscript 's' is used for performance standards.
14. Although the number of firms n is a discrete variable, we will treat it mathematically as a continuous variable. Because n will be large in a perfectly competitive industry, this will not make a big difference.
15. Note that $C_E < 0$ with environmental policy.
16. One's *a priori* sense may also be wrong.
17. Suppose that it would. This would mean that with firm bubbles, firms would still be making a profit at P^s, with n^b exceeding n^s and thus q^b below q^s, but with E^b/q^b equal to E^s/q^s. This is impossible, because given E/q, average cost is at a minimum, equal to P^s, at q^s. Thus, at $q < q^s$, there is a loss.
18. With a permit auction and emission charges we have, substituting (3.1^m):
$$\pi = Pq - C(q,E) + EC_E = qC_q + EC_E - C(q,E)$$
With standards we have, substituting (3.1^s):
$$\pi = Pq - C(q,E) = qC_q + EC_E - C(q,E)$$
19. This result can also be obtained by comparing the charge bill without abatement $tf(q)$ to the charge bill plus abatement costs (A.3):
$$tE + C_a(q,E) = tE + w\sigma\left(\frac{f(q)}{E} - 1\right)$$
20. Of course, this is only a problem with bubbles in the long run.
21. For the significance of this common property, see section 3.5.
22. The signs are derived from the conditions mentioned after the expressions. One should also bear in mind that $P' < 0$, $C_E \le 0$, and $C_{qE} = C_{Eq}$.

4. Interest Group Preferences: Other Literature

1. INTRODUCTION

In Chapter 3 we started the analysis of interest group preferences for environmental policy instruments. We looked at the existing literature and developed it further. We continue the analysis of interest group preferences in this chapter. Whereas in Chapter 3 we looked at interest group preferences derived from an industry model, we now look at the other sources from which to derive preferences. In Chapter 3 we mainly discussed the preferences of shareholders, workers and consumers. In this chapter we also discuss the preferences of the environmental bureaucracy and the environmental movement. There are also differences in the way the analysis is carried out. Chapter 3 was quite formal and theoretical. In this chapter we take a more verbal and applied approach. Furthermore, there is more discussion of existing literature and less original analysis in this chapter than in Chapter 3.

In section 2 we review the literature on the polluting industry, other than the formal analysis reviewed in Chapter 3, section 2. In section 3 we discuss the environmental bureaucracy, and in section 4 we look at the environmentalists' preferences. In section 5 we focus on economists as an interest group. We shall discuss economists' motives and see why economists are not regarded as an interest group in this setup.

Section 2 on industry and section 4 on environmentalists also contain a review of surveys conducted to enquire after their preferences. In 1978, a survey was conducted among Congressional staff members and environmental and industry lobbyists in the US. The results are reported in Kelman (1981, 1983). The ideological objections against market instruments, especially voiced by environmentalists in this survey, inspired Kelman to a book-length treatment of the subject (Kelman, 1981), which we shall discuss in section 4.2. Svendsen (1998) interviewed environmentalists and industry representatives in the US and Denmark. Wallart and Bürgenmeier (1996) report about a survey among the major Swiss firms about their attitude towards environmental charges.

We conclude our discussion of the literature and our theoretical analysis from this chapter and Chapter 3 with a tentative preference ordering for the interest groups in section 6.

2. THE POLLUTING INDUSTRY

2.1 Introduction

In this section we shall see what has been said about the preferences of the polluting industry in settings that are more realistic than the stylized model studied in Chapter 3. We shall first discuss the descriptive literature in sections 2.2 and 2.3. The authors cited here typically do not make a distinction between shareholders and workers in the industry. When writing about the polluting industry, they seem either to have shareholders in mind, or to assume that shareholders' and workers' interests are aligned. In section 2.2 we review the arguments that industry is against market instruments, and in section 2.3 the arguments why industry may be in favour of market instruments.

In section 2.4 we discuss the results of a number of surveys. In section 2.4.1 we discuss the survey among US industry lobbyists in 1978 (Kelman, 1981, 1983), in section 2.4.2 the survey among Swiss firms in 1994 (Wallart and Bürgenmeier, 1996) and in section 2.4.3 the survey among US and Danish industry representatives in 1994 (Svendsen, 1998). We conclude with section 2.5.

2.2 Reasons to Oppose Market Instruments

It is widely argued that the producers of polluting products are against the financial instruments of charges and an auction. This is reason 8 from Bohm and Russell's (1985) list of why market instruments are not more widely implemented in practice. Part of their explanation of industry resistance is that for the industry, costs will be higher with these instruments (reason 8a): with direct regulation, firms only have to pay the emission reduction costs, whereas with financial instruments, they also have to pay for the remaining emissions.

Another reason for industry to prefer direct regulation is that direct regulation is more open to industry influence. Bohm and Russell (1985) stress industry influence before the regulation is implemented: government is more inclined to listen to the views of polluters before any action is taken (reason 8b), and polluters can delay the introduction of direct regulation with drawn out negotiations and appeals (reason 8c). White (1976) also stresses the latter point. Other authors stress industry influence when direct regulation is already in place (Freeman et al., 1973: 105, 106). Industry influence will be especially large when direct regulation consists of firm-specific licences. A firm can then capitalize on its superior knowledge about technologies and their costs. The firm will use its bargaining power to obtain a lenient licence and to avoid convictions in case of violations. A firm's bargaining power will be largest when understaffed and under-resourced local bureaucrats on a low government level have to implement the licence giving. Bureaucrats at this level cannot credibly threaten to shut down the plant if the firm does not comply to the environmental standards. Instead, the firm will threaten to shut down the plant if it does not obtain a more lenient licence (White, 1976). This threat will be effective, because the economic benefits of the plant are concentrated at a local level, and the environmental benefits of a strict licence are spread across a larger geographical area.[1]

Bargaining in the implementation phase is impossible with charges. In general, all the details of the charge are specified in formal legislation.

But the above argument does not completely explain the polluters' preference for direct regulation above charges (De Savornin Lohman, 1994a). Not all direct regulation can be manipulated at the implementation phase, and charges also depend on information about technologies and their costs.

Moreover, industry can also try to influence environmental policy when charges are applied. With the example of the French effluent charge, Majone (1989) shows that industry can still have a large say in the administrative stage of a charge. Andersen (1996) argues that in France and Germany, the implementation of the charge was more subject to political pressure than in the Netherlands.[2] This is due to the nature of the regional authority that has to implement the charge. In the Netherlands, the regional water boards were only interested in clean water. But the municipalities in Germany and the water authorities in France were also sensitive to the cost of cleaning up.

Another reason to qualify industry's lack of influence on a charge, is that if industry influence in the administrative arena is small, then it can focus on the political arena.[3] With direct regulation, industry can leave the formal legislation alone, and try to make it 'toothless' at the implementation stage, in the administrative arena that is relatively invisible for the general public. But with charges, the industry must act before the charge is laid down in a law. Industry will try to reduce the charge rate, obtain exemptions and refunds, etc., in the highly visible political arena. De Clercq (1996) observes this difference for Belgium. Therefore it may seem that industry is more opposed to charges than to direct regulation, whereas they are simply forced to act in a more visible arena.

Another reason why polluters prefer direct regulation is that often new plants have to satisfy more stringent rules than existing plants. This may be an efficient form of direct regulation, because it is cheaper to build a plant with environmentally friendly equipment than to retrofit abatement equipment in an already existing plant. But at the same time it constitutes a barrier to entry, because new firms have to make extra costs when setting up a new plant, whereas incumbent firms can continue producing relatively cheaply with their existing plants. Dewees (1983) considers the effects of differential standards on profit and employment in his partial equilibrium model of a polluting industry.

With charges, on the other hand, all firms are treated equally. The picture is somewhat less clear for tradable permits. This is because in practice, the permit market may not work perfectly.[4]

With grandfathering, incumbent firms receive the permits for free and entrants have to pay for them. This difference in itself does not constitute an entry barrier, because the incumbent firm incurs the opportunity costs of using the permits: instead of using them, it could have sold them. However, grandfathering does result in an entry barrier when entrants have to make transaction costs to buy permits or when capital markets work imperfectly (Koutstaal, 1997).

Furthermore, the incumbents may be able to keep new firms out by making an agreement not to sell to entrants or by raising the permit price (Tietenberg, 1985; Misiolek and Elder, 1989; Koster, 1996; Koutstaal, 1997). Thus, tradable permits may result in entry barriers, but the conditions for this to happen (incumbent firms of one industry have market power on the permit market, permit costs are a substantial part of production costs) are unlikely to occur. Moreover, in the permit trading systems in the United States, new firms can buy permits from the government at a fixed (albeit rather high) price (Klaassen and Nentjes, 1997).

The reverse can also occur: the non-tradability of pollution permits protects incumbent firms (Maloney and McCormick, 1982). Tradable permits are an asset that firms can sell when they go out of business, while non-tradable permits are not. Ailing firms that consider going out of business, will evaluate this option more favourably when they can sell their permits. But the buyer of these permits (eager to enter industry x or already incumbent) will probably be more aggressive than the ailing firm. Thus the other firms in industry x would like to be shielded from this aggressive buyer and prefer that the ailing firm, which does them little (when the firm is in industry x) or no (when it is not) harm, stay in business.

A final point to be made about the imperfect functioning of the permit market is the uncertainty for firms. Firms may have difficulties finding out the price for buying or selling permits, and finding a trading partner. When a trading partner is found, the environmental authorities may disapprove of the trade and environmentalists may challenge it in court. They may argue, for instance, that the firm's increase in emissions with purchased permits is not allowed under the emission norms the firm still has to comply with. Another problem is that the environmental authority may confiscate the permits that a firm wants to store for future use. This uncertainty is a factor that works against tradable permits for industry.

Leidy and Hoekman (1994) argue that an industry that is exposed to foreign competition has yet another reason to prefer direct regulation: it increases the probability of protection. It does so, because first, direct regulation provides a formal institutional setting for cooperative behaviour that reinforces their ability to pursue other (non-pollution abatement) areas of mutual interest, including protection. Secondly, the regulatory regime establishes a precedent for market sharing that may pave the way for the inclusion of foreign firms. Thus, foreign firms will also prefer direct regulation. Thirdly, because direct regulation has established a barrier to entry, the extra profits from protection will not be competed away.

2.3 Reasons to Prefer Market Instruments

One can also think of reasons why industry would favour market instruments (Beder, 1996). In the class of market instruments, they will favour grandfathering to the financial instruments, because with grandfathering they do not have to pay for the residual emissions. Industry's appreciation of the financial instruments will depend heavily on the redistribution of the revenue to the industry. If industry does not receive any of the revenues, they will most probably prefer direct regulation to the financial instruments.

The great attraction of market instruments to industry is that the decision of how, and by how much, to reduce emissions is up to the firms. They do not have to reduce emissions in a specific way, prescribed by the government, but they can do it in their own way, which is potentially a lot cheaper and involves less paperwork. The size of this cost advantage depends on the nature of the instrument of direct regulation. If this instrument already gives firms considerable freedom in how to reduce emissions, the extra cost advantage of market instruments will be small.

This cost advantage makes it very likely that industry will prefer grandfathering to direct regulation. De Savornin Lohman (1994a) even argues that emission reduction costs with financial instruments may be so much lower that in fact financial instruments have a smaller cost burden for the polluters. But this does not seem to be very realistic.

Another advantage of market instruments is that they imply a neutral attitude toward pollution and polluters, whereas direct regulation implies a condemnation. We shall return to this subject in section 4.2. There we shall see that environmentalists dislike market instruments for this reason. But for the polluting industry, this is a point in favour of market instruments, because industry does not like to be stigmatized.

2.4 Surveys

2.4.1 Kelman (1981, 1983)
In the 1978 survey (Kelman, 1981, 1983), 17 out of 20 US industry respondents were against charges. Only the Democratic staff members were more hostile against charges. As a group, the industry respondents were the least knowledgeable about charges. But they showed a clear suspicion that charges would cost them more than direct regulation, because they would have to pay for the residual emissions.

2.4.2 Wallart and Bürgenmeier (1996)
Wallart and Bürgenmeier (1996) report the results of a survey among the major Swiss firms about their attitudes toward environmental taxation. The researchers

qualified 44 of the responding firms as 'polluters' (active in a polluting industry) and 58 as 'non-polluters'.

The most surprising finding is the answer to question 51: 'Are you, generally speaking, in favour of charges providing better environmental protection?' About two thirds of all firms were in favour of environmental charges, with the percentage for polluters (63.6) only slightly below the percentage for non-polluters (69.0). The no-reply percentage was particularly high for polluters (9.1 versus 3.4 for non-polluters). Wallart and Bürgenmeier (1996) suggest this may be due to a conflict between the ideas of the respondent as a person and as a representative of the firm.

Question 13 invited firms to compare different policy instruments. Of the respondents, 43.2% agreed with the statement 'Charges are not the best means to reduce pollution'. When asked 'Which means is more effective?', 10 firms named direct regulation, 5 named tradable emission permits, and 5 named negotiations.

We shall first go through the rest of the questionnaire and then comment on the high reported acceptance of environmental charges. Questions 1 to 6 suggested different destinations for the charges revenue. The firms prefer the revenues to be spent on extra environmental protection. The other possible destinations are ordered as follows: reducing direct taxes, a lump-sum rebate of the environmental charges, reducing social premiums and reducing indirect taxes. The least favourite destination is the augmenting of government funds, which is out of the question for 75.5% of the respondents.

Questions 7 to 47 treat all kinds of objections that one could possibly have against the introduction of environmental charges. Bürgenmeier and Wallart (1996) present a top 10 of objections that the firms deemed most founded.

The firms' prime objection against environmental charges is that they would necessitate extra investments. Second on the list is that environmental charges would increase production costs.

Number three is the uncertainty about the conflict between the environmental and the revenue-raising goal of the charges. Firms' doubts about this are also apparent from two other statements: 67.7% agreed to the statement 'The charges level will be set to meet a fiscal, instead of an environmental, goal', which is not enough to reach the top 10 of objections. The statement 'There will be institutional problems of competence between the Departments of Finance and Environment' made it to number 8.

Numbers 4 and 5 on the list are relocation of firms abroad or to other regions and decreased international competitiveness, respectively. Seven firms also mention these objections when answering question 51, as the reason why they oppose environmental charges. In the 'remarks' section at the end of the questionnaire, eleven firms stress the need for international coordination of environmental policy.

Objection number 6 is that the administrative costs of environmental charges are too large. Objection number 7 is the increased influence of the state on the economy. This objection also appears elsewhere in the survey. Twelve firms that are against environmental charges (question 51) express their distrust in the state and in bureaucracy and their aversion to an increasing government sector. Five firms also mention state intervention as a general problem in the 'remarks' section, asserting that the government share in the economy should not rise, that charges should be transparent and announced well in advance, and that they should be justified.

Objection number 9 is the uncertainty about the effect of charges on industries and individual firms. Objection number 10 is that charges are more costly for consumers.

It is also interesting to see which objections the firms rejected. They *disagreed* with the following:

- charges have little or no effect on polluters;
- polluters will continue polluting, relocating their polluting activities abroad;
- environmental problems are already well under control;
- direct regulation is less costly for the economy as a whole;
- charges cannot be introduced without abolishing direct regulation;
- environmental charges would depress general economic growth, employment and productivity, or activity in their own industry;
- the poor would pay more than the rich;
- some people would pay more than others, which is unacceptable;
- environmental problems pertain to the long run, there are more urgent economic problems;

Opinions were divided on whether there would be a moral problem, because paying for pollution allegedly gives a certain legitimacy to the act of polluting.

In question 48, firms were asked about the necessity of a delay between the announcement and the implementation of charges, to give everyone the time to adapt. Of all the firms, 53.9% (and 65.9% of the polluters) called a delay indispensable, 32.4% (27.3%) called it important. A gradual increase of the charges rate to the final level (question 49) was deemed important by 43.1% of all firms and indispensable by 36.3%. Question 50 asked whether firms were able to raise their selling price in order to recover possible extra costs due to regulatory charges. Of all the firms, 22.5% (and 18.2% of the polluters) reported they had no ability at all to raise their prices, 48.0% (54.5%) said they could recover the extra cost only partially.

Let us now look more closely at the high percentage of firms favouring environmental charges. This percentage is surprisingly high, considering firms' aversion to environmental charges reported in the rest of the literature.

Questions 13 and 51 asked firms to judge the instrument of environmental charges. Question 13 asked: 'Are charges the *best* instrument, and if not, which instrument is more *effective*?' This is a different question than: 'Do you *prefer* charges?' It is possible that firms acknowledge the effectiveness of charges in reducing pollution, but at the same time prefer a different instrument that is less effective and more in line with their own wishes.

Question 51 does inquire after the firms' preference. In light of our remark on question 13, it is striking that the response to question 51 is more favourable to charges than the response to question 13 (66.7% vs. 56.8%). However, there are several reasons to be sceptical about this high support for environmental charges.

First, question 51 was the last question of the questionnaire. In questions 1 to 6 the firms could indicate whether certain destinations for the charges revenue were acceptable or not. In questions 7 to 50, firms were asked about all kinds of objections firms could possibly have to environmental charges. Having reached the end of the questionnaire, the respondents might have thought: 'If the government spends the revenues in the way I prefer, and does something about the objections I have just identified, environmental charges are acceptable'. The researchers may have encouraged this kind of reasoning by asking for the respondents' attitude toward environmental charges in a very general fashion.

It is also worth noting that the researchers did not directly inquire after one of the main drawbacks of charges for a firm: they reduce profits. If there had been a question about profits, the acceptance of charges would probably be lower. Now the respondents may not have taken proper account of this reason for rejecting charges.

Secondly, it is not clear from the question what is the alternative to a stricter environmental policy with taxation. Is it a stricter environmental policy with a different instrument, the existing environmental policy, or something else? In the preceding questions about the effects of environmental charges, the existing environmental policy was taken as a benchmark. A number of respondents must have taken the existing environmental policy as a benchmark for question 51 as well, because 32 of the firms in favour of charges mentioned the effectiveness of charges and the necessity to improve environmental quality as the reason for their preference. However, firms may agree to a stricter environmental policy, but prefer a different instrument than charges.

Thirdly, the questionnaire was sent to employees of a firm's financial department. Compared with employees who deal with the environment, these employees are less familiar with the current regulatory approach in environmental policy and more familiar with financial policy instruments. This would make them more favourable toward environmental taxation.

Finally, there is always a tendency in questionnaires to give the 'socially acceptable' answer and to please the researchers. To start with the latter, the respondents must have noticed by the end of the questionnaire that the researchers were interested in environmental charges. Some respondents may have felt bad about having to disappoint the researchers at this stage, and indicated that they were in favour of environmental charges. This argument reinforces the first reason we gave above.

We have already noted, as part of our second reason, that it was unclear whether question 51 was only about different instruments, or also about a tightening of environmental policy. To the extent that respondents thought they were asked whether they favoured a tighter environmental policy, the socially acceptable answer is to be in favour of environmental charges.

For another aspect of social acceptability, recall that in the literature one of the reasons for firms to be against charges and in favour of regulation is that firms can make regulation ineffective in an inconspicuous way. Assuming for the moment that some respondents were aware of this argument against charges, they would probably not want to mention it (and in fact, no one did) for fear of being exposed as a 'dirty firm'.

2.4.3 Svendsen (1998)

Svendsen (1998) finds that in the US, private industry and the public electricity sector are in favour of grandfathering, because it is cost-effective and flexible. The preferences of the Danish industry with respect to CO_2 are different. The preferences of Danish private industry are:

1. voluntary agreements;
2. grandfathering of tradable permits;
3. emissions charges.

The reason that industry puts forward for its preference of voluntary agreements is that it wants to settle things on its own without state intervention. But according to Svendsen (1998), industry would like to delay and postpone regulation.

The Danish electricity sector is in favour of charges for two reasons. First, there are too few units for trade in permits among utilities in Denmark. Secondly, it is easy to charge fuel input as long as CO_2 cannot be removed from emissions.

Svendsen (1998) attributes the differences in preference between the electricity sector in the US and Denmark to the fact that the US electricity sector is more deregulated. Thus, it has more eye for efficiency and it favours grandfathering, just like US private industry. The Danish electricity sector is less interested in efficiency. Its preferences are more aligned with the State. According to Svendsen (1998) the State is interested in maximizing its revenues, and therefore prefers emission taxation.

2.5 Conclusion

The review of a whole range of issues in sections 2.2 and 2.3 enables us to paint a richer picture of industry preferences than we did in Chapter 3. While the analysis of this section does not prompt us to amend the preference ordering we presented in Table 3.6 of Chapter 3, it does make clear that the value of general statements about industry preferences is limited.

While there are large differences in design between the three surveys reviewed in section 2.4, industry attitude toward charges is a recurring theme. We have seen that, according to Kelman (1981, 1983) and Svendsen (1998), US industry is against charges. According to Svendsen (1998), the US electricity sector and Danish industry are against charges as well, but the Danish electricity sector is in favour of charges. The latter may be explained by pointing out that this sector is heavily regulated and has a public monopoly. This also brings home the point that an analysis of the electricity sector, as distinct from other polluting industries, could be worthwhile.

In Wallart and Bürgenmeier's (1996) survey, the majority of Swiss firms is in favour of charges. However, we have given a number of reasons to doubt this finding. All in all, the surveys do not give us cause to change industry's preference ordering as we derived it in Chapter 3.

3.   THE ENVIRONMENTAL BUREAUCRACY

3.1   Introduction

When writing about instrument choice in environmental policy, most authors only spare a few remarks on the preferences of the environmental bureaucracy. The authors ascribe a variety of motivations to the environmental bureaucracy, but the result is invariably that the bureaucracy prefers direct regulation. Nentjes and Dijkstra (1994) offer the most comprehensive theoretical treatment to date. We shall discuss their analysis in section 3.3 and the rest of the literature in section 3.2.

3.2   Observations

Nentjes (1988) suggests that certainty of effectiveness of the instrument is a main criterion. His references to Dutch government reports support his postulate. The official view is that environmental targets will be met with more certainty if direct regulation is applied than if emission charges are used. For that reason direct regulation is the preferred instrument. Other factors that could help explain the environmental bureaucracy's preference for direct regulation are the force of custom and the costs of systems change, for environmental policy (and policy in other areas of government regulation) has traditionally consisted of the imposition of standards.

De Savornin Lohman (1994a: 61) speculates:

A preference for permit giving may be accounted for by a logic of budget maximisation, making bureaucrats prefer more cumbersome regulation. Also the nature of bureaucrats' work connected to charging is less attractive. Administering a charge is a routine job, with low prestige, comparing unfavourably with the work of permit giving where one is visibly in the business of 'protecting the environment'.

Frey (1992) and De Clercq (1996) argue that the environmental bureaucracy prefers direct regulation to emissions charges, because direct regulation gives them more influence on environmental policy. The bureaucracy is involved in the formulation and the implementation of direct regulation. With charges, the politicians and the Department of Finance have a larger say.

It has also been noted that it may be wrong to regard the environmental bureaucracy as a homogeneous group. Liroff (1986) distinguishes command minimalists and command expansionists within the US Environmental Protection Agency (EPA) in the mid-1970s. Both groups recognized the failure of the existing direct regulation, but had different opinions about the remedy.

The command minimalists, primarily officials in EPA's Regulatory Reform Staff, wanted to restrict emission trading as little as possible. The command expansionists, including officials in EPA's air programme and enforcement offices, were more sceptical of emissions trading. They had 'large investments in the status quo, direct accountability to suspicious environmentalists, and perspectives formed by past dealings with recalcitrants'.[5] The views of the command expansionists, among which Liroff (1986) also counts the environmentalists, will be further explored when we discuss environmentalists' preferences in section 4. According to Liroff (1986), the states were also sceptical about the emergence of emissions trading, because they feared it would increase their workload.

In general it seems that in the US, government officials in charge of the practical policy implementation, and with contacts with industry, are more sceptical of emissions trading. The government officials charged with strategic issues, more detached from implementation, are more enthusiastic about emissions trading.

3.3   Nentjes and Dijkstra (1994)

Nentjes and Dijkstra (1994) offer the most systematic and comprehensive treatment of the environmental bureaucracy's preferences. They consider the following instruments: a firm bubble, emissions charges and tradable emission permits, that are either auctioned or grandfathered.

Nentjes and Dijkstra (1994) assume that the main objective of the environmental bureaucracy is to maximize the certainty that the environmental target is met. Outcomes above the target are disliked as much as outcomes below the target. A related objective is that the bureaucracy, taking its responsibility very seriously, wants to maximize its influence on emissions per firm. Next to the main objective, secondary objectives could play a role. Nentjes and Dijkstra (1994) discuss two indicators for these objectives.

The environmental bureaucracy cannot be blind to the polluters' costs of meeting the environmental targets. The higher these costs, the more reluctant industry will be to comply with environmental policy, and the more tense the relation between environmental bureaucracy and industry will be. This latter point is most relevant to those civil servants with close contacts with industry. Furthermore, the higher industry costs, the more industry will complain about environmental policy to bureaucratic sectors within government and political parties that are sensitive to industry complaints. These bureaucratic sectors and political parties might try to thwart environmental policy.

Taking into account the possibility that a bureaucratic organization can have internal goals, or organizational slack, next to its formal goal (Williamson, 1963, 1964; Migué and Bélanger, 1974; Duizendstraal and Nentjes, 1994a,b) an indicator has to be added to reflect this third criterion; for example a preference for instruments that demand maximum input of bureaucratic labour.

The three criteria can be conceived as elements of the environmental bureaucracy's utility function. The difficulty is that the trade-off between the three components is not known. Therefore Nentjes and Dijkstra (1994) start with constructing a table which shows how the different instruments score on the three criteria. This table, with a slight amendment for the second criterion, is given here as Table 4.1. In this table, a number 1 indicates highest preference and a number 4 the lowest order of preference. Two numbers at one place represent a shared set of places in the ranking order.

For the ranking in column (1), indicating bureaucratic control, we first look at whether the target emission level for the industry will be realized with certainty. To keep in line with the model from Chapter 3, section 3, from which we deduced shareholders' and workers' preferences, we look at certainty in the short run, given the number of firms.[6]

With tradable permits, there is certainty that the emission target will be met, because the government directly controls the total number of permits. With firm bubbles there is also certainty, because the government controls emissions per firm, and the number of firms is given. With emissions charges, there is no certainty that the emission target will be met. The government sets the charge rate such that it expects that the emission target will be reached. The expectation will only come true if a number of relevant variables assume their expected values. If emission reduction, or the production of the commodity, turns out to be cheaper than the government expected, or demand for the product is higher than expected, emissions will be above the target level.

Table 4.1   Bureaucratic preferences for instruments

	Control (1)	Cost (2)	Labour (3)
Firm bubbles	1	1/2	3/4
Tradable permits, grandfathering	2	1/2	1/2
Tradable permits, auction	3	3/4	3/4
Emissions charges	4	3/4	1/2

Thus, in column (1), emission charges are ranked lowest of all instruments, because of the uncertainty about their effect on emissions. The other three instruments are ranked in descending order of bureaucratic influence on the firm level. With firm bubbles, the bureaucracy can determine firm emissions. With grandfathering, it can only determine initial firm emissions. With a permit auction, it cannot even determine that.

Column (2) of Table 4.1 gives the ranking on the compliance cost criterion. As an indicator of compliance cost, Nentjes and Dijkstra (1994) take the reduction in the number of firms from the industry model we presented in Chapter 3, section 3. According to this indicator, bubbles have the lowest compliance cost, and there is no difference between the market instruments.

But this indicator does not take the shareholders' preference for grandfathering into account. Therefore we take a different indicator of compliance cost here, namely a combination of shareholders' and workers' preferences. We have summarized our knowledge on shareholders' and workers' preferences from Chapter 3 in Table 3.6. There we see that workers prefer bubbles to market instruments, and shareholders prefer grandfathering. Thus, bubbles and grandfathering are ranked at a shared first and second place in column (2) of Table 4.1. The financial instruments, disliked both by workers and shareholders, are ranked on a shared third and fourth place.

In column (3) of Table 4.1 the instruments are ranked according to the amount of bureaucratic labour that has to be spent on making the instrument work. When bubbles are applied, the main task for the bureaucracy is to translate total allowed emission for the industry into emission ceilings per firm. Under a charge system, the appropriate charge rate has to be determined: next to information about technical options for controlling pollution, information on pollution control costs has to be collected. Next to that additional labour is needed for collecting the charge. Therefore, an emissions charge might be preferable to firm bubbles. On the other hand, permits with auction probably demand less bureaucratic labour than bubbles: the labour effect of organizing the auction and supervision of trade might be lower than that of collecting technical information and keeping up to date. Since Nentjes and Dijkstra (1994) are uncertain on this point, bubbles and auctioned permits are given the same ranking. Permit systems with grandfathering demand more labour than an auction because the problem has to be solved of finding a fair base level of emissions of established firms. It is unclear to Nentjes and Dijkstra (1994) whether the system will be ranked higher or lower than charges.

Since Nentjes and Dijkstra (1994) consider certainty of effectiveness and control to be the main objective, they take column (1) as decisive in ranking the preferences of the bureaucracy.

4.   THE ENVIRONMENTAL MOVEMENT

4.1   Introduction

It is clear that the environmentalists' main goal is to minimize emissions. It may be less clear at first sight how this goal translates into a preference ordering for instruments that all yield the same emission reduction.

Let us first recall the statements about environmentalists' preferences from the literature reviewed in Chapter 3, section 2.3. According to Dewees (1983), reviewed in Chapter 3, section 2.3.2, environmentalists prefer market instruments. This is because in Dewees' model, all instruments yield the same emissions to output ratio. Because market instruments yield the lowest industry output, they also yield the lowest industry emissions. That is why environmentalists prefer market instruments.

According to Leidy and Hoekman (1994), reviewed in Chapter 3, section 2.3.3, environmentalists prefer firm bubbles to charges. This is because with bubbles, the environmental goal is reached with certainty. Furthermore, more firms stay in the industry with bubbles, and they may even have supernormal profits. These two factors make it easier to require firms to clean up their own environmental degradation from the past.

Now we move on to the rest of the literature. The literature has mainly dwelt on the environmentalists' aversion to market instruments. This will be the subject of section 4.2. In section 4.3 we shall present the positive features of market instruments for environmentalists. We shall treat the preference ordering derived by Nentjes and Dijkstra (1994) in section 4.4. In section 4.5 we discuss the surveys: in section 4.5.1 the 1978 US survey (Kelman, 1981, 1983) and in section 4.5.2 the 1994 US and Danish survey (Svendsen, 1998).

4.2   Reasons to Oppose Market Instruments

Most environmentalist movements were hostile to the development of emissions trading in the USA (Liroff, 1986; Dudek and Palmisano, 1988; Hahn and Hester, 1989a,b; Hahn and Noll, 1990). Several reasons can be given for this.

Firstly, there was a fear that total emissions would increase due to so-called 'paper trades'. For emissions trading to work, each firm should have a right to a certain amount of emissions. These rights sometimes exceed the firm's actual emissions, for three reasons. First, the allocation of emission reduction obligations under the regulatory approach was sometimes based on dubious models and outdated information supplied by the industry (Liroff, 1986). Liroff gives several instances of bubbles that reduced allowed emissions, but not actual emissions. Looking at these bubbles benevolently, one can say they 'recognize past cleanup effort'. Looking at them malevolently, they 'legalize noncompliance'.

A second reason why emissions trading may increase total emissions is given by Liroff (1986: 114). Suppose previous regulation has required a firm to install a certain piece of abatement equipment at a certain emission point. With this equipment, the emissions from this point are supposed to be, say, 115. But this figure of 115 reflects the performance of the equipment under 'the worst, reasonably-to-be-expected situation'.[7] The firm may be able to demonstrate that the expected emission with the equipment is only 100 and use the remaining 15 to increase emissions elsewhere. Thus, the firm appropriates the emission room that was meant as a safety margin. This kind of trade is forbidden in the emissions trading program, but the application of this prohibition to specific trades is contestable.

The third reason is that there may be indivisibilities in pollution abatement. For example, suppose the government prescribes two firms to abate their pollution by at least 80%. However, the firms can only abate 70 or 90%. As a result, both firms abate 90%. This phenomenon is called 'overshooting': it is technically impossible for an individual firm to abate pollution by exactly the prescibed amount, so that it is forced to abate much more. When emission permits become tradable, one firm can sell the permits it does not use to the other. One firm now abates 70%, the other abates 90%. Thus, 'paper trades' (selling emission rights without reducing emissions) increase total emissions.

A lot of environmentalists, when they belong to the camp of the 'command expansionists' (Liroff, 1986),[8] will also frown upon the sale of permits by a firm that was going to reduce its emissions anyway, e.g. because it starts operating a new plant, or because it goes out of business. The environmentalists see these events as an opportunity to reduce total emissions. The tradability of permits makes this impossible, because a firm will now sell the emission permits it does not need anymore. This objection against tradability is especially relevant in areas where the concentration norm for a certain pollutant is not met yet. These are the so-called nonattainment areas. One-to-one trade is clearly out of the question here for environmentalists, and is not permitted in the emissions trading program either. In the offset rules, applicable to nonattainment areas, emissions at one point have to be reduced more than they are increased elsewhere. But still, environmentalists may feel that the trading ratio is too lenient, or trading should be prohibited in nonattainment areas.

Some command expansionists dislike the whole idea that a firm that reduces its emissions (for whatever reason), can sell the emission permits to another firm. Command expansionists feel that if a firm sees a chance to reduce its emissions, it should do so without the opportunity to sell the permits. Command expansionists would like to confiscate these permits, so that total emissions will decrease.

This first set of objections against market instruments, which we have just presented, directly emanates from the environmentalists' main goal to reduce emissions. The second set of objections, to which we now turn, does not directly or explicitly follow from this main goal. These are the 'moral' or 'ethical' objections, elaborated most deeply by Kelman (1981). One manifestation of these objections is the idea that it is wrong to look for a market-oriented solution of the environmental problem, because the environmental problem is due to the failure of markets (Nentjes, 1988).

Some environmentalists see market instruments as a licence to pollute. When applying financial instruments, the government says: 'It is okay to pollute, as long as you pay for it.' With grandfathering, the government even gives away the right to pollute. But, according to environmentalists, environmental quality is fundamentally a right to which the public is entitled. Furthermore, environmentalists care about the reason why people behave environmentally friendly. Firms should cut back pollution because pollution is wrong, not because they can make (or save) money. The instruments of environmental policy should convey a public condemnation of pollution.

Another set of environmentalists' misgivings of market instruments can be summarized by the phrase: 'One cannot set a monetary price on health or the environment.' When environmental quality is made part of the price system, it is no longer 'priceless', and its perceived value may drop. In a wider context, the introduction of market instruments in environmental policy makes the market (as opposed to the government and self-regulation) more prominent as an organizing principle of society. As a result, calculation and self-interest (concepts associated with the market) become more important in society. Environmentalists, and perhaps others as well, tend to feel uneasy at this prospect.

Although these moral or ethical objections may at first seem unrelated to the goal of protecting the environment, there is a connection (Kelman, 1983: 325):

debate on the stringency of environmental demands that is phrased in terms of 'What should the level of a charge be?' focuses attention on costs and thus hurts environmentalists, whereas debate that is phrased in terms of 'What should a standard be?' focuses attention on health protection and thus helps environmentalists.

The connection between the environmentalists' moral objections and their goal of improving environmental quality is that market instruments imply a certain way of looking at the environmental problem. This way of looking at the problem does not only differ from the environmentalists' own stance, but environmentalists would also like to keep the general public from adopting this stance. Otherwise, they fear, public support for more stringent environmental policy may decrease.

Frey (1992) models this consideration. In his model, the introduction of market instruments in one sector increases pollution in another sector because of lower environmental awareness. In this other sector, environmental policy is either nonexistent or not enforced, or the environmental policy goals are in the process of being formulated.

A third category of reasons why environmentalists can be opposed to market instruments are the tactical objections: market instruments are indirectly detrimental to the goal of increased environmental protection. As we have just seen, one can also interpret the moral objections against market instruments as tactical objections.

Another tactical objection against market instruments, especially charges, is that the jurisdiction goes from the environmental policy arena (parliamentary committee, department) to the financial policy arena.[9] The actors in the financial policy arena will not give as much consideration to the environment as the actors in the environmental policy arena. Thus, a market instrument devised in the financial policy arena will lead to less environmental protection than direct regulation devised in the environmental policy arena.

A third tactical objection is mentioned by Kelman (1981, 1983). Some of the environmentalists interviewed in the 1978 survey were afraid that the revision of environmental law, needed for the introduction of market instruments, would also result in a reformulation of the environmental policy goals. Because this would happen at a time when the environmental movement was not as strong as when the original laws were written (the early 1970s), the new goals would be less ambitious.

Keohane et al. (1998) mention yet another tactical objection against market instruments: once implemented, they may be difficult to change. Suppose that a market instrument is in place and the government wants to tighten environmental policy. It will be difficult to raise environmental charges, because raising tax rates in general is difficult. If tradable permits are given the status of 'property rights', the government's plan to reduce their value or number will meet with resistance from industry, probably resulting in court action. But even if permits do not have the formal status of property rights, industry will argue that in order to give the instrument a chance, the government should promise not to interfere to impose tighter regulation in the near future.

4.3 Reasons to Prefer Market Instruments

Of course one can also think of reasons why environmentalists should be in favour of market instrument, although they receive less attention in the literature. Indeed, environmental organizations in the US, after initial hostility, were in favour of emissions charge proposals in the 1970s. There even was an environmental lobbying group called the Coalition to Tax Pollution (Anderson et al., 1977).

The first reason for environmentalists to favour market instruments is that abating pollution becomes cheaper, because market instruments are efficient. As a result, it will be easier to press for more environmental protection. The second reason is that financial instruments yield government revenue. This government revenue can be used for additional environmental protection.

Keohane et al. (1998) argue that an environmental interest group is interested in its own well-being, next to environmental quality. This can be a reason for an environmentalist organization to support market instruments. As an example, Keohane et al. (1998: 36) present the Environmental Defense Fund's (EDF) support for the Sulphur Allowance Trading scheme:[10]

> EDF had already become a champion of market-based apporaches to environmental protection in other, less nationally prominent, domains. Now it faced an opportunity to strengthen that position and solidify its reputation as a pragmatic environmental organization willing to adopt new strategies involving less confrontantion with private industry. By supporting tradeable permits, EDP could seize a market niche in the environmental movement, distinguishing itself further from other groups.

In accordance with what we said above, Keohane et al. (1998: 36) also present another reason why EDF supported the trading scheme:

> Importantly, EDF was able to make a powerful argument for tradeable permits on environmental, as opposed to economic, grounds: the use of a cost-effective instrument would make it politically possible to achieve greater reductions in sulfur dioxide emissions than would otherwise be the case.

4.4 Nentjes and Dijkstra (1994)

In this section, we shall discuss Nentjes and Dijkstra's (1994) treatment of the preferences of environmental organizations. Nentjes and Dijkstra (1994) state that the dominant aim of environmental organizations is to maximize environmental quality. This implies that they would like emissions to be below the target level as much as possible. According to Nentjes and Dijkstra (1994), a second property of the environmentalists' utility function is that they have a risk-averse attitude.

*Table 4.2   Environmental organizations' criteria for assessing instruments,
            according to Nentjes and Dijkstra (1994)*

	Certain emission reduction	Uncertain emission reduction
Extra funds	Auctioned permits	Emission charges
No extra funds	Grandfathered permits, bubbles	(Emission charges with refunding)

In case of a symmetrical distribution of possible outcomes around the environmental target the result with smallest standard deviation is preferred. Two reasons
can be given for this risk aversion. The first is that there may be threshold effects:
when emissions are slightly above the target, there is a large increase in
environmental damage. The second reason is that the environmentalists expect it
will be difficult to tighten environmental policy when it is discovered that
emissions exceed the target level.

We first discuss the consequences of risk aversion. As we have seen in section
3.3, the impact of the emissions charge on total industry emissions is uncertain,
but the impact of firm bubbles and permits is certain. The environmental
organizations have no reason to believe that the government systematically
estimates emission control costs too high or too low. For this reason environmental
organizations would prefer firm bubbles and tradable permits to an emissions
charge.

Since it is expected that the target for industry emissions is realized under all
instruments, it seems impossible to base a preference ordering of instruments on
their contribution to maximal environmental quality. This changes if we take into
account the possibility to improve environmental quality in other ways than by
decreasing the emissions of industry. Emissions charges and auctioned permits
differ from the other instruments in that they yield public revenue next to realizing
the emission target for industry. Because the money is collected in the context of
environmental policy, environmentalists are in a good position to organize a lobby
for allocating these funds to additional environmental protection. To get an extra
share from general funds will usually be harder. For this reason emissions charges
and auctioned permits are preferred to direct regulation and grandfathered tradable
permits. According to Nentjes and Dijkstra (1994), this preference will be
supported by 'moral' views which prevail under environmentalists that the
polluter should pay for the use of the environment instead of getting permission
to pollute for free.

In Table 4.2 the two components that affect the environmental organizations'
preference for instruments are brought together. Nentjes and Dijkstra (1994)

Table 4.3 Preferences of environmental organizations for instruments, according to Nentjes and Dijkstra (1994)

1.	Tradable emission permits, auction
2/3.	Tradable emission permits, grandfathering, and firm bubbles
4.	Emission charges

assess that certainty of emission reduction is valued higher by environmental organizations than extra funds and that for that reason bubbles and grandfathering of permits will be preferred to emissions charges. The environmentalists' preference ordering is then as given in Table 4.3.

4.5 Surveys

4.5.1 Kelman (1981, 1983)
In the 1978 survey in the US, the 19 environmentalists interviewed were split on the issue of charges (Kelman, 1981, 1983): 32% were in favour, 16% favoured experiments and 37% were hostile. As a group, the environmentalists were the most knowledgeable about charges. The most frequently mentioned arguments in favour of charges were:

- charges are an efficient instrument;
- charges make it in one's self-interest to reduce pollution;
- charges make polluters pay for residual emissions.

The most frequently mentioned arguments against charges were:

- one should not have a choice of polluting if willing to pay a charge; charges are a 'licence to pollute';
- health damage should never be allowed; one cannot set a monetary value on health or the environment;
- the charge rate will be too low to have the desired effect.

4.5.2 Svendsen (1998)
Svendsen (1998) finds that in 1994 the US environmental groups no longer opposed emission trading. They have abandoned their ethical objections, identified in the 1978 survey and summarized by Svendsen (1998) as the symbolic goal of zero pollution. Nowadays, the environmental movement is in favour of tradable permits, if they yield a clear environmental benefit.

Presently, the general attitude of Denmark's largest conservation organization is in favour of economic instruments (Svendsen, 1998). In 1988, Danish environmentalists still opposed tradable permits. They argued that a large firm should not be allowed to pollute all it wished and a polluter should not be allowed to ruin an area of natural beauty. But nowadays, the environmentalists promote a CO_2 tax. They are still sceptical with respect to tradable CO_2 permits. Svendsen (1998) attributes this to lack of knowledge.

5.   ECONOMISTS?

Most studies of the political choice of instruments in environmental policy begin with the question: 'Why are there so little market instruments, despite the economists' pleas?' In that light, it may seem strange that we have not yet discussed economists as an interest group. In this section, I will first look at economists' motives and then explain why they are not seen as an interest group in this setup.

A possible reason for not regarding economists as an interest group is that economists do not have an interest of their own in instrument choice. In this view, an economist is in favour of market instruments, because he can calculate that they are welfare-maximizing for the economy as a whole. His task is then to explain these instruments to others, so that they get to know and appreciate market instruments.

It takes some mental flexibility to support the view that economists are the only altruistic participants in the discussion on environmental policy instruments. After all, the fundamental assumption of mainstream economics is that man is motivated by self-interest. In experiments, economists and economic students are often found to be more selfish than others.[11]

Before we focus on economists' self-interested motives, we note that they may also be motivated by something in between self-interest and altruism, namely ideology.[12] Economists may have a faith in the market mechanism as a superior way of social organization. This faith is not only based on the efficiency properties of the market. It also encompasses the ideas that the government should meddle as little as possible with people's freedom to choose, and that it is a good thing to make use of people's self-interest to solve the environmental problem.

Now we turn to possible self-interested motives of economists promoting market instruments. Economists may be concerned with environmental degradation, and offer their professional expertise to help solve the problem. Alternatively, economists may realize that the environment is an ongoing social concern, and decide to pursue a career as an environmental economist.

Daly and Cobb (1989) and Beder (1996) offer a different suggestion. They point out that non-economists are liable to see environmental degradation as a failure of the market economy. Apparently the economists' claim that the market provides the best means of allocating scarce resources, is wrong. Economists react to this by asserting that the problem is not the market system as such, but the fact that there is no market for the environment. The solution they offer is to extend the market system. Economists hope to prove in this manner that traditional economics is relevant to environmental policy. They try to save their stature and to avoid the restructuring of economics, in order to protect their previous investment in learning economics.

Although economists may promote market instruments out of self-interest, this is not enough to qualify as an interest group. The difference between economists and the interest groups we previously encountered, is that the interest groups can apply political pressure. They can threaten to withhold their support for politicians that do not do what they want. They can threaten to sabotage policy implementation. Economists do not have that power.

When analysing instrument choice in environmental policy as an argumentative process (as in the literature reviewed in Chapter 2, section 3, and like Beder (1996), to be reviewed in Chapter 6, section 2.2), one cannot ignore the role of the economist. But here, we analyse instrument choice as a political decision that is subject to pressure, and then the economist is not an active player. In this model, the players know how market instruments work. In that sense, the work of the economist has already been done. The interest groups may employ (or partly consist of) economists, but economists play no role as a group with a distinct agenda.

6.   CONCLUSION, TENTATIVE ORDERING

By way of conclusion, we present a tentative preference ordering of environmental policy instruments for the four main interest groups: the shareholders and workers in the polluting industry, the environmentalist movement and the environmental bureaucracy. These preference orderings, presented in Table 4.4, will be used in Chapter 7, section 2, to illustrate the workings of the institutional model of instrument choice.

One should not attach too much significance to these preference orderings. Actual preference orderings may differ from the ones presented here for many reasons. These reasons can be classified as:

− different specification of the instruments;
− different criteria on which instruments are judged;
− a different model to derive the effects of instruments.

Having said this, we now move on to the explanation of the preference orderings presented here. We have not included the preference ordering of the consumers

Table 4.4   Tentative preference orderings

	Share- holders	Workers	Environmen- talists	Environmental bureaucracy
Bubbles	2	1	2/3	1
Standards	3	2	5	4/5
Tradable permits, grandfathering	1	3/4/5	2/3	2
Tradable permits, auctioning	4/5	3/4/5	1	3
Emissions charges	4/5	3/4/5	4	4/5

in Table 4.4, because in general, the consumers will not be organized in a lobby. It is difficult for the consumers to organize, because they are a large group with small per capita stakes. However, we do note here that product price may also be of interest to the policymaker who tries to control inflation.

We have two possible sources for the orderings for the shareholders and workers. One is the partial equilibrium model from Chapter 3, section 3. The other is the literature that tries to take into account more aspects from reality than the partial equilibrium model. However, this second strand of the literature, reviewed in section 2, does not give enough reason to amend the preference orderings found in Chapter 3.

Thus, in Table 4.4, we have copied the preference ordering for shareholders from Table 3.6. For workers, we have ranked standards and bubbles according to the case that seems most likely. Workers would only prefer bubbles to standards if long-run demand is inelastic and the long-run effect is more important than the short-run effect.

For the environmental bureaucracy and the environmentalists, we base the orderings on Nentjes and Dijkstra (1994). Their orderings for the environmental bureaucracy were given in column (1) of Table 4.1, and for the environmentalists in Table 4.3.

To Nentjes and Dijkstra's (1994) ordering we add the instrument of perfor-mance standards. Environmentalists and the environmental bureaucracy rank this instrument very low, because its effect on industry emissions is uncertain. With performance standards, the government controls total emissions indirectly, via the emissions to output ratio. If output turns out to be lower (higher) than the government had expected, emissions will be below (above) the target.

Because we have taken certainty of emission reduction as the most important criterion for the environmental bureaucracy, they rank standards lowest, together with emissions charges. The environmental movement is also very interested in certainty of emission reduction. It ranks standards even below emissions charges, because emissions charges generate government revenue, and standards do not.

NOTES

1. Slow compliance with direct regulation is also compounded by the fact that firms only start to incur costs the moment they start abating. Perhaps the firm will be prosecuted for delaying abatement, but it may be willing to take that risk. With charges, a firm has to pay for its emissions, so that delaying abatement is costly. Russell (1979) discusses this argument, doubting its validity.
2. See also Chapter 6, section 3.2.
3. See Chapter 2, section 5, for the notion of arenas.
4. See also point 1 from Chapter 2, section 2.
5. Michael Levin, head of EPA's Regulatory Reform Staff, quoted in Liroff (1986: 40).
6. In the long run, the emission target will always be met with certainty, because by nature of the long run, the government can adjust its policy until the target is met.
7. This is a term from an EPA document.
8. See also section 3.2.
9. The notion of arenas is discussed in Chapter 2, section 5.
10. See also Chapter 6, section 2.3.
11. Marwell and Ames (1981), Carter and Irons (1991) and Frank et al. (1993) find economists are more selfish than others. However, Isaac et al. (1985) do not find a significant difference.
12. Kelman (1981, 1983) discusses the economists' ideological arguments in favour of market instruments.

5. Survey among Dutch Interest Groups

1. INTRODUCTION

There are different ways to study interest groups' preferences for environmental policy instruments. From behind his desk, the researcher can read what others wrote about the subject and think about it himself. The results of this approach were presented in Chapters 3 and 4. Another approach, which was also pursued, is to go out and ask representatives from interest groups directly about their preferences.

This chapter is the report of our survey among Dutch interest groups in late 1996, early 1997.[1] Representatives from environmental organizations, the civil service, industry organizations and trade unions received a questionnaire and responded. The survey consisted of two rounds. In the first round, we stayed quite close to the theoretical framework of Chapters 3 and 4. We presented the respondents with the instruments and their effects, as we examined them in this theoretical analysis.

However, we found that the respondents did not have much use for this theoretical approach. The main points of their criticism were the partial character of the approach and the assumptions with respect to efficiency. The dissonance between the theoretical approach and the respondents' frame of reference is also evident from the respondents' reluctance to give a preference ordering for instruments.

Because of the gap between the respondents' frame of reference and the ideas behind the questions from the fist round, we decided to add a second round. In this second round, we asked a number of questions inspired by the respondents' reactions in the first round. Thus, the questions in the second round were better related to the respondents' frame of reference. Next to that, the second round was used to ask a number of clarifying questions.

There is some overlap between this section and Chapter 6, section 3, on market instruments in Dutch environmental policy. In both sections we treat the discussion on regulatory energy charges (Chapter 6, section 3.4) and the current discussion on tradable emission permits that started in 1995 (Chapter 6, section 3.5). Our intention is to present the interest groups' *preferences* in this chapter, and their *actions* in Chapter 6, section 3. But to avoid a fragmentary treatment in either section, we shall have to repeat ourselves occasionally.

This chapter is organized as follows. In section 2 we see which organizations were approached and who responded. In section 3 we present the answers to the first round questionnaire and the subsequent correspondence. In section 4 we discuss the answers to the second round questionnaire. We conclude with section 5.

2.   RESPONDENTS

In all organizations, we approached respondents as high up in the hierarchy as possible, with experience in, or charged with, instrument choice in particular or environmental policy in general. Suggestions for respondents were given by Nentjes (University of Groningen), De Vries (SNM) and Van Namen (VNCI).

Environmental organizations
The environmental organizations approached were:

– Stichting Natuur en Milieu (Nature and Environment Foundation);
– Aktie Strohalm (Action Straw);[2]
– Stichting MilieuDefensie (Environmental Defense Foundation);
– Wereld Natuur Fonds (World Wide Fund for Nature);
– Waddenvereniging (National Association for the Preservation of the Wadden Sea);
– Greenpeace.

The first four organizations responded to the survey. Of these organizations, SNM's strategy is mainly to negotiate with government and industry. AS and MD are more 'action'-oriented.[3] WNF has recently started to try and influence environmental policy, because it has realized that nature is threatened by pollution.

Civil service[4]
Civil servants from the following branches of government were approached:

– VROM: the Department of Housing, Physical Planning and the Environment;
– EZ: the Department of Economic Affairs;[5]
– DCMR: the environmental agency for the Rijnmond area (around Rotterdam);
– IPO: the interprovincial consultation platfom.

Four civil servants from VROM were approached, two of whom responded. IPO and DCMR were approached because both organizations played an important role in setting up the Tradable Emission Permit project (Chapter 6, section 3.5). The

Table 5.1 Respondents to the survey 'Instrument choice in environmental policy'

Respondent	Organization	Category[a]	Contribution[b]	Publications	Representativeness[c]
P. van der Veer and A. van den Biggelaar	SNM	E	1 2 i	Van den Biggelaar (and co-authors), SNM (1996)	a
H. Wieringa and A. de Savornin Lohman	MD	E	1 2		b
M. van der Valk	AS	E	1 2		c
S. Schöne	WNF	E	1 2	Blok et al. (1996)	*director*
C. Dekkers	VROM	C	2 i		c (see section 3.3.3)
P. Ruyssenaars	VROM	C	1 2	Letter from the Minister (VROM, 1996)	c (see section 3.3.3)
F. van Brenk	DCMR	C	1 2		a
K. Hensems	EZ	C	2	Bovenberg et al. (1991)	
W. Zijlstra and W. Klerken	VNONCW	I	1 2 i		a
J. van der Kooij	SEP	I	1	SEP (1988, 1990, 1993)	a
P. Thomassen	OCC	I	1 2 i	Buys (1994), OCC (n.d.)	a
H. Leemreize	FNV	L	1 2	FNV (1993)	a (see section 3.2.5)
C. van der Knaap	CNV	L	1 2		a

Notes
a. E = environmental movement   C = civil service   I = industry   L = trade union
b. 1 = first round respondent   2 = second round respondent   i = interview
c. a = knows/supposes everyone will give approximately the same answers.   b = does not know.
c. c = knows/supposes some will give different answers.

118

search for a respondent from IPO eventually led to an employee of DCMR. Since there already was a respondent from DCMR, the IPO was dropped.

Industry
The industry organizations approached were:

- VNONCW: the general industry and employers' organization;[6]
- OCC: the oil refineries organization;
- SEP: the organization of energy producers;
- VNCI: the chemical industry organization;
- FME: the base metal industry organisation.

The first three organizations responded to the survey. Initially, the VNCI was represented by Van Namen, but his successor cancelled VNCI's contribution, probably for strategic reasons, of which we shall have more to say in the conclusion.

Labour
The trade unions approached were:

- FNV: the general, and largest, trade union;
- CNV: the christian, and second largest, trade union.

Both unions responded to the survey.

The respondents are listed in Table 5.1. Table 5.1 also presents the form of their contribution, including interviews and publications from their organization they referred to or sent. In the first round, the respondents were also asked how they thought others in their organizations would answer the questions. Their reactions are presented in Table 5.1 under the heading of representativeness. Only Schöne (WNF) did not answer this question. But because he is the director of WNF, we may expect his opinions to carry considerable weight, although not everyone at WNF might agree with his answers.

3. THE FIRST ROUND QUESTIONNAIRE

3.1 Introduction

The first round questionnaire was sent in November 1996. It contained questions on the respondents' and their organizations' preferences for instruments. It also contained information on the effects of instruments on several criteria that might interest the respondents.

Some of the respondents' answers gave rise to additional questions. These questions were sent to the respondents in the second round, together with the second round questionnaire we shall discuss in section 4. However, we shall discuss the answers to the additional questions in this section.

In section 3.2 we shall present the criteria on which the respondents would like to judge instruments. In section 3.3 we discuss the interest groups' preferences for instruments. The respondents' favourite destinations for the revenue of the financial instruments are discussed in section 3.4. Section 3.5 concludes our report of the first round.

3.2   Criteria

3.2.1 Introduction
In question 1.3, the respondents were asked on which criteria they would like to judge the instruments. The respondents were asked not only to mention the criteria, but also to rank them if they could. The question explicitly presented eight criteria, but the respondents were not restricted to these. The questionnaire contained a discussion of the effects of instruments on these eight criteria, which were taken from the literature and our own theoretical analysis, as presented in Chapters 3 and 4.

Tables 5.2a and 5.2b present the criteria mentioned by the respondents. Table 5.2a contains the eight criteria explicitly presented in question 1.3. Table 5.2b contains the criteria mentioned by the respondents themselves. In order to facilitate comparisons and to keep the table's size manageable, the criteria originally mentioned by the respondents have sometimes been renamed. Criteria that pertain specifically to one instrument (most notably to tradable emission permits) have been excluded from the table. These criteria will appear in section 3.3, when we discuss interest groups' preferences.

It should be noted that some criteria are very closely linked. For instance, certainty of emission reduction and enforceability may be seen as aspects of effectiveness. Support for environmental policy will depend on employment and income distribution effects, and so on. The implication of this remark is, that a respondent may attach importance to criteria that he did not mention explicitly. For instance, he mentions effectiveness as a criterion, but he does not explicitly mention enforceability, because this is implied in effectiveness. This is the result of giving the respondents the opportunity to mention criteria of their own.

We shall now discuss the criteria for the environmental organizations (section 3.2.2), the civil service (section 3.2.3), industry (section 3.2.4) and labour (section 3.2.5). We conclude with section 3.2.6.

Table 5.2a *Criteria on which to judge instruments, presented in question 1.3*

	SNM	MD	AS	WNF	VROM	DCMR	SEP	VNO	OCC	FNV	CNV
Number of firms left	7	2	2					3			1
Innovation	2	2	1	*	(*)	*				*	3
Objections of principle against market instruments	*		2				(*)				8[a]
Product price, quantity produced	6							1			5
Implementation costs for government	4		2	*	*	*		4		*	6
Employment	3	3[b]	1		*			6		*	2
Profits	5							5		*[c]	4
Certainty of emission reduction	1	1	1	*	*	*	*	2			7

Notes
Number: place in ordering
*:   named in written answer or in interview
(*):   named in relation to other criteria, in written answer or in interview
a.   None
b.   On a macro level
c.   'not really necessary'

121

Table 5.2b Criteria on which to judge instruments, named by the respondents

	SNM	MD	AS	WNF	VROM	DCMR	SEP	VNO	OCC	FNV	CNV
Effectiveness	1[a]		1	+		*	*	*	*	*	*
Efficiency			2		+	*	*	*	*	*	*
Support, public opinion	*				+	*	*	*		*	*
International competitiveness, scale				*				*	*	(*)	
Toward sustainable development	*	*								*	
Income distribution, social effects	*									*	
Compatibility with (international) policy principles					*		*				
Monitoring and enforcement			1						*		
Cost for firms								*			*
Polluter pays, working of market intact, prices reflect environmental cost			1							*	
Argumentation, urgency									*	*	*
Do not reward laggards			*								

North-South relation	*				+
Reach		*			*
Predictable policy				*	
Source-oriented	*			*	
No abuse of financial instruments				*	
Objections of principle against government interference	2				
Potential of strategic behaviour by firms		*			
Equal treatment of firms				*	

Notes
Number: place in ordering
*: named in written answer or in interview
(*): named in relation to other criteria, in written answer or in interview
+: named in publication, not in written answer or interview
a. Consisting of feasibility and certainty of emission reduction.

3.2.2 Environmental organizations

The most important criterion for the environmental organizations is effectiveness or certainty of emission reduction. They also find it very important that the instrument stimulates innovation. Employment, and the implementation costs for government, are mentioned by three out of four respondents. Other criteria are mentioned by at most two respondents.

It is striking that the criterion of efficiency plays such a minor role in the environmental organizations' responses. Although this criterion was not explicitly presented in the survey, it was mentioned by all respondents outside the environmental movement. But within the environmental organizations, only Van der Valk (AS) mentions efficiency, and only as a minor criterion. In the WNF report (Blok et al., 1996) efficiency is not mentioned as a reason for introducing market instruments.

Perhaps we should not make too much of this apparent neglect of efficiency, because (as we shall see in section 4.4) the respondents from the environmental organizations did criticize the survey's assumptions about efficiency. Furthermore, they did mention the effects of instruments on innovation, i.e. the dynamic efficiency of instruments, as a criterion. However, the respondents who did not mention efficiency were asked why they did not. Wieringa (MD) replied that efficiency is very important for finding support.[7] Van den Biggelaar and Van der Veer (SNM) replied that given effectiveness, efficiency is important. Thus, efficiency is a criterion of secondary or indirect importance for them.

Objections of principle against market instruments still linger in environmental organizations, but they do not seem to play a large role. Van den Biggelaar and Van der Veer regarded anti-market sentiments as typical for the 1970s, when the environmental movement was more of an anti-capitalist movement. Although they do not have objections of principle against market instruments, some of their colleagues within SNM are still opposed to tradable emission permits out of principle.

When asked about objections of principle against market instruments at MD, De Savornin Lohman answered that they were present. While admitting he might be overly optimistic, De Savornin Lohman felt these objections were mainly due to lack of understanding and they could be overcome by a good explanation. He also indicated that design details, like enforceability and distributional aspects, were crucial.

Van der Valk (AS) mentions ethical objections as a criterion of minor importance. The fact that he mentions this criterion at all may seem strange, considering his preference ordering of instruments: he ranks tradable permits with auction first and emission charges second. When confronted with this apparent contradiction, Van der Valk emphasized that his ethical objections against market instruments do not play a decisive role. He was also willing to amplify on his objections against market instruments:[8]

The market tends to result in concentration of power and wealth, despite the appearance of the opposite, and I would not wish to enhance that process by creating environmental markets. Unless there are good reasons to assume they do not enhance that concentration. Moreover, it sometimes gives me a bad taste in the mouth when price tags have to be attached to all kinds of things. What is the cost of a dead Dutchman, of a Bangla Deshi, of a deep sea fish, of a rare beetle?

But Van der Valk also has objections of principle against government interference:

When I pollute the environment, hit me with the whip of a tough ecotax, but do not put me in a re-education camp.

This serves to qualify his objections of principle against market instruments. As we have seen in Chapter 4, section 4.2, one may be concerned that with market instruments, polluters reduce pollution because it is in their financial interest, and not because pollution is bad. Obviously, Van der Valk does not share this concern.

The ultimate goal of SNM is a sustainable society.[9] According to Van den Biggelaar and Van der Veer:[10]

There is more to that than a clean environment. It also involves social justice: a fair distribution of income and sufficient employment. It is a society that is stable in all respects.

3.2.3 Civil service

The respondents from the civil service all mention efficiency, innovation and certainty of emission reduction as criteria. Ruyssenaars (VROM) links innovation to certainty of emission reduction: the emission target can only be realized with innovation.

In VROM publications[11] (VROM, 1996; Versteege and Vos, 1995) it is argued that tradable emission permits are not reconcilable with the internationally adopted ALARA (As Low As Reasonably Achievable) principle and the precautionary principle. According to these principles, the polluter should reduce his emissions as much as possible. But with tradable permits, a polluter can buy permits instead of reducing his emissions, even when it is technically possible to reduce emissions. Thus, the introduction of a system of tradable permits would necessitate a time-consuming rewriting of the environmental laws.

3.2.4 Industry

For the industry respondents, efficiency, the product price and international competitiveness are important criteria. A certain suspicion against government is apparent from their criteria that financial instruments should not be abused as a revenue-raising device, and that environmental policy should be predictable.

Contrary to what we assumed in our theoretical analysis, the industry respondents place little emphasis on profits. This is understandable for Van der

Kooij (SEP), because electricity producers are not supposed to make profits. Van der Kooij himself emphasizes that the issue is not profits, but cost reduction, and that SEP has always made a plea for cost-effective environmental policy. Thomassen (OCC) regards profit-making as a responsibility for the firms themselves, and not as a concern for the industry organization. Zijlstra (VNO-NCW) ranks profits no higher than fifth. This is the same ranking as Van den Biggelaar and Van der Veer's (SNM) and lower than Van der Knaap's (CNV). Zijlstra was confronted with these comparative rankings, combined with the conjectures that VNONCW represents entrepreneurs' interests and entrepreneurs are interested in profits. He argued firstly that an entrepreneur is primarily interested in continuity of his company within the boundaries of the market (product price and quantity produced), and in accordance with the environmental regulations. Secondly, he answered that he had been meaning to indicate that profits are not the first thing that springs to mind when thinking about the environment: entrepreneurs have their own responsibility toward the environment.

A similar reluctance to judge environmental policy instruments on non-environmental grounds is found in Van der Kooij's (SEP) answer:

> Your criteria have very little to do with the environment.

The criterion of 'Objections of principle against market instruments' does appeal to Van der Kooij:[12]

> The new instruments are at odds with current policy and demand a complete reorientation of government policy. In the public opinion, emission reduction and buying tradable emission permits will not be seen as equivalent.

Thomassen (OCC) places great emphasis on the equal treatment of firms: there should be a level playing field. Environmental policy should not result in the differential treatment of firms, because this would give some firms an unfair competitive advantage over others.

3.2.5 Labour

For the respondents from the trade unions, employment, innovation, profits and effectiveness are the most important criteria. Certainty of emission reduction is ranked quite low. Leemreize (FNV) also mentions international competitiveness, indicating that this is implicitly contained in the criteria of innovation, employment and profits/value added.

To his answer that he supposes that everyone within FNV will give approximately the same answers as he did, Leemreize adds that instrument choice should be made on a case-by-case basis. Other FNV people might make a different trade-off between short-run and long-run effects, and between business economic and socio-economic considerations than he does.

3.2.6 Conclusion

In this conclusion, we shall compare the criteria named by the respondents to the criteria ascribed to them in the theoretical treatment of Chapters 3 and 4.

All respondents name effectiveness of environmental policy or certainty of emission reduction as a criterion. In the theoretical treatment, we only mentioned this criterion for the environmental movement and the environmental bureaucracy. However, we should note that we assumed that all instruments were expected to result in the targeted emission reduction. Thus, we played down the importance of effectiveness. But in reality, one instrument may be expected to result in more emission reduction than another.

Because effectiveness as a potential criterion is not treated in the questionnaire, we cannot be sure what exactly the respondents meant by it. It encompasses some notion of certainty of emission reduction, but this could be 'rather the certainty than the expectation that x tons will be emitted' or 'certainty that the officially stated goal will be attained'. The other aspect of effectiveness is feasibility. Feasibility implies that the government is able to measure and check firm emissions and enforce policy, so that firms will comply with it. It may also imply making 'realistic' demands on industry.

Speaking in general, one may wonder whether respondents whom we did not expect to name effectiveness, mention this criterion to promote their environmentally friendly image, or because they are genuinely concerned about effectiveness. However, we should also recognize another reason for industry to mention effectiveness. This is that the effectiveness of an instrument depends on the reaction of industry to it, and thereby on the acceptability of the instrument to industry. Thus, when industry mentions effectiveness, it can be seen as a warning: 'When the instrument is not acceptable to us, it will not be effective.'

In Table 5.2b we see that a lot of respondents mention efficiency as a criterion. The criterion of efficiency as such did not figure in our theoretical treatment. The idea behind that is that interest groups are only interested in the efficiency gains of an instrument if they can appropriate part of these gains, e.g. in the form of profits. One can think of two main reasons why the respondents mentioned efficiency:

- they assume they will be able to appropriate a considerable part of an instrument's efficiency gains. Industry expects higher profits, whereas the other interest groups are more interested in the efficiency gains that are realized in the form of revenues of financial instruments (see section 3.4);
- they see efficiency as a way to make environmental policy more acceptable to those who will receive the efficiency gains. Wieringa (MD) explicitly made this argument, although he did not mention efficiency or acceptability initially as criteria. We may assume this argument is also relevant for the respondents who mention both criteria (see Table 5.2b).

Let us now look at the criteria per category of organization. That the environmental organizations attach great importance to effectiveness, or certainty of emission reduction, and innovation, is in line with our theoretical analysis. The same goes for implementation costs for government, which can be seen as an aspect of effectiveness. Employment, however, was not mentioned in our theoretical treatment. The environmental organizations could be interested in employment for several reasons. First, it can be an aspect of their view of a sustainable society, that encompasses more than just a healthy environment (see the quote from Van den Biggelaar and Van der Veer). Secondly, environmentalists are mostly oriented to the political left, and people on the left care about employment. Thirdly, environmental organizations may be interested in employment for strategic reasons. When they can combine environmental and employment policy, they will not antagonize, or even have an ally in, the powerful trade unions and more generally, people whose jobs are threatened by environmental policy.

As we had expected, the civil service is interested in effectiveness and certainty of emission reduction. When environmental policy is effective, this means they have done a good job. Efficiency, in which the civil service also displays an interest, contributes directly and indirectly, via its positive effect on acceptability, to effectiveness and to good relations between civil service and society, especially industry. The criterion of implementation costs for government is mentioned, but as something to be minimized rather than maximized, as in our theoretical treatment. Two reasons can be given for this. First of all, one can hardly expect civil servants to openly admit that they want to maximize the amount of work for themselves and thus the implementation costs. Secondly, when it takes a lot of effort and time to implement a certain instrument, e.g. to adapt legislation to tradable permits, effectiveness is harmed.

For the industry organizations, the most conspicuous difference with the theoretical treatment is the low ranking of profits. The respondents' reactions to this difference were presented in section 3.2.4. As we had expected, the trade unions are interested in employment. Furthermore, as we discussed earlier in this conclusion, the industry organization and the trade unions are interested in the effectiveness of environmental policy.

3.3   Preferences for Instruments

3.3.1 Introduction
The respondents were asked to give their favourite instruments for the abatement of industrial SO_2/NO_x and CO_2 emissions. They were asked to choose from, or rank, the following instruments:

− direct regulations in the form of:
  * a non-tradable emission ceiling per firm;

* a standard, specifying a maximum ratio of emissions to output or input;
– market instruments:
    * emissions charges, the revenue of which is added to general government funds;
    * tradable permits with an auction, the revenue of which is added to general government funds;
    * tradable permits with grandfathering.

The respondents were also asked for previous statements of their organization about instrument choice. The publications they referred to, and sometimes sent, are given in Table 5.1.

In sections 3.3.2 to 3.3.5 I will present the respondents' answers about their own preferences. We shall see that most respondents were not willing to order the instruments presented to them. In section 2.3.6 we will see what the respondents thought the preferences of other organizations would be. We conclude with section 3.3.7.

3.3.2 Environmental organizations
The environmental organizations have on several occasions undertaken action for the introduction of market instruments, but they have not made any general statement that they prefer market instruments.

Wieringa (MD) ranks tradable permits first and emissions charges second. MD and Friends of the Earth (FoE), the international organization to which MD is affiliated, have come out in favour of market instruments when instrument choice was at stake. Wieringa (MD) mentions the ecotax, also on a European level, and the idea to experiment with tradable permits. However, neither MD nor FoE has stated a general preference market instruments. This is because the political choice of instruments is made on the basis of the expected economic effects. Thus it is important to reach consensus about the direction of sustainable economic development:

> Research has shown that the macroeconomic effects of a stringent environmental policy are often positive. With that consensus (and conviction) it becomes easier to agree on instruments.

Van der Valk (AS) ranks an auction of tradable permits first and emissions charges second. He prefers withdrawal rights to emission rights, and input charges to emissions charges, because the intervention should take place as close as possible to the root of the pollution.

Schöne (WNF) names standards on specific details and efficiency improvement targets as his favourite instruments for CO_2 abatement. Standards and grand-fathering of tradable permits are his favourite instruments for SO_2 and NO_x.

The WNF report (Blok et al., 1996) investigates by which policies and measures the European Union can reduce its 1990 level of anthropogenic CO_2 emissions by 20 percent by the year 2005. The introduction of a CO_2 charge is advocated,[13] but it is assumed that the charge rate will not be high enough for the charge alone to result in the targeted emission reduction. The report discusses the heavy industry, the light industry, the residential sector, the service sector, transport and the energy supply sector separately. It also considers the opportunities for renewable energy, material efficiency improvement and changes in consumption patterns. The report indicates by how much and with which instruments the CO_2 emissions per sector can be reduced. This results in the following list (Blok et al., 1996: 10):

- Standards and regulation may play a role in order to improve energy efficiency for dwellings and office buildings, and for electric appliances used in all sectors. Company-wide standards may be applied for cars. Furthermore, obligations can be set for energy companies with respect to the application of renewable energy and combined generation of heat and power (CHP).
- Subsidies may be applied for increasing the rate of retrofit insulation of buildings and for the application of compact fluorescent lamps.
- Voluntary agreements may play a role – on a European scale – in reaching energy efficiency improvement in heavy industry and – on a national scale – in reaching energy efficiency improvement in light industry.
- A number of other instruments are added, among them fiscal measures for renewable energy investments, improved buy-back tariffs for electricity from CHP and renewables, and building infrastructure for public transport.

The selection of instruments in the report is primarily based on policy instruments that have shown their effectiveness in a country or sector for a certain time, but perhaps more effective instruments may be available (Blok et al., 1996: 10). This approach may explain the very minor role for tradable permits in the report. When asked about this, Schöne replied that he did see tradability of CO_2 permits between countries as a long run option.

In their written reply, Van den Biggelaar and Van der Veer (SNM) did not give a preference for certain instruments, because the effectiveness of instruments is strongly dependent on the situation, and often a mix of instruments will be appropriate. In its publications, SNM states a preference of binding measures above voluntary measures, and endorses financial instruments.

In the interview, Van den Biggelaar and Van der Veer (SNM) did mention specific instruments. For CO_2 they named:

- charges for smaller firms;
- emission ceilings for larger firms;
- standards for construction and electrical appliances.

For SO_2, where there are a limited number of large sources, Van den Biggelaar and Van der Veer prefer emission ceilings and tradable permits. For the point sources of NO_x, they propose prescribing technical measures, or norms that are so strict that every firm has to take the most drastic technical measures.

Van den Biggelaar and Van der Veer (SNM) presented the following implications of the criterion of feasibility for instrument choice:

- regulating charges can damage the international competitiveness of firms;
- a well-functioning market is needed for tradable permits to work. Further research is necessary before this instrument can be considered;
- issuing licences does not work with hundreds of small firms. The implementation costs are too high, and local authorities will be too lenient with licence issuing and monitoring;
- the right moment to tighten environmental norms for a firm is when it renews its plant.

As a general remark on their preferences, Van den Biggelaar and Van der Veer said:

> *We might prefer a particular instrument ourselves, but when the other parties concerned do not like it, we had better promote a different instrument that is still acceptable to us.*

However, their preferences for instruments as stated above are their own, without taking into account others' preferences.

As we shall see in our discussion of the regulatory energy charge (Chapter 6, section 3.4.8), SNM attaches great importance to the implementation of the principle of the regulatory charge. Within SNM, the opinions on whether to support tradable emission permits in the current discussion (Chapter 6, section 3.5) are divided. The proponents argue that it will make environmental policy less costly, and that therefore total emissions can be further reduced. The opponents have objections of principle, but also practical objections:

- the local environmental groups now have the right to go to court if they are against the changes in a firm's environmental licence. With tradable permits, they will probably not have this right;
- tradable permits are a new instrument, and will result in new problems. There is no need for new instruments. Instead, better use should be made of the existing instruments;
- because tradable permits are a new instrument, research is necessary about how the instrument works and how it should be implemented. While the research is carried out, advance in environmental policy is impossible;
- only recently, SNM decided to promote emissions charges. Promoting another new instrument at this moment would cause confusion about what SNM stands for.

3.3.3 Civil service

Van Brenk (DCMR) ranks grandfathering of tradable permits first and firm bubbles second. He notes that others within DCMR might have different preferences, as we have already indicated in Table 5.1. For instance, according to Van Brenk, the licence issuing and enforcement departments would like to keep direct regulation. DCMR has not taken a public position on instrument choice. The subject has been discussed internally, but without a formal conclusion.

Ruyssenaars and Dekkers (VROM) point out that opinions within VROM about instrument choice are divided,[14] although there is a general desire to enhance flexibility. Dekkers gave the following outline of what he expected the VROM position to be in the Tradable Emission Permits discussion (Chapter 6, section 3.5):

The TME study indicates that there are already considerable cost advantages to be had from enhancing flexibility within the current regulatory framework and with some additional measures. Then we are talking, for instance, about bubbles on the firm level. We don't need impressive policy changes to achieve sizeable cost advantages.

In her report on the contemporary discussion on tradable permits (Chapter 6, section 3.5), VROM Minister De Boer (Department of VROM, 1996) emphasizes that a tradable permit system can only be considered if there is support for it in society. Society must accept that emitting is seen as a right instead of as a necessary evil. The target groups will have to accept a 'hard' emission ceiling. Whether the target groups will accept tradable permits, depends largely on the cost advantages above the current regulation. With respect to the cost saving, the Minister remarks:

– the current covenants already take cost differences between firms into account;
– with the current emission norms, all technologies currently known will be implemented in 2010;
– on the other hand, a tradable permit system could stimulate innovation in environmental technology.

The Minister concludes that a tradable permit system stands more to reason for SO_2 and NO_x than for CO_2, because it is difficult to introduce 'hard' ceilings for CO_2, given international agreements and resistance from the target groups. If a system of tradable permits were introduced for SO_2 and NO_x, it should be applied nationally to large(r) firms, and trade between the target groups should be allowed.

According to Dekkers, the differences in opinion within VROM can be traced back to the question of how much responsibility industry can handle in reducing emissions. There is a group that wants to come to agreements about reduction goals with target groups, and then leave the implementation (while monitoring it) to industry. This group also contains the proponents of tradable emission permits.

When the implementation of agreements is left to industry, they can set up a tradable emission permit system, or something similar.

The other group within VROM argues that one cannot always, and unconditionally, leave the responsibility of meeting the emission reduction goals to industry. Dekkers places himself in this group:

> *Speaking from my own experience with firms I can say they will only take measures voluntarily if they cost little or nothing, or if their direct surroundings force them to. For substances like NO_x and CO_2, and other large scale environmental problems without directly identifiable damage or nuisance to the direct surroundings, one should not put one's trust in voluntary agreements. Firms cannot explain to their shareholders that they should make large investments because of 'voluntary agreements'. That does not work, and is not compatible with corporate culture and the internal decision making process about large investment projects.*

Dekkers found it hard to give reasons for the divergence in opinion within VROM:

> *There are simply differences between people, that is a fact of life.*

He thinks it has to do with the experiences of people, the environmental problems they are working on, and general societal opinions. Contacts and responsibility also play a role:

> *Perhaps someone who is responsible for the target group policy with respect to industry, appreciates good contacts with industry more, and is more inclined to listen to firms.*

Dekkers also indicated that every directorate within VROM has its own culture and its own way of looking at problems. However, the differences on instrument choice transcend the directorates. Dekkers does not think the differences in education are important in explaining the differences in opinion.

Dekkers is against the tradable emission permit system that has recently been studied (Chapter 6, section 3.5) for two reasons. First, tradable emission permits are at odds with the ALARA principle and the precautionary principle, as we have seen in section 3.2.3.

Secondly, there is the problem of initial distribution. When the permits are distributed according to current emissions, the firms that have already reduced their permits drastically are punished, because they receive a small amount of permits. The firms that have not done much about the environment yet are rewarded, because they receive a lot of permits. This will be seen as unfair. According to Dekkers, this problem did not occur with the SO_2 emission market in the US, because the firms had not done much yet to reduce SO_2 emissions.[15]

Elsewhere (Tabak, 1997), Dekkers also doubts whether industry will commit to a 'hard' emission ceiling. He expresses the fear that when government sets aside the current regulations to make way for the tradable permit system, it has to start all over again negotiating emission reductions from industry.

Dekkers is a proponent of an NO_x charge, notably of a charge with a rate that will increase in time. He does not expect problems with international trade, because the charge revenue would be returned to the firms by way of an investment subsidy.

Ruyssenaars (VROM) thinks a combination of the current agreements (covenants) with tradable permits, within the target group, is the best instrument. This instrument has the advantage that it can be quickly implemented.

3.3.4 Industry

The SEP has repeatedly stated its preference for a covenant to reduce emissions. The SEP already optimizes electricity production nationally, so it should also optimize emission allocation nationally. The SEP also looks beyond electricity production, because other measures may be more cost-effective in reducing environmental damage. In this context, the SEP has payed for flue gas de-sulphurization in Poland, and it is involved, in the framework of the FACE Foundation in afforestation in order to compensate for CO_2 emissions. SEP sees prospects for Joint Implementation provided credits are granted.[16] From Van der Kooij's criteria, which we reviewed in section 3.2.4, we can conclude that the SEP's attitude toward tradable emission permits is reserved.

Thomassen (OCC) prefers standards to firm bubbles, because there should be a level playing field. For the same reason he is against voluntary agreements. Thomassen is sceptical about tradable permits.

> *Such a system would have to apply to the whole of Europe, or there will be relocation effects. And how will the initial distribution of permits take place: will firms that have already done a lot about the environment not be punished because they receive a small number of rights? One must also beware of monopoly positions in the tradable permit market.*
>
> *We fear a system of tradable permits will be added to the existing laws. Then the tradability of permits is severely impaired by the national and European rules that a firm still has to comply with.*

Like Dekkers (VROM), Thomassen (OCC) argues that a tradable emission permit system is more viable when the bulk of the emission reduction has yet to be done.

According to Thomassen (OCC), an energy charge does not work. The charge would have to be dramatically high to discourage energy use. Thomassen does see a role for financial instruments to encourage or discourage the use of a particular kind of fuel.

According to Klerken and Zijlstra, VNONCW is not against charges as such, but they opposed the regulatory energy charge (see Chapter 6, section 3.4), because of the large negative side effects. Klerken and Zijlstra argued the government could achieve more by making agreements with industry than with a charge, at least with a charge rate the government dares to introduce.

Klerken and Zijlstra (VNONCW) are enthusiastic about covenants. They result in cost savings, because the decision how and when to reduce emissions is left to the firm. Consequently, emissions can be reduced further than would otherwise be acceptable. Covenants also increase the environmental awareness of firms and their motivation to reduce emissions. Thus, the government can be more confident that the emission reduction targets will be met. Finally, covenants reduce paperwork in which neither firms nor the government has any faith.

Klerken and Zijlstra see tradable permits as a possible complement to covenants. Firms could make a deal with the government that one firm reduces emissions drastically, and that the other firms do not have to reduce emissions. The firms could then make their own arrangements about sharing the costs of emission reduction.

Klerken and Zijlstra do not expect tradable permits will be applied in the Netherlands in the same way as in the US, with a full-blown market and money explicitly changing hands:

> *That is not our culture. The reasoning in our society is that you cannot have the right to pollute, because pollution should be reduced as much as possible. A tradable permit system implies that you reduce your pollution less than is technically possible. It is questionable whether the Dutch public opinion and the environmental movement will accept that.*

3.3.5 Labour
Van der Knaap (CNV) ranks firm bubbles first, emissions charges second and grandfathering of tradable permits fifth and last. CNV has not publicly taken position on instrument choice. There has been an internal discussion on instruments, but this did not lead to a general preference for certain instruments, or an ordering. The assessment of the best instrument (mix) to apply will be made on a case-by-case basis.

Leemreize (FNV) begins his letter with the remark that the FNV has not occupied itself profoundly with instrument choice. It has spoken out in favour of market instruments above direct regulation, most notably in FNV (1993). It has also contributed to SER (Socio-Economic Council) advices.

However, the FNV has also pointed out the practical problems of market instruments, so that one should be cautious about applying them. Furthermore, the FNV has stated that a combination of instruments often works best in practice.

FNV's reasons for preferring market instruments were that they leave more freedom of choice, and are thus most appropriate in a market economy, and they are efficient, especially dynamically efficient. Whereas the FNV has not spoken out in favour of a particular market instrument, Leemreize prefers tradable permits. However, he admits he lacks insight in the practical applicability of this instrument for CO_2 and SO_2/NO_x.

3.3.6 About each other

The respondents were also asked what they thought the preferences of other organizations were. Van der Knaap (CNV), Van Brenk (DCMR) and Ruyssenaars (VROM) have no clear picture of the preferences of other influential organizations. According to Ruyssenaars, these preferences also depend on the design of the instruments.

According to Van den Biggelaar and Van der Veer (SNM), industry organizations adopt the view of the most environmentally unfriendly firm(s) in their industry. Industry favours voluntary agreements. According to Van der Veer (SNM), the cost savings of tradable permits are interesting for industry, but only if emissions have to be reduced drastically.

For NO_x, nothing might happen. Then tradable permits are not relevant to industry.

Van den Biggelaar and Van der Veer (SNM) claim that generally speaking, government is on the side of business. This is also true for most top level VROM bureaucrats. The middle level is more environmentally-minded.

According to Van den Biggelaar and Van der Veer (SNM), the current cabinet is on the side of business, because it is pro-market. There is a tendency to obscure the tension between environment and ecology by focusing exclusively on win–win situations: measures that are good for the environment and economically viable. The government's pro-market attitude is criticized by the opposition, and also by some members of the coalition parties PvdA and D66.

As we have seen in section 3.3.4, Klerken and Zijlstra (VNONCW) claim that the environmental movement is not comfortable with tradable emission permits.

Dekkers (VROM) argues that industry prefers complicated regulation:

Sometimes they complain to us that it is all too complicated, but it is their wish that every specific situation is taken into account. Clear and simple regulation is perceived as too harsh.

3.3.7 Conclusion

The most important conclusion with respect to preferences is that the organizations that were surveyed do not wish to state a general preference for a particular instrument. They want to judge the appropriateness of instruments on a case-by-case basis, and indicate that an instrument mix will often be most appropriate.

Bearing this in mind, one can discern a general tendency toward more use of market instruments than is current in Dutch environmental policy. The representatives from the environmental organizations are most enthusiastic about market instruments, and industry is least enthusiastic. But there are differences between organizations of the same kind. Of the environmental organizations, WNF is least enthusiastic about market instruments. There are even differences within organizations, as we have seen for SNM, DCMR and VROM.

With respect to direct regulation, most respondents did not differentiate between standards and firm bubbles. The difference between regulation imposed by the government and regulation involving the target group (i.e. covenants) was felt as more acute. VNONCW and SEP are enthusiastic about covenants. WNF also acknowledges that covenants can be a useful instrument. On the other hand, OCC and SNM are very sceptical about covenants.

The differences between the 'outsiders'' and the 'insiders'' answers (section 3.3.6) on the preferences of an organization are small. Van den Biggelaar and Van der Veer's (SNM) statement that industry prefers covenants could be too simplistic, considering the apprehensions expressed by Thomassen (OCC). As was to be expected, the industry respondents did not confirm Van der Veer's (SNM) statement that, while they are interested in tradable permits, they would rather have a lenient environmental policy.

The difference between the preference for tradable permits expressed by the respondents from the environmental organizations, and the statement by Klerken and Zijlstra (VNONCW) that the environmental movement is not comfortable with tradable permits, can be traced back to different opinions within the environmental organizations.

3.4 The Revenue of Financial Instruments

Question 3.2 asked what the respondents would like the government revenue of financial instruments to be spent on. The industry respondents did not answer this question. Thomassen (OCC) did not entertain the illusion that the revenues would wind up anywhere else than in the treasury.

From the environmental organizations, Van der Veer and Van den Biggelaar (SNM) and Wieringa (MD) answered the question. Both would like to spend the revenue on a reduction in the labour tax and a (temporary) subsidy on environmentally friendly investments.

Ruyssenaars (VROM), as well, mentions the options of greening the fiscal system and subsidizing environmentally friendly investment. As we have seen in section 3.3.3, Dekkers (VROM) is in favour of a charge for NO_x, the revenue of which he wants to redirect to the firms by way of an investment deduction.

According to Van der Knaap (CNV), the revenues of financial instruments should be returned to the sector from which the revenues were generated. Leemreize (FNV) takes a different approach. He states that relatively dirty products and activities should be made more costly compared to relatively clean products and activities. Thus, the government revenue should be spent on reducing tax burdens elsewhere. However, Leemreize also states that in practice, (part of) the revenue could be redirected to the sector itself, in the form of a targeted subsidy to force a breakthrough to cleaner products or technologies.

When comparing the small number of answers, we find a consensus among six of them (excluding Van der Knaap, CNV): the revenues from financial instruments should be spent on (temporary) subsidies to environmental investments and on reducing tax burdens elsewhere, especially on labour. Strangely enough, the environmental movement is more outspoken than the trade unions about reducing labour taxes. Leemreize and Van der Knaap were asked about this lack of emphasis on reducing labour taxes.

Leemreize (FNV) replied he might not have explicitly mentioned reducing labour taxes. However, he sees this as a very obvious destination for the revenues of financial instruments, because the fiscal system should be ecologized: the tax burden should be shifted from the production factor of labour and possibly the production factor of capital to the production factor of the environment. He also indicated that the most appropriate destination of the revenues depends on the economic circumstances. When unemployment is high, a reduction in labour taxes stands most to reason. However, in other circumstances (low unemployment and a high interest rate), a reduction on capital tax is more appropriate.

Van der Knaap (CNV) applies the general principle, that the revenues taken from a sector should be returned to that sector, to environmental policy:

> Employees have not done anything special or extra in this context, and for that reason their claim to the revenues collected is less justifiable than the firms'. This approach seems fair to us as CNV.

In light of this remark, it is strange that Van der Knaap (CNV) does not prefer grandfathering to financial instruments, with the revenues going to public funds (see section 3.3.5). Grandfathering can be seen as a way to let the sector keep the revenues, and should thus be preferred by Van der Knaap. In a reaction to the above argument, Van der Knaap stated he had ranked grandfathering low because this instrument had hardly been applied in the Netherlands. However:

> When I go along with your line of reasoning that grandfathering is a practicable instrument that can be applied without too much red tape, then I also go along with your line of reasoning that this option should be ranked highly, if not highest.

3.5 Conclusion

The first thing to note about the first round of the survey is that the information in the questionnaire was of very little use to the respondents. The respondents who did pay attention to the information, did so in a critical manner. The partial character of the analysis was criticized, as well as a number of specific assumptions, especially on efficiency. Considering the dissonance between the model behind the information and the questions from the questionnaire and the experience of the respondents, gratitude is in order to those who responded in spite of this dissonance.

The most significant finding from the first round is that it is difficult, if not impossible, to summarize an interest group's preferences in an ordering. An interest group's preferences will depend on the specific design of the instruments. This is all the more true for interest groups that have not profoundly occupied themselves with instrument choice (yet). Furthermore, there may be differences of opinion within the interest group, as we observed for the environmental agency DCMR, the Department of VROM and the trade union FNV. We also found that the respondents from the environmental organizations were quite enthusiastic about market instruments, but that others in the environmental movement still have objections of principle and practice against market instruments.

On certain points, the motivations of interest groups and the criteria on which they judge instruments differ from the motivations we ascribed to them in the theoretical analysis. The most striking difference is that in our theoretical analysis we did not ascribe any independent role to the efficiency of instruments. Therefore we did not present it as a possible criterion in the survey either. But almost all respondents themselves named efficiency as an important criterion.

We also found that the trade unions, especially the FNV, are interested in ecologizing the economy and the tax system. The resulting job loss in polluting sectors is in itself no reason for the trade unions to resist this ecologization.

Whereas the trade unions are also interested in the environment, the environmental movement is also interested in employment. This is clear from the fact that the respondents from the environmental movement mention employment as an important criterion to judge instruments on, and would like to reduce labour taxes with the revenues of financial instruments.

Let us now compare our results to other surveys, reviewed in Chapter 4, sections 2.4 and 4.5. The preferences of Dutch industry (including the electricity sector) are most akin to the preferences of Danish private industry, reported by Svendsen (1998): voluntary agreements first, grandfathering of tradable permits second and emission charges third. Unlike the Danish electricity sector, which according to Svendsen (1998) prefers charges, the Dutch electricity sector prefers a covenant. The Dutch industry is less in favour of tradable permits with grandfathering than the US industry according to Svendsen (1998). The Dutch industry is critical about charges, which is in line with Kelman's (1981, 1983) finding for the US, and runs counter to Wallart and Bürgenmeier's (1996) finding for Switzerland.

Objections of principle against market instruments still exist, but do not seem to play a large role for the Dutch environmental movement. This is in contrast with the US environmental movement in 1978 according to Kelman (1981, 1983), and in line with the contemporary US environmental movement (Svendsen, 1998). The position of the Dutch environmental movement is akin to the Danish environmental movement (Svendsen, 1998). Both are in favour of economic instruments, especially charges. They still have misgivings about tradable permits.

In our survey, industry respondents argue that a low price elasticity is an impediment for introducing effective charges: it is politically infeasible to set the charge rate high enough to reach the desired emission reduction. In the US survey (Kelman, 1981, 1983), the environmentalists raised this point. But when industry makes this argument, it has a different connotation to it than when environmentalists make it. Used by the environmental movement, it is an assessment of the political situation. Used by industry, it is more of a threat, because it is industry that will resist a high charge rate.

4.   THE SECOND ROUND QUESTIONNAIRE

4.1   Introduction

The respondents' answers to the first round questionnaire gave rise to a lot of questions. In the second round, which started in March 1997, we took the opportunity to ask these questions.

Some of the questions were addressed to a single respondent. This was when this person had made a remark that was in need of clarification or amplification. We have reported on their answers in section 3.

Other questions were addressed to all respondents. This was when we thought it worthwhile to elicit the opinions of all respondents about a remark from one or more respondents in the first round. This second set of questions was presented in the form of ten statements.

In this section, we shall report the answers to this second round questionnaire. In section 4.2 we consider statements 1 and 2, on the targets of environmental policy: should they be stated in absolute or in relative terms? In section 4.3 we consider statements 3 and 4, on the impact of market instruments on international competitiveness. In section 4.4 we consider statements 5, 6 and 7, on the efficiency of market instruments compared with direct regulation. In section 4.5 we consider statements 8 and 9,[17] on the design of a tradable emission permit system. Section 4.6 gives the conclusions.

4.2   Targets of Environmental Policy

It is interesting to enquire after the respondents' preferences for targets of environmental policy (*what* should be achieved), next to their preferences for the instrument (*how* it should be achieved).

In the first round of the survey, the respondents were asked to compare instruments given that the target was a certain industry emission level. But this might be a controversial target. It is an absolute target, i.e. stated in tons of emissions. The Dutch government has also stated its national targets in absolute terms. But some interest groups, especially industry, might prefer a relative target, stated in tons of emissions per unit of output or input. This gives industry more flexibility: when they increase production, they can also increase emissions.[18]

Indications about a possible controversy on the targets of environmental policy can be found in the letter of VROM Minister De Boer (Department of VROM, 1996), which refers to industry resistance against an absolute ceiling on emissions. Dekkers (VROM) also makes this point (see section 3.3.3). Furthermore, VNONCW president Blankert and Van 't Hullenaar from EnergieNed, the energy distributors' organization, refuted absolute targets for CO_2 before the Dutch Parliamentary Research Committee on the greenhouse effect (Klimaatcommissie, 1996). The argument used against absolute targets is that they would make it very difficult for Dutch CO_2 emitting firms to expand. As a result, the Dutch firms, or their competitors, would expand abroad. Because environmental policy abroad is probably more lenient, global CO_2 emissions will increase more than if expansion in the Netherlands were allowed. Thus, having relative instead of absolute targets would increase Dutch CO_2 emissions, but reduce global CO_2 emissions. Because CO_2 emissions contribute to the global environmental problem of the greenhouse effect, relative national targets are also preferable on environmental grounds.

However, FNV president Stekelenburg and MilieuDefensie representative Buitenkamp stated their preference for absolute national CO_2 targets before the Parliamentary Committee (Klimaatcommissie, 1996). Stekelenburg expressed his fear that a relative target would attract energy-intensive industry, which would make the Netherlands economically vulnerable in the long run. Buitenkamp was afraid relative targets would result in a global increase of CO_2 emissions and advocated tradable CO_2 permits between countries. With this instrument, an increase in emissions in one country will be compensated by an equal reduction in emissions elsewhere.

Statements 1 and 2 in the second round of the survey inquired after the respondents' preferences for relative or absolute targets for CO_2 and SO_2/NO_x. We hypothesize that industry prefers relative targets, and the environmental organizations prefer absolute targets. The position of the trade unions is difficult to predict. Relative targets may be better for short run employment, but worse for long run employment, as Stekelenburg (FNV) indicated.

Furthermore, it can be expected that the positions are more favourable for absolute targets for SO_2/NO_x than for CO_2. The reason is that SO_2/NO_x contribute to acid rain, which is a regional, instead of a global, environmental problem. Thus, when firms leave the Netherlands because they cannot expand under the absolute SO_2/NO_x targets, they will probably go to a country where acid rain is less of a problem. Then the increase in SO_2/NO_x is less damaging abroad, and there is no environmental reason for preferring relative national SO_2/NO_x targets.

Let us now look at the responses, presented in Table 5.3. Statements 1 and 2 are the most controversial statements from the survey. With the exception of Van den Biggelaar and Van der Veer (SNM), the environmental respondents are

Table 5.3   Targets of environmental policy

---

1. The target of Dutch CO_2 policy should be stated in relative instead of in absolute terms.
2. The target of Dutch SO_2/NO_x policy should be stated in relative instead of in absolute terms.

	Completely agree	Agree	Do not agree, do not disagree	Disagree	Complete- ly disagree
1.	OCC VNO EZ		CNV	DCMR FNV De SNM Ruy	WNF AS MD
2.	OCC VNO		CNV	DCMR FNV De SNM EZ	WNF AS MD Ruy

Note: In Tables 5.3 to 5.7, the respondents' positions are presented by the name of their organization, except for Dekkers (De) and Ruyssenaars (Ruy), both from VROM.

extremely in favour of absolute targets. The industry respondents are extremely in favour of relative targets. The other respondents take a more moderate position. Dekkers and Ruyssenaars (VROM) and Leemreize (FNV) prefer absolute targets. Van der Knaap (CNV) takes the middle ground. Hensems (EZ) prefers relative CO_2 targets and absolute SO_2/NO_x targets.

To the statement of his preference for relative targets, Thomassen (OCC) adds that allowed emissions should also be related to product quality. He refers to the reduction of the lead and sulphur content of fuels. This reduction has been achieved at the expense of increased CO_2 emissions, because it costs energy to remove sulphur and lead. Thomassen (OCC) would like to see an increase in allowed emissions for such an improvement in the (environmental) quality of the product.

The positions of the environmental movement (for absolute targets) and of industry (for relative targets) are as we had expected. That the positions are more in favour of absolute targets for SO_2/NO_x than for CO_2 also conforms to our expectation. But the similarity between the positions on the two statements is most striking. Only two respondents' positions on the second statement differ from the first. However, we should take the extreme positions into account. When one completely agrees with absolute targets for CO_2, one cannot agree even stronger with absolute targets for SO_2/NO_x. Conversely, when one completely agrees with relative targets for SO_2/NO_x, one cannot agree even stronger with relative targets for CO_2. Taking this into account, we see that five respondents take an extreme position, five respondents take the same non-extreme position on both statements

Table 5.4 International competitiveness

Suppose all other OECD countries' environmental policy is as stringent as the Dutch.

3. If in that case only the Netherlands introduce tradable emission permits with grandfathering, this would hurt the international competitiveness of Dutch industry.
4. If in that case only the Netherlands introduce emissions charges, this would hurt the international competitiveness of Dutch industry.

	Completely agree	Agree	Do not agree, do not disagree	Disagree	Complete-ly disagree
3.	OCC		WNF VNO Ruy FNV MD	AS De CNV SNM	DCMR EZ
4.	OCC VNO EZ	AS CNV FNV	WNF Ruy MD DCMR SNM	De	

and two respondents differentiate their answer between statements 1 and 2.

4.3 International Competitiveness

In Table 5.2b we see that a number of respondents, mainly from industry, named international competitiveness as a criterion for judging instruments. This criterion is often used with respect to the stringency of environmental policy: a stricter environmental policy in the Netherlands than abroad would damage the competitive strength of Dutch industry. Statements 3 and 4 were included in the survey to gauge the opinions on whether international competitiveness is affected by instrument choice, given the strictness of domestic and international environmental policy. The hypothesis is that international competitiveness is more hurt by charges than by tradable emission permits with grandfathering, because of the extra financial burden of charges for firms. Furthermore, we can expect that industry will be most worried about industry competitiveness.

The positions of the respondents are shown in Table 5.4. We see that only Thomassen (OCC) thinks that grandfathering will hurt the competitiveness of Dutch industry. The other respondents either disagree or take the neutral position. With charges, the results are the other way around: only Dekkers (VROM) thinks they will not hurt the competitiveness of Dutch industry. The other respondents think charges will be detrimental to competitiveness, or take the neutral position. This difference between grandfathering and charges conforms to our expectations. As we had expected, the industry respondents are most worried about the effects of grandfathering and charges on international competitiveness.

Van Brenk (DCMR) and Hensems (EZ) are most adamant in their conviction that grandfathering will not hurt Dutch competitiveness. According to Van Brenk, the effect of charges depends on the destination of the charge revenues. These could for instance be used to finance emission reduction. Hensems (EZ) makes the largest jump: from 'completely disagree' on statement 3 to 'completely agree' on statement 4.

Wieringa (MD) and Schöne (WNF) take the neutral position on both statements. Schöne points out that the impact of a charge differs per sector. According to Wieringa (MD), international competitiveness is used too much as an excuse against good environmental policy:

'The models' tell us, empirical practice shows, that environmental costs are only a small part of total costs.

4.4   Efficiency of Market Instruments Versus Direct Regulation

Statements 5, 6 and 7 inquire after the differences in efficiency between market instruments and direct regulation. In our presentation of the effects of instruments in the first round questionnaire, we stated that market instruments stimulate innovation, and direct regulation does not. Schöne (WNF) and Van den Biggelaar and Van der Veer (SNM) criticized this statement. They claim that innovation can also be stimulated with direct regulation, when this is combined with progressive standard setting.[19]

In our presentation of instruments in the first round questionnaire, we had made the assumption that with direct regulation, the emissions are efficiently reduced. This means that we had assumed that in one way or the other, perhaps by way of covenants, all possibilities for reducing total abatement cost by letting one firm emit more and another firm less, had been exhausted.[20] In the first round, Van den Biggelaar and Van der Veer (SNM), Van der Valk (AS) and Ruyssenaars (VROM) contested the plausibility of this assumption.

Because the efficiency assumptions met with criticism from some respondents, it was decided to explicitly present the assumptions to all respondents. As we can see from Table 5.2b, efficiency is an important criterion for the respondents. Therefore it is important to know how they assess the efficiency of market instruments relative to direct regulation. When someone is convinced of the efficiency advantages of market instruments, he will be more favourable toward market instruments. Thus, we hypothesize that there is a correlation between a respondents' positive (negative) judgment of the relative efficiency of market instruments, as reported in the statements 5, 6 and 7, and his strong (weak) preference for market instruments, as reported in the first round of the survey.

Next to the assumptions from the survey (statements 5 and 6), the respondents were presented with a statement (statement 7) from Jan de Vries of the environmental organization SNM (Tabak, 1997). The idea behind statement 7 is that efficient instruments make it less costly, and thus easier, to attain a given environmental target. Thus, if market instruments are efficient, they should make it easier to attain an ambitious environmental target. *A priori,* statement 7 can be seen as redundant. When a respondent agrees with the dynamic and static efficiency of market instruments, he should agree that ambitious environmental targets can more easily be achieved with market instruments than with direct regulation. In other words, when a respondent disagrees with statement 5 and agrees with statement 6, he should agree with statement 7.

The respondents' positions are shown in Table 5.5. Van der Valk (AS) supposes market instruments are necessary for an efficient distribution of the emission room. But he points out that market instruments cannot function in a vacuum. Other kinds of instrument should still be used. A combination of instruments is needed, and it depends on the environmental problem which instrument mix is best:

> For e.g. nuclear energy, direct regulation (in this case: a ban) is best; a market instrument is unnecessary. I suspect the 'rebound effect' will occur earlier or harder with market instruments, so that in that respect market instruments may be less effective. The very reason that they are cost-effective makes one expect the 'volume effect' will compromise their environmental effectiveness.

The 'rebound' and 'volume' effects Van der Valk refers to, are also known under the names of substitution and income effects. We shall consider two examples of these effects. Suppose that a charge is levied on energy. Then demand for energy will drop. If the supply curve of energy is rising, the producer price of energy will drop. Thus, first the consumer price of energy rises, because of the charge. Then it declines, because the producer price declines. This latter effect is the 'rebound' effect, which works in the 'wrong' direction: the energy price declines, and energy consumption rises.[21] Another example is the following. When market instruments are efficient, society can save resources in attaining the environmental goals. When these resources are then used in an environmentally unfriendly manner, the environmental gain from market instruments declines. Note that rebound and volume effects will primarily occur with charges, because with tradable permits, the environmental goal will always be achieved.

Let us now look at the positions per statement. We see the opinions on statement 5 differ widely. The 'disagree' position is the one most frequently taken. Thus there is a slight tendency to confirm the dynamic efficiency advantage of market instruments over direct regulation, in other words to confirm the assumption from the first round questionnaire.

Table 5.5   Efficiency of market instruments versus direct regulation

5.   Innovation in environmental technology can be stimulated just as well
     with direct regulation, including progressive standard setting, as with
     market instruments.
6.   Only with market instruments can the available emission room be distri-
     buted efficiently across firms.
7.   Ambitious environmental goals can be more easily attained with market
     instruments than with direct regulation.

	Complete-ly agree	Agree	Do not agree, do not disagree	Disagree	Complete-ly disagree
5.	WNF	Ruy CNV SNM	AS EZ	OCC VNO DCMR De MD	FNV
6.		DCMR AS FNV	VNO De Ruy SNM	OCC WNF EZ CNV MD	
7.		DCMR AS De FNV MD	OCC VNO CNV SNM	WNF EZ Ruy	

On statements 6 and 7, only the three middle positions are taken, and all three
positions are taken by at least three respondents. The 'disagree' position is the one
most frequently taken on statement 6. Thus there is a slight tendency to doubt the
static efficiency advantage of market instruments over direct regulation, in other
words to confirm the assumption from the first round questionnaire. Van den
Biggelaar and Van der Veer (SNM) take the neutral position, although they
pointed out the static efficiency of market instruments in the first round.

The 'agree' position is the one most frequently taken on statement 7. Thus there
is a slight tendency to prefer market instruments in the attainment of ambitious
targets.

Now we shall examine the correspondence between the respondents' positions
on statements 5, 6 and 7. We hypothesized that when a respondent disagrees
(agrees) with statement 5, and agrees (disagrees) with statement 6, he should agree
(disagree) with statement 7. This hypothesis is borne out for all respondents but
Van der Knaap (CNV). Van der Knaap agrees with statement 5 and disagrees with
statement 6. We would therefore expect him to disagree with statement 7. But
instead he takes the neutral position on statement 7.

The correlation in the respondents' positions allows us to classify them with
respect to their opinions on efficiency. The result is shown in Table 5.6, where we

Table 5.6   Respondents' positions on efficiency, derived from their answers to statements 5, 6 and 7

	Only market instruments are efficient	Mixed	Direct regulation is efficient as well	Differ-ent
Strongly in favour of market instruments	FNV AS	MD	SNM	
Average	VNO DCMR		Ruy EZ	CNV
Weakly in favour of market instruments	De	OCC	WNF	

have cross-tabulated the respondents' judgment of efficiency against the degree of their preference for market instruments. We see that the respondents are fairly evenly spread between 'only market instruments are efficient' and 'direct regulation is efficient as well'. There is no relation between the kind of interest group and their position on efficiency. Although the classification of respondents with respect to their attitude toward market instruments in general is somewhat arbitrary, the overall picture is clear: there is no relation between the agents' efficiency judgment and their general attitude toward market instruments.

4.5   Design of a Tradable Emission Permit System

Statements 8 and 9 of the second round questionnaire pertain to the design of a tradable emission permit system. Statement 8 refers to a problem one encounters with grandfathering: how to distribute the tradable permits initially. The most obvious way to distribute the permits is on the basis of present emissions. However, this may be seen as unfair. Firms that have already reduced their emissions drastically are punished, because they receive a small amount of permits. Firms that have not done much about reducing emissions are rewarded, because they receive a large amount of permits. As we have seen in section 3.3, Thomassen (OCC) and Dekkers (VROM) mentioned this problem in the first round. Van der Valk's (AS) criterion 'Do not reward laggards' also applies to it. Thus, it seems the problem of the initial distribution of tradable permits is widely acknowledged.

The respondents' positions on statement 8, presented in Table 5.7, confirm this. With the exception of Ruyssenaars (VROM) and Van den Biggelaar and Van der Veer (SNM), who take the neutral position, all respondents recognize it will be

Table 5.7 Design of a tradable emission permit (TEP) system

8.	If it is decided to introduce a TEP system, then it will be difficult to find a basis for initially distributing the rights that is acceptable to all.			
9.	If a TEP system is introduced, the permits should be tradable between target groups as well.			

	Completely agree	Agree	Do not agree, do not disagree	(Completely) disagree
8.	OCC VNO De EZ	WNF CNV MD DCMR AS FNV	Ruy SNM	
9.	EZ	WNF AS VNO De Ruy CNV FNV MD	OCC DCMR SNM	

difficult to find an acceptable basis for distributing the permits. The industry respondents strongly agree with the statement, and find Hensems (EZ) and Dekkers (VROM) on their side.

Thus, we may conclude that agreeing on the initial distribution of tradable permits will be difficult. This will be a major obstacle when it is decided to introduce tradable permits. However, we should realize it is difficult to disagree with statement 8, due to its wording. If the statement had read 'it will be (practically) impossible' instead of 'it will be difficult', or 'acceptable for most parties involved' instead of 'acceptable for everyone', respondents might have disagreed.

Statement 9 refers to tradability of permits between target groups. As we shall see in Chapter 6, section 3.5.4, the TME report gives figures for a SO_2/NO_x permit market with and without tradability between the target groups of electricity producers, chemistry, refineries and base metal. Tradability between target groups enhances the cost advantages of tradable permits. The political issue is not only: 'Tradable permits or not?', but also 'Tradability between target groups or not?' As we have seen in section 3.3.3, VROM Minister De Boer was in favour of tradability between target groups in March 1996. We have also seen that the VROM civil servants Dekkers and Ruyssenaars were against tradability between target groups at the time of the survey.

A priori, the position of industry is unclear. On the one hand, tradability between target groups increases the cost advantages. On the other hand, target groups may prefer to set up their own tradable permit system, so that they can design it according to their own wishes, and have the option of discontinuing it if they wish. Other respondents can be expected to favour tradability between target groups, the reasoning being: 'If we are going to have tradable permits, we are going to do it properly, with maximum efficiency advantages.'

The respondents' positions are presented in Table 5.7. As we had expected, tradability of permits between target groups meets with wide, although not all too enthusiastic, approval. Hensems (EZ) is the only enthusiastic proponent of tradability between target groups. Thomassen (OCC), Van Brenk (DCMR), and Van den Biggelaar and Van der Veer (SNM) remain neutral. Thus, it seems that Thomassen (OCC) recognizes the disadvantages of full-blown tradability for a target group, as we have identified them above. Klerken and Zijlstra (VNONCW), the other industry respondents, are in favour of tradability between target groups, perhaps because they have the interests of the whole of Dutch industry at heart.

It may seem strange that Dekkers and Ruyssenaars (VROM) favour tradability between target groups, whereas we saw in section 3.3.3 that they were against it. The explanation could be that statement 9 presumes the introduction of a Tradable Emission Permit (TEP) system, while Dekkers and Ruyssenaars would rather not have a full-fledged TEP system. A different wording of statement 9 (which we shall call statement 9') with which Dekkers and Ruyssenaars would *disagree*, is: 'The current discussion about a TEP system should result in the introduction of a TEP system with tradability between target groups.' Dekkers and Ruyssenaars favour a very limited tradability, without tradability between target groups. It is dubious whether this deserves the label 'tradable emission permits'. On the other hand, Dekkers and Ruyssenaars agree with statement 9: '*If* a TEP system is introduced, *then* the permits should be tradable between the target groups.' With this discussion we have meant to show that someone who disagrees with statement 9', can agree with statement 9.[22]

4.6 Conclusion

From the second round questionnaire we can conclude the following. There is a controversy among Dutch interest groups about how national environmental targets should be stated. Industry prefers relative targets, where the allowed emissions are related to e.g. output. The other interest groups prefer absolute targets, stating the level of allowed emissions. The environmental organizations are the most outspoken advocates of absolute targets. There is little difference in the respondents' positions on targets for CO_2 and SO_2/NO_x.

In the first round, we saw that the industry respondents were not very enthusiastic about market instruments. In the second round, we see they are adamant advocates of relative environmental targets. Both market instruments and relative targets can be seen as a means to achieve flexibility. They give a firm the opportunity to increase its emissions when it increases its production. With market instruments, a firm can increase its emissions by paying more on charges, or by buying extra rights. With relative targets, a firm can increase its emissions, because the allowed emissions are related to output or input. Industry is in favour of flexibility, but we saw that the industry respondents prefer the flexibility of relative targets to the flexibility of market instruments. A possible explanation for the industry respondents' preference is that they want what is best for the industry as a whole. With market instruments and absolute targets, a firm can increase its emissions, but at the expense of decreased emissions elsewhere. With relative standards, a firm can increase its emissions, without the need for other firms to decrease their emissions.

According to most respondents, grandfathering does not hurt international competitiveness, but charges do. The industry respondents are the most worried about the effect of instruments on international competitiveness.

Opinions are divided over the efficiency of market instruments compared to direct regulation. There is a slight tendency to doubt the static efficiency of market instruments and to confirm their dynamic efficiency. Furthermore, there is a slight tendency to acknowledge the statement that ambitious environmental targets can more easily be attained by market instruments. When we consolidate the respondents' positions on the three statements about efficiency, we see that they are quite evenly distributed between 'only market instruments are efficient' and 'direct regulation is efficient as well'. There is no relation between the respondents' efficiency judgment and either the kind of organization or their general attitude toward market instruments.

Almost all respondents recognize that with grandfathering, the initial distribution of tradable permits will be problematic. The respondents are in favour of tradability of permits across target groups.

5.   CONCLUSION

In this conclusion, we shall reflect upon the relevance of the survey. The conclusions with respect to the results can be found in sections 3.5 and 4.6.

We may conclude the survey gives a good impression of the issues related to instrument choice, that are relevant to interest groups. From the trade unions the response rate was excellent, from the environmental organizations and civil service it was good, and from industry it was somewhat disappointing.

The responses were different from what we had expected, or hoped for. For instance, the respondents were very reluctant to give a preference ordering of instruments, or even state their preferences for instruments in general. This difference between expected and actual responses emanates from the difference in the way interest groups and the theoretical researcher look at instrument choice. The overly theoretical approach of the first round questionnaire may have contributed to the potential respondents' decision not to respond. Furthermore, we might have been able to get more information from the respondents if the questions had been more in tune with their perceptions. However, we have still been able to extract useful information. This is due to the following factors:

- the respondents' willingness to answer questions emanating from ideas that were not theirs;
- the interviews with the respondents;
- the second round, used for clarification, and for questions that were more in line with the respondents' perceptions.

Next to finding out what was relevant to interest groups, we have amply documented that they do not have much use for the theoretical approach of Chapter 3. If we had tried, from the beginning of the survey, to connect more to the practical world of the interest groups, there would have been a large difference between the theoretical and the empirical treatment of interest group preferences. We would not have been able to justify this difference. Now we know this difference is justified. But we had to conduct a survey to find that out.

Simultaneously with the survey, there was a discussion about and research into a tradable permit system (see Chapter 6, section 3.5). This may have affected the respondents who were involved in this discussion, in a positive and in a negative way.

On the positive side, it made the respondents realize that tradable emission permits were not just a hypothetical possibility, but an alternative to be taken seriously. The discussion has also channelled the respondents' thoughts about the design and the effects of a tradable permit system. Moreover, more or less latent differences of opinion about a certain instrument surface when the introduction of this instrument is seriously considered. This is what happened in the environmental movement, especially in SNM.

On the negative side, the respondents may not have felt free to philosophize about the advantages and disadvantages of tradable permits, because they wanted to keep their powder dry, or their hands free. The respondents may have been unwilling to disclose their own points of view, or their interpretation of their organization's point of view, before a formal discussion within the organization about the position and the actions to take. The respondents may have been unwilling to give arguments that their organization might want to use in a later stage of the discussion, or, worse still, run the risk that their organization may use an argument that runs counter to what they have said in the survey.

The extent of this negative effect is difficult to assess. It may have played a role for Van der Kooij (SEP). It may also have contributed to VNCI's decision to withdraw their contribution to the survey.[23] On the other hand, it did not seem to bother Dekkers (VROM) and it did not prevent us from obtaining a complete picture of the opinions within SNM.

NOTES

1. For a more extensive report, including the full text of the first and the second round questionnaires, see Dijkstra (1997a) in Dutch or Dijkstra (1997b) in English.
2. The name calls to mind the Dutch expression for clutching at straws.
3. See Pleune (1997) for the strategies of Dutch environmental organizations.
4. Although we shall frequently discuss the answers from the civil servants together under the heading of 'civil service', it should be borne in mind that the category of respondents from the civil service is quite heterogeneous.
5. In the first round, Hensems (EZ) only referred to an EZ discussion paper (Bovenberg et al., 1991). I will not treat this paper here, because it discusses instruments more than taking a stand.
6. The increasingly closer cooperation between the christian industry organization NCW and the general industry organization VNO resulted in the Association VNO–NCW in 1996 and a complete merger by 1 January 1997.
7. Apparently, he had initially forgotten to mention support as a criterion.
8. It should be noted that, since the survey was conducted in Dutch, quotes cannot possibly be literal. Quotes in normal script are taken from written answers. Quotes in italics are taken from authorized interview reports.
9. This is probably the goal of the other environmental organizations as well, although only Wieringa (MD) mentions it explicitly.
10. Quotes in italics are taken from authorized interview reports. Quotes in normal script are taken from written answers.
11. We shall review Versteege and Vos (1995) more elaborately in Chapter 6, section 3.5.2.
12. For an explanation of Van der Kooij's first remark in the following quote, see section 3.2.3.
13. Schöne himself did not initially mention emissions charges as an instrument for CO_2 abatement, but later replied that he was in favour of this instrument.
14. This is the reason why Ruyssenaars indicated some people within VROM would answer the questions differently (see Table 5.1).
15. See Chapter 6, section 2.3.
16. Joint Implementation means that (a firm from) a developed country is involved in a project to reduce emissions in a developing country. Crediting means that the emission reduction is regarded as an achievement of (the firm from) the developed country.
17. Statement 10 is not treated here, because it caused considerable confusion.
18. The relative target should not be confused with the instrument of a performance standard (i.e. a maximum emissions to output ratio). In our analysis until now, the aim of government was to reduce industry emissions to a certain level (i.e. an absolute target), but it could try to realize this target with the instrument of a standard.
19. With progressive standard setting, the government sets the emission norms for the future at a level that cannot be achieved with the technology that is presently known (or applied).
20. The reason for making this assumption was not mentioned in the questionnaire. The reason is that some of the effects of instruments presented in the questionnaire were derived from the partial equilibrium model in Chapter 3. In this model, it is assumed that all firms are equal, so that there are no cost differences between firms. To enhance the applicability of this model to the actual situation, it was assumed that direct regulation, as well as market instruments, would result in the elimination of cost differences.
21. See Chapter 6, section 3.4.4, for CPB's (1992a) estimate of this effect for an energy charge.
22. Ruyssenaars (VROM) himself says: 'I am not opposed to the introduction of a full-blown TEP system (i.e. with tradability between target groups); however, weighing the pros and cons I think that in practice a variant to such a system (i.e. application on a sectoral level) offers larger advantages.'
23. See also Chapter 6, section 3.5.6.

6. Market Instruments in Practice

1. INTRODUCTION

In this chapter we look at market instruments in practice: how they have been applied across the world (section 2), and how they have been discussed and applied in the Netherlands (section 3). This chapter is an empirical investigation of both central questions of our research, as we presented them in Chapter 1:

1. What are the preferences of interest groups for environmental policy instruments?
2. How do the interest groups, with their preferences, try to influence the government's decision on instrument choice, and how is the political decision made?[1]

Because this chapter combines both questions, we have placed it in between the treatment of the first question in Chapters 3 to 5 and the treatment of the second question in Chapters 7 to 11.

Let us now reflect upon what we can learn about the first question in this chapter. More specifically, let us compare the relevance of what interest group representatives say about their preferences in surveys (like the surveys we reviewed in Chapter 4 and our own survey, presented in Chapter 5) and the positions they take in actual policy debates about instrument choice.

One might make the point that the position taken in actual policy debates is more informative about an interest group's preferences than answers in a survey. In a survey, a representative from an interest group is presented with a theoretical, hypothetical choice between instruments, that has no further consequence. In an actual policy situation, however, the position that an interest group takes has more serious consequences than in a survey. Thus, a position in a policy situation will be better founded. Let us illustrate this with the hypothetical example of a trade union. In a survey, the environmental spokesman of the trade union expresses a preference for market instruments, because he thinks the tax system and the economy should be ecologized, or perhaps just to make the trade union look good. But now the government seriously considers an emissions charge. The spokesman cannot simply follow his sympathy for market instruments. He must find out how many jobs the charge will cost. He may find that this job loss is so large, that he has to take a position against this particular charge. Or perhaps the environmental spokesman is in favour of a charge, despite the jobs lost, but other sections of the trade union, more concerned with jobs, overrule him. In that sense, the positions taken in a policy debate are more representative of an interest group's preferences than the answers to a survey.

But there is also a case for the opposite argument that answers to a survey are more informative of an interest group's preferences than positions in a policy debate. This is because the position an interest group takes in a policy debate reflects two considerations: what does the interest group want, and how does it try to get it. An interest group may prefer a particular (design of an) instrument A, but support a different instrument (design) B, for which it has a weaker preference, in the policy debate. An interest group may do so, because it thinks the other interest groups will reject its most favourite instrument A, but accept their second choice B.

2.   THE APPLICATION OF MARKET INSTRUMENTS

2.1   Introduction

Although the central question of this dissertation is 'Why are market instruments not more widely applied?', we should recognize that market instruments are actually applied in environmental policy. They are applied on a modest scale, but their importance is increasing.

In this section we shall look at the applications of market instruments in practice. We shall not give a general overview of market instruments in practice, since such overviews can be found elsewhere.[2] Instead, we shall focus on the factors that contributed to the application of market instruments, like the positions taken by interest groups and government, and the policy process.

In section 2.2, we shall present some reasons that are given for the emergence of market instruments in general. Then we shall go on to specific market instruments: tradable permits in the US (section 2.3) and charges in Europe (section 2.4). We conclude with section 2.5.

2.2   The Emergence of Market Instruments

Barde (1996) gives the following list of reasons for the increased importance of market instruments:[3]

– the often limited performance of direct regulation, costly and difficult to enforce;
– the move toward deregulation or regulatory reforms in various areas of public

intervention;
- the search for economically more efficient policy instruments;
- the search for revenue either for the general government budget or for financing specific environmental programmes;
- the need for an effective integration between economic and environmental policies;
- the urgent need to implement tax reforms implying the removal of distortionary subsidies and taxes and their replacement, at least in part, by environmental taxes.

Beder (1996) takes a different outlook. She sees the emergence of market instruments as the success of economists.[4] Economists have been advocating market instruments for decades, but only recently have they been able to convince interest groups of the advantages of market instruments. The 'pro-market' fashion in politics in the 1980s and 1990s has worked in the economists' favour.

According to Beder (1996), economists have enrolled the support of industry by emphasizing the flexibility that market instruments bring. Firms can determine themselves how and by how much to reduce pollution, without interference from the government. Furthermore, economists have pointed out that market instruments are morally neutral about pollution, whereas direct regulation tends to stigmatize pollution.

According to Beder (1996), the support of politicians and bureaucrats was won by stating that market instruments would take environmental decision making out of the political sphere, and into the market sphere. This appeals to politicians and bureaucrats, because they see the political process as divisive and confrontationist, and giving rise to wasteful lobbying activities. The market, by contrast, offers the promise of taking care of environmental problems in a smooth, technocratic, and non-participatory way.

Beder (1996: 60) calls environmentalists 'perhaps the most surprising converts' to market instruments. Following Kelman's (1983) advice, economists have been able to convince the environmentalists that they should attach more weight to the efficiency advantages of market instruments, and less to their ideological disadvantages. Furthermore, environmental organizations have found it necessary to employ their own economists in order to be heard in an increasingly economics-dominated environmental policy arena. Beder (1996) suggests that the environmental organizations have actually brought in the Trojan horse, because the economists have given the environmentalists what they do not really want: market instruments.

Keohane et al. (1998) also mention a number of Barde's (1996) points, as well as the 'pro-market' fashion. They also point at the attention to new, unregulated environmental problems without constituencies for the status quo approach of direct regulation.

2.3   Tradable Permits in the US

The use of tradable emission permits is largely restricted to the US, where they are used in addition to existing (direct) regulation. Thus, one can say that in the US, tradable permits were grandfathered.

Emissions trading arose in the 1970s, not by conscious design, but as an emergency solution. Under the regulation of that time, firms could not get an emission permit for expanding or settling in nonattainment areas (areas where emissions had to be reduced). In order to enable economic development in nonattainment areas, the Environmental Protection Agency (EPA) decided to allow an increase in emissions from new and expanding firms, if these or other firms could reduce emissions elsewhere by even more. The emissions trading system evolved in a halting fashion (Liroff, 1986). Politicians[5] and some EPA bureaucrats[6] were reluctant to give up detailed control of emissions. Sceptical environmentalists challenged emission trades.[7] The EPA and the courts released contradictory statements. Industry hesitated to participate, because it was uncertain whether EPA would approve of trades and the courts would vindicate them.

In the end, Emissions Trading consisted of the following rules:

– netting, introduced in 1974, allows new emissions from plant modification to be met with an equal decrease in emissions from another source within the same plant;
– offsets, introduced in 1976, allow emissions from new sources if emissions from existing sources are reduced by even larger amounts;
– the bubble rule, introduced in 1979, allows emissions from existing plants in excess of the standards if emissions from other sources are reduced by at least 20% more than the standard requires;
– banking, introduced in 1979, allows firms to store their emission reduction credits for later use.

In the 1980s, the Emissions Trading programme gradually became more comprehensive, institutionalized, consistent and accepted. At the same time, new tradable emission permit (TEP) systems were designed with clear trading rules. The first large-scale, consciously designed TEP system was the Sulphur Allowance Trading (SAT) programme of 1990 for the SO_2 emissions of electric utilities.[8] Basically, the reason why this programme got to be accepted, is that it implied a 'deal' between the environmental movement and industry (Rico, 1995). The environmentalists got a drastic and 'hard' emission reduction and industry got flexibility. Kete (1992) and Stavins (1997) provide more elaborate accounts.

The SAT programme was proposed by the Bush administration. President Bush wanted to show the electorate he was 'the environmental President' by doing something about acid rain. Congress had intensively discussed the acid rain problem in the 1980s, but this had not resulted in any legislation (Kete, 1992). The use of market instruments conformed with the 'moderate Republican' ideology of the Bush administration (Stavins, 1997).

Kete (1992) names the following reasons why the environmental movement accepted, or even supported, the programme. First, the programme implied a drastic and 'hard' reduction of SO_2 emissions by 55%. Secondly, the SAT programme was an addition to existing regulation, rather than replacing it. Thirdly, it was explicitly stated that the emission allowances were no property rights. Thus, the government was not giving away the 'right to pollute'.

Stavins (1997) and Keohane et al. (1998) also point at the 'niche-seeking' strategy of the Environmental Defense Fund, which strongly advocated market instruments.[9] Furthermore, Stavins (1997) argues that there were no vested interest in the direct regulation approach to acid rain, because there was hardly any acidification policy before the SAT programme.

Making the programme mandatory for utilities, but only optional for industry, made it more acceptable for Congress in two ways. There were only a few Congress members with constituencies where utilities had to make large SO_2 reductions. On the other hand, virtually all constituencies contained firms that would be adversely affected. Furthermore, there were concerns about the economic viability and international competitiveness of industry. Utilities, on the other hand, are regulated monopolies that can pass most of the extra cost on to the customers.

The most hotly debated aspects of SAT in Congress were the initial distribution of allowances and the compensation of displaced coal miners. In Chapter 2, section 6, we saw that in the 1970s regulation that forced the utilities to scrub, protected the Midwest coal mines. With the SAT programme, utilities could choose between scrubbing and switching to low-sulphur coal. However, a number of measures were taken to placate Mid Western Congress members. Utilities that decided to scrub instead of switch fuel, received extra allowances. A total of $250 million was made available to help displaced high-sulphur coal miners.

2.4　Charges in Europe

For a long time, the Dutch water pollution charge was the only environmental charge with an incentive effect. We shall discuss this charge in section 3.2.

In the 1990s, there was a marked increase in the use of regulatory charges in Europe, especially in the Scandinavian countries. Despite a lot of discussion about a regulatory energy charge on an EU level, such a charge is not in place yet (Skjærseth, 1994). Common features of the existing charges are that they are an addition to the regulatory framework and that energy intensive industry is (partially) exempted.

The Dutch regulatory energy charge will be discussed in section 3.4. Here we will look somewhat closer at the Swedish case (Lövgren, 1994; EEA, 1996; Cansier and Krumm, 1997; OECD, 1997). The decision to levy environmental taxes was part of the reform of the highly distortionary tax system. In 1991 Sweden unilaterally introduced a sizable carbon/energy tax. However, employment and competitiveness concerns prompted a study by an official commission into the effect of charges. The commission concluded that industry should not pay any taxes that were motivated by fiscal rather than local or regional environmental considerations. Thus, the energy tax was lowered considerably in 1992.

The Swedish NO_x and sulphur charges are still in place. The NO_x charge is levied on a limited group of large emitters. To avoid distortion between large emitters subject to the charge and their smaller competitors, the whole charge revenue is given back to the large emitters, in proportion to their energy output. The revenue of the sulphur charge, on the other hand, is added to the general government funds.

EEA (1996) provides a list, based especially on the Scandinavian experience, of how most barriers (such as the potential negative impacts on competitiveness, employment and lower income groups) to the implementation of charges can be overcome:

- careful design;
- the use of environmental taxes and respective revenues as part of policy packages and green tax reforms;
- gradual implementation;
- extensive consultation and information.

2.5   Conclusion

Market instruments are gradually becoming more important in environmental policy across the world, but at the moment direct regulation is still by far more important. Furthermore, market instruments, when applied, are always additional to direct regulation.

The application of tradable emission permits is largely restricted to the US. Since the first trading rules emerged in the 1970s, the TEP systems have gradually become more comprehensive and consistent, i.e. they developed toward the textbook TEP system. We have seen that the introduction of a TEP system requires a careful balancing act between regional interests, industry and the environmental movement.

The interest of European governments in regulatory charges surged around 1990, especially prompted by the CO_2 problem. A number of energy and other environmental charges have been in place since then in Northwest Europe. If the introduction of an EU-wide energy charge fails, the pressure on national energy charges can be expected to increase. Industry will lobby for lower rates, more exemptions and more targeted redirection of charge revenues. But when industry has its way, the support for the energy charge will erode, because the support is based on the effectiveness of the charge and the use of its revenues to reduce labour taxes.

3.   MARKET INSTRUMENTS IN DUTCH ENVIRONMENTAL POLICY

3.1   Introduction

In this section we discuss market instruments in Dutch environmental policy. We will see how they work and how they came to be accepted. We shall also look at proposals for market instruments that were not accepted. Our sources of information are publications by interest groups, government documents,[10] interviews with interest group representatives, research reports, newspaper and magazine articles and scholarly publications.

Before presenting the contents of this section in more detail, let us first look at Dutch politics. Parliament consists of a First Chamber and a Second Chamber. Bills are first treated by the Second Chamber and then by the First Chamber. The Second Chamber has more rights than the First Chamber. Whereas the Second Chamber votes more on political grounds, the First Chamber votes more on formal grounds. The majority of the bills that have passed the Second Chamber are passed by the First Chamber without too much discussion. But there are exceptions, as we shall see in section 3.4.8.

Table 6.1 presents the major Dutch political parties with the number of seats in the Second Chamber. The electoral system being based on proportional representation, no single party holds a majority in the Second Chamber. Thus, a majority government consists of a coalition of parties. Table 6.2 presents the governments from 1982 onward. Since 1982, environmental policy has been the responsibility of the Minister of VROM (housing, physical planning and the environment). The names and party affiliations of the VROM Ministers from 1982 onward are also given in Table 6.2.

The rest of this section is organized as follows. In section 3.2 we treat the water pollution charge, introduced in 1970. Although this charge was meant to raise revenue for collective water purification, it did have a regulatory effect. In section 3.3 we discuss the idea of an equalizing charge or (anti-)acidification fund. This idea was not put into practice. The regulatory energy charge is discussed in section 3.4. This charge was heavily discussed around 1992, but only became law in a watered-down version by 1 January 1996. In section 3.5 we review the current discussion about tradable permits for industrial SO_2 and NO_x emissions, which

Table 6.1   Dutch political parties

Name	Description	Seats 1989[a]	Seats 1994[a]
PvdA	Social Democrats	49	37
CDA	Christian Democrats	54	34
VVD	conservative liberals	22	31
D66	progressive liberals	12	24
SGP, GPV, RPF	orthodox protestant	6	7
GL	Green Left	6	5

Note: a. Seats in the Second Chamber (150 seats) after the elections of September 1989 and May 1994, respectively.

Table 6.2   Dutch cabinets and VROM ministers

Years	Coalition parties	VROM Minister (party)
1982–1986	CDA, VVD	Winsemius (VVD)
1986–1989	CDA, VVD	Nijpels (VVD)
1989–1994	CDA, PvdA	Alders (PvdA)
1994–1998	PvdA, VVD, D66	De Boer (PvdA)

started in 1995.

There is some overlap between this section and the presentation of our survey in Chapter 5, with respect to the regulatory energy charge and especially with respect to the current discussion about tradable permits. We have tried to present the interest groups' *preferences* in Chapter 5 and their *actions* in sections 3.4 and 3.5 of this chapter. But to avoid a fragmentary treatment in either chapter, we shall have to repeat ourselves occasionally.

This section is not a complete overview of all market instruments in Dutch environmental policy. In the 1980s, there were very effective tax breaks for unleaded petrol and cars with a catalytic converter (Klok, 1991). From 1994 until now, there has been a system of tradable manure production rights (Dijkstra, 1998).

3.2   The Water Pollution Charge

From its introduction in 1970 until the early 90s, the Dutch water pollution charge was practically the only environmental charge in the world with a regulatory effect. However, officially the charge was not meant to reduce water pollution by firms, but to finance collective water purification treatment.[11] Regulation in the form of standards was supposed to be the main instrument to reduce industrial pollution. But the charge rate on the residual effluent was so high that firms found it cheaper to take more purification measures than they were obliged to, rather than pay the charge. Since the government did not anticipate this, there was an overcapacity of purification plants in the 1980s (Schuurman, 1988).

The charge is only one instrument in the policy to reduce water pollution, but it is an important instrument. This is clear from Bressers' (1983) survey among water quality managers, Bressers' and Schuurman's regression of the pollution reduction on several explanatory variables and Schuurman's survey among representatives of discharging firms.

We shall now review the positions of the environmental movement and industry on the charges. In the late 1960s, when it was decided to implement a water pollution charge, the Dutch environmental movement was not organized yet (Tellegen, 1981). Thus, it could not speak out in favour of or against the charge. In the 1970s, when the environmental movement became organized, it was sceptical about the charge. One environmental action group called upon households to refuse the payment of the charge, because the polluting industries instead of the households should pay for purification (Tellegen, 1981).

In 1975, the environmental organization MilieuDefensie discussed the water pollution charge at its general meeting (VMD, 1976). MilieuDefensie was also very critical of the charge, because the organization of collecting charges and purifying waste was nontransparent, undemocratic and too decentralized. MilieuDefensie advised households to pay the charge under protest, or after the water quality manager had answered a number of questions. For biologically non-degradable waste, MD advocated an inhibiting charge, i.e. a charge with a rate that should prevent pollution.

In a later publication (VMD, 1979), MilieuDefensie is more critical of charges for firms. MD approves of charges for households (although they would rather call the charges contributions), because households have no opportunity to purify their waste themselves. But MD is against charges for industry, because charges that finance purification abate the causes of discharges, without directly affecting the discharges themselves. MD did not think much of the regulatory effect of charges (VMD, 1979: 104–105):

> The rare occasion that the charges prompted a firm to purify rather than discharge, is no more than an exception confirming the rule.

MD advocated progressively stricter discharge standards, ultimately (after ten years) resulting in discharges that would not upset the natural balance. Then there would be no need for collective treatment of discharges, and thus no need for charges. Another reason why MD opposed charges was that they were against the idea of conferring a 'right to pollute'.[12]

Now we turn to industry. For some industries, the charge constituted a major financial burden. Some firms, especially in the starch industry, would have had to close down if they had had to pay the charge. However, such firms were exempted for a number of years. At the end of the period of exemption, they had to pay the charge for the whole period, based on the pollution level they had reached at the end. Furthermore, the government facilitated the firms' adjustment with subsidies for abatement and information dissemination (Andersen, 1996).

In our theoretical analysis we have seen that industry is against charges. So how did this charge come to be accepted in the first place, in spite of the resistance we may expect from industry? Andersen (1996) presents two reasons for this.

The first reason is that it was the Department of Transport and Public Works that decided to apply the charge (Andersen, 1996: 148–9):

> The Department of Transport and Public Works has traditionally been an influential Department, able to control the resources necessary for its responsibilities. It has a profile commanding somewhat more respect than the joint Department of Housing, Planning and Environment, especially in the eyes of industrialists and local authorities. The water administration has a tradition of financial autonomy, which explains not only why effluent charges were introduced, but also why the economic Departments do not interfere in this sector.

The second reason Andersen gives for the introduction of water pollution charges is that the charge rate is determined by the regional water boards. In these water boards, farmers typically hold a majority, and industry is in a minority position. Farmers are interested in clean water, and they are not major polluters themselves. Thus, they want the dischargers to bear the cleanup cost in proportion to their pollution. That this means large costs for industry is of no concern to the farmers. And because farmers control a majority in the water board, they can have their favourite policy implemented.

In the Netherlands, water pollution control was delegated to the water boards rather than to the municipalities, because the municipalities were deemed too small and too weak for this task (Andersen, 1996; Bressers, 1983). In Denmark, France and Germany, the other countries Andersen (1996) studied municipalities and other local authorities have a large role in water pollution control.[13] It seems more than a coincidence that these countries either have no charge (Denmark) or a low charge (France and Germany). Local authorities, for which water pollution control is only one of many tasks, are also interested in other issues, like local employment. Therefore, they will be wary of scaring industry away with high water purification costs.[14]

However, when we adopt this argument for the high charge rates in the Netherlands, we have difficulty in explaining the initial resistance of water boards to charges, also mentioned in Andersen (1996). The water boards initially asked for a subsidy scheme, which would allow general tax revenues to be used for water pollution control. However, the government rejected this request (De Goede et al., 1982: 6–7).

We can conclude that the regulatory effect of the water pollution charge was achieved by accident, because the charge was meant to raise revenue for water purification. It was a fortunate accident to the extent that the regulatory effect of the charge has contributed to the reduction in industrial discharges. However, if the government had been faster in recognizing this regulatory effect, the package of instruments used in water pollution management could have been made more efficient.

3.3 The Equalizing Charge, or: The Anti-Acidification Fund

3.3.1 Introduction
The idea behind an equalizing charge is that efficiency requires some polluters to make substantially higher emission reduction costs than others. In order to spread the costs, the polluters with low emission reduction costs pay an equalizing charge, with the revenues of which the government subsidizes abatement by the polluters with high emission reduction costs. Thus, some polluters pay to a fund from which other polluters draw. In acidification policy, this fund became known as the (anti-)acidification fund.

The idea of an equalizing charge first appeared in Dutch environmental policy in a note from VROM Minister Winsemius to the Second Chamber in July 1984 (18 474: 1–2).[15] In 1987, the equalizing charge was considered as an instrument in acidification policy. We review the early discussion of this idea in section 3.3.2. In section 3.3.3 we treat the report of the Boorsma committee on the anti-acidification fund. The reactions to this report are given in section 3.3.4. There we shall also see that the government ultimately discarded the ideas of the Boorsma committee. We conclude with section 3.3.5.

3.3.2 The equalizing charge considered for acidification policy
In July 1987, the Environmental Committee of the Second Chamber and the Ministers of VROM and Economic Affairs (EZ) (19 598: 2) discussed a report from the platform of environmental organizations LMO (Klaassen, 1985) to reduce acidification. Eisma (D66) and Oomen-Ruijten (CDA) expressed an interest in regulatory charges, the revenues of which could be used to subsidize emission reduction. In his reaction, Minister Nijpels said that VROM was already studying the potential of charges in several forms: regulatory charges, equalizing charges and charges to finance specific programmes, like a damage fund.

On 22 December 1987, the Ministers of VROM, Transport and Public Works and Agriculture, Nature and Fisheries sent an interim evaluation of the acidification policy to the Second Chamber (18 225: 22). The Ministers argued there was a need for an intensification of acidification policy, because of the economic growth, the sharp increase in car traffic, and because emissions caused more harm than had been assumed until then. They announced a package of extra measures, in which the government would determine the emission reduction by each sector on the basis of cost-effectiveness. In the view of the Ministers, an equalizing charge could be introduced to charge the sectors that would incur relatively low emission reduction costs. The revenues of this charge, collected in an anti-acidification fund, could then be used to subsidize costly emission reduction in other sectors. Because the equalizing charge would be levied on emissions, it was in line with the 'Polluter Pays Principle' that the government would like to apply.

The report cited preliminary results from the research VROM had ordered from DHV (DHV, 1988). The Ministers concluded that there were great objections of principle and practice against an equalizing charge. The objection of principle was that the charge should not lead to an increase in the collective tax burden. But then there would be a separate circuit of revenues and expenditures, largely outside of political control. The practical objections were how to determine the bases for the charge and for the subsidy. The Ministers announced that the research would nevertheless be completed, and a definitive position would be determined.

VROM Minister Nijpels was glad that the cabinet had decided to continue the study of the anti-acidification fund (Aarden, 1987). He preferred firms to come to an agreement among themselves, without government intervention. Then there would be no 'semantic' discussion about whether the equalizing charge was a part of the collective tax burden.

The industry organizations VNO and NCW were against the anti-acidification fund. They wanted each polluter to pay for his own abatement. Furthermore, they feared the high administrative cost of a fund.

The environmental movement was in favour of an anti-acidification fund. In December 1987, the environmental organization Stichting Natuur en Milieu (SNM) released its own fund plan (Fransen, 1987). This SNM report gives two reasons in favour of an anti-acidification fund. First, it can be used to reach a good distribution of the costs of emission reduction measures across all polluters. This will reduce (the threat of) firm closurers and socially inacceptable situations (especially in cattle farming) as much as possible. Secondly, the emissions charges levied to feed the fund will give a financial incentive to reduce emissions. The SNM report (Fransen, 1987) proposed a fund consisting of three compartments:

- the reconstruction fund, financed by a base charge on emissions, to finance part of the cost of costly abatement measures;
- the damage fund, financed by a damage charge on emissions, to finance compensatory payments for damage;
- the structure fund, financed by general government funds, to finance a reduction in the volume of car traffic and of the intensive cattle farming sector.

The DHV report (DHV, 1988) was released in March 1988. In this report, the principle of the anti-acidification fund is that the fraction of national abatement costs that a polluter should pay equals his contribution to acidification in the reference year 1985. The report gives the abatement costs per sector of a package of measures with which the government's targets can be achieved. To redistribute the abatement costs across the sectors, a charge is levied on emissions, and abatement measures are subsidized. The authors of the report conclude that an equalizing acidification fund is technically feasible. They also indicate that in the setup they have chosen, the charge will not have much of a regulatory side-effect. This is because every sector (or every polluter, the distinction is not always very clear in the report) always has to pay a share in the national cost, proportional to its past pollution.

The result of the redistribution is that households, agriculture, refineries, other manufacturing and other sectors will pay more than their own abatement measures. Road traffic and utilities will pay less than their own abatement. The position of cattle farming depends on the redistribution scheme. The report concludes that the regulatory side-effect of a charge warrants further research.

In March 1988 Nijpels installed the Advisory Committee on the Financing of Acidification Abatement. This committee, headed by Prof. Boorsma, had to investigate the possibilities of an equalizing charge and an anti-acidification fund for abating acidification. The government did not wish the charge to result in an increase in the government budget or the collective burden.

In a combined meeting with the Agricultural Committee on 25 April 1988 (UCV 52), the Environment Committee discussed the interim report about acidification policy and the DHV report. Oomen-Ruijten (CDA) was worried that the government had already discarded the idea of an equalizing charge, while research was still going on. She favoured an integral approach to the financing of abatement measures, taking into account the competitive position and financial strength of firms and sectors. Taking this integral approach, she, unlike employers' organizations, did not mind that industry would have to pay for abatement in intensive cattle farming.

Verspaget (PvdA) would rather see abatement subsidized from general funds than from an anti-acidification fund. She noted the acceptability of such a fund could be enhanced by reducing the financial transfer from other sectors to intensive cattle farming, foreseen in the DHV report. This was a good idea anyway, because intensive cattle farming had to be reduced. Verspaget would like to make more use of the regulatory effect of a charge. In that respect, she preferred the SNM system to the DHV system.

Braams (VVD) argued that every polluter should reduce his pollution as much as possible. Charging the polluter to finance someone else's abatement would only have a discouraging effect.

Many speakers argued that the government's precondition of no increase in the collective tax burden should not impede the search for a good financing system for abating acidifying emissions. Minister Nijpels answered he would convey this point to the cabinet and to the Boorsma committee.

3.3.3 The Boorsma report

The report (Boorsma et al., 1988) of the Boorsma committee appeared in August 1988. With respect to the preconditions of no increase in the collective burden or the government budget, the committee pointed out that any definition of 'collective burden' is quite arbitrary. However, both conditions could be met by letting an independent environmental institution run the system. In the rest of this section, we shall call this institution the 'emission bank'.

The Boorsma committee presented a combination of direct regulation, charges, subsidies and tradable permits. It did not limit the system to any sector, implying that it could also be used for agriculture and traffic. We shall now give an outline of the system.

Firms have to pay a charge to the emission bank, in return for which they receive coupons that give the right to emit a certain amount of acidifying substances within a specified period (1, 2 or 3 years). The emission bank is obliged to sell the firm the amount of coupons that corresponds to the emission level that the firm's existing licence specifies.[16] The firm is free to buy less coupons than its permit enables it to. It can also sell coupons back to the emission bank. The emission bank determines the charge rate, cq the coupon price. With its revenues, the emission bank subsidizes emission reduction. When a firm reduces emissions with a subsidy from the emission bank, the emission bank receives the coupons the firm does not need anymore. Thus, one can also say the emission bank buys the coupons back from the firm.

When a firm expands, its licence will be adjusted. A new firm receives a licence. Thus, in both cases, a firm can buy coupons from the emission bank to the amount that corresponds with its new licence.

The committee advocates 'limited' tradability of coupons between firms. Firms should be allowed to trade coupons, as well as the future right to buy coupons from the emission bank. But the 'limits' on tradability are unclear. The report reads (Boorsma et al., 1988: 26):

> Thus, trading is only useful if the buyer of environmental coupons or of the rights to these can increase his emissions within the regulatory requirements imposed upon him. This buyer ... does not acquire any extra right to emission that he did not already have.

According to this passage, the future right to buy coupons cannot be traded, because a firm can never buy more coupons from the emission bank than its licence allows. The only way around this, which the committee presents elsewhere (p. 27), is that the licence itself stipulates that a firm is allowed to emit more (up to a certain margin) than the amount specified in the licence, provided it has bought enough coupons from another firm.

3.3.4 Reactions to the Boorsma report and final policy decision

VROM Minister Nijpels was practically the only one who reacted positively to the Boorsma report. Although the illustrative calculations in the Boorsma report showed that agriculture would benefit from their system, the agricultural sector and its Minister Braks (CDA) were negative. They feared the plans would threaten the profitability of the sector, because there was little room to pass on the costs in the form of higher prices. Furthermore they did not see how the emissions from every single farm could be measured. The industry organizations VNO and NCW were against the plan because it would increase the collective burden, it was complicated and would lead to much 'red tape' and the pumping around of funds.[17]

The environmental organization MilieuDefensie (MD) gave the Boorsma plan 'the benefit of the doubt' (De Bruin, 1988). Buitenkamp (MD) called the regulatory effect of the charge the most important aspect of the plan. She did not see reasons of principle to reject the plan on the ground that firms could buy the right to pollute. She argued that firms already had that right via the licence, but with a charge, they would have to pay for that right. Buitenkamp was against allowing firms to buy permits in order to emit more than their licence stipulated.

The first National Environmental Policy Plan (NMP, Department of VROM, 1989) appeared in May 1989, after considerable delay. The NMP did not mention the anti-acidification fund. In his Abatement Plan for Acidification (18 225: 31), published in July 1989, Minister Nijpels explained that the advice of the Boorsma committee had been taken into consideration. But the financing of acidification policy, as laid down in the NMP,[18] made the creation of an anti-acidification fund, as proposed by the Boorsma committee, superfluous.

3.3.5 Conclusion

In this conclusion, we shall discuss why the plan of the Boorsma committee was not accepted. An important reason was that the plan was not only a unique, but also an intricate and sometimes obscure mixture of tradable permits, charges, subsidies and direct regulation.[19]

Looking at the interest groups, we see that the environmental movement cautiously endorsed the plan for an anti-acidification fund. Industry was against it, because of the administrative complexity and because they would have to pay for emission reduction in agriculture.

However, the agricultural sector was also against the fund, although they would be subsidized for their emission abatement. Presumably, the agricultural sector thought they could avoid drastic emission reduction measures altogether with the aid of the Department of Agriculture, Nature and Fisheries. Seen in this light, the Boorsma committee's decision to apply the fund to agriculture as well decreased its viability. It was another reason for industry to oppose the plan, whereas the agricultural sector would not support it anyway.

The cabinet already had its apprehensions against the acidification fund before the Boorsma committee started its investigation, as is clear from the interim evaluation of acidification policy in December 1987 (18 225: 22). Combining this with the cabinet's guidelines to the Boorsma committee that the fund should not increase the budget deficit nor the collective burden, we may wonder whether the cabinet ever gave the idea of the anti-acidification fund and the equalizing charge a fair chance.

It is also interesting to look at the reason Minister Nijpels gives for the cabinet's decision to reject the proposal from the Boorsma committee (18 225: 31).[20] He refers to the cabinet's choice in the NMP (Department of VROM, 1989) to let every sector pay for most of its own emission reduction measures. The idea of the anti-acidification fund was that one sector would partly pay for another sector's emission reduction. The cabinet's proposal to let every sector pay for its own emission reduction measures was presumably inspired by the growing environmental consciousness in society and industry at the time.

However, Minister Nijpels does not refer to the market mechanism in the proposal from the Boorsma committee. Apparently, the cabinet was not interested in this aspect. The Boorsma committee may have missed an opportunity here. In the early VROM documents about the equalizing charge it was suggested that one firm could pay the charge to another firm, which is very similar to a bubble. Minister Nijpels and the CDA were also interested in the idea. However, the Boorsma committee decided to combine the equalizing charge and market instruments in its own way.

3.4   The Regulatory Energy Charge

3.4.1 Introduction
In the early 1990s the Netherlands, like a lot of other European countries, contemplated the introduction of a regulatory energy charge, preferably on an international scale. In this section we shall present the Dutch discussion.

The centrepiece of our exposition will be the research on energy charges by the Steering Group. We begin with the preparations for the research by the civil service (section 3.4.2). Then we review the events that took place while the Steering Group was conducting its research (section 3.4.3). In section 3.4.4 we briefly present the findings of the Steering Group. In section 3.4.5 we review the comments on the report. The positions taken by advisory boards and interest groups are presented in section 3.4.6. Section 3.4.7 presents the positions of the cabinet and the political parties. We shall see that the main discussion points were the minimal scale at which an international charge should be introduced, and whether or not to introduce a national small user charge. In section 3.4.8 we discuss the government's decision to introduce a small user charge by 1 January 1996. We conclude with section 3.4.9.

3.4.2 The run-up to the research

From the 1970s on, energy saving traditionally was a task for the Department of Economic Affairs (EZ). When the hypothesis that the CO_2 emissions from the burning of fossil fuels contribute to the greenhouse effect gained acceptance, VROM also became interested in energy saving. In 1990, both Departments professed an interest in regulatory charges to curb energy use.[21] VROM and EZ saw the efficiency and the fact that it reduces the need for government intervention as positive points of this instrument.[22] However, VROM and EZ had different views about the use of regulatory charges (Jaarsma, 1993). VROM was very much in favour of a national charge for small users. EZ would only agree to a charge on an international level.

In the summer of 1990, an interdepartmental working group was installed to prepare the research into a regulatory energy charge. It was decided that a Steering Group should order and coordinate the research from several research institutes. This Steering Group would consist of external experts and a VROM and an EZ representative. The secretariat would consist of two civil servants from EZ and one from VROM. An EZ civil servant would do the writing for the Steering Group.

The Steering Group, headed by Prof. Wolfson, was set up in January 1991. The purpose of their research was (Stuurgroep, 1992: 1):

> to investigate the extent to which regulatory energy charges can generate energy savings, and to provide insight into the other effects of such charges on economic life.

3.4.3 During the research

We shall now discuss the events that took place while the Steering Group conducted its research, and that directly or indirectly had an impact on its work.

In March 1991, the government asked the Steering Group to investigate whether regulatory energy charges could be a substitute for energy saving subsidies, because the government was looking for ways to cut spending and increase revenues. The government also asked the Steering Group to precipitate the results of a domestic charge on small users (the C-version). The Steering Group complied with the first request, but eventually decided not to comply with the second request, because publishing these results during the Dutch EU-presidency (the second half of 1991) would counteract the Dutch activities for an EU-wide regulatory charge. However, the request did result in increasing the political weight of the C-version, long before any results were disclosed.

In July 1991, EZ Minister Andriessen (CDA)[23] sent a letter to the Steering Group, indicating that the Government was especially interested in the option of reducing labour taxes with the revenues of the energy charge. Thus, the government professed an interest in the 'double dividend', or as it is commonly called in the Netherlands, the 'double-edged sword'.

In the summer of 1991, the government decided to drastically increase the fuel tax over the next years. The revenues of this tax were to finance the government's expenditures on environmental policy. Protests against this measure, especially from the fuel-intensive, export-oriented industry, culminated in a letter from seven Dutch captains of industry.[24] They claimed that the increase in the fuel tax was more about raising revenue than about protecting the environment. The tax would cost the firms money, that they could otherwise spend on the environment.[25] Industry was willing to decrease its emissions after a process of consultation with the government, resulting in covenants. With covenants, industry cost would be much lower, and there would be no danger of large firms leaving the Netherlands. But with a further increase in environmental taxes, firms might start leaving the Netherlands. This protest, which was a bad omen for the introduction of a regulatory energy charge, led the government to exempt the large industrial users from the increase in the fuel tax.

In October 1991, EZ proposed to calculate the effects of another version of the charge: a national charge, only on households (to be called the C'-version), because EZ found the negative effects of the C-version on industry too large. Initially, the Steering Group was initially not willing to comply with this request, because they would not be seen as motivated by policy considerations. But then Prime Minister Lubbers (CDA) discussed the matter with President Wolfson of the Steering Group and a CPB representative. They concluded that simulation of the C'-version would not cause any delay. After that, the Steering Group agreed to including the C'-version.

In December, Bovenberg and Cnossen (1991) argued that the double-edged sword idea, to use the revenues from an energy charge to boost employment by reducing labour taxes, is an illusion. Jaarsma and Mol (1994) interpret this as a sign that EZ was worried about a positive reception of an energy charge (especially in the C-version), because Bovenberg was working part-time at EZ, and the authors thank the EZ representative in the Steering Group for his contribution.

The initial planning was for the Steering Group to publish its findings by the end of 1991. When it became clear that this was not feasible, the Steering Group decided to release the results of the partial studies it had ordered into the potential for energy reduction in several sectors. In January 1992, the findings of the CPB for the A-version (a charge in all OECD countries) leaked. Both the partial studies and the CPB findings were quite disconcerting with respect to the elasticity of energy demand and the employment and other economic effects.

The interventions of EZ reached a climax with the speech of Minister Andriessen on 30 January 1992. On the eve of the Steering Group's final meeting, Andriessen called the regulatory energy charge a 'blunt potato peeler making frayed wounds' rather than a 'double-edged sword'. Andriessen ruled out the introduction of the charge in the Netherlands alone, even if it were only on small users, and said a charge could only be introduced on at least a European scale. Andriessen said he felt urged to take a stand against the regulatory energy charge, before the research was published, because 'others' (including VROM Minister Alders) had already prematurely spoken in favour of the charge. He had noticed that industry was unsettled and hesitant to make new investments as the government kept producing plans to increase taxation, at a time of recession. Jaarsma (1993) and Van Venetië (1992) add to this that Andriessen wanted to boost his profile. He had frequently been criticized for not sufficiently defending industry interests, especially with the increase of the fuel tax.

The Steering Group was very irritated by Andriessen's statements. They suspended their activities, because apparently Andriessen (one of the Ministers that had commissioned the research) had already made up his mind and was no longer interested in the results of the research. After a meeting between the Steering Group and Andriessen, in which the Steering Group emphasized they would present research results, and not policy advice, and Andriessen confirmed he was still interested in research results, the Steering Group resumed its work. The independent members of the Steering Group took the opportunity to dispose of the Departmental representatives and rewrite the part on the economic effects.

3.4.4 The Steering Group's report
The report of the Steering Group (Stuurgroep, 1992) was released on 26 February 1992. Because the danger of misinterpretation of the Steering Group's findings was obvious by then, Chairman Wolfson wrote in his letter of recommendation:

> Our task was not to advise, but to provide insight into the possible consequences of such a measure [a regulatory energy charge, BRD] for the benefit of the subsequent policy process of consultation, decision making and implementation. That task has been focal for our approach. We have aimed not at formulating feasible policy considerations, but we have tried instead to illustrate the ultimate consequences of the investigated versions. With this, we have as it were delineated the playing field, within which the game can be played. ...
> The Steering Group has decided to highlight the problems that occur with the introduction of a regulatory energy charge, as sharply as possible. The sharpness of this investigative choice is not meant to discourage the introduction of regulatory energy charges, but to clarify which complications have to be surmounted and which accommodating measures are necessary to be well-prepared in case the introduction has been decided upon.

Jaarsma and Mol (1994: 125) call this:

> a well-meant and relevant message, that was to be greatly ignored in a wildly flaring political and social debate.

The main element of the report is the simulation of the macroeconomic effects of

Table 6.3   Effects of a 50% regulatory energy charge, cumulative deviations from the reference path in 2015

	A-version[a]	B-version[b]	C-version[c]
Reduction in energy use, %	30	35	3[d]
– due to relocation and reduction in production and income	20–25	25–30	
– due to increase in energy efficiency	5–10	5–10	3
Reduction in disposable wage, %	8	7	0.1
Reduction in industrial production, %	8	4	0.2
Reduction in employment, 1000	224	71	1

Notes
a. All OECD countries.
b. In the Netherlands only.
c. For small users in the Netherlands only.
d. The reduction in the energy use of small users is 7%.

Source: Stuurgroep (1992)

energy charges, performed by the CPB (1992a). The Steering Group first ordered a number of partial studies into the effects of an energy charge in several sectors. The results of these studies would be used as inputs for the CPB simulations. The CPB calculated the effects of an energy charge until the year 2015, as deviations from the reference scenario, in which there would be no policy aimed at reducing energy use.

The Steering Group decided to study the effects of two charge rates: 50% and 100% of the user price. The following versions of the charge were studied:

– A-version: in all OECD countries;
– B-version: only in the Netherlands;
– C-version: on small users, only in the Netherlands;
– C'-version: on households, only in the Netherlands.[26]

Table 6.3 summarizes the main quantitative findings for the 50% charge. Only the results of the 50% charge are shown, because this rate is already above the rates actually proposed by the EU. We note that the impacts of the 100% charge on most variables are less than double the impacts of the 50% charge.

In the A-version, the reduction in global energy demand puts considerable pressure on the producer prices for energy.[27] As a result, the consumer price for energy in 2015 is only 6.6% (11.5%) higher with the 50% (100%) charge than in the reference scenario. According to the CPB study (1992a), the whole fertilizer industry will leave the Netherlands for a non-OECD country. Considerable parts[28] of the non-ferrous metal, pottery, and wool and cotton industries will also leave.

The B-version features more drastic effects than the A-version, for two main reasons. First, it is easier for firms to escape the charge: they have to leave the Netherlands, instead of the whole OECD area. Secondly, the energy price in the Netherlands will be higher, because there is no depressing effect on the producer price. A larger part of the energy-intensive industry will leave the Netherlands. Next to the industries mentioned above, the base chemical, brick, iron and steel, cement, paper, foundry and rubber industries will be severely affected.

3.4.5 Comments
Under this heading, we shall discuss a number of comments on the Steering Group's report. These comments come from the General Energy Council (AER) (1992), Verbruggen (1992),[29] Van den Biggelaar and Van der Veer (1992), Van den Burg et al. (1993)[30] and the scientific bureau of the political party GL (Snels, 1992). The gist of these comments is that a number of decisions and assumptions by the Steering Group have contributed to the meagre results:

- the Steering Group intentionally did not investigate, or even indicate, how the negative effects of an energy charge could be mitigated;
- in the reference scenario, with which the report compares the effects of the energy charge, there is no policy aimed at reducing energy use. Thus, it may seem that the negative effects are due to the charge only, but these effects are a result of decreasing energy use with a charge. According to Verbruggen (1992), opponents of the charge should also come up with alternative proposals to save energy;
- the reference scenario assumes that energy prices will rise considerably. Thus, there is already sizable energy saving without the charge, and the additional energy saving effect of the charge is small;
- in the reference scenario, there is full employment in 2015, at the end of the period under research. As a result, any positive employment effects from lowering the labour tax with the revenues of the energy charge are only transitory;
- the Steering Group assumes a price elasticity of energy use of 0.2–0.3. Compared with other research, this is a low value. As a result, a price rise of energy results in a comparatively small reduction in energy use. The reason that the Steering Group finds such a low price elasticity is, that it decided only to take the presently known abatement technology. The Steering Group decided to abstract from the incentive effect of a high energy price on research and development activities into new abatement technology, because this effect is hard to quantify (Stuurgroep, 1992: 21).

3.4.6 Reactions in society

In this section we review the positions that advisory boards to the government and interest groups took on regulatory energy charges.

In the spring of 1992, the Scientific Council for Government Policy (WRR), headed by the former chairman of the Steering Group Wolfson, published a report on which instruments to use for which environmental problems (WRR, 1992). On the ground of the so-called 'situational characteristics method', it concluded that regulatory charges were most appropriate for reducing energy use. The reason is that charges place low demands on enforcement, they are effective and efficient, they do not increase the overall tax burden and satisfy the polluter pays principle. The WRR advocated a small user charge in the Netherlands and a charge on all users on at least an EU scale.

The SER (Socio-Economic Council) had some difficulty with the government's request for advice on the Steering Group report. In a letter to the Minister of EZ, the SER president said the SER was used to giving advice on the government's policy intentions, but neither the report, nor the letter from the government, contained any policy intentions (SER, 1993). The Minister replied that the government was favourable toward the charge proposed by the EU, but that unlike the EU, they did not want to condition its introduction upon simultaneous introduction in the US and Japan (SER, 1993).

Because the SER also considered the EU proposals for a regulatory energy charge and because there was considerable disagreement within the council, the SER took a lot of time for its advice. Initially, the representatives from the employers' organizations only supported a charge at the OECD level. Later they consented to a charge at the EU level (Anonymous, 1993a). At the final stage however, industry rejected the draft of the SER advice (Anonymous, 1993b). Unlike their SER representatives, industry ruled out a national or Northwest European charge, in case an EU charge would not be feasible. Ultimately the SER advice, released in February 1993, consisted of two parts (SER, 1993). The SER was unanimous about the point that the Dutch government should first do its best for the introduction of a regulatory energy charge on as wide a scale as possible, but at least in the whole of the EU. Opinions were divided on the subsequent course of action, should it become clear by 1995 that an EU charge was not feasible. According to the trade union representatives and the crown members, all options were open for that eventuality. For the industry representatives, a charge on a national or Northwest European scale was out of the question in any case.

In their reaction to the increase in the fuel tax, industry had already intimated that it was against a further increase in environmental taxes. On 30 January 1992, six of the seven captains of industry that had written the angry letter against the increase in the fuel tax met with Prime Minister Lubbers (CDA), EZ Minister Andriessen (CDA), VROM Minister Alders (PvdA) and Finance Minister and vice-Prime Minister Kok (PvdA). Although the cabinet was very secretive about what had been discussed, it is significant that on the same evening Andriessen launched his attack on the regulatory energy charge (section 3.4.3).

The industry organizations VNO and NCW applauded Andriessen's statements. They even went one step further, rejecting an EU-wide charge as well (e.g. VNO and NCW, 1992).

According to Klerken and Zijlstra (1997), VNO and NCW were against the regulatory energy tax, because of the large negative side effects:

> Research by the CPB and the Wolfson Committee showed that the price elasticity of energy demand was only 0.15. Then the side-effects, especially the economic effects, are not compensated by the environmental effect. We might have thought differently about the energy tax if the price elasticity were 2 or 3. Then you have a large effect with a small charge, and you accept the side-effects.

Industry had already made a binding long-term agreement with the government to improve energy efficiency by 20% in ten years. According to Klerken and Zijlstra, this is more than the government can ever achieve with a charge, at least with a charge rate the government dares to introduce. If the regulatory charge had been introduced, industry might not have regarded the long-term agreement as binding anymore.

Thus, according to Klerken and Zijlstra (1997), industry did not oppose the charge because it was against a tightening of environmental policy. They even argued that with agreements and covenants (which they favoured), energy use could be reduced more than with charges (which they opposed).

The proponents of the regulatory energy charge participated in the 'Study Group on regulatory energy charges' established in 1990. The following organizations and persons participated in the Study Group (Van der Veer, 1997):

- the environmental organizations Stiching Natuur en Milieu, Aktie Strohalm, Wereld NatuurFonds and Stichting MilieuDefensie;
- the trade unions FNV and CNV;
- working groups of the Council of Churches;
- the Consumers' Union;
- members of the Council for Medium and Small Firms, on a personal basis;
- civil servants from the Department of VROM, on a personal basis.

In May 1992, the organizations participating in the Study Group, together with other environmental organizations and research institutes, sent a 'Plea for a Dutch energy charge' to the Second Chamber (Consumentenbond et al., 1992), pleading for an international energy charge or, if this was not feasible, for a national charge on small users. In this plea, the trade unions FNV and CNV promised to refrain from demanding wage compensation for the price increases due to a regulatory energy charge.

In an earlier stage, the environmental movement had tried to make the charge more palatable for large users as well. As we have seen, the Steering Group did not pay special attention to mitigating policies. The environmental movement, however, produced many options to soften the blow, especially for the energy-intensive industry, by way of exemptions and targeted redistribution of the charge revenue. According to Van der Veer of the environmental movement SNM (1997), some of these ideas would have been worth elaborating. However, industry was not willing to discuss mitigating policies (Klerken and Zijlstra, 1997; Van der Veer, 1997). The reason Klerken and Zijlstra (VNONCW) put forward for this is that industry was against the charge as such, and was therefore not willing to discuss the way it should be introduced.[31]

Despite the fact that the FNV was a prominent member of the coalition for a regulatory charge, the chairman of the industrial union of the FNV Van der Weg proclaimed in February 1992 that he agreed with Andriessen's apprehensions against a charge (Wirtz, 1992). Although the idea of reducing labour taxes with the revenues of the energy charge appealed to him, he said a charge could only be introduced on an EU-wide level, and doubted whether a national small user tax would be worthwhile. Van der Veer (1997) called Van der Weg's statements 'a considerable setback'. However, he saw the incident mainly as an internal FNV matter and pointed out that Van der Weg had never publicly repeated these statements.

3.4.7 Politics
In this section, we shall discuss the reactions, statements and positions of the political parties in the Second Chamber and the government regarding the Steering Group's research and regulatory energy charges in general.

The government, in a first reaction, concluded: 'the report is thorough and balanced, but does not lend itself to rash policy conclusions'. But there was disagreement within the government. As we have seen, EZ Minister Andriessen (CDA) was against introduction of the charge in the Netherlands alone. But vice-Prime Minister and Minster of Finance Kok and VROM Minister Alders (both PvdA) were in favour of a national charge for small users, to be introduced at 1 January 1993, even if there would be no international charge.

Second Chamber members already started giving their opinions in February 1992, before the Steering Group's report was published. Table 6.4 shows the positions of the major Second Chamber parties. As a matter of course, all parties were in favour of introducing the charge in as large a region as possible. Thus, Table 6.4 shows which parties were in favour of an EU charge, a charge in a number of EU countries, and in the Netherlands alone, in case a charge on a wider scale would be infeasible.

Te Veldhuis (VVD) stated in the Environmental Committee Meeting of May 1992 (UCV 39) the VVD wanted to wait for the results of the research into the

Table 6.4   Positions of Second Chamber parties about the introduction of a regulatory energy charge

	GL	D66	PvdA	CDA	VVD
On an EU level	+	+	+	+	?
In a number of EU countries	+	+	+	–	–
In the Netherlands alone[a]	+	+	?	–	–

Notes
\+ = in favour;   ? = doubts;   – = against.
a. With exemptions or special arrangements for large users.

Sources: Aarden and Van den Hende (1992), Anonymous (1992), 1991/2: UCV 39.

economic effects of an EU-wide charge, before it determined its position. Te Veldhuis also doubted whether the government could explain a small user charge to the small industrial users and the households: why would they have to pay the charge, whereas the large industrial users were exempted?

Although the PvdA Ministers Kok and Alders were in favour of a national small user charge, PvdA MP member Van der Vaart still expressed some doubts in February (Aarden and Van den Hende, 1992).

CDA MPs Lansink and Van Houwelingen pointed out in February that the mood in the country was anti-environmental taxes (Aarden and Van den Hende, 1992). They argued the cabinet had itself to blame for this, because it had raised the fuel tax.

Tommel (D66) stated in February (Aarden and Van den Hende, 1992) he was not going to 'pull a dead horse', i.e. argue for a lost case, because VVD and CDA were against a regulatory charge in any form. However, in the Committee Meeting in May 1992, he tried to 'revive the dead horse' by stating D66 would support regulatory charges, even if they would only be introduced in the Netherlands, in which case special provisions for large users were necessary.

In the Environmental Committee Meeting of May 1992 (UCV 39), Willems (GL) submitted a motion asking the government to make an effort for the introduction of an energy charge in a number of like-minded countries by January 1993, in case the introduction of an EU-wide charge would fail. VROM Minister Alders advised against the motion, on strategic rather than substantial grounds. He argued the Netherlands should first do its utmost for an EU-wide charge, without publicly discussing what to do in case it failed.

The Second Chamber voted on the Willems motion on 25 June. The fractions of D66, GL, SGP, GPV and RPF voted in favour. The other fractions voted against, so that the motion was rejected.

From the summer of 1992 onward, the political attention was focused on the EU wide charge, the introduction of which would ultimately be rejected. In December 1993, the government spoke again on the issue of a national energy charge. In the Second National Environmental Policy Plan (NMP2, Department of VROM, 1993) the government announced it would start the preparations for a national introduction of an energy charge. The Netherlands could then introduce the charge in 1995, hopefully together with all, or some, EU countries. In the absence of an international agreement, the Netherlands could introduce a small user charge by 1995. The government left the concrete decisions to the next cabinet, that would take office after the elections of May 1994.

3.4.8 The introduction of the small user charge

In the summer of 1994 a new cabinet, consisting of PvdA, VVD and D66, took office. PvdA and D66 had stated in their election programmes that they were in favour of a national energy charge, starting with the small users, and that the Netherlands should do its best for an international energy charge.[32] The VVD, in whose election programme the energy charge was not mentioned at all, wanted to reduce energy use with other instruments.

The coalition agreement of the new government of 13 August 1994 (23 715: 11) stated that the Netherlands would continue to work vigorously for a European energy charge. However, should this prove impossible, a national energy charge on small users would be introduced by January 1996, if possible together with other countries. The revenue of the charge would be used for relieving the tax burden and stimulating employment and purchasing power. The position of the greenhouse horticulture sector would be scrutinized. The reason for this (not mentioned in the coalition agreement) is that this sector consists of small, energy-intensive firms that compete internationally.

In July 1995, the Ministers of VROM and EZ and the Deputy Minister of Finance submitted a bill (24 250: 3) to introduce a regulatory energy charge in the Netherlands, because agreement in the EU was not to be expected shortly. The government proposed to tax annual natural gas consumption between 800 and 170,000m^3,[33] and electricity consumers with an annual consumption between 800 and 50,000 kWh.[34] Thus, the large users would have to pay for their natural gas consumption in the bracket between 800 and 170,000 m^3, but were exempt from the electricity charge. The greenhouse horticultural sector would have to pay the electricity charge, but was exempt from the natural gas charge. The charge rates were to rise in two annual steps, and would raise energy prices in the bracket by approximately 20% at its final level, in accordance with the original EU proposal for a regulatory energy charge.

The bills about the introduction of the charge and the recycling of all of its revenues (24 344: 2) were bound to one another in the sense that one could not come into force without the other. With the design of the recycling plan, the government tried to strike a balance between the simplicity of the system, compensating the average user in every sector and household category and stimulating employment.

The Second Chamber discussed the introduction of a regulatory energy charge on 10 and 11 October 1995. PvdA, D66 and GL supported the proposal, although they only saw it as a first step toward a broader application of the charge. Of these three parties, the PvdA was least impatient and GL was most impatient. Remkes (VVD) made it crystal clear that the VVD was against the charge, and would only vote in favour because it was part of the coalition agreement. Lansink (CDA) was against the charge, because of its limited effect on energy reduction and the negative net effect of charge and recycling for certain sectors and households.

Giskes (D66) and Crone (PvdA) submitted an amendment to charge everyone's electricity consumption below 50,000 kWh, including the large users. Remkes and De Vries (VVD) submitted an amendment stating that the Minister could reimburse all or part of the charge revenues for firms with an energy reduction covenant. EZ Minister Wijers (D66) was against the amendments taken in isolation, but he suggested to link them. Then a large user would only have to pay for his electricity consumption below 50,000 kWh if he did not have a covenant. Giskes and Crone then withdrew their amendment to submit another amendment stating that the Minister *could* charge large users for their electricity consumption below 50,000 kWh. Furthermore, Giskes and Jorritsma-Van Oosten (D66) submitted a motion to link the possibility to charge large users with the possibility to reimburse firms with a covenant.

The broad concern about the negative consequences of the charge for particular households (large families, the elderly, low income groups, the handicapped and the chronically ill) and particular sectors (agriculture, catering, non-profit sector) was translated into two motions. One motion asked the government to make proposals in case any sector or group of households would be particularly harmed. The other motion asked the government for an annual report of the environmental, economic and financial effects of the charge.

The Second Chamber voted on 12 October 1995. The bill as well as the above-mentioned amendments and motions were all accepted. PvdA, VVD and D66 voted for all of these. CDA voted for the Remkes/De Vries amendment and the motions, but against the Crone/Giskes amendment and the bill. GL voted for the Crone/Giskes amendment, the bill and the motions, but against the Remkes/De Vries amendment.

Quite out of the ordinary, the First Chamber expressed severe apprehensions about the regulatory charge. The First Chamber discussed the charge and recycling bills on 4 and 5 December 1995. We shall highlight the critical contributions from PvdA and VVD here.

De Haze Winkelman (VVD) seriously doubted whether the expectedly small effects on energy use outweighed the expectedly large negative effects. He mentioned the negative effects for the image of the Netherlands as a country for firms to invest in. Furthermore, he referred to the problems in internationally competing small and medium firms, agriculture, catering, private transportation and the non-profit sector. He would like the government to draw up an energy reduction covenant with these sectors and exempt them from the charge. Zijlstra (PvdA) was also worried about the low effectiveness of the charge and the negative effects on agriculture, catering and the non-profit sector. Furthermore, he emphasized the financial loss of low income families. VROM Minister De Boer (PvdA) and Deputy Minister of Finance Vermeend (PvdA) promised to investigate the plight of these families and, if necessary, propose compensatory measures.

On 12 December, Zijlstra (PvdA) announced the PvdA would vote in favour of the bill, because he was satisfied with this promise from the government. De Haze Winkelman (VVD) was pleased with Minister Wijers' (EZ) promises that there would be no expansion of the charge on a purely national scale in the near future and that the decision to exempt firms with a covenant would be applied generously. He announced that, despite the great problems the VVD fraction still had with the bill, they were going to vote in favour. They would do so not for substantial, but for political reasons: the cabinet was preparing some bills that the VVD had a great interest in.

The First Chamber accepted the bill to introduce the regulatory charge with the votes of PvdA, VVD, D66 and GL. The bill to recycle the revenues was accepted with the votes of PvdA, CDA, VVD, D66 and GL. Thus, the regulatory energy charge came into effect on 1 January 1996.

We conclude with the strategy of the environmental organization SNM in this debate. SNM supported the energy charge all the way, even when it became clear it would only be a shadow of the charge they would like to see. According to Van der Veer (1997):

> We took an opportunistic approach: let us first secure the introduction of the charge, and then after that we can discuss its reach and its rate. So now that the charge is in place, we do argue that its rate is too low and its reach too limited.

It is important to SNM that the government has adopted the principle of the regulatory tax, to be distinguished from the revenue-raising tax. That is why SNM found it important that the proposals for implementing the charge and for recycling its revenues were presented together. SNM has even tried to make the restitution of the energy tax revenue visible to the tax payer on the tax form. However, this was not feasible.

3.4.9 Conclusion
In this conclusion, we shall give two main reasons why the introduction of a national regulatory energy charge failed before 1994 (the first period) but

succeeded after 1994 (the second period).

The first reason is the most important one. In the first period, the issue came up in the course of the cabinet period, and the cabinet consisted of one party (CDA) that was against a national charge, and one party (PvdA) that was in favour of it. In the second period, the issue was settled in the coalition programme, as part of a package deal, between two parties (PvdA and D66) that were in favour of a national charge, and one party (VVD) that was against it.

The second reason why the introduction of the charge succeeded in the second period, is that there was a clear plan by the government, which allowed for a more structured discussion. There are three elements to this clarity. First, the government proposed charge rates, charge brackets and recycling measures resulting in less dramatic financial setbacks for disadvantaged sectors and income groups than the illustrative calculations by the Steering Group. Thus, if anyone based his resistance against the charge on the quantitative results of the Steering Group, this resistance would disappear or be softened by the government's proposals.

Furthermore, the government proposed a national charge for small users with an exemption for greenhouse horticulture, starting on 1 January 1996. This means that large users and greenhouse horticulture had little to fear, and would thus not oppose the charge. Other opponents of the charge could not postpone the discussion about a national charge by arguing that a charge should be introduced internationally. They had to come out in favour or against the national charge, starting on 1 January 1996.

Thus, the small user charge did not meet with opposition from the large users and the greenhouse horticulture sector. The elimination of the opposition from the large users was important, because this is a small group of firms where each firm has a large interest in opposing the charge. Thus, as public choice theory predicts (Chapter 2, section 4) the large users are well-organized. The principal opponents to the small user charge were the industrial sectors and the categories of households that would lose from the charge despite of the recycling. But these were large groups, where each firm or household only had a small stake in opposing the charge. Thus, these groups could not organize as much opposition as the large users could.[35] Furthermore, the Consumers' Union was a proponent of the charge and concentrated on compensation for everyone through the refunding scheme.

Of course, the disadvantage of a large group of agents with small per capita stakes also applies to the industrial sectors and households that would gain from the charge and the recycling. However, since the government itself proposed the charge, it was more vulnerable to opposition than it was dependent on support.

The effect of proposing only a small user charge on the lobbying effort by the environmental movement is unclear. On the one hand, the environmental movement could concentrate its support on the small user charge, because a large user charge was not at stake. On the other hand, the environmental movement would be more enthusiastic about a large user charge. However, when we overview the whole constellation of groups in favour of and against a charge, the probability of getting the charge accepted is higher for the small user charge than for the comprehensive charge.

Finally, the government presented the charge and the recycling of its revenues as a package deal. In the early phase, when the government did not structure the discussion about the charge and its revenues at all, industry could dictate that the charge itself would be discussed first. As a result, the charge could not be introduced. We shall establish this point formally in Chapter 10.

3.5   Tradable Emission Permits From 1995 Onward

3.5.1 Introduction
The most serious discussion about tradable emission permits for industry in the Netherlands until now is still taking place at the moment. In section 3.5.2 we shall discuss the DHV report (Versteege and Vos, 1995) about the applicability of Tradable Emission Permits (TEPs) in acidification policy. Ordered by the Department of VROM, this report was the first manifestation of the recent interest of government in TEPs. Although the report concluded rather abruptly that there was no need for a full-fledged TEP system, this was not the end of the discussion, but rather a false start. As we shall see in section 3.5.3, the regional environmental agency DCMR ordered another study and organized a workshop in June 1995 with representatives from government, industry and the environmental movement. At this workshop it was decided to order a quantitative study into the financial gains from tradability for industry. The results of this study (TME et al., 1997), published in May 1997, are given in section 3.5.4. The reactions to the study are presented in section 3.5.5. In June 1997, the chemical industry organization VNCI presented its own version of a TEP system. We treat this plan, the details of which are still being discussed, in section 3.5.6. We conclude with section 3.5.7.

3.5.2 The DHV report
Late 1993, the Air and Energy directorate of the Department of VROM ordered a study from DHV into the practicability of tradable emission permits (TEP). VROM would like to see an investigation into the following issues:

1. the target groups and substances, for which a TEP system could be used in acidification policy;
2. the preconditions under which such a system could be introduced in the Netherlands;
3. the consequences that the preparations for the introduction of a TEP system would have and the costs of introduction of this system for government and the target groups.

The DHV report (Versteege and Vos, 1995) was published in June 1995. With respect to the first question, the report states that TEPs are an appropriate instrument for the NO_x and SO_2 emissions of the target group of industry (not including refineries and utilities). The characteristics that point in the direction of TEPs are:

– the cost differences between the firms are large, because the target group is heterogeneous;
– the number of sources is high, so that a TEP market can be expected to work well and implementation costs are low relative to the number of sources;
– the target levels for the NO_x and SO_2 emissions of the target group are already expressed in emission ceilings;
– there is ample opportunity for firms to implement and develop new emission reduction technologies.

For the target groups of refineries and utilities, all but one of the above points apply. Taken on their own, both groups are too small for a well-functioning TEP market. But if tradability across target groups is allowed, TEPs can also be applied to refineries and utilities.

The DHV report suggests the following design of the TEP system. There should be no tradability between SO_2 and NO_x. The permits should initially be grand-fathered on the basis of the emission requirements in the starting year. Entrants on the market have to buy their TEPs, firms that leave can sell their TEPs. The provinces have to ensure that trades do not result in the violation of local air quality standards and that certain minimal emission restrictions (mandated by the EU) are satisfied.

With respect to the third research question, DHV estimated the time needed for preparation of a TEP system. The report concludes that the TEP system can be expected to start operating somewhere between 2000 and 2005. The time that civil servants from Departments and provinces would have to spend preparing for the TEP system, is estimated at about 225 months.

The final chapter of the study discusses the issues that remain open after the research, and then offers a conclusion. The issues that await further research are:

– by the time the TEP system can be introduced, most firms will have had to apply the strictest emission reduction technology presently known. Then there is not much need for trade. On the other hand, a TEP system can give an impulse to innovation. Then again, so can progressive standard setting;
– the benefits of a TEP system should be further analyzed, but this is only possible when the design of the system to be introduced is known;
– one great benefit of TEPs is that the government controls the total amount of emissions. On the other hand, TEPs could frustrate economic development. The

government might want to keep TEPs in reserve to accommodate expansions and new establishments of firms;
- it will be very troublesome to reach an agreement with the target groups about the initial distribution of rights and their devaluation in time. This will be more difficult in the Netherlands than it was in the US, because Dutch firms have to reduce their emissions much further;
- trade could be seriously hampered by the preconditions imposed by the EU and the necessity to satisfy local air quality standards;
- it is doubtful whether firms are willing to participate in a TEP experiment;
- a TEP system like the one studied in this report seems to be at odds with the current integral approach to environmental policy. Furthermore, the TEP system violates the ALARA principle.[36]

The report concludes that the introduction of a TEP system will cost much time, whereas its flexibility and efficiency benefits are unclear. Therefore one may wonder whether it is not possible and perhaps even more useful to achieve a more flexible and efficient way of dealing with acidification in the Netherlands within the current regulatory framework.

Tabak (1997) notes that the concluding chapter is far more negative about the potential of TEPs than the rest of the report warrants. Co-author Vos' reaction to this is (Tabak, 1997: 122):

> We wrote that summary together with VROM civil servants. Their hand is clearly recognizable. The whole story is politically laden. It is about policy security and existing agreements with firms that took great pains to achieve.

Thus it seems that the VROM directorate of Air and Energy itself was not interested in TEPs, but that it was forced by others (elsewhere in VROM, in politics and in industry) to produce an investigation. It tried to give the report a negative twist, in the hope of nipping the interest in TEPs in the bud.[37]

3.5.3 The DCMR initiative

However, at the same time the attitude of another government institution was far more positive toward TEPs. Rozenburg and Van Brenk, employees of the environmental agency for the industrial Rijnmond area (around Rotterdam) DCMR, ordered research from CE (the Center for Energy saving and clean technology) about the possibilities for applying TEPs to the industrial SO_2 and NO_x emissions. The report (Davidson and De Wit, 1995a) was to serve as a discussion paper for a workshop in June 1995. The purpose of this workshop was for government institutions, industry and the environmental movement to discuss the potential advantages of TEPs.

Like the DHV report, the CE report proposes that newly entering and expanding firms should buy TEPs, and firms that reduce their size or leave the market can sell their TEPs. Instead of introducing a national system right away, the TEP system could first be applied to the 22 largest sources in the Rijnmond area. The advantages of starting with a regional system are that the lower number of parties concerned makes it easier to reach an agreement about the design of the system, and there is no need for an active market and a price for TEPs to arise. The disadvantage is that the small number of firms impedes an efficient functioning of the TEP market.

A later version of the CE report (Davidson and De Wit, 1995b) also includes a report of the workshop on TEPs. The report summarizes the presentations made by the government, industry and the environmental movement, the discussions and the decisions about how to proceed.

The government sees the following advantages to a TEP system:

- the total amount of emissions is fixed;
- the efficiency of emission reduction is enhanced;
- there is a permanent incentive to innovate;
- the government can regulate 'at a distance';
- TEPs for the NO_x and SO_2 emissions of large industries (refineries, utilities, chemistry) can be implemented in the existing framework of target group policy;
- with grandfathering, there is no extra financial burden for firms.

The government signals the following 'points of attention':

- TEPs are at odds with the current culture of negotiation. The government should be willing to relinquish its influence on the company level;
- the existing regulation must be adapted;
- local air quality standards should still be enforced and may impede trade;
- the introduction of a TEP system should be final, because industry investment is a long term decision;
- society should accept that firms can buy TEPs rather than reduce their own emissions.

Industry pointed out that the existing target group consultations and covenants already enable industry to a large extent to reduce emissions there, where it is least costly. First, a thorough investigation is needed to establish the financial advantage of TEPs to the present Dutch system.

According to industry, it is too late to introduce TEPs in acidification policy, because this policy is already well-developed. Industry saw more possibilities for CO_2 TEPs. A TEP system for SO_2 and NO_x should be introduced on at least a national scale, preferably with parts of Belgium and Germany as well. Industry doubted whether the government would be willing to 'retreat', as it is supposed to in the transition to a TEP system. Emission ceilings should be fixed for a long time ahead. The fastest and best way to benefit from TEPs is to introduce them in the implementation of environmental policy within and between target groups:

> The instrument can function without government intervention, industry can act as a broker and the government checks and accepts the results.

It should be acceptable in public opinion that a firm buys emission rights rather than reducing its own emissions.

In the environmental movement there are supporters of and opponents to TEPs. The following points of attention can be distinguished:

– TEPs offer more certainty that the emission ceilings will be reached. The ceilings can be set at a lower level than with direct regulation, because emission reduction is less costly;
– the government and the environmental movement will have less control on a firm level. Neighbours and environmental organizations should have a say in matters like the initial distribution of rights and the emission ceiling;
– TEPs are at odds with the integral approach to environmental policy;
– local air quality standards still have to be met;
– the objection of principle against grandfathering is that the polluter should pay. A slowly rising charge on emission rights should be contemplated to skim the capital gift to firms implicit in grandfathering.

The workshop participants concluded that all parties saw the theoretical advantages of TEPs. Problems with respect to administrative and international preconditions were seen as solvable. The public opinion with respect to TEPs is unpredictable. It was doubted whether the government could make the change in attitude necessary for a TEP system. At the request of industry, it was decided to order a study into the financial advantages of a TEP system. Industry promised to supply the information needed for the study.

3.5.4 The TME study
The Interprovincial Platform IPO ordered the study into the financial advantages of a TEP system from TME (main contractor and project leader), Tebodin, Grontmij and the University of Groningen. The study was paid for by IPO and the Departments of VROM and EZ.

The TME study was published in May 1997 (TME et al., 1997). Data on emissions, emission reduction measures and their cost were supplied by firms. In the simulations of the TEP market, it was assumed the market would work perfectly.

The report gives the results for SO_2 and NO_x TEP systems for the sectors of base metal, chemistry, electricity and refineries. Three kinds of tradability are studied:

- internal trade: within companies;
- sectoral trade: within the four sectors;
- suprasectoral trade: across the four sectors.

The emissions and costs of these variants of tradability are compared to a 'regulation' scenario, in which the emission from every single smokestack is regulated. The authors indicate that this is an overly restrictive rendition of actual policy. Obviously, cost savings increase with the trading possibilities. With suprasectoral trade, the savings in the period 1995–2010 are 50% for NO_x and 39% for SO_2. Cost savings are highest for the chemical industry. The less flexible the system, the more actual emission reduction is above the required emission reduction (presented under 'ceiling'), i.e. the more 'overshooting' there is.[38]

With NO_x, the largest cost reductions are achieved in the step from regulation to internal trade (especially for the base metal, refineries, and utilities), and from internal trade to sectoral trade (especially for the chemical sector). With suprasectoral trade, the chemical and refinery sectors buy permits from the base metal industry and the utilities.

With SO_2, the largest cost reduction is achieved in the step from internal trade to sectoral trade. Tradability in whatever form hardly makes a difference for the utilities. With suprasectoral trade, the refineries will buy permits from the base metal and chemical sectors.

3.5.5 Reactions

Reactions to the TME research can be found in the TME report itself (TME et al., 1997), Tabak (1997) and Jehae (1997). The TME report presents some reactions of the firms that were visited for the research. Firms were quite interested in design issues, like the initial distribution of TEPs and the way expansion of existing firms and entry of new firms would be accommodated.

The firms also displayed some distrust of government. They wondered whether the government could manipulate the TEP price by an interim decrease of the emission ceiling or by withholding emission rights. Furthermore, firms suspected the government would still want to hang on to parts of the existing permit system, tightening the emission standards.

Finally, the firms doubted whether the emission targets for 2010 were feasible. They accepted the emission techniques that the researchers used to determine how the 2010 targets would be met with regulation, but only for research purposes.

Now we shall look at the reactions of the interest groups to the research. In Chapter 5, section 3.3, we saw that VROM representative Dekkers is against this TEP system. There we also saw that the environmental organization SNM is divided. Proponents argue that environmental policy becomes less costly and thus more acceptable. Opponents have objections of principle, but also practical objections.

Stoppelenburg of the Association for the Protection of the Wadden Sea is also sceptical, primarily because he sees great enforcement problems. He is also afraid that there will be no room for new firms with clean technology, because they have to buy their emission permits (Jehae, 1997). De Vries of SNM also mentions the enforcement problem, but on balance his attitude is positive. He suggests that the government can keep permits in reserve for new firms and emphasizes the incentive for firms to implement new technology (Jehae, 1997).

Hensems (EZ) mentions a number of problems (Jehae, 1997): enforcement, the initial distribution of permits,[39] how to incorporate small firms and the fact that permits would only be tradable for a limited number of pollutants. As a result of the latter point, firms might only make an effort to reduce their emissions of these pollutants. Furthermore, it becomes more difficult to assess a firm's overall environmental performance and to issue a comprehensive environmental licence. Jehae (1997) also reports that all parties concerned express grave doubts about the enormous potential for cost saving found in the TME study (TME et al., 1997).

Rozenburg (DCMR), one of the initiators of the project, sees very large advantages, provided monitoring is good (Tabak, 1997). Late 1996, he assessed that there was going to be a TEP system, if industry was positive about it. Tabak (1997) also reports some cautiously optimistic reactions from Shell representative Gaasbeek and VNCI representative Van Namen.

3.5.6 The VNCI plan

In June 1997, the chemical industry organization VNCI approached the industry and the Department of VROM with a plan for 'cost equalization', which implies some kind of tradability of NO_x emissions within the chemical industry.[40] Some details of the plan transpired in a newspaper article in September 1997 (Aarden, 1997). In the chemical industry, small firms have much higher emission reduction costs than large firms. Thus, the idea is that small firms should pay large firms, in return for which small firms can emit more and large firms will emit less than current regulation prescribes. Koster (Shell) notes that this requires a change in environmental legislation: the government cannot prescribe abatement measures and emission levels for each firm separately (Aarden, 1997).

Different ideas were expressed with respect to entrants. According to Quik, (VNCI), participating in the cost equalization system would not be advantageous for entrants, because they have to comply with the state-of-the-art environmental technology when they enter. However, he did not object principally to the participation of new firms. According to Koster (Shell), on the other hand, entrants should have the opportunity to buy permits if this were cheaper than installing state-of-the-art technology.

It was expected that firms that pollute the air primarily on one location would not be able to participate in the cost equalization system. Quik (VNCI) indicated that the system, if successful, could be introduced in (or expanded to) other sectors as well.

The quote from Van der Veer (SNM) in Aarden (1997) suggests that the environmental movement is all for cost equalization. However, Van der Veer had some apprehensions:

– SNM feared that VNCI would introduce a new NO_x target for 2005, which is so lenient that the government's NO_x target for 2010 would be very difficult to reach;
– cost equalization should be seen as an experiment which, if successful, should be applied to other sectors as well. It should also be seen as a step toward a tradable emission permit system, because a TEP system is more transparent and enables environmental organizations and government to reduce emissions by buying permits.

In February 1998, it became clear that the VNCI had failed to convince the firms in the chemical industry of the advantages of cost equalization. It was more successful with the government. In its Third National Environmental Policy Plan (NMP3, Department of VROM, 1998), the government announced its intention to introduce a cost equalization scheme for NO_x, although it had not succeeded (yet) in reaching an agreement about the scheme with industry.

3.5.7 Conclusion

Because the discussion about tradable emission permits (TEPs) is still taking place at the moment, we cannot draw any definite conclusions from this section yet. However, it is interesting to observe the differences between and within organizations of the same category that emerge from the discussion until now.

As we saw in section 3.5.2, the Department of VROM was quite negative about TEPs. In section 3.5.3 we saw that the regional environmental agency DCMR was far more positive about TEPs. The platform of provinces IPO has also displayed an interest in TEPs. Thus, the Dutch civil service on the regional level is more enthusiastic about TEPs than the national civil service,[41] whereas we saw that in the US it was just the other way around (Chapter 4, section 3). The reason why the regional civil service is more interested in TEPs seems to be that they have to conduct the painstaking negotiations with firms about compliance with the existing environmental licences and drawing up new and revised licences. TEPs promise to make the jobs of the regional civil service much easier. The national VROM civil servants, on the other hand, do not have the experience of trouble-some contacts with firms and are more worried about the cost of changing national legislation.

The current discussion has also brought the differences within the environmental movement to the surface. When speaking in general terms, the economic experts of the environmental movement can claim that TEPs should be introduced. But when there is a more concrete plan to introduce TEPs, it becomes clear that there are still opponents of this instrument in the environmental movement.

Finally, there are differences between and within industries. If we had to predict which industry would be most positive about TEPs after the TME study, we would have picked the chemical industry, because expected cost savings are largest for this industry. And in fact, the chemical industry did react most positively: the chemical industry organization VNCI introduced its own plan for TEPs, called cost equalization. However, the VNCI failed to rally the support of all the firms it represents. Thus, there are also differences of opinion within the chemical industry.

Nevertheless, the VNCI did succeed in convincing the government of the merits of cost equalization. The national government seems to be more serious than ever about introducing some form of tradability. To explain this change in attitude, one might suggest that the government was waiting for a sign from industry of its interest in tradability.

4.   CONCLUSION

In our introduction we announced that this chapter would comprise a treatment of both our research questions, about interest group preferences as well as about the political process. Now we shall see what we have learned about these questions in this chapter. We shall mainly refer to our discussion of market instruments in the Netherlands.

With respect to the Dutch environmental movement, the additional value of this chapter is the insight into the historical development of its preferences. We see that the preference of the environmental movement has evolved in time and depends on the specific instrument. In the 1970s, the Dutch environmental movement was against the water pollution charge. In 1988, they cautiously endorsed the plan of the Boorsma Committee (Boorsma et al., 1988) for an anti-acidification fund. In the 1990s, they enthusiastically supported the regulatory energy charge, but were divided on tradable emission permits.

As we had expected from the theoretical survey and the literature, industry lobbied against the financial instruments of the anti-acidification fund and the regulatory energy charge. It is worth noting that existing emission trading schemes are based on grandfathering and most existing regulatory charges have exemptions or special recycling schemes for large polluters.

Trade unions only played a role in our discussion of regulatory energy charges in the Netherlands, which they supported (section 3.4.6). They promised not to demand wage compensation for the price increase due to a regulatory charge.

However, we also saw that at one point a trade union leader rejected any national charge. This abberation illustrates Leemreize's remark from our survey (Chapter 5, section 3.2.5) that within the FNV, people might make different trade-offs between employment and environment.

The civil service played a prominent role in sections 3.4 (the regulatory energy charge) and 3.5 (tradable emission permits). The Departments of VROM and EZ jointly commissioned the research into the regulatory energy charge, but they were diametrically opposed to each other, up to their Ministers. We will return to the subject of controversies between the Department of the Environment and other Departments in Chapter 7, section 2.4.

With respect to the regulatory energy charge, EZ was against any national charge, whereas VROM was in favour of a national charge, at least for small users, in the absence of international agreement. The controversy was clearly present in the CDA/PvdA cabinet around 1992, but seems to have disappeared in the following PvdA/VVD/D66 cabinet. A number of possible reasons can be given for this. For one thing, the PvdA/VVD/D66 coalition agreement stipulated the introduction of a national small user charge. The opponents of a charge at EZ may have been satisfied that the 'worst danger' (a more comprehensive national charge) had been averted, and started concentrating on a good recycling scheme for the small industrial users. Furthermore, EZ Minister Wijers (D66) was more environmentally-minded than his predecessor Andriessen (CDA).

From the interest group of the environmental bureaucracy it is but a small step to our second research question, which is concerned with the political process. One thing to be noted here is the large influence of politicians and the civil service on research reports, written by 'outside' committees or institutes. Jaarsma and Mol (1994) already described this for the Regulatory Energy Charges Steering Group, but the same is true for the Boorsma committee and the DHV research into tradable emission permits. The task of the Boorsma committee to design an anti-acidification fund was practically made impossible by the cabinet's precondition of no increase in the collective tax burden. The hand of VROM is clearly visible in the negative conclusion of the DHV report (Versteege and Vos, 1995) on tradable emission permits.

We have seen that until 1990, the national Dutch government showed little interest in market instruments. The water pollution charge, which can be seen as an 'accident' and the tax breaks for cars with a catalytic converter and unleaded petrol were the only market instruments used in environmental policy. Of course we must take into account the positions of industry (against financial instruments) and environmental movement (slowly starting to appreciate market instruments) to explain this relative absence of market instruments. In 'The Hague' itself, the bureaucracy maintained there was no need for market instruments and the politicians were not interested enough to make a big point of it.

Finally, we note the impact of the coalition agreement, drawn up by the parties that are going to form the new government. Writing a coalition agreement is a process of 'give and take' between the parties, or in a political science term, 'logrolling'. In the 1994 elections, PvdA and D66 were in favour of a national regulatory energy charge on small users, in the absence of international agreement. The VVD was against such a charge. The coalition agreement of the PvdA/VVD/D66 government stipulated the introduction of a national energy charge for small users. Although the VVD was against the charge, it cast its pivotal vote in favour of it, because the charge was part of the coalition agreement that also contained many points the VVD felt strongly about.

NOTES

1. For the purpose of this chapter, we have formulated the second research question somewhat more broadly than in Chapter 1.
2. For instance: Opschoor et al. (1994), Klaassen (1996), EEA (1996), Cansier and Krumm (1997) and Svendsen (1998).
3. A similar list can be found in OECD publications (OECD, 1993; Opschoor et al., 1994; OECD, 1997).
4. Kete (1992), in a more appreciative tone, also credits economists.
5. See Chapter 2, sections 3, 4.3.3 and 5.
6. See Chapter 5, section 3.2.
7. See Chapter 4, section 4.2.
8. See Rico (1995), Burtraw (1996) and Klaassen and Nentjes (1997) for assessments of this programme. See Fromm and Hansjürgens (1996) for an analysis of RECLAIM, the other major new tradable permit system in the US.
9. See also Chapter 4, section 4.3.
10. The *Handelingen der Staten-Generaal* (Acts of Parliament) will be cited as follows. Sessions of the First and Second Chamber are referred to by their date. Extended (Second Chamber) Committee Meetings are referred to by the code UCV, the number of the meeting and if necessary the year of session. Other government documents are referred to by their file number, their document number and if necessary the year of session. Only government documents that are published separately as well (like the NMP) are included in the list of references.
11. Andersen (1996:162) claims that 'Dutch policy-makers had read their economic textbooks and, in fact, praised the regulatory effects of environmental charges', but he only gives one quote, taken from the Acts of Parliament (1964/5, 7 884: 3, p. 12), to sustain this claim.
12. For the same reason, they were not so keen on the term 'discharge licence' and on the 'polluter pays principle'.
13. In France, river basin authorities are also important, but industry has a large say in the policy of these authorities.
14. Danish municipalities even tried to lure industry with discounts on waste water treatment and lax controls (Andersen, 1996).
15. The ensuing discussion is treated in Dijkstra (1998).
16. The committee recognized the problem that the existing licences did not always specify the exact amount of emissions, and not all firms had adequate licences yet.
17. Headlines like 'Good for the collection of curiosities. Anti-acidification fund: an armchair proposal' (Anonymous, 1988b) in the NCW magazine and 'Industry does not believe in environmental coupon game' (Anonymous, 1988a) suggest that industry refused to take the idea seriously.
18. Of the cost of additional emission reduction measures, the respective target groups had to pay 86% themselves. A raise in the diesel excise would pay for making trucks and buses cleaner. Part of the measures to reduce agricultural NH_3 emissions were to be financed from the fuel tax (Department of VROM, 1989).

19. Compare Peeters (1992).
20. When I asked former Minister Nijpels why the cabinet had not tried to implement the Boorsma plan, he only answered that the plan was 'politically infeasible'.
21. VROM in NMP-plus (Department of VROM, 1990), and EZ in Nota Energiebesparing (Department of EZ, 1990).
22. Van der Schot (1992) links the political interest in regulatory charges to the exit of the VVD from the government coalition and the entry of the PvdA, and the critique from a.o. the SER (Socio-Economic Council) (1989) on the small role of regulatory charges in the National Environmental Policy Plan (Department of VROM, 1989) from the CDA/VVD government.
23. Note the congruence between the priorities of the Ministers' respective parties and Departments. CDA as well as EZ is relatively more concerned with industry. PvdA as well as VROM is relatively more concerned with the environment.
24. Akzo, Dow, DSM and Hoechst (chemical), Shell (oil), Hoogovens (metal) and KNP (paper).
25. In their reaction to the 'letter of the seven', Van den Biggelaar and Wams (1991) from the environmental organizations Stichting Natuur en Milieu and Milieudefensie, respectively, called this argument 'bizarre': 'Can we infer from this that with rising energy prices they would reduce energy saving?'
26. This version received only a brief treatment.
27. This is the so-called 'rebound' effect to which Van der Valk (Aktie Strohalm) referred in our survey (Chapter 5, section 4.4).
28. Defined here as a reduction in both domestic sales and exports of at least 30% with the 50% charge.
29. The economist Verbruggen was a crown member of the SER at that time.
30. The authors of the latter two contributions work at, or have connections with, the environmental organization Stichting Natuur en Milieu.
31. In Chapter 10, section 5.4, we will give an interpretation of the environmental movement's willingness, and industry's refusal, to discuss revenue distribution.
32. The 1994 election programmes are collected in DNPP (1994).
33. 800m^3 is the benchmark consumption of a household with state-of-the-art heating and insulation.
34. Note that the Dutch regulatory energy charge is not levied on petrol and diesel. However, excise taxes on petrol and diesel were raised considerably in the 1990s.
35. The case of the medium and small industries was further weakened by the fact that they based themselves on a study from their own research institute EIM which, according to the cabinet, was based on outdated data that overstated the charge revenue and thus the burden for industry. Therefore, the government was not willing to discuss the effects of the charge based on the EIM figures.
36. We discuss the tension between TEPs and the ALARA (As Low As Reasonably Achievable) in Chapter 5, section 3.2.3.
37. This may serve as an answer to Tabak's (1997: 122) question of why VROM had TEPs researched in the first place.
38. Overshooting is discussed in Chapter 4, section 4.2.
39. In our survey of Dutch interest groups, we found that almost all respondents (among them Hensems) saw this as a problem (Chapter 5, section 4.5).
40. Note that the VNCI withdrew its contribution to our survey of interest groups (Chapter 5, section 2). They may have made this decision, (partly) because they were hatching their own TEP plan.
41. However, as we saw in our survey (Chapter 5, section 3.3.3), opinions within DCMR are also divided.

7. Models of Interest Group Influence

1. INTRODUCTION

In Chapter 1 we identified two research questions:

1. What are the preferences of the relevant interest groups for environmental policy instruments?
2. Given the preferences of everyone affected by instrument choice, and given that market instruments are efficient, why does the political process so often result in the choice of direct regulation?

In Chapters 3 to 5 we treated the first question. Chapter 6, about market instruments in practice, addressed both questions. We now move on to the second question, which will occupy us in Chapters 7 to 11. In this chapter, we introduce two models of interest group influence on political decision making. We shall see whether we can explain the political choice for direct regulation in these models.

In section 2, we discuss the institutional model from Nentjes and Dijkstra (1994). As we have seen in Chapter 2, section 5, the literature that takes into account the institutional aspects of political decision making has been mainly US-oriented. We shall present a model that reflects the situation in the Netherlands and other Western European countries, with proportional representation in elections, strong party discipline and an important role for the cabinet.

In section 3 we introduce the rent seeking model, where agents make an effort to get their favourite policy alternative accepted. This model has already been discussed briefly in Chapter 2, section 4.2. In section 3 we treat the model elaborately. We shall see how we should extend the model to make it applicable to instrument choice in environmental policy. Finally, we give the mathematical solution to the 'standard' rent seeking game. Section 4 concludes the chapter.

2. THE INSTITUTIONAL MODEL

2.1 Introduction

Our analysis seeks to model a democracy where a parliament is elected on the basis of proportional representation. Proposals to change policy are prepared by the bureaucracy of a Department. They are brought forward and defended in Parliament by the Minister. Ultimately the vote in Parliament decides whether the bill is accepted, or not. Although most parliamentary democracies are bicameral, we shall concentrate on the chamber that votes first. For instance in the Netherlands, this is the Second Chamber. We assume that the First Chamber votes for the proposal that the Second Chamber has accepted. Two reasons can be given for that:

– the First Chamber judges the proposal on formal criteria. We assume that the proposal satisfies the formal criteria;
– the vote of the First Chamber is (partly) a political one. We assume the seat distribution in the First Chamber does not differ significantly from the seat distribution in the Second Chamber.

Thus, the players in the political process of decision making on instruments of environmental policy are: members of Parliament (as united in political parties), the Minister of the Environment and the environmental bureaucracy. We shall first discuss the preferences of parliamentary parties (section 2.2). In section 2.3 we analyse the formation of government. In section 2.4 we see which instrument will be proposed by the Minister of the Environment, who has to take into account (or is influenced by) the preferences of the coalition parties and the environmental bureaucracy. Section 2.5 concludes the section.

2.2   Parliamentary Parties

2.2.1 Parties as unitary actors
The members of Parliament (MPs) are united in several parties. We interpret these parties as unitary actors for our purposes. This means that a party goes into or stays out of government as one block, and all MPs vote in the same way.[1] In the Dutch Parliamentary Survey of 1990, the question was asked, 'When a member of the Second Chamber has to vote, but his opinion differs from his parliamentary party's, should he then vote according to his party's opinion or according to his own opinion?' Of the Second Chamber members, 20% answered 'the party's opinion', 11% 'his own opinion', and 69% 'it depends'. The members of the coalition parties tended more towards 'the party's opinion' and less to 'his own opinion' (Van Schendelen, 1992a; Thomassen and Zielonka-Goei, 1992).

Several reasons can be given to explain why all MPs of a party vote in the same way (Daalder, 1987):

1. MPs are disciplined, either because the party leaders will punish them if they vote another way, or more informally, because the parliamentary party consists

of a small number of members with close personal contacts.
2. The MP realizes that the voters did not vote for him personally (as in a district system of elections) but for the party or more specifically, the party's election programme. Thus the MP has no mandate from the voters to go his own way.
3. The parliamentary party mainly consists of specialists. A specialist feels strongly about his own subject, and not about the other subjects. Thus, the specialist votes for a proposition recommended by the specialist of that specific subject, expecting the others to vote for his proposals in turn.

With regard to the first reason, there are some instances in which Dutch Second Chamber members that did not conform to the party line, were ineligible to stand in the next election. In the Dutch Parliamentary Survey of 1990, support can be found for the second and third reason. With regard to the second reason, 72% of the Second Chamber members agreed to the statement, 'When there are conflicting opinions within the party, the role of the election programme is important in the discussion' (Thomassen and Zielonka-Goei, 1992). With regard to the third reason, to the question, 'In general, who makes the pivotal decisions within your parliamentary party?', 13% of the members of the three largest Second Chamber party members answered 'the party specialist' and 53% answered 'the party committee', a small group of specialists in the same field.

2.2.2 Interest group influence
The starting point of our analysis is that instrument choice in environmental policy is influenced by interest groups. Our theoretical analysis of the preferences of interest groups is found in Chapters 3 and 4. In the conclusion to Chapter 4 we derived the tentative preference orderings, presented in Table 4.4. They are repeated in Table 7.1.

It should be noted once more that these orderings cannot possibly summarize all information about interest group preferences. However, they are useful in explaining how our model works.

Political parties differ in the weights they attach to the interests of societal groups. For instance, a party on the left will attach more importance to the interest of workers than a party on the right.

In our model, we group the parties together in four *blocks*. The parties in one block have the same ordering of importance they attach to the preferences of workers, shareholders and environmentalists.[2] By focusing on blocks instead of parties we simplify the analysis (there are more parties than blocks) and we make it more universally applicable (a party existing in one country may not exist in another country).

The blocks, with their rankings, are presented in Table 7.2. The table also gives the Dutch political parties, presented in Table 6.1, that are contained the blocks.[3] Substituting the interest groups' rankings of instruments into the parties' ranking

Table 7.1 Tentative preference orderings

	Share-holders	Workers	Environmen-talists	Environmental bureaucracy
Bubbles	2	1	2/3	1
Standards	3	2	5	4/5
Tradable permits, grandfathering	1	3/4/5	2/3	2
Tradable permit auction	4/5	3/4/5	1	3
Emissions charges	4/5	3/4/5	4	4/5

Table 7.2 Political blocks and their relation to interest groups

Block	Dutch party	Ranking of Environmentalists	Shareholders	Workers
Left-liberal and green	GL, D66	1	3	2
Traditional left (social-democrat)	PvdA	2	3	1
Traditional centre (christian-democrat)	CDA	3	1/2	1/2
Traditional right (con-servative)	VVD	3	1	2

Table 7.3 Political party preference for environmental policy instruments

	Green	Left	Centre	Right
Bubbles	2	1	1	2
Standards	5	2	2/3	3
Tradable permits, grandfathering	3	4	2/3	1
Tradable permits, auction	1	3	4	4
Emissions charges	4	5	5	5

of interest groups, we obtain the parties' ranking of instruments, shown in Table 7.3. The ranking is based on the preferences of the interest group that comes first in the political party's ordering. Further specification is based on the preferences of the interest group that comes next in the ordering.

2.3   The Cabinet

We assume that none of the blocks identified in Table 7.2 has a majority of seats in parliament, but there will be a majority government. Thus, the cabinet will consist of a coalition of at least two blocks.

Let us first look at the empirical justification for these assumptions. According to Laver and Schofield's (1990) overview of twelve post-war European democracies,[4] one party held more than half of the legislative seats in only 20 out of 218 parliaments. Of course, there will be more parliaments in which one block has a majority, because there can be more than one party in a block.[5] But it seems reasonable to focus on the situation in which no block commands a majority of seats.

In Laver and Schofield's (1990) overview, a minority government formed in 73 out of 198 parliaments (37%) without a majority party. Because on average, minority governments are in power for a shorter period, a minority government was in power for 27% of the time in parliaments without a majority party. There are large differences between countries. In Denmark, Ireland, Norway and Sweden, minority governments occur very frequently. Finland and Italy are in the middle category. In the other countries (Austria, Belgium, Germany, Iceland, Luxembourg, the Netherlands) there is hardly ever a minority government. Thus, the assumption that there will be a majority government is more applicable to some countries than to others.

Now we turn to the question of which blocks will be in government. To this end we order the blocks on a left-right scale. From left to right this yields: Green, Left, Centre, Right. We assume that a government will consist of parties from two contingent blocks. Thus, there are three possible coalitions: Green–Left, Left–Centre, and Centre–Right. When each parliamentary party belongs to one of the four blocks, either Green–Left or Centre–Right will command a majority. Next to that, Left–Centre may or may not command a majority.

On the subject of left-right scaling, we find the following in Laver and Schofield (1990: 113):

> Over 80 per cent of the coalitions formed either contained the median party on the left–right scale or were supported by it, which implies that a single left–right scale does indeed give us considerable analytical leverage in explaining coalition formation in these systems. This suggests that one-dimensional representations of coalition bargaining capture many important elements of government formation.

Van Roozendaal (1992) comes to the same conclusion, while dealing with some specific criticisms.

However, in the Dutch Parliamentary Survey of 1990, 18% of the Second Chamber members did not relate to the left–right division (Hillebrand and Meuleman, 1992). Next to the left–right scale another scale, based on ethical issues and correlated to MPs' sympathy for other parties, can be distinguished.[6]

I will discuss two theories of coalition formation that can explain why a coalition will consist of two, instead of three, blocks.[7] The first theory is the 'closed minimal range' concept, introduced by De Swaan (1973). The closed minimal range coalition is the minimal connected winning coalition with the smallest ideological range. A minimal connected winning coalition is a coalition where the omission of one party would make the coalition either not winning or not connected (on a left–right scale). When in our model we consider the blocks instead of the parties as relevant actors, and the distances between the blocks are not too unequal, the closed minimal range coalition consists of two contingent blocks.

The second theory is a modification of Grofman's (1982) hierarchical model of coalition building. Grofman assumes that coalition building takes place in a number of steps. In the first step, the parties closest to each other enter a protocoalition. This (and any subsequent) protocoalition acts as one party for the rest of the coalition formation process. In the following steps, the parties and/or protocoalitions that are closest to each other form a new protocoalition. This process continues until there is a protocoalition with a majority. This will be the government coalition.

Applied to our model, the parties within a block will first come together and form a protocoalition. When each block has formed a protocoalition, the two blocks that are closest to each other will come together. However, and contrary to the Grofman (1982) model, if this combination of two blocks does not command a majority, the combination breaks up into the constituent blocks.

When there is a combination (arrived at in one way or the other) of two contingent blocks that commands a majority, some parties may drop out of the combination. This is no problem, as long as the remaining parties still command a majority.

2.4 The Environmental Minister and Bureaucracy

A proposal about which instrument to apply in a particular field of environmental policy will come from the Minister who is in charge of the environment. Following the finding of Laver and Shepsle (1994a) that government policy is affected by the partisan composition of the coalition, we assume the proposal will depend on the preferences of the coalition parties.[8] The reasons for this are:

- the proposal may depend on the Minister's party affiliation, but we do not know beforehand which party will occupy the Department of the Environment. Laver and Shepsle (1994a) conclude that government policy is affected by the allocation of cabinet portfolios between parties.[9] However, with one exception,[10] there are no simple links between a certain Department and a certain party, although there is some support for broader tendencies (Budge and Keman, 1990);
- cabinet agreement on the proposal may be called for. However, this check upon a Minister's discretion may prove ineffective, as the other Ministers (all specialists, except for the Prime Minister) usually vote for his proposal (Laver and Shepsle, 1994b). This is the same mechanism within the cabinet as Daalder (1987) identified within a parliamentary party;
- the proposal must be accepted in Parliament. The question of changing the instrument of environmental policy seems important enough for a requirement of agreement between the Minister and the coalition parties. The Minister will be disappointed when the coalition parties do not support him. Likewise, a coalition party will be disappointed when the Minister's proposal is accepted with the aid of the opposition;
- instrument choice is arranged in the coalition agreement, drawn up when a new cabinet takes office.

Table 7.4 presents the coalition rankings of environmental policy instruments. To produce these rankings, we have summed and ranked the rankings of the political parties involved.

The number one instrument in the ranking is the instrument that the coalition is *expected* to apply. It is not the only *feasible* instrument for the coalition. The way in which the coalition's ranking is obtained produces a 'compromise solution' for the number one instrument. But instrument choice in environmental policy can be made a part of a more comprehensive 'package deal' between the coalition partners. This package deal can be implicit or explicit, i.e. laid down in the coalition agreement. This is what happened with the regulatory energy charge in the Netherlands (Chapter 6, section 3.4.8). The coalition agreement of August 1994 between PvdA, VVD and D66 stipulated that a national regulatory energy charge on small users be introduced in the absence of international agreement. The VVD was against the charge, but PvdA and D66 had their way on this point.

Table 7.4 suggests that a switch from direct regulation to tradable permits can appear on the political agenda under a centre–right coalition (grandfathering) and under a green–left coalition (auction).

The Minister's proposal will also be affected by the preferences of the environmental bureaucracy. For this reason, the preference ordering of the environmental bureaucracy is added to Table 7.4.

In the theory of government decision making, the influence of the civil service

Table 7.4 Compromises of parliamentary coalitions

	Green–Left	Centre–Left	Centre–Right	Environmental bureaucracy
Bubbles	1	1	1	1
Standards	3/4	2	3	4/5
Tradable permits, grandfathering	3/4	3	2	2
Tradable permits, auction	2	4	4	3
Emissions charges	5	5	5	4/5

is carried to its extreme in the model of bureaucratic government,[11] in which it is assumed that the bureaucracy has the effective power both to make and to implement public policy.

> The most typical justification for this assumption is that cabinet Ministers are just politicians, more or less amateurs in particular policy fields, who move into and out of their jobs like birds of passage. Senior civil servants, in contrast, are more or less permanent professionals in a given field, with access to a vast pool of specialist expertise. If civil servants have a policy agenda of their own – whether this arises from particular personal tastes, a desire for professional advancement, or even from sincerely held views about what is best for the country – then they are in a very strong position effectively to determine government policy outputs. (Laver and Shepsle, 1994a: 6)

However, Laver and Shepsle (1994a) find no support for the model of bureaucratic government, as is clear from their conclusions, already cited here, that partisan composition of the coalition and the party affiliation of the Minister do affect government policy.[12] But almost all authors in the overview acknowledge the power of the civil service. Laver and Shepsle (1994b) conclude that this power is especially large in the Netherlands, Norway and Sweden.[13] For instance, Andeweg and Bakema (1994) report that about three quarters of all MPs, questioned in the Dutch Parliamentary Survey of 1990, agreed with the statement, 'It is often difficult for Cabinet Ministers to press their point when senior bureaucrats dissent'.

Another piece of evidence of the power of the civil service in the Netherlands is the existence of so-called tribal wars between the civil servants in different departments, apparently uncontrolled by the Ministers involved. The Dutch

Department of VROM (Housing, Spatial Planning and the Environment) has had its share of tribal wars (Van der Straaten, 1990). For a long time, other Ministers' policies openly frustrated Government goals on acid rain. In the late 1980s it was officially recognized that other Ministers' policies could contribute to the Government environmental goals. But this is still one step away from actually taking the environment into account.

In Chapter 6, section 3.4, we saw that the Dutch Department of Economic Affairs (EZ), the Minister as well as his civil servants, was far more reserved about the use of the regulatory energy charge than the Department of VROM. Attempting to thwart VROM, EZ tried to influence the research of the Steering Group and the ensuing discussion.

Klabbers et al. (1993) conclude from interviews with policy actors and scientists in the Netherlands that the various governmental departments were positioned in different phases of the development of climate change policies. As a consequence, government did not speak with one voice.

This description of the influence of bureaucracy suggests two points:

- the environmental bureaucracy's ideas will strongly influence the Minister's policy;
- for a far-reaching reform of environmental policy, cooperation of other Departments is necessary. Then, not only the environmental bureaucracy, but also the bureaucracy of other Departments have to be persuaded. This last task is particularly hard if, as is likely, this bureaucracy is used to defending interests that run counter to the reform.

We shall concentrate on the first aspect. A Minister who considers proposing new instruments of environmental policy has to take the preferences of (the top of) his bureaucracy into account. On the other hand his success depends on the approval of the coalition parties in parliament. In the worst case, for the Minister, his freedom to bring forward proposals is restricted to the instruments for which the preferences of the coalition and the environmental bureaucracy coincide.

2.5   Conclusion

As is shown in Table 7.4, all government coalitions rank the instrument of bubbles highest. Since this is also the most preferred instrument of the bureaucracy, we can conclude that the prospects of introducing market instruments are rather bleak.

The initiative for introducing market instruments would have to come from the Minister of the Environment. From Table 7.4, we see that a Minister from the Green party would like to introduce an auction of tradable permits and a Minister from the Right party would like to introduce grandfathering of tradable permits. From Table 7.4, we see that the environmental bureaucracy will oppose an auction more than they would grandfathering. From Table 7.4, the resistance of the coalition partner (the Left, respectively the Centre) may be less fierce against grandfathering than against an auction, as well.

Thus, there is not much hope for the introduction of market instruments in this model. The best chance seems to be for grandfathering under a Centre–Right government with a Minister of Environment from the Right. Auctions may also stand a chance, under a Green–Left government with a Minister from the Green party. Charges do not stand a chance in this model.

3.   RENT SEEKING: INTRODUCTION

3.1   Introduction

The second model we introduce in this chapter is the model of the rent seeking contest (the rent seeking model), which we have already discussed briefly in Chapter 2, section 4.2. In the rent seeking model the interest groups, which we shall call rent-seeking agents, do their best, i.e. they make an effort, to obtain a favourable policy decision. Every agent makes an effort for his own favourite alternative, so that they are engaged in a contest against each other.

The big difference with the institutional model from section 2 is that the players involved in the institutional model (the interest groups and the politicians) act mechanically as if they were 'machines'. The interest groups compile their preference orderings for instruments, and the political parties process these orderings. In a later stage, the government coalition processes the parties' orderings. In the rent seeking model, however, the interest groups 'come alive'.[14] They have to decide whether and how intensively they are going to lobby, and for which instrument.

When we let an agent 'come alive', and make his own decisions, we have to specify how, and on the basis of which information, the agent will make his decisions. We shall now investigate this subject.

In its simplest and most general form, agent i's payoff function from the rent seeking contest is:

$$U_i = \rho_i(x_1,...,x_i,...,x_n)v_i - x_i \tag{7.1}$$

where:

ρ_i = the contest success function (csf), that translates the agents' efforts into the probability that agent i will win;

v_i = agent i's stake, i.e. his difference in payoff between when he wins the contest and when he loses;

x_i = agent i's effort, i.e. the resources he spends in trying to influence the political decision.

We shall now treat each of these terms, beginning with agent i's effort x_i. As we shall see when we treat the contest success function, the higher agent i's effort, the higher the probability that the political decision will have the outcome that agent i made an effort for. It is important to realize that in the rent seeking model, the efforts are made before the political decision is made. Thus, the agents incur these costs regardless of the outcome of the political decision. Therefore, when we speak of rent seeking costs, we are not talking about the costs of promises to politicians like: 'If you decide in favour of us, we will contribute to your campaign fund, vote for you...' etc.

So what are these efforts that influence the political decision? We can think of downright bribes, although this category seems to apply more to less democratic countries. But bribes can also take more subtle forms, like presenting one's case over dinner. Another cost category is the direct cost of the time spent talking to civil servants and politicians, the cost of publishing reports and actions like demonstrations, strikes, etc.

But perhaps the most important cost component is the indirect cost, mainly in terms of time, of preparing the activities that directly influence the decision maker. In Chapter 11 we shall see that our interviewees from the interest groups and the civil service ascribe a large influence to the force of arguments on the political decision. We should realize that the production of arguments is costly.

As a first step in the 'production process' of arguments, an interest group must think of arguments that could sway the decision maker. The interest group can try to pursue arguments of its own, to relate to issues the decision maker has professed an interest in or to counter arguments from its opponents.

In the second stage, the interest group further elaborates its arguments, conducting, if possible, research into the quantitative aspects. For instance, an environmental organization tries to quantify the environmental benefits of environmental policy, and industry tries to quantify its cost. But the environmental movement will also try to find evidence that industry overstates the cost, and industry will try to find evidence that the environmentalists overstate the benefits.

Finally, an interest group must decide which arguments to use, and how to present them in a way that appeals to the decision maker.

Although we shall not model the production of arguments formally, it seems plausible that the more resources an interest group spends on the production of arguments, the more convincing these arguments will be, and the more influence the interest group will have.

After having discussed what exactly an interest group does to influence a decision, we shall now look at a different interpretation of rent seeking costs. This is the interpretation from the models of asymmetric information, discussed in Chapter 2, section 4.2. In these models, the decision maker does not know the interest group's stake, but the interest group knows its own stake. The interest group may be able to undertake a costly action to convince the decision maker that it has a high stake. Thus, in this interpretation, it does not matter what exactly an interest group does, because any costly action will influence the decision maker.

We now move on to another element of the payoff function (7.1), namely the contest success function (csf) ρ_i. It gives the probability that agent i will win the contest (i.e. agent i's success probability), given the efforts of all agents.

The rent seeking literature features a number of different contest success functions, but they all have the following two properties in common. First, the higher agent i's effort, the higher his success probability. And secondly, the higher the other agents' efforts, the lower agent i's success probability.

The rent seeking model does not explain how the decision maker is influenced by the agents' efforts. We have already devoted some attention to this subject in our discussion of an agent's effort. We shall not expand on this discussion here, but we do note that it is a weak point of the rent seeking model that the csf is not motivated by an analysis of the decision maker's behaviour. This weakness becomes especially prominent when we assume a specific functional form for the csf. We shall assume in our analysis of the rent seeking contest between two agents that when agent i spends twice as much as agent j, agent i's (j's) success probability will be 2/3 (1/3). But we cannot justify why agent i's success probability will be exactly 2/3, and why it cannot be 0.6 or 0.8. We cannot refer to an underlying model of decision maker behaviour, nor to an empirical estimate of the csf.[15]

A possible justification for the csf is that the rent-seeking agents themselves do not know exactly how the decision maker arrives at his decisions. The agents make an effort to influence the decision, they 'give it their best shot', and hope that the decision will be favourable. However, we shall assume that the rent-seeking agents know the csf that gives the probability that the decision maker will choose a particular alternative as a function of the agents' efforts. It seems somewhat strange that an agent does not know how exactly the decision maker makes his decision, but does know the exact success probability with which he chooses a certain alternative.

We have now come to the discussion of the last element in agent i's payoff function (7.1). This is agent i's stake v_i: his valuation of the prize of the contest. It is his difference in payoff between when he wins (i.e. when the decision maker selects the alternative the agent has made an effort for) and when he loses (i.e. when the decision maker selects a different alternative). Thus, in (7.1) the political decision is a *private good*: when an agent's favourite alternative is not accepted, he does not care which alternative is selected. In that case we can (as we did in (7.1)) normalize to zero agent i's payoff from any other alternative than his own. We shall discuss the nature of the prize more extensively in section 3.3.

Finally, we shall make two remarks on the form of agent i's payoff function.

The form (7.1) is the one most commonly used, but some articles feature different forms, based on different assumptions. Here we shall highlight two assumptions behind (7.1).

First, we have assumed constant marginal cost of effort. We have simply put x_i in agent i's payoff function (7.1), so that agent i's payoff is declining as fast in the first unit of x_i as in any following unit. Alternatively, we could let the marginal cost of effort increase, as in Riaz et al. (1995).

Second, we have assumed the rent-seeking agents are risk-neutral. This is evident from the fact that we simply multiply agent i's success probability with his stake. Alternatively, we could let the agents be risk-averse, as in Hillman and Katz (1984) and Hillman and Samet (1987). Then the agents would attach less value to the uncertain outcome of the contest.

The rest of this section is organized as follows. We shall first give a historical overview of the rent seeking literature (section 3.2). In section 3.3, we shall see how rent seeking analysis should be expanded in order to apply it to instrument choice in environmental policy. In section 3.4, I will give a preview of the expansions that will be made in Chapters 8 to 10. Section 3.5 contains the mathematical analysis of the basic model of the rent seeking contest.

3.2   Historical Overview

The first article on rent seeking *avant la lettre* is Tullock (1967). Tullock points out a previously neglected category of cost of government intervention. We shall look at his argument in case of a monopoly, illustrated in Figure 7.1. In this figure, D is the demand curve for the good, MR is the marginal revenue curve and MC is the marginal cost curve. If the market is competitive, the producers take the product price as given. In the market equilibrium, product price equals marginal cost. This occurs at point B, with production Q_0 and product price P_0. Producer surplus is zero, consumer surplus is ABP_0.

Now suppose the market is not competitive, but there is only one producer. This firm has a licence from the government to produce and sell this product, and the government only issues one licence. Thus, there is a monopoly. The monopolist will produce the profit-maximizing quantity.[16] This is quantity Q_1, where marginal cost equals marginal revenue. Product price will be P_1. Producer surplus is P_1FEP_0, and consumer surplus is AFP_1. Compared to the competitive situation, the consumers have lost the area P_1FBP_0. Of this area, P_1FEP_0 has gone to the producers, and FBE is lost. FBE is known in economics as the deadweight loss or the Harberger triangle (Harberger, 1954).

But according to Tullock (1967), the area P_1FEP_0 is not just a transfer from consumers to the monopolist. The existence of a producer surplus makes it attractive to become a monopolist. Thus, firms will make an effort to try and get the government to establish monopoly licences and to obtain these licences. In

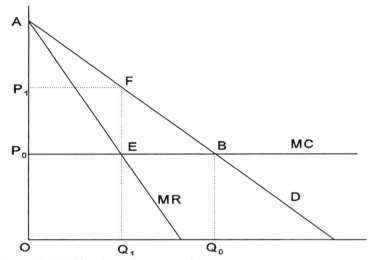

Figure 7.1 Welfare loss of a monopoly

other words: they engage in rent seeking activities. These activities are productive from the firm's point of view (otherwise, it would not make an effort), but they are not productive from society's point of view. Factors of production are used to obtain the producer surplus which is there, whether or not anyone tries to obtain it.

Although Tullock (1967) himself is somewhat obscure on the point, Posner (1975) equates the sum of rent seeking efforts to the producer surplus, under the following assumptions:

- obtaining monopoly is itself a competitive activity, with free entry;
- the long-run supply of the inputs into the efforts is perfectly elastic;
- the efforts produce no socially valuable by-products.

Thus, if a monopoly licence were issued for one market period, i.e. the period for which the demand curve is defined, not only the area FBE, but also the area P_1FEP_0 would be lost to society. Tullock suggests that the loss would be larger, but this seems partly due to the assumption that the licence is issued for longer than one market period. He also mentions the consumers' expenses in attacking the monopoly and the producer's expenses in defending it. However, it should be noted that the former is a separate cost category, whereas the latter is not. The prospective producers will take these expenses into account when trying to obtain the monopoly in the first place.[17]

Krueger (1974) and Posner (1975) developed the rent seeking theory further. Krueger coined the term 'rent seeking', applying it to firms' efforts to obtain import licences. Posner tried to estimate the social cost of monopoly.

Tullock (1980) gave a major injection to the rent seeking literature by introducing a specific contest success function (csf). As we have seen in section 3.1, the csf translates the size of the agents' efforts into their success at influencing the decision maker. Hillman and Riley (1989) baptize the contest that this csf causes the imperfectly discriminating rent seeking contest. The imperfectly discriminating rent seeking contest is like a lottery: the more tickets you buy, the higher is the probability that you win the prize. The name derives from the fact that the agent who makes the smaller effort can still win the contest. This is in contrast with the perfectly discriminating rent seeking contest Hillman and Riley (1989) also discuss, where the agent with the highest effort wins for certain. The perfectly discriminating rent seeking contest can be seen as a special kind of auction, namely an all-pay auction. Everyone has to pay his own bid, but only the highest bidder obtains the prize.

The imperfectly discriminating rent seeking contest is the concept most widely used in the literature. The perfectly discriminating rent seeking contest is less frequently employed. Sometimes, a general contest success function compatible with several functional forms is used (e.g. Baik, 1993; Körber and Kolmar, 1996). Other functional forms, like the difference model by Hirschleifer (1989) have been scarcely applied.

3.3   Expanding Rent Seeking Analysis

In this section we shall identify the directions in which we have to adapt rent seeking analysis to make it more applicable to instrument choice in environmental policy. The literature until now, reviewed by Nitzan (1994), has mainly dealt with rent seeking for a *private good*.

The *private good* nature of the rent means that an agent only gains when she wins the contest. If she does not enter the contest, she does not care who wins it. Her preferences can be called *dichotomous*: 'If I win the contest, I gain v_i. If I lose, I have nothing'. One can think for example of several firms contesting for a monopoly licence. The term v_i is called the *stake* of an agent.

Opposed to a private good is a *public good*. When the rent is a public good, an inactive agent is interested in who wins. Instrument choice in environmental policy can be seen as a public good. For example, suppose the shareholders lobby for grandfathering and the workers lobby for standards. The environmental movement is not active itself, but it hopes that the shareholders will win. Thus, when we want to model instrument choice as a rent seeking contest, we should model it as a rent seeking contest for a public good. But this area has scarcely been studied in the rent seeking literature until now.

The public good class can be subdivided into pure and impure public goods. When the rent is a *pure public good*, there is a set of agents with the same dichotomous preferences. One can think of identical individuals, spread across two polluted locations, A and B. The government has decided to clean up one location (Katz et al., 1990). The individuals in location A that stay out of the contest would rather see the agent active for A win, than the agent active for B. Moreover, since the agents in the same location have identical preferences, they all have the same stake in the political decision.

In the case of an *impure public good* (Linster, 1993b), an agent's preferences are more than dichotomous. Instrument choice in environmental policy, as we have discussed it, is an example: an interest group prefers instrument A, but it is not necessarily indifferent between instruments B and C.

With public goods, the interests of different agents can (partly) run parallel, for example two agents prefer instrument A to instrument B. Cooperation between these agents is then an obvious area for research. Cooperation has been studied most widely in rent seeking contests for a private good, starting with Nitzan (1991a,b).[18] The principle is that a number of agents form a group, that will compete for the prize as a group and share the prize if the group wins. In that way, cooperation transforms the prize from a private into a public good.

Another particular feature of instrument choice in environmental policy is, that there are instruments that yield government revenue. Thus, there are two government decisions that are influenced by interest group pressure: the choice of instrument and the division of revenue in case a financial instrument is chosen. Until now, such a combination of two rent seeking games has not been studied.

3.4   Overview of Chapters 8 to 10

In section 3.3 we have identified two directions in which rent seeking analysis should be developed to make it more applicable to instrument choice in environmental policy. The first direction is the study of rent seeking contests for impure public goods. The second direction is the combination of the contests for instrument choice and revenue division.

We shall analyse the rent seeking contest for an impure public good in Chapters 8 and 9. In Chapter 8 we shall analyse the noncooperative equilibria, where each agent maximizes his own payoff. In Chapter 9 we analyse cooperation in a rent seeking contest for a political decision that can have two outcomes. Cooperation is modelled as the establishment of agreements between agents on the same side, i.e. in favour of the same outcome, prior to the actual rent seeking contest. We shall analyse the novel cooperation concept of support, where an inactive agent pays part of the efforts of the agent who is active in the rent seeking contest.

In Chapter 10 we shall look at a two-stage rent seeking contest between two agents. The one stage is for the instrument: either direct regulation or a financial instrument. The other is for the revenue of the financial instrument.

In the 'Application' sections of each chapter, we apply the analysis to instrument choice in environmental policy. There we address the central question of our study, formulated in Chapter 1: 'Given the preferences of everyone affected by instrument choice, and given that market instruments are efficient, why does the political process so often result in the choice of direct regulation?' In the rent seeking model, the preferences of the agents are given by their stakes. The assumption that market instruments are efficient means that the aggregate valuation of (or aggregate stake in) a market instrument exceeds the aggregate valuation of (or aggregate stake in) any instrument of direct regulation. A rent seeking contest will 'often' result in the choice of direct regulation when the success probability of direct regulation is high. Thus, rephrasing our second research question for the rent seeking model, we have: 'Can the model explain that the market instrument, which is the alternative with the highest aggregate valuation, has a low,[19] or even zero, success probability?'

This question can be split into two parts. First we have to find out whether it is possible that the alternative with the highest valuation has the lowest success probability. We have to identify and analyse the factors which can cause this to happen. The second step is to ask whether these factors apply to a contest between the proponents of a (particular) market instrument and (a particular instrument of) direct regulation. For instance, we will see that the success probability of an instrument will be low, when there are many agents with low stakes in favour of the instrument. Then the question is whether there will actually be many agents with low stakes in favour of the market instrument.

In our application, we shall restrict ourselves to the five instruments and the four interest groups we have analysed extensively in Chapters 3 and 4. This analysis was summarized in Chapter 4, section 6, and Table 4.4. We shall assume the environmental bureaucracy is an interest group like the others: the shareholders, the workers and the environmental movement. Thus, we shall not take into account that the other interest groups may try to influence the environmental bureaucracy.

Regarding the interest groups identified above as one agent may be seen as quite restrictive. We assume that all shareholders act as one agent, but perhaps the shareholders of different industries or different firms do not act as one. Then many results of our applications would change. However, we shall maintain our classification of the four interest groups in our applications. Splitting the interest groups up will quickly result in a proliferation of possibilities, some of them quite arbitrary. Of course, nothing prevents the reader from generating his own applications by plugging in his own interest groups and stakes.

But first we shall give the analysis of the rent seeking contest for a private good. This analysis can also be found a.o. in Hillman and Riley (1989) and Linster (1993b). It is presented here so that we can refer to it in the following chapters.

We shall only analyse imperfectly discriminating rent seeking contests, because they are the most analysed and the most manageable.

3.5 A Rent Seeking Contest for a Private Good

3.5.1 Introduction
When a rent seeking contest is analysed as an imperfectly discriminating contest, two kinds of contests can be analysed. In a 'winner takes all' contest, the prize is indivisible. Only one agent can win, and this agent wins the whole prize. The higher an agent's effort, the higher the probability that he will win. One can think a contest between several TV stations for a cable channel. The 'winner takes all' contest will be analysed in section 3.5.2.

In a 'division of the pie' contest, the prize is divisible. The higher an agent's effort, the larger the part of the prize that he will obtain. The 'division of the pie' contest will be analysed in section 3.5.3.

3.5.2 A 'winner takes all' contest
Suppose n agents confront the opportunity of influencing the outcome of a political decision.[20] All agents who actively participate in the political contest irretrievably lose the efforts which they made in the attempt to influence the outcome of the contest in their favour, whether or not they are ultimately successful. Let agent i spend x_i to influence the political outcome in his favour. Agent i's success probability, i.e. the probability that agent i will be the successful contender is:

$$p_i(x_1,...,x_n)$$

where:

$$x_i \geq 0 \qquad \sum_{i=1}^{n} p_i = 1 \qquad \frac{\partial p_i}{\partial x_i} \geq 0 \qquad \frac{\partial p_i}{\partial x_j} \leq 0 \qquad i,j = 1,...,n \quad i \neq j$$

In words: efforts must be nonnegative. One of the agents i, $i = 1, ..., n$ must win the prize. The probability that an agent wins the prize is nondecreasing in his own effort level, and nonincreasing in any other agent's effort level.

It is assumed that the rent-seeking agents are risk-neutral. The expected payoff of agent i is:

$$U_i = p_i(x_1,...,x_i,...,x_n)v_i - x_i \qquad (7.1)$$

Here, v_i is agent i's valuation of the prize, also called agent i's stake. The value of the stake can differ from agent to agent. In our example of the TV station: a station with a lot of TV stars may have a higher expected profit from broadcasting than The Weather Channel. The former TV station will then have a higher stake in the prize (a cable channel).

For the contest success function ρ_i, we use Tullock's (1980) specification:[21]

$$\rho_i(x_1,...,x_i,...,x_n) = \begin{cases} \dfrac{1}{n} & for \; x_1 = x_2 = ... = x_n = 0 \\[4mm] \dfrac{x_i}{x_i + \displaystyle\sum_{\substack{j=1 \\ j \ne i}}^{n} x_j} & otherwise \end{cases} \qquad (7.2)$$

A rent seeking contest with this ρ_i function is called an imperfectly discriminating rent seeking contest.

Agent i sets his effort x_i such that his payoff is maximized, taking the efforts of the other agents as given. Substituting (7.2) into (7.1), his maximization problem is:

$$\max_{x_i} \; U_i = \frac{x_i}{x_i + \displaystyle\sum_{\substack{j=1 \\ j \ne i}}^{n} x_j} v_i - x_i \qquad (7.3)$$

The first order condition is:

$$\frac{\partial U_i}{\partial x_i} = \frac{\sum x_j}{\left(\sum x_i\right)^2} v_i - 1 = 0 \qquad (7.4)$$

where:

$$\sum x_i \equiv x_i + \sum_{\substack{j=1 \\ j \ne i}}^{n} x_j$$

Differentiating (7.4) once more with respect to x_i:

$$\frac{\partial^2 U_i}{\partial x_i^2} = \frac{-2\sum x_j}{\left(\sum x_i\right)^3} v_i < 0$$

Thus the second order condition for a maximum is satisfied. The first order condition (7.4) yields a global interior maximum of expected payoff for agent i.

However, we may find that agent i's effort level that satisfies (7.4) is nonpositive. In that case, agent i's payoff is declining for all $x_i > 0$, and agent i should remain inactive. From (7.4) with $x_i = 0$, this will happen when:

$$\sum x_j \geq v_i \qquad (7.4')$$

Thus, when the aggregate spending level of the other agents equals or exceeds agent i's stake, agent i should remain inactive. When agent i's stake exceeds the aggregate spending level of the other agents, he should become active.

Let us first assume there are only two agents involved. The two active agents are labelled 1 and 2, with $v_1 \geq v_2$. Agent 1 sets the effort level x_1 that maximizes his expected payoff U_1, taking agent 2's effort level x_2 as given:

$$\max_{x_1} \quad U_1 = \frac{x_1}{x_1 + x_2} v_1 - x_1 \qquad (7.5)$$

The first order condition is:

$$\frac{x_2}{(x_1 + x_2)^2} v_1 = 1 \qquad (7.6)$$

From the first order condition we can derive a *reaction function* or *best response function*. This function yields the x_1 that maximizes U_1 given the value of x_2. The reaction function of agent 1 is:[22]

$$R_1(x_2) = \begin{cases} -x_2 + \sqrt{v_1 x_2} & \text{if } x_2 \in (0, v_1] \\ 0 & \text{if } x_2 > v_1 \end{cases} \qquad (7.7)$$

This reaction function is drawn in Figure 7.2.

For agent 2, the first order condition is, analogous to (7.6):

$$\frac{x_1}{(x_1 + x_2)^2} v_2 = 1 \qquad (7.6')$$

Agent 2's reaction function is, analogous to (7.7):

$$R_2(x_1) = \begin{cases} -x_1 + \sqrt{v_2 x_1} & \text{if } x_1 \in (0, v_2] \\ 0 & \text{if } x_1 > v_2 \end{cases}$$

This reaction function is drawn in Figure 7.2 as well. The Nash equilibrium occurs at point A, where the two reaction curves intersect. At that point, neither agent would like to change his effort level, given the other agent's effort level.

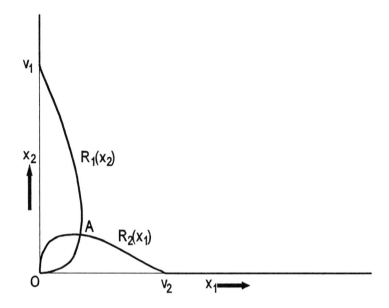

Figure 7.2   Reaction curves for agents 1 and 2

The equilibrium effort levels can be determined by solving both agents' first order conditions, (7.6) and (7.6'), simultaneously:

$$x_1 = \frac{v_1^2 v_2}{(v_1 + v_2)^2} \qquad x_2 = \frac{v_1 v_2^2}{(v_1 + v_2)^2} \qquad (7.8)$$

Substituting these spending levels into (7.2), we find the success probabilities:

$$p_1 = \frac{x_1}{x_1 + x_2} = \frac{v_1}{v_1 + v_2} \qquad p_2 = \frac{x_2}{x_1 + x_2} = \frac{v_2}{v_1 + v_2} \qquad (7.9)$$

Substituting (7.8) and (7.9) into (7.3), we find the agents' expected payoffs:

$$U_1 = \frac{v_1}{v_1 + v_2} v_1 - \frac{v_1^2 v_2}{(v_1 + v_2)^2} = \frac{v_1^3}{(v_1 + v_2)^2} \qquad (7.10)$$

$$U_2 = \frac{v_2^3}{(v_1 + v_2)^2}$$

We see that $U_1 \geq U_2 > 0$. Thus, agent 2 will make an effort, no matter how small its v_2 relative to v_1.

But what will happen when there are more than two agents? Suppose that $v_1 \geq v_2 \geq ... \geq v_n$. When (for instance) v_1 and v_2 are relatively large, x_1 and x_2 will be high. Applying (7.4'), when $v_3, ..., v_n$ are relatively small, the agents $3, ..., n$ will not find it worthwhile to participate actively in the contest: they will spend $x_i = 0$, $i = 3, ..., n$.

To find out how large his v_i must be for agent i to participate, let us assume that $m \leq n$ agents, $k = 1, ..., m$, actively participate in the contest. The first order conditions for the agents $k = 1, ..., m$ are, from (7.4):

$$\frac{\sum x_f}{\left(\sum x_k\right)^2} v_k - 1 = 0 \qquad k = 1,...,m \qquad f = 1,...,k-1,k+1,...,m \quad (7.4'')$$

From (7.4''):

$$\sum x_f = \left(\sum x_k\right)^2 \left(\frac{1}{v_k}\right)$$

Summing over m:

$$(m-1)\sum x_k = \left(\sum x_k\right)^2 \sum_{k=1}^{m} \left(\frac{1}{v_k}\right)$$

Solving for Σx_k:

$$\sum x_k = \frac{m-1}{\sum \left(\frac{1}{v_k}\right)} = \frac{m-1}{m} \tilde{v}_k \qquad (7.11)$$

where

$$\tilde{v}_k \equiv \frac{m}{\sum\limits_{k=1}^{m} \left(\frac{1}{v_k}\right)}$$

is the so-called *harmonic mean* of the valuations $v_1, ..., v_m$.

Now suppose the agents $k = 1, ..., m$ believe that only they will actively participate. Then the effort of an individual agent is determined by (7.4'') and the total effort by (7.5). The condition under which the agent $m+1$ will indeed set $x_{m+1} = 0$ has been derived as (7.4'):

$$\sum x_k \geq v_{m+1}$$

Table 7.5   Rent seeking contests with three active agents

v_1	v_2	v_3	x_1	x_2	x_3
144	144	120	33.75	33.75	22.50
144	72	60	33.96	13.06	7.84
144	48	40	27.92	7.98	1.99
144	36	30	23.39	5.40	0.60

Table 7.6   Rent seeking contests with two active agents

v_1	v_2	v_3	x_1	x_2	ρ_1	ρ_2
144	144	120	36	36	0.50	0.50
144	72	60	32	16	0.67	0.33
144	48	40	27	9	0.75	0.25
144	36	30	19.2	4.8	0.80	0.20

Substituting from (7.11), the condition for $x_{m+1} = 0$ is:

$$v_{m+1} \leq \frac{m-1}{\sum_{k=1}^{m}\left(\frac{1}{v_k}\right)} = \frac{m-1}{m}\tilde{v}_k \qquad (7.12)$$

If (7.12) is satisfied, the belief of the agents $k = 1, ..., m$ that only they will actively participate, is justified. Thus, when there are n agents involved, $v_1 \geq v_2 \geq ... \geq v_n$, the agents $1, ..., m$ will be active, with m the lowest number that satisfies (7.12).

Tables 7.5 and 7.6 give a numerical illustration of the workings of the rent seeking model. In Table 7.5, all three agents with a stake in the contest are active. In Table 7.6, only the two agents with the largest stakes are active. The stake of the third agent is such that he will just not be active. If his stake were any higher, he would become active.

3.5.3 A 'division of the pie' contest
For the 'division of the pie' contest, we can use the same analysis as in section 3.5.2, only now ρ_i is the *part* of the prize that goes to agent i, instead of the *probability* that agent i wins the whole prize. Another difference with the 'winner takes all' contest is the assumption that all agents value the whole prize equally. Thus, calling this prize R (for government revenue), we have $v_1 = v_2 = ... = v_n = R$. Using expression (7.2) for ρ_i, agent i's expected payoff is:

$$U_i = \frac{x_i}{\sum\limits_{j=1}^{n} x_j} R - x_i$$

In section 3.5.2 we derived inequality (7.12), that limited the number of active agents in case the agents' stakes differed. In a 'division of the pie' game, all agents have the same stake, so that condition (7.12) will never be satisfied. All agents that are admitted to the contest will make a positive effort.

When there are two agents, with $v_1 = v_2 = R$, their equilibrium spending levels are, analogous to (7.8):

$$x_1 = x_2 = \frac{R}{4} \qquad (7.8')$$

The success probabilities are, analogous to (7.9):

$$p_1 = p_2 = \frac{1}{2} \qquad (7.9')$$

The agents' expected payoffs are, analogous to (7.10):

$$U_1 = U_2 = \frac{1}{2}R - \frac{R}{4} = \frac{R}{4} \qquad (7.10')$$

4. CONCLUSION

In this chapter we discussed two models of political decision making: the institutional model (section 2) and the rent seeking model (section 3). In this conclusion, we shall compare these two models.

We begin with a formal difference. The actors in the institutional model behave quite 'mechanically': the political parties process the preferences of the interest groups and the coalitions process the preferences of the political parties. In the rent seeking model, the interest groups have 'come alive': they make their own decisions. In that sense, the rent seeking model is a 'richer' model. Thus, the rent seeking model lends itself better for further expansion.

We shall undertake this expansion of rent seeking analysis in the following three chapters. After that, in Chapter 11, we assess both models, confronting them with empirical evidence from interviews with interest group representatives, and identifying directions for future research.

The advantage of the institutional model is that it takes account of the fact that there are different political parties, which differ in the weights they attach to different interest groups. The second advantage is that the role of the environmental bureaucracy is different from the other interest groups. The bureaucracy has a more direct influence on the political decision.

While it would be an option to develop a rent seeking model that shares these features, we shall take a different route. We shall develop a rent seeking model that can address the issues that the institutional model, as presented here, cannot.

The first drawback of the institutional model is that is does not take into account the government revenues from the financial instruments. If the interest groups take into account that they will (or may) receive part of these revenues, financial instruments will rise in their preference ordering. This has a favourable effect on the possibility that financial instruments will be accepted. One might even say that neglecting the revenues from the financial instruments artificially depresses the predicted possibility of their political success.

In Chapters 8 and 9 we assume that the revenue division is not a political issue when instrument choice is at stake. The agents have already secured a certain part of the revenue of the financial instrument. In Chapter 10 we analyse the combination of a contest for the instrument and a contest for the revenue.

The second drawback of the institutional model is that it does not take into account the preference intensities. A ranking of instruments is not a complete representation of an interest group's preferences. The parties who take the interests of different groups into account might also like to know whether which instrument is chosen makes a big difference to an interest group. When the parties know the intensities of the interest groups' preferences, they can translate these preferences into their own preferences in a more sophisticated way.

In the rent seeking model, the preference intensities, or stakes, are taken into account. When an agent has a large stake in an instrument, he will make a great effort to increase the success probability of that instrument.

The drawbacks of the rent seeking model, including the developments announced here, are that there is only one decision maker, and all interest groups are treated alike. Furthermore, it is not clear what motivates the decision maker: he is assumed to react mechanically to the pressure he is exposed to.

NOTES

1. See Laver and Schofield (1990), Appendix A, for a country by country overview of whether parties can indeed be seen as unitary actors in this respect.
2. The environmental bureaucracy is not distinguished as a separate group because its size is too small to be of decisive electoral importance.
3. It is difficult to place D66 in this scheme. With respect to environmental policy, we can place it in the 'green' block. But with respect to broader socioeconomic issues, D66 could also be placed in the block with PvdA or even CDA. This is one reason why the current PvdA/VVD/D66 coalition seems to defy our theory of coalition formation by 'skipping' the CDA block.
4. The countries are Austria, Belgium, Denmark, Finland, West Germany, Iceland, Ireland, Italy, Luxemburg, The Netherlands, Norway and Sweden. The period reviewed is 1945–1987.

5. For instance, until the 1967 elections the three main Dutch Christian Democratic parties held a majority in parliament.

6. On this second scale, the CDA occupies a relatively extreme position, whereas on the left–right scale they are in the middle. This can be seen as another reason why the CDA has been in the opposition since the 1994 elections, with a party to their left (PvdA) and a party to their right (VVD) in government.

7. The current Dutch PvdA/VVD/D66 government consists of three blocks (or at least three large parties). This is because the smaller parties can either not be placed in one of 'our' four blocks, or are unwilling or considered unfit to participate in a government coalition.

8. In the Dutch Parliamentary Survey of 1990, when the question was asked, 'Who determines the main directions of public policy?', 19% answered 'the government' and 55% 'the government and the coalition parties' (Andeweg and Nijzink, 1992).

9. They also conclude that government policy is not affected by the allocation of cabinet portfolios within parties. Thus, we can treat parties as unitary actors in this respect as well.

10. The Department of Agriculture goes to the Agrarian Party or the Christian Democrats (Laver and Schofield, 1990).

11. It is carried even further in the BBC TV series *Yes Minister*.

12. Budge and Keman (1990) come to the same conclusions.

13. It is even larger in France, but France has a district system of elections.

14. However, as we shall see, the political decision maker is still a 'machine' in the rent seeking model.

15. If anything, the empirical evidence suggests that rent seeking expenditures are lower than what 'our' csf would give rise to (Tullock, 1997).

16. Assuming that the government licence does not restrict his pricing or producing behaviour.

17. One should also take into account that social welfare rises when the consumers defeat the monopoly. Ellingsen (1991) analyses what happens when the consumers oppose the monopoly, either when or after the firms try to obtain the monopoly licence. He shows that in a perfectly discriminating contest, this reduces social cost. In an imperfectly discriminating contest, social cost is reduced when there are many firms competing for the licence, the Harberger triangle is large and the Tullock rectangle is small.

18. See Chapter 9, section 2, for an overview of the literature on cooperation and delegation in rent seeking contests.

19. With low we mean: lower than one half (one third), if the political choice is between two (three) alternatives.

20. This description of the contest leans heavily on Hillman and Riley (1989).

21. Tullock's (1980) original formulation is more general:

$$\rho_i = \frac{x_i^r}{x_i^r + \sum x_j^r}$$

This more general formulation is treated a.o. in Pérez-Castrillo and Verdier (1992). In this chapter and in our own analysis in Chapters 8 to 10, we will set $r = 1$. The reasons for this choice are:

- mathematical convenience;
- when $r < 1$, all agents with a positive stake are active in a rent seeking contest for a private good;
- when $r > 1$, there may not be a noncooperative equilibrium in pure strategies and when there is, the agent with the highest stake may be inactive.

22. The reaction function R_1 is not defined for $x_2 = 0$.

8. Noncooperative Rent Seeking

1. INTRODUCTION

In this chapter, we will analyse noncooperative behaviour in a rent seeking contest for an impure public good. In a rent seeking contest for an impure public good, an agent is interested in the outcome of the contest, even though he is not active himself. Instrument choice in environmental policy is an example of an impure public good. For instance, the shareholders promote grandfathering and the workers promote standards. The environmental movement is inactive, but hopes that the shareholders will win. Thus, in order to understand instrument choice in environmental policy, we should examine the rent seeking contest for an impure public good.

In a rent seeking contest for an impure public good, agents (in the above example: the shareholders and the environmental movement) have common interests. However, in this chapter we will assume that the agents behave noncooperatively. That is: they follow the strategy that yields the highest payoff for themselves. They do not make agreements with the other agents about a concerted action to increase their joint payoffs. We defer the analysis of cooperation to Chapter 9.

In section 2, we will analyse the rent seeking contest for an impure public good with two alternatives. In section 3, we analyse the contest with more than two alternatives. Sections 2.1 and 3.1 contain the formal analysis and sections 2.2 and 3.2 give the application to instrument choice in environmental policy. The central question in these applications is: can the model explain that market instruments have a low, or even zero, success probability, although they are the instruments with the highest aggregate valuation?

In section 2, we apply Baik's (1993) general result to our specification of the rent seeking contest. We find that only the agents with the highest stake on either side will be active. This implies that market instruments will be disadvantaged when there are many agents with a small stake in the market instrument, opposed to one agent with a large stake in direct regulation.

In section 3, we extend Linster's (1993b) analysis. We find that the market instrument will not be promoted in a contest with firm bubbles and standards, if the proponent of bubbles is very much against standards, the proponent of standards is very much against bubbles and the proponent of the market

instrument not very much against standards or bubbles.
  Section 4 concludes the chapter.

2.   TWO ALTERNATIVES

2.1   Analysis

In this section we shall look at a political decision that can have two outcomes, which we call A and B. There are n agents that prefer outcome A, $i = 1, ..., n$, with stakes $v_{1,A} \geq v_{2,A} \geq ... \geq v_{n,A} > 0$. There are m agents that prefer outcome B, $j = 1, ..., m$, with stakes $v_{1,B} \geq v_{2,B} \geq ... \geq v_{m,B} > 0$.
  The payoff of agent k on the A-side is:

$$U_{k,A} = \rho_A v_{k,A} - x_{k,A} \tag{8.1}$$

For the specification of the success probability, we use the function introduced by Katz et al. (1990). Analogous to (7.2), the probability that the outcome will be A is:

$$\rho_A = \frac{\displaystyle\sum_{i=1}^{n} x_{i,A}}{\displaystyle\sum_{i=1}^{n} x_{i,A} + \sum_{j=1}^{m} x_{j,B}} \tag{8.2}$$

Thus, all the efforts of agents promoting instrument A are added up, and so are all the efforts of agents promoting instrument B. Only the aggregate effort counts in determining the success probability, regardless of how many agents make an effort or who makes an effort.
  Substituting (8.2) into (8.1), the payoff for agent k on the A-side, $k = 1, ..., n$, is:

$$U_{k,A} = \frac{x_{k,A} + \displaystyle\sum_{\substack{f=1 \\ f \neq k}}^{n} x_{f,A}}{x_{k,A} + \displaystyle\sum_{\substack{f=1 \\ f \neq k}}^{n} x_{f,A} + \sum_{j=1}^{m} x_{j,B}} v_{k,A} - x_{k,A}$$

In a noncooperative rent seeking game, every agent sets his effort level in order to maximize his own payoff, taking as given the effort levels of other agents on his own side as well as on the other side. Thus, agent k will set his $x_{k,A}$ according to the first order condition:

$$\frac{\partial U_{k,A}}{\partial x_{k,A}} = \frac{\sum_{j=1}^{m} x_{j,B}}{\left(x_{k,A} + \sum_{\substack{f=1 \\ f \neq k}}^{m} x_{f,A} + \sum_{j=1}^{m} x_{j,B}\right)^2} v_{k,A} - 1 = 0 \qquad (8.3)$$

We will derive the noncooperative equilibrium for this game. A special case of this game, where all agents on the same side have the same stake, has been studied by Katz et al. (1990). However, Katz et al. were wrong in stating that there is only one equilibrium. Baik (1993) has studied a more general form of the game than we do here, with two or more possible outcomes of the political decision, and with a general contest success function. Our analysis is thus an application of Baik.

We will start our analysis with the special case from Katz et al. (1990), where all agents on a side have the same stake. In that case, the rent is a pure public good.

Let v_A (v_B) be the stake of an individual agent on the A- (B-) side. Katz et al. (1990) identify one equilibrium for this contest:

$$x_{i,A} = \frac{v_A^2 v_B}{n(v_A + v_B)^2} \qquad i = 1,...,n$$

$$x_{j,B} = \frac{v_A v_B^2}{m(v_A + v_B)^2} \qquad j = 1,...,m \qquad (8.4)$$

We will check whether this is an equilibrium for agent k,A. From (8.4):

$$\sum_{\substack{f=1 \\ f \neq k}}^{n} x_{f,A} = \frac{(n-1)}{n} \frac{v_A^2 v_B}{(v_A + v_B)^2} \qquad \sum_{j=1}^{m} x_{j,B} = \frac{v_A v_B^2}{(v_A + v_B)^2} \qquad (8.4')$$

Substituting (8.4') into (8.3), the first order condition for agent k is:

$$\frac{dU_{k,A}}{dx_{k,A}} = \frac{v_A^2 v_B^2 (v_A + v_B)^2}{\left(x_{k,A}(v_A + v_B)^2 + \frac{n-1}{n} v_A^2 v_B + v_A v_B^2\right)^2} - 1 = 0$$

Solving the first order condition for $x_{k,A}$, we find:

$$v_A v_B (v_A + v_B) = x_{k,A}(v_A + v_B)^2 + \frac{n-1}{n} v_A^2 v_B + v_A v_B^2$$

This can be rewritten as:

$$\frac{v_A v_B}{v_A + v_B} = x_{k,A} + \frac{(n-1)v_A^2 v_B}{n(v_A + v_B)^2} + \frac{v_A v_B^2}{(v_A + v_B)^2}$$

from which we can solve:

$$x_{kA} = \frac{v_A^2 v_B}{n(v_A + v_B)^2}$$

Thus, (8.4) is an equilibrium. But there are more equilibria. Lemma 8.1 gives a characterization of all equilibria.

Lemma 8.1 Suppose there are n agents with a stake v_A in outcome A: $v_A \equiv v_{1A} = v_{2A} = \ldots = v_{nA} > 0$, and there are m agents with a stake v_B in outcome B: $v_B \equiv v_{1B} = v_{2B} = \ldots = v_{m,B} > 0$. In the noncooperative equilibrium, there are N active agents on the A-side, $1 \le N \le n$:

$$
\begin{aligned}
x_{kA} &> 0 & k &= 1, \ldots, N \\
x_{fA} &= 0 & f &= N+1, \ldots, n \\
\sum_{i=1}^{n} x_{iA} = \sum_{k=1}^{N} x_{kA} &= \frac{v_A^2 v_B}{(v_A + v_B)^2} & i &= 1, \ldots, n
\end{aligned}
\tag{8.5}
$$

Analogously, there are M active agents on the B-side, $1 \le M \le m$:

$$
\begin{aligned}
x_{g,B} &> 0 & g &= 1, \ldots, M \\
x_{h,B} &= 0 & h &= M+1, \ldots, m \\
\sum_{j=1}^{m} x_{j,B} = \sum_{g=1}^{M} x_{g,B} &= \frac{v_A v_B^2}{(v_A + v_B)^2} & j &= 1, \ldots, m
\end{aligned}
\tag{8.6}
$$

Proof Note first that, according to the Lemma, the aggregate effort on either side is independent of N and M, the number of active agents on either side. Thus, we only have to prove that (8.5) is a noncooperative equilibrium on the A-side, when the aggregate effort on the B-side is given by (8.6).

To prove the lemma, we will show that:

a. when the aggregate effort of all other agents on the A-side equals or exceeds the equilibrium Σx_{iA} given in (8.5), agent i will not spend anything;
b. when the aggregate effort of all other agents on the A-side is below the equilibrium Σx_{iA} given in (8.5), agent i will spend so much that the aggregate effort becomes the equilibrium Σx_{iA}.

Substituting (8.6) into (8.3), the first order condition for agent i on the A-side is:

$$\frac{dU_{i,A}}{dx_{i,A}} = \frac{v_A^2 v_B^2 (v_A + v_B)^2}{\left[\left(\sum_{\substack{t=1 \\ t \neq i}}^{n} x_{t,A} + x_{i,A} \right) (v_A + v_B)^2 + v_A v_B^2 \right]^2} - 1 = 0$$

Solving the first order condition for $x_{i,A}$:

$$v_A v_B (v_A + v_B) = \left(\sum_{\substack{t=1 \\ t \neq i}}^{n} x_{t,A} + x_{i,A} \right) (v_A + v_B)^2 + v_A v_B^2$$

This can be rewritten as:

$$v_A^2 v_B = \left(\sum_{\substack{t=1 \\ t \neq i}}^{n} x_{t,A} + x_{i,A} \right) (v_A + v_B)^2$$

from which we can solve:

$$x_{i,A} = \frac{v_A^2 v_B}{(v_A + v_B)^2} - \sum_{\substack{t=1 \\ t \neq i}}^{n} x_{t,A}$$

Thus, agent i adds to the efforts of the other agents when their efforts fall short of the equilibrium effort (8.5), and when their efforts equal or exceed the equilibrium effort, there is no need for agent i to contribute. ∎

This concludes our treatment of the noncooperative equilibrium for the pure public good, where all agents on the same side have the same stake. We now turn to the impure public good, where the agents on the same side can have different stakes. Our first question is: when is there more than one active agent on a side?

Lemma 8.2 When there is more than one active agent on the A-side:
a. all active agents on the A-side have the same stake $v_{c,A}$;
b. their aggregate effort equals the effort that one agent with stake $v_{c,A}$ would make if he were the only active agent on the A-side.

Proof Let us look at two agents, k and f, both active on the A-side. The aggregate effort on the B-side is x_B.
Combining the first order conditions for agents k and f, from (8.3):

$$\frac{x_B}{\left(\sum_{i=1}^{n} x_{i,A} + x_B \right)^2} v_{k,A} = \frac{x_B}{\left(\sum_{i=1}^{n} x_{i,A} + x_B \right)^2} v_{f,A} = 1$$

This equality can only be satisfied for $v_{k,A} = v_{f,A}$. It follows that all agents with $x_{i,A} > 0$ must have the same stake. This proves part a. of the Lemma.

The first order condition for the active agents on the A-side, all of whom have stake $v_{c,A}$, is, from (8.3):

$$\frac{x_B}{\left(\sum_{i=1}^{n} x_{i,A} + x_B\right)^2} v_{c,A} = 1$$

If there were only one agent with stake $v_{c,A}$ active on the A-side, the first order condition for his effort $x_{c,A}$ would be, analogous to (7.6):

$$\frac{x_B}{(x_{c,A} + x_B)^2} v_{c,A} = 1$$

This proves part b. of the Lemma. ∎

Now that we know when there will be more than one active agent on a side, we want to know when there is only one active agent, and who this will be.

Lemma 8.3 When the agents have stakes $v_{1,A} > v_{2,A} \geq ... \geq v_{n,A} > 0$ and $v_{1,B} > v_{2,B} \geq ... \geq v_{m,B} > 0$, there is a unique noncooperative two-agent equilibrium with the agents 1 on either side active.

Proof First we prove that when the agents 1 are active, the other agents do not have an incentive to enter. Thus, the agents $1,A$ and $1,B$ are active, and they assume that no other agents will be active.

The first order condition for agent 1 on the A-side is, analogous to (7.6):

$$\frac{x_{1,B}}{(x_{1,A} + x_{1,B})^2} v_{1,A} - 1 = 0 \tag{8.7}$$

Now we look at the expected payoff of an agent k, $k \neq 1$, on the A-side. From (8.3), his marginal payoff is:

$$\frac{\partial U_{k,A}(0, x_{1,A}, x_{1,B})}{\partial x_{k,A}} = \frac{x_{1,B}}{(x_{1,A} + x_{1,B})^2} v_{k,A} - 1 = \frac{v_{k,A}}{v_{1,A}} - 1 < 0$$

The second equality follows from (8.7). The inequality follows from $v_{k,A} < v_{1,A}$. Thus, agent k's marginal payoff is negative for $x_{k,A} = 0$. Furthermore, it is declining for all $x_{k,A} \geq 0$:

$$\frac{\partial^2 U_{kA}(x_{kA}, x_{1A}, x_{1B})}{\partial x_{kA}^2} = \frac{-2x_{1B}v_{kA}}{(x_{1A} + x_{kA} + x_{1B})^3} < 0$$

The marginal expected payoff of the inactive agents on the B-side is negative and declining as well, so that no other agent will want to enter when agent 1 is already active. Conversely, if there were a contest between two agents without the agent 1 active on either side, agent 1 would want to enter.   ∎

We have now discussed all the aspects of the noncooperative equilibrium of a rent seeking contest for a public good. In Proposition 8.1 we collect all these aspects from the preceding lemmas.

Proposition 8.1 Suppose there are n agents who prefer outcome A, with stakes $v_{1A} \geq v_{2A} \geq \ldots \geq v_{nA} > 0$, and there are m agents that prefer outcome B, with stakes $v_{1B} \geq v_{2B} \geq \ldots \geq v_{mB} > 0$. Then, in the noncooperative equilibrium:

a. the aggregate effort on the A-side x_A and the aggregate effort on the B-side x_B are given by:

$$x_A = \frac{v_{1A}^2 v_{1B}}{(v_{1A} + v_{1B})^2} \qquad\qquad x_B = \frac{v_{1A} v_{1B}^2}{(v_{1A} + v_{1B})^2} \tag{8.8}$$

b. when $v_{1A} > v_{2A}$, agent 1 is the only active agent on the A-side, and likewise on the B-side.
c. when there are $N > 1$ agents on the A-side with stake v_{1A}, there are multiple equilibria. Only these N agents can be active on the A-side, but they do not all have to be active, and the active agents do not all have to spend the same amount, just as long as the aggregate effort on the A-side is given by x_A from (8.8). The same applies to the B-side.

Baik (1993) proves these same points for a general csf and two or more possible outcomes. Thus, we can conclude that Baik's (1993) general result carries over directly to the imperfectly discriminating rent seeking contest with two possible outcomes.

2.2   Application

In section 2.1 we discussed the noncooperative equilibrium of the rent seeking contest in which the choice for the decision maker is between two alternatives. Applying the analysis to instrument choice in environmental policy, the political choice is between an instrument of direct regulation[1] and a market instrument. Either instrument may have more than one proponent. The central question in our application is our second research question, reformulated in Chapter 7, section 3.4, as: 'Can the model explain why the instrument with the highest aggregate valuation (i.e. the market instrument) has a success probability below 1/2?' We shall see that the answer is yes.

In section 2.1, we saw that in the noncooperative equilibrium only the agents with the highest valuation on either side are active. Thus, when there is one agent with a large stake in direct regulation and the agents in favour of the market instrument have small per capita stakes, direct regulation will have a large success probability.[2] The market instrument has a small success probability, even when the aggregate stakes for the market instrument exceed those for direct regulation.

This result is not unique to rent seeking theory. It is common to the political economy of regulation, as we saw in Chapter 2, section 4.2. In general, an inefficient policy proposal, that confers large per capita benefits to a small group and takes a small per capita amount away from a large group, is more likely to be accepted than an efficient policy, that does the exact opposite.

The argument of Buchanan and Tullock (1975), treated in Chapter 2, section 4.3.2, can be cast in terms of a rent seeking game. Buchanan and Tullock (1975) assume the revenue of an emissions charge will be distributed across the whole population. Then the polluting industry (seen as one agent) has a large stake in direct regulation, whereas the individual citizen has a small stake in emissions charges. As a result, direct regulation has a high success probability.

Hillman (1989: 70–71) treats a similar case explicitly with rent seeking analysis. A protectionist proposal yields a gain of W to agent 1 who is the beneficiary of protection. W is the loss in income incurred by $(n-1)$ agents. Agent 1's stake in protection is $v_1 = W$. The other agents' per capita stake in free trade is $v_j = W/(n-1), j = 2, ..., n$. As we know from section 2.1, the probability that the protectionist proposal will be accepted is:

$$\frac{v_1}{v_1 + v_j} = \frac{n-1}{n} \tag{8.9}$$

This is larger than 0.5, which would have been agent 1's success probability in case there were only one agent with stake W opposed to him. When the loss of W is spread among more than one agent, each agent j sets his effort x_j such that his own payoff is maximized. He does not take into account the fact that an increase in his x_j also increases the payoff of the other agents on his side. That is why the aggregate effort from the free trade lobby is too low.[3]

To what extent does the choice between a market instrument (in the role of free trade) and direct regulation (in the role of protection) resemble the rent seeking contest just described? A first difference is that in Hillman's (1989) example, the aggregate stakes in protection and free trade are equal (although a lower stake in protection might be more appropriate). With instrument choice, the aggregate stake in the market instrument exceeds the aggregate stake in direct regulation.

Given n, the success probability of direct regulation will be lower than in (8.9).

From our theoretical analysis, summarized in Table 4.5 of Chapter 4, it follows that when the market instrument considered is grandfathering, one interest group will be very much in favour of it, namely the shareholders. The workers, the environmental bureaucracy and possibly the environmentalists will be against grandfathering and in favour of direct regulation. Thus, there is a large probability that grandfathering will be accepted. The advantage of a concentrated interest over a dispersed interest works in favour of the market instrument of grandfathering.

When the market instrument considered is a financial instrument, the outcome of the rent seeking contest depends on the way in which its revenues are distributed. Due to our assumption that market instruments have the highest aggregate valuation, there are distributions of the revenue that will turn everyone into a proponent of the financial instrument. We can also calculate a minimum success probability for the financial instrument. This minimum is reached when all proponents of the financial instrument have the same stake, and there is one proponent of direct regulation, who has received nothing from the financial instrument's revenues.

To give a numerical example, suppose four agents have a stake of 100 in direct regulation, if they do not receive anything from the revenue of the financial instrument. The total revenue from the financial instrument is 450. This revenue can be split among the four agents in a way that they all prefer the financial instrument: give everyone at least 100. Thus, the maximum success probability for the financial instrument is one. The minimum success probability is reached when three agents each receive 150 and the fourth agent receives nothing from the revenues. Then the proponents of the financial instrument all have a stake of 50. Thus, the minimum success probability for the financial instrument is $1/3$.

We can conclude that the advantage of one agent with a large stake against many agents with a small stake works in favour of grandfathering, and thus cannot explain why this market instrument has a low success probability. Financial instruments may be disadvantaged, depending on how their revenues are divided among the agents.

In Chapters 8 and 9 we assume that the distribution of the revenues from the financial instruments is exogenously given. In general, however, revenue distribution will be contested, just like instrument choice itself. In Chapter 10 we will treat the combined contest for instrument choice and revenue distribution.

3.   MORE THAN TWO ALTERNATIVES

3.1   Analysis

The rent seeking contest for an impure public good with more than two alternatives is treated in Linster (1993b), whose notation we shall follow. Like Linster, we shall assume that every agent has his own favourite alternative. We will extend Linster's analysis with a discussion of the uniqueness of equilibria.

In the case of impure public goods, agent i's valuations are represented by a vector $\mathbf{v}_i = (v_{i1}, v_{i2}, ..., v_{in})$, where v_{ij} is the value to agent i if agent j wins the prize.

The agents' expected payoffs can be summarized in matrix form as:

$$
\begin{pmatrix}
v_{11} & v_{12} & \cdots & v_{1n} \\
v_{21} & v_{22} & \cdots & v_{2n} \\
\cdot & \cdot & & \cdot \\
\cdot & \cdot & & \cdot \\
\cdot & \cdot & & \cdot \\
v_{n1} & v_{n2} & \cdots & v_{nn}
\end{pmatrix}
\begin{pmatrix}
x_1/s \\
x_2/s \\
\cdot \\
\cdot \\
\cdot \\
x_n/s
\end{pmatrix}
-
\begin{pmatrix}
x_1 \\
x_2 \\
\cdot \\
\cdot \\
\cdot \\
x_n
\end{pmatrix}
=
\begin{pmatrix}
U_1 \\
U_2 \\
\cdot \\
\cdot \\
\cdot \\
U_n
\end{pmatrix}
$$

or $\mathbf{U}(\mathbf{x}) = \mathbf{V}\mathbf{x}/s - \mathbf{x}$, where $s \equiv \Sigma x_i$.

Maximizing U_1 with respect to x_1, we find:

$$
\frac{\partial U_1(x_1,...,x_n)}{\partial x_1} = \frac{v_{11}s - v_{11}x_1}{s^2} - \frac{v_{12}x_2}{s^2} - \cdots - \frac{v_{1n}x_n}{s^2} - 1 = 0
$$

This can be rewritten as:

$$
\frac{(v_{11}-v_{12})x_2}{s^2} + \cdots + \frac{(v_{11}-v_{1n})x_n}{s^2} = 1
$$

Doing the same for all other agents and summarizing in a matrix, we have:

$$
\begin{pmatrix}
0 & v_{11}-v_{12} & \cdots & v_{11}-v_{1n} \\
v_{22}-v_{21} & 0 & \cdots & v_{22}-v_{2n} \\
\cdot & \cdot & & \cdot \\
\cdot & \cdot & & \cdot \\
\cdot & \cdot & & \cdot \\
v_{nn}-v_{n1} & v_{nn}-v_{n2} & \cdots & 0
\end{pmatrix}
\begin{pmatrix}
x_1/s^2 \\
x_2/s^2 \\
\cdot \\
\cdot \\
\cdot \\
x_n/s^2
\end{pmatrix}
=
\begin{pmatrix}
1 \\
1 \\
\cdot \\
\cdot \\
\cdot \\
1
\end{pmatrix}
$$

or $(\mathbf{J}_{n\times n} - \mathbf{V})\mathbf{x}/s^2 = \mathbf{1}_n$, where $\mathbf{J}_{n\times n}$ is the $n\times n$ matrix which has v_{ii} as every element in the ith row and $\mathbf{1}_n$ is the $n\times1$ column vector of ones. Thus $\mathbf{x}/s^2 = (\mathbf{J}_{n\times n} - \mathbf{V})^{-1}\mathbf{1}_n$, where $s = \mathbf{1}'_n(\mathbf{J}_{n\times n} - \mathbf{V})^{-1}\mathbf{1}_n$.

Now I will extend the analysis by Linster (1993b) with a discussion of the equilibria of this game. Let us define a *private equilibrium* as an equilibrium in which the inactive agents do not want to enter.

What is the connection between the x-vector and the occurrence of a private equilibrium?

1. If all the x_i are positive, then there is a private equilibrium with all n agents active. But this is not necessarily the only private equilibrium.
2. If there are negative x_i, then there is no private equilibrium with all n agents active. There is not necessarily a private equilibrium with the agents j with positive x_j active.

Only for $n = 3$ can we state the general rule that when all x_i are positive, there is a unique three-agent equilibrium, and when one x_i is negative, there is a unique two-agent equilibrium, with agent i inactive. This can be seen as follows.

An alternative way to find an x_i is by Cramer's rule. Since $(\mathbf{J}_{3\times3} - \mathbf{V})\mathbf{x}/s^2 = \mathbf{1}_3$, we have $x_i/s^2 = |(\mathbf{J}_{3\times3} - \mathbf{V}_i)|/|(\mathbf{J}_{3\times3} - \mathbf{V})|$. In this expression, $(\mathbf{J}_{3\times3} - \mathbf{V}_i)$ is $(\mathbf{J}_{3\times3} - \mathbf{V})$ with the ith column replaced by $\mathbf{1}_3$. We are interested in the sign of x_i, which has the same sign as x_i/s^2. The determinant of $(\mathbf{J}_{3\times3} - \mathbf{V})$ is always positive:

$$\begin{vmatrix} 0 & v_{11}-v_{12} & v_{11}-v_{13} \\ v_{22}-v_{21} & 0 & v_{22}-v_{23} \\ v_{33}-v_{31} & v_{33}-v_{32} & 0 \end{vmatrix} =$$

$$= (v_{11}-v_{12})(v_{22}-v_{23})(v_{33}-v_{31}) + (v_{11}-v_{13})(v_{22}-v_{21})(v_{33}-v_{32}) > 0$$

Thus, the sign of x_i is the sign of $|(\mathbf{J}_{3\times3} - \mathbf{V}_i)|$. Consider, without loss of generality, $|(\mathbf{J}_{3\times3} - \mathbf{V}_2)|$:

$$\begin{vmatrix} 0 & 1 & v_{11}-v_{13} \\ v_{22}-v_{21} & 1 & v_{22}-v_{23} \\ v_{33}-v_{31} & 1 & 0 \end{vmatrix} = (v_{22}-v_{23})(v_{33}-v_{31}) + (v_{11}-v_{13})[(v_{22}-v_{21})-(v_{33}-v_{31})] \quad (8.10)$$

Dividing (8.10) by $[(v_{11} - v_{13}) + (v_{33} - v_{31})]$, we have:

$$\left(v_{22} - \frac{v_{21}(v_{11}-v_{13}) + v_{23}(v_{33}-v_{31})}{(v_{11}-v_{13}) +(v_{33}-v_{31})} \right) - \left(\frac{(v_{11}-v_{13})(v_{33}-v_{31})}{(v_{11}-v_{13}) + (v_{33}-v_{31})} \right) \quad (8.11)$$

When only agents 1 and 3 are active, their stakes are $v_1(1,3) \equiv v_{11} - v_{13}$, and $v_3(1,3) \equiv v_{33} - v_{31}$. The stake of the inactive agent 2 then equals $v_2(1,3) \equiv v_{22} - \rho_1(1,3)v_{21}$

$- \rho_3(1,3)v_{23}$. Thus we can rewrite (8.11):

$$\left[v_{22} - \frac{v_1(1,3)v_{21} + v_3(1,3)v_{23}}{v_1(1,3) + v_3(1,3)} \right] - \frac{v_1(1,3)v_3(1,3)}{v_1(1,3) + v_3(1,3)} \equiv$$

$$\equiv v_2(1,3) - \frac{1}{2} \frac{2}{1/v_1(1,3) + 1/v_3(1,3)} \tag{8.11'}$$

This is the familiar difference (see (7.12)) between the inactive agent's stake and $(m-1)/m$ times the harmonic mean of the active agents' stakes, which determines whether the inactive agent will enter.

If (8.11) is negative, then agent 2 is inactive and agents 1 and 3 are active in the equilibrium. In our application in section 3.2, we will further analyse (8.11). There we will see that when there is a two-agent equilibrium, the alternative with the highest aggregate valuation may not be promoted.

If (8.11) is positive, then agent 2 is active in the equilibrium. Then we still have to check the expressions analogous to (8.11) for the agents 1 and 3, to find out whether they will be active in the equilibrium.

For $n > 3$, things are not so clear cut, as is illustrated by some numerical examples in the Appendix. In general, for $2 < m < n$, one must check whether there is a private equilibrium with m agents active, in the following way:

1. The agents i supposedly active in the private equilibrium should have $x_i > 0$.
2. The agents j supposedly inactive in the private equilibrium should have $v_{jj} - \Sigma \rho_i v_{ji} \leq \Sigma x_i$, $i = 1, ..., n$.

3.2 Application

In this section we apply the analysis of section 3.1 to a rent seeking contest with three agents and three instruments. We will not apply the analysis to more than three instruments, because there may be multiple equilibria in this case, and we do not know which equilibrium will be played. Moreover, since we only consider four interest groups and five instruments in total, an example with four interest groups, each with its own favourite alternative, would seem quite artificial and far-fetched.

Anyway, the three-alternative, three-agent case allows us to demonstrate the most important finding from section 3.1 for our purposes. This is that the alternative with the highest aggregate valuation can have a low, and even zero, success probability. Thus, with this model we can give an affirmative answer to our central question: 'Is it possible that the market instrument is not selected, although it is the instrument with the highest aggregate valuation?'

The key expression from section 3.1 is (8.11'):

$$\left[v_{22} - \frac{v_1(1,3)v_{21} + v_3(1,3)v_{23}}{v_1(1,3) + v_3(1,3)} \right] - \frac{v_1(1,3)v_3(1,3)}{v_1(1,3) + v_3(1,3)} =$$

$$\equiv v_2(1,3) - \frac{1}{2} \frac{2}{1/v_1(1,3) + 1/v_3(1,3)} \qquad (8.11')$$

In this expression, v_{ij} is agent i's valuation of agent j's favourite alternative, and $v_i(1,3)$ is agent i's stake in a contest between agents 1 and 3.

If (8.11') is positive, then agent 2's stake in his own alternative is so large that he will enter the contest between agents 1 and 3. Then agent 2 will be active in the equilibrium. If (8.11') is negative, agent 2's stake in his own alternative is so low, that he will keep out of a contest between agents 1 and 3. Then there is a two-agent equilibrium, with agents 1 and 3 active.

It is possible for expression (8.11') to be negative, while at the same time, agent 2's favourite alternative has the highest aggregate valuation:

$$\sum v_{i2} > \sum v_{i1} \qquad\qquad \sum v_{i2} > \sum v_{i3} \qquad\qquad i = 1,2,3$$

To understand how this can happen, I develop an example by Linster (1993b). Then I will give the general rule. Finally, the rule is applied to instrument choice.

Linster (1993b) gives an example with a relatively low success probability for the alternative with the highest aggregate valuation. With a slight modification, we can reduce this probability to zero. Linster discusses the political decision about the location of a street light in a street. It will be placed in front of a resident's house. There are three residents: one on the left, one on the right and one in the middle. A resident's utility from the street light is:

- 1 if it is in front of his own house;
- $\gamma < 1$ if it is in front of his neighbour's house;
- $\gamma^2 < \gamma$ if it is two houses away.

From Table 8.1 we see that placing the street light in the middle yields the highest aggregate payoff, namely $1+2\gamma$. Placing the street light on either side yields an aggregate utility of $1+\gamma+\gamma^2$.

Table 8.1 is also the V-matrix, introduced in section 3.1. The reader can go through the calculations laid out in this section, or follow Linster's calculation to find that the left and right resident both spend $2(1-\gamma)/(3-\gamma)^2$, and the middle resident spends $2(1-\gamma)^2/(3-\gamma)^2$. Thus, the middle resident spends a fraction $1-\gamma$ < 1 of what the right (and the left) resident spends. This implies that the probability that the alternative with the highest aggregate utility (street light in the middle) is chosen is less than one third. In fact, it is:

Table 8.1   Residents' valuations of the street light

	Light left	Light middle	Light right
Left resident	1	γ	γ^2
Middle resident	γ	1	γ
Right resident	γ^2	γ	1

$$p_2 = \frac{1-\gamma}{3-\gamma} < \frac{1}{3}$$

Intuitively, the left (right) resident spends a lot, because he is afraid the street light might be placed at the right (left). The stakes of the left and right resident are higher than the stake of the middle resident, who knows that the street light will be close to him anyway. Therefore he spends less than his left and right neighbour. The consequence is that the probability of the light being placed in the middle is lowest, although this position yields the highest aggregate payoff.

We can adapt the valuations in the above example, so that the middle resident will not make an effort at all. To this end we adapt a resident's valuation of the street light that is two houses away. Originally, this valuation was γ^2. We will now make this valuation, which we call u, variable. If the middle resident is inactive, the stake of the right and the left resident is $1-u$: the difference between having the street light in front of their own house and having it two houses away. We know from (7.8) that the sum of their expenditures will be $\frac{1}{2}(1-u)$. We know from (7.4') that the middle resident will be inactive when his stake does not exceed this spending level. The middle resident's stake is the difference between having the street light in front of his own house and having it in front of his neighbour's house, or $1-\gamma$. Thus, when $1-\gamma \leq \frac{1}{2}(1-u)$, or $u \leq 2\gamma-1$, the middle resident will be inactive. The adaptation of the original V-matrix (Table 8.1) with the highest possible value of u for which the middle resident is inactive, is shown in Table 8.2.

Placing the street light in the middle yields an aggregate utility of $1+2\gamma$, while placing it on either side yields an aggregate utility of 3γ. Since $\gamma < 1$, placing the street light in the middle still maximizes aggregate utility.

Stranger yet: in Table 8.1, the valuation of the street light two houses away was γ^2. In that case, the middle resident was active, so that there was still a chance that the street light would be placed in the middle. In Table 8.2 we reduced the valuation of the street light two houses away to $2\gamma-1 < \gamma^2$. Thus, the aggregate valuation of the street light on either side declines, but the probability that the

Table 8.2   Residents' valuations of the street light, middle resident inactive

	Light left	Light middle	Light right
Left resident	1	γ	2γ−1
Middle resident	γ	1	γ
Right resident	2γ−1	γ	1

street light will be placed on either side rises to one. The aggregate valuation of the street light in the middle remains the same, but the probability that the street light will be placed in the middle declines to zero. This is because the right (left) resident becomes more 'aggressive' when his valuation of the street light on the left (right) declines.

Before we turn from this example to instrument choice, we present the general rule stating when the alternative with the highest aggregate valuation will not be promoted. The general rule is this: suppose there are three agents involved, labelled 1, 2 and 3, each with his own favourite alternative, labelled 1, 2 and 3 respectively. Let alternative 2 have the highest aggregate valuation.

Now suppose agent 1 dislikes alternative 3 very much and vice versa. Agent 2, on the other hand, does not have a strong preference for alternative 2 above alternatives 1 and 3. Then agent 2 will be inactive, so that the alternative with the highest aggregate valuation will not be promoted.

Now we turn to instrument choice. Suppose the choice is between the two instruments of direct regulation (standards and bubbles) and one market instrument (grandfathering or a financial instrument). Is it possible that the market instrument will not be promoted?

Again, there is a difference between grandfathering and a financial instrument. Grandfathering has one strong proponent (the shareholders), who will certainly be active. With a financial instrument, there are revenue divisions with which the proponent of auctions or an emissions charge will remain inactive.

We will consider a numerical example, given in Table 8.3, with three interest groups and three instruments (the 3x3 case). The preference orderings of each group are based on our theoretical discussion in Chapters 3 and 4, summarized in Chapter 4, section 6, and Table 4.4.

Table 8.3 presents the interest groups' valuations of an auction when they do not receive anything from the government revenue. This revenue, which will be divided among the three interest groups, is also given in the table.

This numerical example illustrates that in the 3x3 case, there is not necessarily a division of government revenue that will make the auction the number one

Table 8.3 Interest group valuations of instruments

	Bubbles	Standards	Auction
Shareholders	100	30	0
Workers	30	100	0
Environmentalists	10	0	20
Revenue	0	0	150

alternative for all interest groups, even though the auction has the largest aggregate payoff. The shareholders need a revenue of 100 from the auction in order to prefer the auction to bubbles. The workers also need a revenue of 100 to prefer the auction to standards. But the revenue from the auction is only 150.

Which instruments will be promoted in the equilibrium depends upon the distribution of government revenue. Figure 8.1 gives the equilibria. On the horizontal axis is the revenue that goes to the shareholders. On the vertical axis is the revenue that goes to the workers. The revenue that is left from the total of 150 goes to the environmentalists.

The equilibria are identified by a three letter combination, giving the instrument promoted by the shareholders, workers and environmentalists, respectively. The letter 'O' means that the interest group will remain inactive. For example: BAO means that the shareholders will promote bubbles, the workers will promote an auction and the environmentalists will remain inactive. The areas where the equilibria apply, are separated from each other by thick lines.

In the equilibrium BSO, the auction will not be promoted. In Figure 8.1, this equilibrium is the white area at the middle of the outer diagonal. When the environmentalists receive a small part of the revenue (less than 20), and the rest is divided relatively equally among shareholders and workers (neither receives more than 100), the auction is not promoted.

When either the shareholders or the workers receive more than 100, this interest group will promote the auction. When the environmentalists receive more than 20 (and neither the shareholders nor the workers receive more than 100), they will promote the auction.

In the dotted area of Figure 8.1, the auction is promoted, but its success probability is below one half. In the cross-hatched areas, the success probability of the auction exceeds one half. Note that these areas are located at the corners of the triangle: one interest group receives a lot of the revenue. This interest group will then be a fervent advocate of the auction. The success probability of the

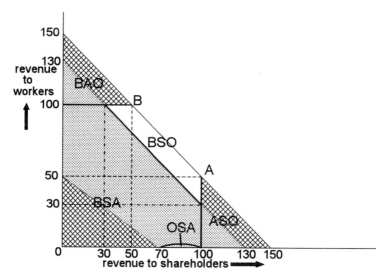

Figure 8.1 Equilibria for different revenue distrubutions

auction is highest at 0.58 in ASO at point A and in BAO at point B.

Thus we see that when there are three agents, each with its own favourite instrument, the market instrument may not be promoted at all. This result is especially likely to obtain for financial instruments, when their revenue is divided fairly evenly across the interest groups.

4.   CONCLUSION

In this chapter, we have analysed noncooperative behaviour in a rent seeking contest for an impure public good. Instrument choice in environmental policy can be seen as a rent seeking contest for an impure public good, because interest groups have certain preferences in common. For instance: workers and the environmental bureaucracy both prefer bubbles to grandfathering.

In section 2 we analysed the two-alternative case, where one group of agents (the A-side) prefers policy alternative A, and the other group (the B-side) prefers alternative B. We have seen that only the agent with the highest stake on either side will be active. Applying this to instrument choice in environmental policy, a market instrument can have a low success probability in a contest against an instrument of direct regulation. This will happen when there are many agents with a small stake in the market instrument, and there is one agent with a large stake in direct regulation. But how likely is this scenario? With grandfathering, things will probably work the other way around, because there is one group with a large stake in grandfathering: the shareholders. The scenario applies to financial instruments, when the revenues are distributed such that there will be many agents with a small stake in the financial instrument, and one agent with a large stake in direct regulation.

In this context, the question of what one sees as one interest group is also important. For instance, when the shareholders from different industries, or different firms, cannot be seen as one interest group, there will be several groups instead of one group in favour of grandfathering. Then the success probability of grandfathering will be lower.

In section 3 we studied the contest with more than two alternatives, where every agent has his own favourite alternative. We have seen that it is possible that the alternative with the highest aggregate valuation (the market instrument, in our application) is not promoted at all. In the three-alternative case, with a market instrument, firm bubbles and standards, this will happen when the proponent of bubbles is very much against standards, the proponent of standards is very much against bubbles, and the proponent of the market instrument not very much against standards or bubbles.

When we think about the likelihood of this scenario, we come to the same conclusion as for the two-alternative case. It is unlikely to apply to grandfathering, because shareholders are a strong proponent of grandfathering. But it can apply to financial instruments, with certain distributions of the revenue. When the revenue of the financial instrument is distributed fairly evenly among the three agents involved, the financial instrument will not be promoted in a contest with firm bubbles and standards.

APPENDIX. NONCOOPERATIVE EQUILIBRIA WITH MORE THAN THREE ALTERNATIVES

1. Multiple equilibria with all $x_i(n) > 0$

When

$$
V = \begin{pmatrix}
1 & 0 & 0.7 & 0.6 \\
0 & 1 & 0.4 & 0.5 \\
0.6 & 0.5 & 1 & 0 \\
0.7 & 0.8 & 0 & 1
\end{pmatrix}
$$

there is a four-agent equilibrium. But there is also an equilibrium with agents 2, 3 and 4 active and an equilibrium with agents 1 and 2 active.

2. $x_i(n) > 0$ for $m < n$ agents, but no equilibrium with these m agents active

a. When

$$V = \begin{pmatrix} 1 & 0.8 & 0 & 0.5 \\ 0.7 & 1 & 0.6 & 0 \\ 0 & 0.6 & 1 & 0.4 \\ 0.3 & 0.9 & 0.8 & 1 \end{pmatrix}$$

we have $x_1(n)$, $x_3(n)$, $x_4(n) > 0$ and $x_2(n) < 0$. But $x_4(1,3,4) < 0$.

b. When

$$V = \begin{pmatrix} 1 & 0 & 0.7 & 0.6 \\ 0 & 1 & 0.5 & 0.4 \\ 0.4 & 0.6 & 1 & 0 \\ 0.1 & 0.7 & 0 & 1 \end{pmatrix}$$

we have $x_1(n)$, $x_2(n) < 0$ and $x_3(n)$, $x_4(n) > 0$. But $x_2(3,4) > 0$.

NOTES

1. In the following, we will denote this by direct regulation, for short.
2. Remember that, by (7.9), the success probabilities in the Nash equilibrium are proportional to the agents' stakes.
3. Hillman himself seems to miss this point, judging from his own comment on the example just quoted (1989: 71): 'Notice that free-rider type disincentive problems generally associated with collective action are absent in this argument. No public-good attributes of collective action have been introduced.'

9. Cooperative Rent Seeking

1.   INTRODUCTION

As we saw in the introduction to Chapter 8, instrument choice in environmental policy can be seen as a rent seeking contest for an impure public good. In Chapter 8 we studied noncooperative behaviour in such a contest. In this chapter we will look at cooperation. We analyse the attempts to influence the political choice between two alternatives, A and B. There are n agents that prefer alternative A, $i = 1, ..., n$, with stakes $v_{1,A} > v_{2,A} > ... > v_{n,A} > 0$. There are m agents that prefer alternative B, $j = 1, ..., m$, with stakes $v_{1,B} > v_{2,B} > ... > v_{m,B} > 0$. Unlike in the two-alternative case of Chapter 8, section 2.1, we do not allow for two agents' stakes at the same side to be of the same value. Allowing this would be straightforward analytically, but add to the complexity and confusion in the exposition.

For the specification of the success probability, we use the function discussed in Chapter 8, section 2.1. The probability that alternative A will be chosen is:

$$\rho_A = \frac{\displaystyle\sum_{i=1}^{n} x_{i,A}}{\displaystyle\sum_{i=1}^{n} x_{i,A} + \sum_{j=1}^{m} x_{j,B}} \tag{8.1}$$

The noncooperative equilibrium for this case was already discussed in Chapter 8: only the agents with the largest stake on either side (the agents 1) will be active. When the agents on a side behave noncooperatively, they immediately plunge into the rent seeking contest. But perhaps it is better to get together first, to try and work out some sort of arrangement, and then to play the contest against the other side. With 'better' I mean that this alternative approach would yield a higher aggregate payoff for the side as a whole. The actions undertaken in the stage prior to the contest itself can be called 'cooperation', because their aim is to increase the side's aggregate payoff above the payoff in the noncooperative equilibrium.

In this chapter, we will analyse a specific form of cooperation, namely support. With support, an inactive agent pays part of the active agent's effort. This form of cooperation has not been analysed before in the rent seeking literature. We will model the rent seeking game as a five-stage game:

1. The A-side determines who will be the active agent, in order to maximize its aggregate payoff given the identity of the active agent on the B-side. If necessary to reach an agreement on the choice of the active agent, lump sum transfers are agreed upon.

   We will see that when one of the agents $2,...,n$ is designated as the active agent, other agents will support him. When agent 1 is designated as the active agent, no one will support him.[1] Thus, when a side designates agent 1 as the active agent, it chooses to play the noncooperative equilibrium (discussed in Chapter 8, section 2.1).

2. Each agent determines his support rate, i.e. the fraction of the active agent's effort he will pay, in order to maximize his own payoff, given:

   – the support from the other agents on the A-side;
   – the support from the inactive agents on the B-side;
   – the own stake of the active agent on either side.

3. The active agent makes his effort to maximize his own payoff, given:

   – the support from the other agents on the A-side;
   – the effort from the active agent on the B-side.

4. The inactive agents pay the support they promised to the active agent.

5. The political decision is made.

We will derive the subgame perfect equilibrium of this game. This means that in any stage, an agent will always play the equilibrium strategy of that stage, whether or not the events in previous stages are part of an equilibrium path. We solve the game by backwards induction. The analysis of the fourth and the fifth stage can be brief, because the rent-seeking agents do not need to make any decisions in these stages. In the fifth stage, the political decision is a function (8.1) of the active agents' efforts, made in stage three. In the fourth stage, all inactive agents pay the support they promised to the active agent. The transfers are the product of the support rate (determined in the second stage) and the effort level (determined in the third stage). We simply assume that the inactive agents will pay what they promised to pay, because an enforcement mechanism is present in society.

After a review of the literature in section 2, we will analyse the second and the third stage of the game in section 3. In section 4, we discuss the first stage. In section 5 we present the equilibrium paths for the whole game. The model is applied to instrument choice in environmental policy in section 6. We will see that the answer to our central question: 'Can the model explain why the alternative with the highest aggregate valuation has a low or even zero success probability?' is affirmative. Section 7 concludes the chapter.

2. REVIEW OF THE LITERATURE

2.1 Introduction

Although the concept of support is new to the rent seeking literature, other forms of cooperation have been analysed. In this section, we will review the literature on cooperation in rent seeking contests and compare these to our game of support. The cooperation schemes of sharing, rewards and matching will be discussed in a following order that is roughly ascending in similarity of the schemes to support, in sections 2.2, 2.3 and 2.4 respectively.

The structure of the rent seeking game with cooperation is the same for the schemes discussed here and the support scheme. In the first stage (or stages), agreements are made between the agents with a common interest. These agreements change the incentives of the agents in the rent seeking contest. Thus, when the rent seeking contest is played in the second (or later) stage, the equilibrium will differ from the noncooperative equilibrium that would be played without prior agreements.

The overview is summarized in Table 9.1, where we compare the schemes to each other and to the game of support on the following four points:

- whether and how an active agent is designated;
- who receives the payments implied in the cooperation scheme;
- how the nature of the payment changes the incentives of the agent(s) involved in the contest;
- how it is decided by how much to reward or support the active agent.

2.2 Sharing

Cooperation in rent seeking contests for public goods has mainly been studied starting from the assumption that the prize is a private good. The rent-seeking agents cooperate by forming groups. The efforts of the group members are summed to obtain the group effort. Thus, one can say that cooperation changes the nature of the prize from a private to a public good. Without cooperation, agent i's effort to obtain the prize contributes to the probability that agent i wins. Agent i's efforts only benefit agent i himself. With cooperation, agent i's effort contributes to the probability that the group containing agent i wins. The whole group benefits from agent i's efforts.

Cooperation in a rent seeking contest for a private good implies that there must

Table 9.1   Comparison of cooperation and delegation schemes

Scheme	Designation of active agent	Destination of payment	Payment made when/rising in	Determination of payment rate
Loehman et al. (1996)	None	Other agents	Other agents' efforts	Cooperative
Baik and Kim (1997)	Non-cooperative	Active agent	Active agent wins	Exogenous
Konrad (1997)	Exogenous	Active agent	Active agent wins	Cooperative
Guttman (1987)	None	Extra effort	Other agents' efforts	Noncooperative
Support	Cooperative	Active agent	Active agent's effort	Noncooperative

be a sharing rule determining the division of the prize if the group wins. Nitzan (1991a,b) proposes a division partly based on relative effort and partly egalitarian. Lee (1995) endogenizes the specification of this sharing rule: which part of the prize should be divided equally and which part according to relative effort, in order to maximize the group's aggregate payoff. In these three articles, membership of a sharing group is exogenously given. In other contributions (Baik, 1994b; Baik and Shogren, 1995; Baik and Lee, 1997), the agent's decision to join a sharing group is endogenized. Baik (1994b) and Baik and Shogren (1995) assume there will only be one sharing group, with nonmembers acting on their own. Baik and Lee (1997) assume the agent's choice is between two competing groups.

The subject we study in this chapter is a contest for a 'natural' public good: the prize is a public good whether or not the agents cooperate. Inactive agents benefit from the efforts of active agents. For instance, suppose shareholders and environmentalists prefer grandfathering to standards. Workers, on the other hand, prefer standards to grandfathering. When shareholders and workers are active against each other in a contest between grandfathering and standards, the environmentalists benefit from the shareholders' efforts. The environmentalists do not have to cooperate with the shareholders to enjoy this benefit.

Thus, when the prize of the contest is a public good by nature, a sharing rule to determine the division of the prize in case the group wins, is not necessary. There is a 'natural' division of the prize, where every agent i receives his own v_i. However, a side may still employ a sharing rule to increase its aggregate payoff relative to the noncooperative outcome. Another implication of the difference between a contest for a private and a public good is that in the private good case, the agents can choose which group they want to join. In a contest for a public good, the choice between groups is restricted. An interest group whose least favourite instrument is the emissions charge, will not join the group that promotes the emissions charge.

Loehman et al. (1996) adapt the sharing rule for a contest for a 'natural' public good: when a group wins, the agents in the group are rewarded or penalized according to their relative effort. Loehman et al. conduct experiments with this rule in a perfectly discriminating rent seeking contest, but they do not analyse the solution of the game.

We have chosen to analyse support instead of sharing in the adaptation of Loehman et al., because we believe it is more appropriate for a rent seeking contest for an impure public good, for the following two reasons. First, sharing relies more on cooperative behaviour than does support. With sharing, the extent to which deviations from the average effort level are rewarded and penalized is determined cooperatively. With support, every agent determines the support rate that maximizes his own payoff. Secondly, the structure of transfers between agents is more intricate for sharing. As a first step, every group member's effort level must be ascertained. Then it is clear how much each agent should pay or receive. But when there is more than one agent that has to pay, and more than one agent that should receive, then coordination of transfers is necessary. With support, however, only the active agent's effort needs to be observed. Then coordination of transfers is not necessary, because all payments are made to the active agent.

2.3 Rewards

Another method to change the incentives of the active agent is by offering him a reward (also called contingent fee or subsidy), i.e. a payment to the active agent that is only made when he wins the contest (Baik and Kim, 1997; Konrad, 1997). Baik and Kim (1997) analyse a rent seeking contest between two players, where each player can hire a delegate to play the contest for him. There are several delegates, each with a different ability for the contest.[2] The compensation for the delegate consists of two parts. The delegate always receives her fixed fee, which is rising in her ability. When the delegate wins, she also receives her contingent fee, which is a fixed fraction of her client's stake.

There are a number of differences between Baik and Kim's (1997) analysis and ours. First of all, Baik and Kim (1997) analyse a rent seeking contest for a private good, in which only the two players have a stake of their own in the outcome. The delegates do not have a stake of their own in the outcome of the contest. By contrast, we analyse a rent seeking contest for a public good, in which more than one agent has a preference for the same outcome. The delegate (in Baik and Kim's (1997) terms) or active agent (in our terms) also has a stake of his own in the outcome. Furthermore, in Baik and Kim's (1997) analysis, the delegates differ in their ability. In our analysis, all agents have the same ability.

Baik and Kim's (1997) and our analysis also differ in the way the transfer to the active agent is determined. With Baik and Kim (1997), the contingent fee is a fixed fraction of the client's stake. We let the client (or inactive agent) determine the size of the support rate himself.

Baik and Kim (1997) also assume the active agent receives a fixed fee. We do not analyse this fixed fee (or lump sum payment), although a fixed fee may be necessary for an agent to accept the role of the active agent. However, we assume an agent will accept the role of the active agent, when this is in the best interest of the side as a whole.

Konrad (1997) analyses the contest between two firms in different countries for a contract in a third country. First the respective governments decide by how much to subsidize or tax 'their' firm's profits from the contract. Then the firms play the contest against each other.

There are a number of differences between Konrad's (1997) and our analysis. First, Konrad (1997) analyses a perfectly discriminating contest, whereas we analyse an imperfectly discriminating contest. Secondly, in Konrad's (1997) analysis the identity of the active agent is exogenously given: the firms are active and the governments are inactive in the contest. By contrast, in our analysis the identity of the active agent is endogenously determined. The third difference is that Konrad (1997) allows the inactive agent to choose between subsidizing or taxing the active agent. In our analysis, the inactive agent can only subsidize the active agent.

With respect to the degree of cooperation, our game of support can be placed between Baik and Kim's (1997) and Konrad's (1997) games. In Baik and Kim's (1997) game, the client determines by himself, i.e. noncooperatively, whether or not to hire a delegate. In Konrad's (1997) game, the government sets the cooperative reward rate, i.e. the rate that maximizes the aggregate payoff of government and firm. In our game, each agent sets the support rate that maximizes his own payoff, given the identity of the active agent. Thus, the support rates are determined noncooperatively. However, the designation of the active agent is a cooperative decision: the agent with whom the highest aggregate payoff can be achieved is designated as the active agent.

2.4   Matching

The last cooperation scheme we review here is the matching mechanism (Guttman, 1987, 1991). Unlike sharing and rewards, matching has not been applied to a rent seeking contest yet, but only to the broader category of voluntary contributions to a public good. We will present the matching mechanism here in the context of a contest for an impure public good. The agents on a side play a two-stage game. In the first stage, they announce their matching rates. In the second stage, they make their rent seeking efforts. These consist of two components: the flat effort and the matching effort. The matching effort is the product of the matching rate and the sum of other agents' flat efforts.

The similarity between matching and support is that a payment is being made, that is increasing in the active agent's effort. The difference is that with support, the payment goes to the active agent. With matching, the payment consists of a rent seeking effort which is made irrespective of who made the flat effort. As a result, there is no need to designate an active agent with matching.

3. EFFORT LEVEL AND SUPPORT RATE ON THE A-SIDE

3.1 Introduction

In this section we analyse the second and the third stage of the five-stage game of cooperation, presented in section 1. We start our analysis in the third stage, where the active agent makes his effort. After we have solved for this stage, we move on to the second stage, where the inactive agents determine the support they offer to the active agent.

In section 3.2, we assume that in equilibrium there is partial support: aggregate support is below 100%. At the end of the section we will see under which condition this will actually be the case. In section 3.3 we discuss full support: aggregate support at or beyond 100%.

3.2 Partial Support

In this section, we discuss the determination of the effort level (stage 3) and the support rates (stage 2) on the A-side, under the assumption that aggregate support will be below 100% on both sides. The condition under which this will be the case will be derived later in this section.

When agent f on the A-side supports agent g on the A-side with support rate $s_{f,A}$, this means that agent f promises to pay a fraction $s_{f,A}$ of agent g's effort in the rent seeking contest. We begin our analysis in the third stage. We can derive the following proposition:

Proposition 9.1 Agent g on the A-side, with stake $v_{g,A}$, who has been promised an aggregate support rate of $\Sigma s_{f,A} < 1$ from $N < n$ agents, $f = 1, ..., N$, acts as if he had *induced* or *enlarged* stake:

$$T_{gA} \equiv \frac{v_{gA}}{1 - \sum_{f=1}^{N} s_{fA}} \tag{9.1}$$

Proof   Agent g's maximization problem is:

$$\max_{x_{gA}} \frac{x_{gA}}{x_{gA} + x_B} v_{gA} - x_{gA} + x_{gA} \sum_{f=1}^{N} s_{fA} \tag{9.2}$$

Agent g determines the effort level x_{gA} that maximizes his payoff, given the aggregate support Σs_{fA} from the agents $f = 1, .., N$, and given the effort x_B by the active agent on the B-side. The first order condition is:

$$\frac{x_B}{(x_{gA} + x_B)^2} v_{gA} = 1 - \sum_{f=1}^{N} s_{fA} \tag{9.3}$$

Comparing this with (7.6), the first order condition in the two-agent rent seeking contest, we can say that agent g acts as if he had induced stake or enlarged stake $v_{gA}/(1 - \Sigma s_{fA}) > v_{gA}$.   ∎

Proposition 9.1 means that we can always say that the active agent g on the A-side acts as if he had stake T_{gA} or T_A, where T_A is given by (9.1). Of course, what goes for the A-side, goes for the B-side just as well. This means that we can analyse the third stage, i.e. the actual rent seeking contest, as a contest between two agents with stakes $T_{gA} = v_{gA}/(1 - \Sigma s_{fA})$ and T_B, although we do not know at this point how T_B is determined. In Chapter 7, section 3.5.2, we already discussed the Nash equilibrium of a rent seeking contest between two agents with stakes v_1 and v_2. Thus, we can simply replace v_1 and v_2 by T_{gA} and T_B in (7.8) and (7.9) to obtain the equilibrium expressions for agent g's effort level x_{gA} and his success probability ρ_A, respectively:

$$x_{gA} = \frac{\left(v_{gA}/\left(1 - \sum_{f=1}^{N} s_{fA}\right)\right)^2 T_B}{\left(v_{gA}/\left(1 - \sum_{f=1}^{N} s_{fA}\right) + T_B\right)^2} = \frac{T_B v_{gA}^2}{\left(T_B\left(1 - \sum_{f=1}^{N} s_{fA}\right) + v_{gA}\right)^2} \tag{9.4}$$

$$\rho_A = \frac{v_{gA}/\left(1 - \sum_{f=1}^{N} s_{fA}\right)}{v_{gA}/\left(1 - \sum_{f=1}^{N} s_{fA}\right) + T_B} = \frac{v_{gA}}{T_B\left(1 - \sum_{f=1}^{N} s_{fA}\right) + v_{gA}} \tag{9.5}$$

Given the stake of the active agent on the other side T_B, agent g's effort, and consequently his success probability, is higher when he is supported than when he is not.

Now we turn to stage two, where each inactive agent f determines his support rate s_{fA}. Thus, in stage two, the stake of the active agent T_{gA} (given by (9.1)) is determined as a result of the decentralized decisions taken by each agent f individually.

The expected payoff of an agent f, who considers supporting agent g, is:

$$U_{fA} = \rho_A v_{fA} - s_{fA} x_{gA} \tag{9.6}$$

Agent f sets the support rate s_{fA} that maximizes his payoff, taking as given the identity of the active agent on the A-side (agent g), the support by other agents (Σs_{kA}), and the stake of the active agent on the other side (T_B). Substituting (9.4) and (9.5) into (9.6), his maximization problem is:

$$\max_{s_{fA}} U_{fA} = \frac{v_{gA}}{T_B\left(1 - \sum_{\substack{k=1 \\ k \neq f}}^{N} s_{kA} - s_{fA}\right) + v_{gA}} v_{fA} - \frac{s_{fA} v_{gA}^2 T_B}{\left(T_B\left(1 - \sum_{\substack{k=1 \\ k \neq f}}^{N} s_{kA} - s_{fA}\right) + v_{gA}\right)^2}$$

The first order condition is:

$$(v_{fA} - v_{gA})\left(T_B(1 - \sum_{f=1}^{N} s_{fA}) + v_{gA}\right) = 2T_B v_{gA} s_{fA} \tag{9.7}$$

When agent f increases the support rate he promises to agent g, there are three effects on agent f's payoff. Ranked from direct to indirect, these effects are:

1. Given agent g's effort level, agent f has to pay more to agent g.
2. Agent g increases his effort level, so that agent f has to pay even more.
3. The success probability of the A-side rises, so that agent f's expected payoff rises.

The left hand side of (9.7) can be interpreted as the difference between the third and the first effect. The right hand side of (9.7) is size of the second effect.

When agent f supports agent g, $s_{fA} > 0$, and the right hand side of (9.7) is positive. On the left hand side of (9.7), the term $(1 - \Sigma s_{fA})$ is positive, because we assume in this section that $\Sigma s_{fA} < 1$. The condition for the left hand side of (9.7) to be positive is then $v_{fA} > v_{gA}$. Thus, all agents f with $v_{fA} > v_{gA}$, and only the agents f with $v_{fA} > v_{gA}$ support agent g. In other words, the agents $f = 1, ..., g-1$ support agent g. We first said there would be N agents supporting agent g, without knowing the value of N. But now we know how many agents and which agents will support agent g. We found that $N = g - 1$. The intuition is, that from the point of view of an agent f with a higher stake than the active agent g, the active agent does not make a high enough effort. Thus, agent f is willing to pay for part of agent g's effort to get agent g to make a higher effort. On the other hand, from the point of view of an agent with a stake below v_{gA}, agent g is already spending quite enough. Such an agent does not have an incentive to support agent g.

To derive the aggregate support Σs_{fA}, we sum (9.7) over $f = 1, ..., g-1$:

$$\left(\sum_{f=1}^{g-1} v_{fA} - (g-1)v_{gA}\right)\left(T_B(1 - \sum_{f=1}^{g-1} s_{fA}) + v_{gA}\right) = 2T_B v_{gA} \sum_{f=1}^{g-1} s_{fA}$$

Then we can find the expression for Σs_{fA}:

$$\sum_{f=1}^{g-1} s_{fA} = \frac{(T_B + v_{gA})\left(\sum_{f=1}^{g-1} v_{fA} + (1-g)v_{gA}\right)}{T_B\left(\sum_{f=1}^{g-1} v_{fA} + (3 - g)v_{gA}\right)} \tag{9.8}$$

For the rest of the analysis, it is also useful to derive the expression for $1 - \Sigma s_{fA}$:

$$1 - \sum_{f=1}^{g-1} s_{fA} = \frac{v_{gA}\left(2T_B + (g-1)v_{gA} - \sum_{f=1}^{g-1} v_{fA}\right)}{T_B\left(\sum_{f=1}^{g-1} v_{fA} + (3-g)v_{gA}\right)} \tag{9.8'}$$

Substituting (9.8') into (9.7), we solve for s_{fA}, the support by an individual agent f:

$$s_{fA} = \frac{(v_{fA} - v_{gA})(T_B + v_{gA})}{T_B\left(\sum_{f=1}^{g-1} v_{fA} + (3-g)v_{gA}\right)} \tag{9.9}$$

From (9.8') we can derive the condition under which $\Sigma s_{fA} < 1$ in equilibrium, where $f = 1, ..., g-1$:

$$\sum_{f=1}^{g-1} v_{fA} - (g-1)v_{gA} < 2T_B \tag{9.10a}$$

For future analysis, it is also important to know how Σs_{fA} depends on T_B.

Lemma 9.1 Aggregate support on the A-side $\Sigma s_{f,A}$, and thus the enlarged stake of the active agent $T_{g,A}$, is declining in the stake of the active agent on the B-side T_B.

Proof Let us define:

$$K \equiv \frac{\sum\limits_{f=1}^{g-1} v_{f,A} + (1-g)v_{g,A}}{\sum\limits_{f=1}^{g-1} v_{f,A} + (3-g)v_{g,A}} > 0$$

Then (9.8) becomes:

$$\sum\limits_{f=1}^{g-1} s_{f,A} = \left(1 + \frac{v_{g,A}}{T_B} \right) K$$

Differentiating this with respect to T_B, we find:

$$\frac{\partial \sum\limits_{f=1}^{g-1} s_{f,A}}{\partial T_B} = -\frac{v_{g,A}K}{T_B^2} < 0$$

∎

3.3 Full Support

When (9.10a) is not satisfied, i.e when

$$\sum\limits_{f=1}^{g-1} v_{f,A} + (1-g)v_{g,A} \geq 2T_B \qquad (9.10')$$

aggregate support on the A-side cannot be below 100% in equilibrium. In that case, there will always be at least one agent f with $v_{f,A} > v_{g,A}$ whose payoff is rising monotonically in $s_{f,A} \in [0, 1 - \Sigma s_{k,A})$, where $\Sigma s_{k,A}$ is the aggregate support to agent g from the other agents on the A-side. Agent f's first order condition (9.7) cannot be satisfied for $s_{f,A} < 1 - \Sigma s_{k,A}$. Instead, we have:

$$v_{f,A} - v_{g,A} > 2T_B s_{f,A} \qquad \text{for } s_{f,A} + \sum\limits_{\substack{k=1 \\ k \neq f}}^{g-1} s_{k,A} < 1 \qquad (9.7')$$

Thus, it seems like agent f would like to set aggregate support at or perhaps even beyond 100%.

However, we cannot simply allow $\Sigma s_{f,A} \geq 1$. This becomes clear when we look at the behaviour of the active agent g who has been promised $\Sigma s_{f,A} \geq 1$. In the third stage of the game, the active agent sets the effort level $x_{g,A}$ that maximizes his payoff, given the value of x_B. But when x_B is positive, agent g's payoff is rising monotonically in $x_{g,A}$. The more agent g spends, the higher is his success probability. But agent g does not have to pay for his own effort. When $\Sigma s_{f,A} = 1$, the other agents pay for all of his efforts. When $\Sigma s_{f,A} > 1$, agent g even receives a bonus that is increasing in his effort level. Thus, there is no upper limit to what agent g wants to spend when x_B is positive. Of course, the supporting agents are neither willing nor able to pay agent g an infinite amount of money. The active agent on the B-side takes this into account, and thus the promise by the agents f on the A-side to support their active agent g by 100% or more is not credible.

We offer the following solution to this problem. Setting $\Sigma s_{f,A} \geq 1$ is allowed, but the supporting agents will only pay the active agent if his effort level equals a certain prespecified amount $X_{g,A}$. If the active agent sets a higher or a lower effort level, he has to pay everything himself. We set the effort level at which support will be paid at T_B. The reason for selecting T_B becomes clear when we look at (9.4) and (9.5). We see that the higher $\Sigma s_{f,A}$, the higher $x_{g,A}$ and the higher ρ_A. When $\Sigma s_{f,A}$ approaches the value of 1, $x_{g,A}$ approaches the value of T_B and ρ_A approaches the value of 1. Thus, with $\Sigma s_{f,A} < 1$, the agents f can achieve all values of $x_{g,A}$ below T_B and all values of ρ_A below one. But when (9.10') holds, the agents f are not satisfied with that. Their stakes are so large, that they want $\rho_A = 1$. They want to win with certainty. To that end, the active agent should spend at least T_B. In that case the active agent on the B-side with stake T_B will not spend anything at all (cf. (7.7)).

Now suppose that $\Sigma s_{k,A} < 1$. Then agent f will never want to set his $s_{f,A}$ so high that $s_{f,A} + \Sigma s_{k,A} = \Sigma s_{f,A} > 1$. Irrespective whether $\Sigma s_{f,A} = 1$ or $\Sigma s_{f,A} > 1$, the active agent will always spend T_B. When agent f sets $\Sigma s_{f,A} > 1$ instead of $\Sigma s_{f,A} = 1$, he has to pay more to the active agent, but there is no offsetting benefit. Thus, the supporting agents will not make use of the opportunity to set $\Sigma s_{f,A} > 1$.

When (9.10') is satisfied with inequality, there is a continuum of solutions for the individual support rates $s_{f,A}, f = 1, ..., g-1$. This is because there will always be at least one agent f for whom (9.7') applies. Thus, when another agent $k, k = 1, ..., f-1, f+1, ..., g-1$ spends a little less than his equilibrium $s_{k,A}$, agent f will spend a little more than his equilibrium $s_{f,A}$, so that $\Sigma s_{f,A} = 1, f = 1, ..., g-1$. The only restrictions on the equilibrium support rates are:

– $\Sigma s_{f,A} = 1, f = 1, ..., g-1$;
– every agent f's payoff is nondeclining in $s_{f,A}$, so that $s_{f,A}$ is not too high. This implies that for every agent $f = 1, ..., g-1$:

$$v_{f,A} - v_{g,A} \geq 2T_B s_{f,A} \qquad (9.7'')$$

4. THE CHOICE OF THE ACTIVE AGENT

4.1 Introduction

After having treated stages 2 and 3 of the rent seeking game in section 3, we now discuss the first stage: who will be the active agent? The agent who, possibly with the support from other agents, can secure the highest aggregate payoff for a side, will be designated as the active agent.

As in section 3, we shall treat partial support and full support separately. In section 4.2 we assume there will be partial support on both sides in equilibrium. In section 4.3 we see what happens when a side can play full support and we derive the conditions under which full support will be played in equilibrium.

4.2 Partial Support

4.2.1 Introduction

In this section, we analyse the choice of the active agent on the A-side, given that the A-side and the B-side both play partial support. The agent who, possibly with the support from other agents, can secure the highest aggregate payoff for the A-side, will be designated as the active agent. But instead of comparing the aggregate payoff for all possible active agents, it will be more insightful to compare the active agents' enlarged stakes and to apply the following proposition.

Proposition 9.2 Suppose that in stage one, the A-side can choose between designating agent p or agent q as the active agent. The A-side wants to maximize its aggregate payoff $\Sigma U_{i,A}$, given that agent y will be active on the B-side. In stage two, agent p, resp. q, will be endowed with enlarged stake $T_A(p,y)$, resp. $T_A(q,y)$. The enlarged stake of agent y on the B-side will be $T_B(p,y)$, resp. $T_B(q,y)$. Let $T_A(p,y) < T_A(q,y)$, $T_B(p,y) \geq T_B(q,y)$, $\Sigma U_{i,A}(p,y) \geq 0$, $\Sigma U_{i,A}(q,y) \geq 0$.

a. When $\Sigma v_{i,A} \geq 2T_B(q,y)$, then agent q should be the active agent;
b. when $\Sigma v_{i,A} < 2T_B(q,y)$, and $T_A(q,y) \leq T_A^*[T_B(q,y)]$, where T_A^* is given by:

$$T_A^*(T_B) \equiv \frac{\displaystyle\sum_{i=1}^{n} v_{i,A}}{2 - \displaystyle\sum_{i=1}^{n} v_{i,A}/T_B} \tag{9.11}$$

then agent q should be the active agent.

Proof See the appendix.

Proposition 9.2 is not a comprehensive guideline. It does not tell us which agent will be active in any conceivable situation. However, we shall see that Proposition 9.2 is relevant in many cases.

The rest of this section is organized as follows. In section 4.2.2 we analyse the A-side's choice between the agents $2, ..., n$. We know from section 3 that the active agent $g = 2, ..., n$ will receive support from other agents. That is why we will also call the choice between the agents $2, ..., n$ the choice given that the A-side plays support. We shall see that the A-side chooses agent n from the agents $2, ..., n$. In section 4.2.4, the A-side's choice between agent n and agent 1, in other words between playing support and no support, is treated. It turns out that an important factor in this choice is whether the A-side's success probability is above or below one half in equilibrium. Thus we need to know whether the A-side is the favourite or the underdog. That is why this subject is treated in section 4.2.3, before the analysis of the A-side's choice between agents 1 and n.

4.2.2 The choice between the agents $2, ..., n$
In this section, we limit our analysis to the question which one of the agents $2, ..., n$ should be the active agent. We know from section 3 that when one of the agents $2, ..., n$ is designated as the active agent in stage 1, other agents will offer him support in stage 2. We are going to prove that agent n should be the active agent. Before we state this as Proposition 9.3, we will first derive some results that are part of the proof.

Lemma 9.2
a. Given the value of T_B, the enlarged stake of agent g on the A-side, $g = 2, ..., n$ is rising in g.
b. Given the value of T_B, agent n has the highest enlarged stake of the agents $2, ..., n$: $T_{n,A} > T_{h,A}$; $h = 2, ..., n-1$.

Proof
a. The enlarged stakes $T_{g,A}$ of the agents $g = 2, ..., n$ can be calculated from (9.1) and (9.8):

$$\frac{v_{g,A}}{1 - \sum_{f=1}^{g-1} s_{f,A}} = \frac{T_B \left(\sum_{f=1}^{g-1} v_{f,A} + (3-g)v_{g,A} \right)}{2T_B + (g-1)v_{g,A} - \sum_{f=1}^{g-1} v_{f,A}} \tag{9.12}$$

The right hand side of (9.12) is increasing in g, the index number of the active agent. This is because, as can be seen from Table 9.2 and Figure 9.1, the numerator is nondecreasing in $g = 2, ..., n$ and the denominator is decreasing in $g = 2, ..., n$.

Table 9.2 Some useful sequences

g or n	$\sum\limits_{f=1}^{g-1} v_{f,A} + (3-g)v_{g,A}$ $\sum\limits_{i=1}^{n} v_{i,A} + (2-n)v_{n,A}$ (9.13a)	$\sum\limits_{f=1}^{g-1} v_{f,A} + (2-g)v_{g,A}$ $\sum\limits_{i=1}^{n} v_{i,A} + (1-n)v_{n,A}$ (9.13b)	$\sum\limits_{f=1}^{g-1} v_{f,A} + (1-g)v_{g,A}$ $\sum\limits_{i=1}^{n} v_{i,A} - nv_{n,A}$ (9.13c)
2	$v_{1,A} + v_{2,A}$	$v_{1,A}$	$v_{1,A} - v_{2,A}$
3	$v_{1,A} + v_{2,A}$	$v_{1,A} + v_{2,A} - v_{3,A}$	$v_{1,A} + v_{2,A} - 2v_{3,A}$
4	$v_{1,A} + v_{2,A} + v_{3,A} - v_{4,A}$	$v_{1,A} + v_{2,A} + v_{3,A} - 2v_{4,A}$	$v_{1,A} + v_{2,A} + v_{3,A} - 3v_{4,A}$

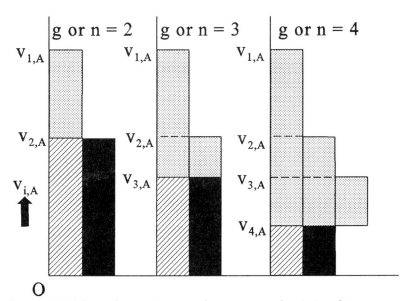

Figure 9.1 Values of (9.13a)-(9.13c) for g or n equal to 2, 3 and 4

b. It follows directly from **a.** that the highest possible value of $T_{g,A}$ is $T_{n,A}$. ∎

The expressions in Table 9.2 are illustrated in Figure 9.1. In this figure, the dotted columns represent the value of (9.13a), which is the sum of the differences between $v_{f,A}$ and $v_{g,A}$ for $f = 1, ..., g-1$. We see that (9.13a) is rising in g. When we go from $g = 2$ to $g = 3$, the first column becomes longer and a second column is added. From $g = 3$ to $g = 4$, the first two columns become longer and a third column is added, and so on.

The difference between (9.13b) and (9.13a) is $v_{g,A}$, which is represented by the hatched columns in Figure 9.1. The hatched column is placed under the first column. Thus, the value of (9.13b) is the dotted plus the hatched columns. When we go from $g = 2$ to $g = 3$, the length of the first column remains the same, and a second column is added. From $g = 3$ to $g = 4$, the length of the first column remains the same, the second column becomes longer and a third column is added. Thus, (9.13b) is rising in g.

The difference between (9.13b) and (9.13c) is another $v_{g,A}$, which is represented by the black columns in Figure 9.1. The black column is placed next to the hatched column. Thus, the value of (9.13c) is the dotted plus the hatched plus the black columns. When we go from $g = 2$ to $g = 3$, the total size of the columns remains the same. From $g = 3$ to $g = 4$, the size of the first two columns remains the same, and a third column is added. Thus, (9.13c) is nondeclining in g.

The reason why the induced stake of the active agent is rising in g is that the higher g, the more agents will offer support. When agent 2 is active, only agent 1 will support him. When agent 3 is active, agents 1 and 2 will support him, etc. Agent 1 may offer less support to agent 3 than to agent 2, but total support to agent 3 exceeds total support to agent 3, because agent 3 receives support from two agents instead of from one.

Lemma 9.3   When $\Sigma v_{i,A} < 2T_B(n,y)$, then:

$$T_A(n,y) < T_A^*[T_B(n,y)] \equiv \frac{\displaystyle\sum_{i=1}^{n} v_{i,A}}{2 - \displaystyle\sum_{i=1}^{n} v_{i,A}/T_B(n,y)}$$

Proof   We can calculate $T_{n,A}$ by substituting $g = n$ into (9.12):

$$T_{n,A} = \frac{T_B\left(\displaystyle\sum_{i=1}^{n} v_{i,A} + (2 - n)v_{n,A}\right)}{2T_B + nv_{n,A} - \displaystyle\sum_{i=1}^{n} v_{i,A}} < T_A^*(T_B) \equiv \frac{\displaystyle\sum_{i=1}^{n} v_{i,A}}{2 - \displaystyle\sum_{i=1}^{n} v_{i,A}/T_B} \quad (9.14a)$$

The inequality follows from the fact that the numerator on the left hand side is decreasing in $v_{n,A}$ whereas the denominator is increasing in $v_{n,A}$. Therefore, $T_{n,A}$ is decreasing in $v_{n,A}$: the lower $v_{n,A}$, the higher is $T_{n,A}$. As $v_{n,A}$ approaches zero, $T_{n,A}$ approaches $T_A^*(T_B)$. But $T_{n,A}$ will always be below T_A^*, because $v_{n,A}$ is positive.   ■

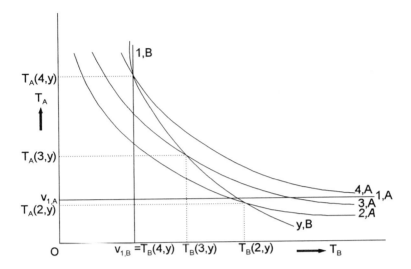

Figure 9.2 Reaction curves for the enlarged stake of the active agent

Lemma 9.4 The equilibrium $T_A(g,y)$ is increasing in $g = 2, ..., n$, and the equilibrium $T_B(g,y)$ is nonincreasing in $g = 2, ..., n$.

Proof When agent 1 is active on the B-side, the equilibrium T_B does not depend on g. Agent 1 will not be supported and thus $T_B(g,1) = v_{1,B}$. As we saw in Lemma 9.2a, $T_{g,A}$ is increasing in g, given the value of $T_{y,B}$. This concludes the proof for $y = 1$.

When agent $y = 2, ..., m$ is active on the B-side, he will be supported. Figure 9.2 depicts the situation. The curve 'y,B' gives $T_{y,B}$ as a function of T_A. The curve '$2,A$' gives $T_{2,A}$ as a function of T_B, etc.

We know from Lemma 9.1 that $T_{g,A}$ is declining in T_B. By the same token, $T_{y,B}$ is declining in T_A. From Lemma 9.2a, we know the curve '$3,A$' is above the curve '$2,A$' and '$4,A$' is above '$3,A$', etc. We see that the higher g, the higher the equilibrium $T_A(g,y)$, and the lower the equilibrium $T_B(g,y)$.   ∎

Now we are ready to state our main result:

Proposition 9.3 When in stage one, the A-side has to choose between the agents $2, ..., n$ for its active agent, given that agent y is active on the B-side, it will choose agent n.

Proof According to Proposition 9.2, the following conditions, taken together, are sufficient for Propostion 9.3 to hold:

a. When $\Sigma v_{i,A} < 2T_B(n,y)$, then $T_A(n,y) \le T_A^*[T_B(n,y)]$, where T_A^* is given by (9.11). We know from Lemma 9.3 that this condition is satisfied.

b. $T_A(n,y) > T_A(h,y)$ and $T_B(n,y) \le T_B(h,y)$, $h = 2, \dots, n-1$. We know from Lemma 9.4 that this condition is satisfied. ∎

4.2.3 Favourite and underdog

In section 4.2.2 we saw that when the A-side has to choose between the agents 2, ..., n for its active agent, it will choose agent n. In section 4.2.4 we will analyse the A-side's choice between agent 1 and agent n. In this analysis, it is important to know whether the A-side is the favourite or the underdog, i.e. whether it has a success probability above or below 1/2 in equilibrium. That is why we discuss this matter in this section. We will first determine which side is the favourite and which is the underdog in case both sides play support.

Proposition 9.4 When both sides play support, then the A-side is the underdog if and only if:

$$\sum_{i=1}^{n} v_{i,A} + (1-n)v_{n,A} < \sum_{j=1}^{m} v_{j,B} + (1-m)v_{m,B} \tag{9.15}$$

Proof On the A-side agent n is active, supported by $n-1$ agents, $f = 1, \dots, n-1$. As we have derived in the proof of Lemma 9.3:

$$T_{n,A} = \frac{v_{n,A}}{1 - \sum_{f=1}^{n-1} s_{f,A}} = \frac{T_B\left(\sum_{i=1}^{n} v_{i,A} + (2-n)v_{n,A}\right)}{2T_B + nv_{n,A} - \sum_{i=1}^{n} v_{i,A}} \tag{9.14a}$$

On the B-side agent m is active, supported by $m-1$ agents, $k = 1, \dots, m-1$. By symmetry:

$$T_{m,B} = \frac{v_{m,B}}{1 - \sum_{k=1}^{n-1} s_{k,B}} = \frac{T_A\left(\sum_{j=1}^{m} v_{j,B} + (2-m)v_{m,B}\right)}{2T_A + mv_{m,B} - \sum_{j=1}^{m} v_{j,B}} \tag{9.14b}$$

Solving (9.14a) and (9.14b) for $T_A = T_{n,A}$ and $T_B = T_{m,B}$:

$$T_A(n,m) = \frac{v_{n,A}\left(\sum_{j=1}^{m} v_{j,B} + (1-m)v_{m,B}\right) + v_{m,B}\left(\sum_{i=1}^{n} v_{i,A} + (1-n)v_{n,A}\right)}{\left(\sum_{j=1}^{m} v_{j,B} + (2-m)v_{m,B}\right) - \left(\sum_{i=1}^{n} v_{i,A} - nv_{n,A}\right)} \tag{9.16a}$$

$$T_B(n,m) \; = \; \frac{v_{n,A}\left(\sum_{j=1}^{m} v_{j,B} + (1-m)v_{m,B}\right) + v_{m,B}\left(\sum_{i=1}^{n} v_{i,A} + (1-n)v_{n,A}\right)}{\left(\sum_{i=1}^{n} v_{i,A} + (2-n)v_{n,A}\right) - \left(\sum_{j=1}^{m} v_{j,B} - mv_{m,B}\right)} \qquad (9.16b)$$

For the relative magnitude of $T_A(n,m)$ and $T_B(n,m)$ we find:

$$T_A(n,m) \; < \; T_B(n,m) \quad \Leftrightarrow \quad \sum_{i=1}^{n} v_{i,A} + (1-n)v_{n,A} \; < \; \sum_{j=1}^{m} v_{j,B} + (1-m)v_{m,B} \quad (9.15)$$

∎

But inequality (9.15) is not only applicable in case both sides play support, as the following proposition shows.

Proposition 9.5 Suppose the B-side plays support. Then, when the A-side is the underdog if it plays support, i.e. if it designates agent n as the active agent, it is also the underdog if it plays no support, i.e. if it designates agent 1 as the active agent.

Proof From (9.14b), with $v_{1,A}$ for T_A:

$$T_B(1,m) \; = \; \frac{v_{1,A}\left(\sum_{j=1}^{m} v_{j,B} + (2 - m)v_{m,B}\right)}{2v_{1,A} + mv_{m,B} - \sum_{j=1}^{m} v_{j,B}} \qquad (9.17)$$

The A-side will be the underdog when $v_{1,A} < T_B(1,m)$. From (9.17), this implies:

$$\sum_{j=1}^{m} v_{j,B} + (2 - m)v_{m,B} \; > \; 2v_{1,A} + mv_{m,B} - \sum_{j=1}^{m} v_{j,B}$$

This can be rewritten as:

$$\sum_{j=1}^{m} v_{j,B} + (1 - m)v_{m,B} \; > \; v_{1,A} \qquad (9.17')$$

When the A-side is the underdog when it plays support, it is also the underdog when it plays no support. In other words, when inequality (9.15) is satisfied, inequality (9.17') is also satisfied, because $\Sigma v_{i,A} + (1-n)v_{n,A} \geq v_{1,A}$ (cf. Table 9.2). ∎

This is all we can say about which side will be the favourite and which side will be the underdog at this stage. We are now ready to analyse the A-side's choice between agent 1 and agent n for its active agent.

4.2.4 Agent 1 or agent n?

In section 4.2 we saw that the A-side prefers agent n for its active agent from the agents 2, ..., n. The only question that still remains is then whether the A-side prefers agent 1 or agent n. We will address this question in this section. Since we know from section 3 that agent n will and agent 1 will not receive support, we can rephrase the question as: will the A-side play support or no support? As we already announced, the answer depends on whether the A-side is the favourite or the underdog.

Let us first discuss the choice between agent 1 and agent n when the A-side is the favourite in case it plays support, i.e. $T_A(n,y) > T_B(n,y)$. Before stating the result as Proposition 9.6, we first present the following Lemma that is part of the proof.

Lemma 9.5   When $T_A(n,y) > T_B(n,y)$, then $v_{1,A} < T_A(n,y)$.

Proof   When $v_{1,A} \leq T_B(n,y)$, then it is clear that $v_{1,A} < T_A(n,y)$, because $T_B(n,y) < T_A(n,y)$. We will now prove that $v_{1,A} > T_B(n,y)$ implies $T_A(n,y) > v_{1,A}$.

Using equation (9.14a), we will prove that

$$T_A(n,y) = \frac{T_B(n,y)\left(\sum_{i=1}^{n} v_{i,A} + (2 - n)v_{n,A}\right)}{2T_B(n,y) + nv_{n,A} - \sum_{i=1}^{n} v_{i,A}} > v_{1,A}$$

This inequality is satisfied when:

$$T_B\left(\sum_{i=1}^{n} v_{i,A} + (2-n)v_{n,A}\right) > v_{1,A}\left(2T_B + nv_{n,A} - \sum_{i=1}^{n} v_{i,A}\right)$$

This inequality can be rewritten as:

$$(v_{1,A} + T_B)\left(\sum_{i=1}^{n} v_{i,A} - nv_{n,A}\right) > 2T_B(v_{1,A} - v_{n,A})$$

The inequality holds because $v_{1,A} + T_B > 2T_B$, since $v_{1,A} > T_B$, and $\Sigma v_{i,A} - nv_{n,A} \geq v_{1,A} - v_{n,A}$, as is clear from Table 9.2.   ∎

We are now ready to state the preference of the A-side when it is the favourite in case it plays support.

Proposition 9.6 When the A-side is the favourite when it plays support, it should play support.

Proof Invoking Proposition 9.2, we will show that:

a. $v_{1,A} < T_A(n,y)$ when the A-side is the favourite when it plays support, i.e. when $T_A(n,y) > T_B(n,y)$. As Lemma 9.5 shows, this condition is satisfied.
b. When $\Sigma v_{i,A} < 2T_B(n,y)$, $T_A(n,y) < T_A^*[T_B(n,y)]$, where T_A^* is given by (9.11). As Lemma 9.3 shows, this condition is satisfied as well. ·
c. $T_B(1,1) = T_B(n,1) = v_{1,B}$, and when $v_{1,A} < T_A(n,y)$, $T_B(1,y) > T_B(n,y)$ for $y = 2, ...,$ n. Figure 9.2 illustrates the inequality. We see that $v_{1,A} < T_A(4,y)$. Because the reaction curve 'y,B' is declining according to Lemma 9.1, $T_B(1,y) > T_B(4,y)$. ∎

We can now combine Propositions 9.4, 9.5 and 9.6 to give the general condition defining the favourite and the underdog:

Proposition 9.7 The A-side is the underdog if and only if:

$$\sum_{i=1}^{n} v_{i,A} + (1-n)v_{n,A} < \sum_{j=1}^{m} v_{j,B} + (1-m)v_{m,B} \tag{9.15}$$

Proof From Proposition 9.4 we know that (9.15) means that the A-side is the underdog when both sides play support. From Proposition 9.5 we know that (9.15) also means that the A-side is the underdog when the A-side plays no support and the B-side plays support. Proposition 9.6 shows that the favourite, i.e. the B-side according to (9.15), will always play support. Thus, when (9.15) is satisfied, the B-side is the favourite and it plays support, and the A-side is the underdog whether it plays support or not. ∎

We see that the A-side can be the underdog although its aggregate stake is higher: (9.15) can hold although $\Sigma v_{i,A} > \Sigma v_{j,B}$. We will elaborate upon this possibility in section 6.2.

Now that we know who will be the active agent for the favourite, and which side will be the favourite and which the underdog, we can discuss the designation of the active agent on the A-side in case it is the underdog. When the A-side is the underdog, it will designate agent 1 as the active agent in some cases and agent n in others. The decision rule is given in the following proposition.

Proposition 9.8 When the A-side is the underdog, i.e. (9.15) is satisfied, it will designate agent 1 as the active agent when $v_{1,A} > T_A(n,m)$ and it designates agent n when $T_A(n,m) > v_{1,A}$. Substituting (9.14b), this means that agent 1 will be the active agent if and only if:

$$v_{1,A} > \frac{v_{n,A}\left(\sum_{j=1}^{m} v_{j,B} + (1-m)v_{m,B}\right) + v_{m,B}\left(\sum_{i=1}^{n} v_{i,A} + (1-n)v_{n,A}\right)}{\left(\sum_{i=1}^{n} v_{i,A} + (2-n)v_{n,A}\right) - \left(\sum_{j=1}^{m} v_{j,B} - mv_{m,B}\right)} \quad (9.18)$$

Proof Available from the author.

4.3 Full Support

In section 4.2 we discussed the designation of the active agent on the A-side, given partial support on both sides. In this section we will discuss the designation of the active agent on both sides in case there is full support on one side. We will also derive the conditions under which there will be full support in equilibrium.

Let us use the labels 'A-side' and 'B-side' such that (9.15) is satisfied, i.e. the B-side is the favourite. We assume that only the B-side might want to play full support. As we shall see shortly, this assumption is justified.

Let us first identify the conditions under which the B-side can play full support. When there is full support on the B-side, the analysis of section 4.2 does not apply, because it results in a nonpositive $T_{m,B}$. From (9.16b), we cannot find a positive $T_B(n,m)$ when:

$$\sum_{i=1}^{n} v_{i,A} + (2-n)v_{n,A} \leq \sum_{j=1}^{m} v_{j,B} - mv_{m,B} \quad (9.16)$$

From (9.17), we cannot find a positive $T_B(1,m)$ when:

$$2v_{1,A} \leq \sum_{j=1}^{m} v_{j,B} - mv_{m,B} \quad (9.17'')$$

Dijkstra (1998) shows that when only one of the inequalities (9.16) or (9.17") is satisfied, the B-side will not play full support. In this section we assume that both (9.16) and (9.17") are satisfied, so that the B-side can play full support, irrespective of who is active on the A-side:

$$\max\left[2v_{1,A}; \sum_{i=1}^{n} v_{i,A} + (2-n)v_{n,A}\right] \leq \sum_{j=1}^{m} v_{j,B} - mv_{m,B} \quad (9.19)$$

Note that (9.19) can only be satisfied for the B-side, because the B-side is the favourite:

$$\sum_{i=1}^{n} v_{i,A} + (1-n)v_{n,A} < \sum_{j=1}^{m} v_{j,B} + (1-m)v_{m,B} \quad (9.15)$$

Inequality (9.15) implies:

$$\sum_{i=1}^{n} v_{i,A} - nv_{n,A} < \sum_{j=1}^{m} v_{j,B} + (2-m)v_{m,B} \qquad (9.15')$$

so that (9.19) cannot be satisfied for the A-side.[3]

We will now analyse the designation of the active agent on the B-side, in case (9.19) is satisfied. When the stakes on the B-side are very high, the inactive agents may also be willing to offer full support when another agent instead of agent m will be active. They will offer full support to agent $y+1$, $y+1 = 2, ..., m$ when:

$$\max\left[2v_{1,A}; \sum_{i=1}^{n} v_{i,A} + (2-n)v_{n,A}\right] \leq \sum_{w=1}^{y} v_{w,B} - yv_{y+1,B} \qquad (9.19')$$

Let agent $y+1$ be the active agent on the B-side, where y satisfies (9.19'). Agent $y+1$ receives full support from the other agents on the B-side. However, as we discussed in section 3.3, support is only paid when agent $y+1$ spends exactly T_A.

We will now consider the equilibrium value of T_A. At first sight, this may seem like a non-issue: no matter what the value of T_A, agent $y+1$ will always spend T_A, so that the 'active' agent on the A-side will not spend anything and the payoff of the agents on the A-side is zero. However, when T_A is very high, offering full support is no longer optimal for the agents on the B-side. Thus, T_A should be at or below a certain threshold value T_{AS}, so that the agents on the B-side will still want to offer full support. From (9.10'), T_A should satisfy:

$$T_A \leq T_{AS} \equiv \frac{1}{2}\left(\sum_{w=1}^{y} v_{w,B} - yv_{y+1,B}\right) \qquad (9.10b)$$

When there is full support on the B-side, the aggregate payoff on the B-side is:

$$\sum_{j=1}^{m} U_{j,B} = \sum_{j=1}^{m} U_{j,B} - T_A$$

which is declining in T_A. Thus, it is clear that the B-side prefers the lowest possible maximum level of T_A. From (9.10b) and Table 9.2, we see that the threshold level T_{AS} is declining in $y+1$, the index number of the active agent. Thus, when the B-side wants to play full support, agent $y+1$ will be the active agent, where y is the lowest number for which (9.19') is satisfied. In other words, y satisfies:

$$\sum_{w=1}^{y-1} v_{w,B} + (1-y)v_{y,B} < \max\left[2v_{1,A}; \sum_{i=1}^{n} v_{i,A} + (2-n)v_{n,A}\right] \leq \sum_{w=1}^{y} v_{w,B} - yv_{y+1,B} \quad (9.19'')$$

However, the B-side does not always want to play full support when it can do so. When T_A is close to or at T_{AS}, agent $y+1$ on the B-side has to make a large effort.

The supporting agents on the B-side are still willing to offer full support, but the aggregate payoff on the B-side might have been higher when another agent had been active and had received partial support. A numerical elaboration of this possibility is given in section 6.3.

Now we turn to the question which agent will be active on the B-side with partial support.[4] We can establish the following:

Lemma 9.6   When the B-side is not the favourite when it plays partial support, its aggregate payoff is higher when it plays full support.

Proof   When the B-side plays full support, agent $y+1$ will be active. The aggregate payoff on the B-side will be, from (9.10b):

$$\sum_{j=1}^{m} U_{j,B} = \sum_{j=1}^{m} v_{j,B} - T_A \geq \sum_{j=1}^{m} v_{j,B} - T_{AS} = \sum_{j=1}^{m} v_{j,B} - \frac{1}{2}\left(\sum_{w=1}^{y} v_{w,B} - yv_{y+1,B}\right) \geq$$

$$\geq \sum_{j=1}^{m} v_{j,B} - \frac{1}{2}\left(\sum_{j=1}^{m} v_{j,B} - mv_{m,B}\right) = \frac{1}{2}\left(\sum_{j=1}^{m} v_{j,B} + mv_{m,B}\right)$$

When the B-side is not the favourite in case it plays partial support, its aggregate payoff is:

$$\sum_{j=1}^{m} U_{j,B} = \rho_B \sum_{j=1}^{m} v_{j,B} - x_B < \frac{1}{2}\sum_{j=1}^{m} v_{j,B} - x_B < \frac{1}{2}\left(\sum_{j=1}^{m} v_{j,B} + mv_{m,B}\right) \qquad \blacksquare$$

Lemma 9.6 implies that partial support is only an option for the B-side when it is the favourite with partial support. Then we can apply Proposition 9.6: when the B-side is the favourite when it plays support, it should play support. This means that agent 1 will not be active on the B-side. Then we can apply a variant to Proposition 9.3 saying that when the B-side can choose between the agents 2, ..., y for its active agent, it will choose agent y.

Thus, we have to compare the B-side's aggregate payoff when agent $y+1$ is active and the stake of the active agent on the A-side is T_{AS} to the B-side's aggregate payoff when agent y is active. Before we can do that, we must determine who will be the active agent on the A-side when agent y is active. As Proposition 9.8 tells us, the agent with the highest (induced) stake will be active. The expression for the induced stake of agent n is derived in section 5.6 as (9.25). Thus, agent 1 will be active on the A-side if and only if:

$$v_{1,A} > \frac{v_{n,A}\left(\sum_{w=1}^{y-1} v_{w,B} + (2-y)v_{y,B}\right) + v_{y,B}\left(\sum_{i=1}^{n} v_{i,A} + (1-n)v_{n,A}\right)}{\left(\sum_{w=1}^{y-1} v_{w,B} + (3-y)v_{y,B}\right) - \left(\sum_{i=1}^{n} v_{i,A} - nv_{n,A}\right)} \qquad (9.25')$$

The aggregate payoff on the B-side when agent y is active against agent 1 is given in section 5.5 as (9.26). Thus, when (9.25') is satisfied, agent $y+1$ will be active on the B-side when:

$$\sum_{j=1}^{m} v_{j,B} - \frac{1}{2}\left(\sum_{w=1}^{y} v_{w,B} - yv_{y+1,B}\right) >$$

$$> \frac{\sum_{w=1}^{y-1} v_{w,B} + (3-y)v_{y,B}}{2(v_{y,B} + v_{1,A})} \sum_{j=1}^{m} v_{j,B} - \frac{v_{1,A}\left(\sum_{w=1}^{y-1} v_{w,B} + (3-y)v_{y,B}\right)^2}{4(v_{y,B} + v_{1,A})^2} \quad (9.26')$$

When (9.25') is satisfied and (9.26') is not, agent y will be active on the B-side.

When (9.25') is not satisfied, agent n will be active on the A-side against agent y. The aggregate payoff on the B-side when agent y is active against agent n is given in section 5.6 as (9.28). Thus, when (9.25') is not satisfied, agent $y+1$ will be active on the B-side when:

$$\sum_{j=1}^{m} v_{j,B} - \frac{1}{2}\left(\sum_{w=1}^{y} v_{w,B} - yv_{y+1,B}\right) > \frac{\left(\sum_{w=1}^{y-1} v_{w,B} + (3-y)v_{y,B}\right) - \left(\sum_{i=1}^{n} v_{i,A} - nv_{n,A}\right)}{2(v_{n,A} + v_{y,B})} *$$

$$* \left[\sum_{j=1}^{m} v_{j,B} - \frac{v_{n,A}\left(\sum_{w=1}^{y-1} v_{w,B} + (2-y)v_{y,B}\right) + v_{y,B}\left(\sum_{i=1}^{n} v_{i,A} + (1-n)v_{n,A}\right)}{2(v_{n,A} + v_{y,B})}\right] \quad (9.27')$$

5. THE EQUILIBRIUM PATH OF THE WHOLE GAME

5.1 Introduction

Now that we have analysed all four stages of the game, we can present the complete equilibrium path. In this section we present the expressions for the equilibrium outcomes. Numerical elaborations can be found in section 6.4.

As we have seen above, there are a number of equilibria. Figure 9.3 shows which agent will be active on either side, depending on the specific parameter values. Section 6.3 contains a numerical elaboration of the conditions involved. Figure 9.3 also refers to the numbers of the sections 5.2 to 5.6 where the complete equilibrium path is presented, given the identity of the active agents.[5] The equations referred to in Figure 9.3 are collected in Table 9.3.

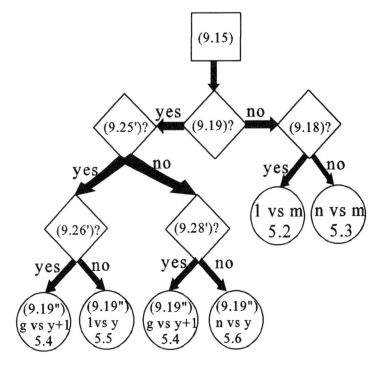

Figure 9.3 Flow diagram for the determination of the equilibrium

Let us now go through the procedure of finding the appropriate equilibrium, as laid out in Figure 9.3. We start by using the labels 'A-side' and 'B-side' such that (9.15) is satisfied. This means that the A-side is the underdog according to Proposition 9.7. Then we check whether the necessary condition (9.19) for full support on the B-side is satisfied. If it is not, agent m will be active on the B-side. When (9.18) is satisfied, agent 1 will be active on the A-side. When (9.18) is not satisfied, agent n will be active on the A-side.

Let us now see what happens when the necessary condition (9.19) for full support on the B-side is satisfied. The B-side must now decide whether it wants to play full support with agent $y+1$ active or partial support with agent y active. Agent y is the last agent who will receive partial support and agent $y+1$ is the first agent who will receive full support, as can be seen from (9.19").

The choice of active agent on the B-side depends upon the question who will be active on the A-side against agent y. When (9.25') is satisfied, agent 1 will be active on the A-side against agent y. Then condition (9.26') is relevant. When (9.26') is satisfied, there will be full support on the B-side with agent $y+1$ active against any agent g on the A-side. When (9.26') is not satisfied, there will be partial support on the B-side with agent y active against agent 1 on the A-side.

Table 9.3 Equations referred to in Figure 9.3

$$\sum_{i=1}^{n} v_{i,A} + (1-n)v_{n,A} < \sum_{j=1}^{m} v_{j,B} + (1-m)v_{m,B} \tag{9.15}$$

$$v_{1,A} > \frac{v_{n,A}\left(\sum_{j=1}^{m} v_{j,B} + (1-m)v_{m,B}\right) + v_{m,B}\left(\sum_{i=1}^{n} v_{i,A} + (1-n)v_{n,A}\right)}{\left(\sum_{i=1}^{n} v_{i,A} + (2-n)v_{n,A}\right) - \left(\sum_{j=1}^{m} v_{j,B} - mv_{m,B}\right)} \tag{9.18}$$

$$\max\left[2v_{1,A}; \sum_{i=1}^{n} v_{i,A} + (2-n)v_{n,A}\right] \le \sum_{j=1}^{m} v_{j,B} - mv_{m,B} \tag{9.19}$$

$$\sum_{w=1}^{y-1} v_{j,B} + (1-y)v_{y,B} < \max\left[2v_{1,A}; \sum_{i=1}^{n} v_{i,A} + (2-n)v_{n,A}\right] \le \sum_{w=1}^{y} v_{j,B} - yv_{y+1,B} \tag{9.19''}$$

$$v_{1,A} > \frac{v_{n,A}\left(\sum_{w=1}^{y-1} v_{w,B} + (2-y)v_{y,B}\right) + v_{y,B}\left(\sum_{i=1}^{n} v_{i,A} + (1-n)v_{n,A}\right)}{\left(\sum_{w=1}^{y-1} v_{w,B} + (3-y)v_{y,B}\right) - \left(\sum_{i=1}^{n} v_{i,A} - nv_{n,A}\right)} \tag{9.25'}$$

$$\sum_{j=1}^{m} v_{j,B} - \frac{1}{2}\left(\sum_{w=1}^{y} v_{w,B} - yv_{y+1,B}\right) >$$

$$> \frac{\sum_{w=1}^{y-1} v_{w,B} + (3-y)v_{y,B}}{2(v_{y,B} + v_{1,A})} \sum_{j=1}^{m} v_{j,B} - \frac{v_{1,A}\left(\sum_{w=1}^{y-1} v_{w,B} + (3-y)v_{y,B}\right)^2}{4(v_{y,B} + v_{1,A})^2} \tag{9.26'}$$

$$\sum_{j=1}^{m} v_{j,B} - \frac{1}{2}\left(\sum_{w=1}^{y} v_{w,B} - yv_{y+1,B}\right) > \frac{\left(\sum_{w=1}^{y-1} v_{w,B} + (3-y)v_{y,B}\right) - \left(\sum_{i=1}^{n} v_{i,A} - nv_{n,A}\right)}{2(v_{n,A} + v_{y,B})} *$$

$$*\left[\sum_{j=1}^{m} v_{j,B} - \frac{v_{n,A}\left(\sum_{w=1}^{y-1} v_{w,B} + (2-y)v_{y,B}\right) + v_{y,B}\left(\sum_{i=1}^{n} v_{i,A} + (1-n)v_{n,A}\right)}{2(v_{n,A} + v_{y,B})}\right] \tag{9.28'}$$

When (9.25') is not satisfied, agent n will be active against agent y. Then condition (9.27') is relevant. When (9.27') is satisfied, there will be full support on the B-side with agent $y+1$ active against any agent g on the A-side. When (9.27') is not satisfied, there will be partial support on the B-side with agent y active against agent n on the A-side.

5.2 Agent 1 Active on the A-Side, Agent m Active with Partial Support on the B-Side

In this section, we go through the equilibrium path for the five stages of the game, presented in section 1, in case (9.19) is not satisfied and (9.18) is. Then agent 1 will be active on the A-side and there will be partial support with agent m active on the B-side.

1. The A-side designates agent 1 as the active agent. The B-side designates agent m as the active agent.
2. The agents $w = 1, ..., m-1$ offer support to agent m on the B-side. The support rate from agent w is, from (9.9):

$$s_{w,B} = \frac{(v_{1,A} + v_{m,B})(v_{w,B} - v_{m,B})}{v_{1,A}\left(\sum_{j=1}^{m} v_{j,B} + (2 - m)v_{m,B}\right)} \tag{9.20}$$

The total amount of support is, from (9.8):

$$\sum_{w=1}^{m-1} s_{w,B} = \frac{(v_{1,A} + v_{m,B})\left(\sum_{j=1}^{m} v_{j,B} - mv_{m,B}\right)}{v_{1,A}\left(\sum_{j=1}^{m} v_{j,B} + (2 - m)v_{m,B}\right)}$$

This results in an enlarged stake $T_B(1,m)$ for agent m of:

$$T_B(1,m) = \frac{v_{1,A}\left(\sum_{j=1}^{m} v_{j,B} + (2-m)v_{m,B}\right)}{2v_{1,A} + mv_{m,B} - \sum_{j=1}^{m} v_{j,B}} \tag{9.17}$$

3. The agents' efforts are, from (7.8) and (9.17):

$$x_{1,A} = \frac{v_{1,A}\left(2v_{1,A} + mv_{m,B} - \sum_{j=1}^{m} v_{j,B}\right)\left(\sum_{j=1}^{m} v_{j,B} + (2 - m)v_{m,B}\right)}{4(v_{1,A} + v_{m,B})^2}$$

$$x_{m,B} = \frac{v_{1,A}\left(\sum_{j=1}^{m} v_{j,B} + (2-m)v_{m,B}\right)^2}{4(v_{1,A} + v_{m,B})^2}$$

4. On the B-side, the agents $w = 1, ..., m-1$ pay the support they promised to agent m. The amount that agent w pays is:

$$s_{w,B}x_{m,B} = \frac{(v_{w,B} - v_{m,B})\left(\sum_{j=1}^{m} v_{j,B} + (2-m)v_{m,B}\right)}{4(v_{m,B} + v_{1,A})}$$

5. The success probabilities are, from (7.9) and (9.17):

$$\rho_A = \frac{2v_{1,A} + mv_{m,B} - \sum_{j=1}^{m} v_{j,B}}{2(v_{1,A} + v_{m,B})} \qquad \rho_B = \frac{\sum_{j=1}^{m} v_{j,B} + (2-m)v_{m,B}}{2(v_{1,A} + v_{m,B})}$$

The aggregate payoffs are:

$$\sum_{i=1}^{n} U_{i,A} = \frac{2v_{1,A} + mv_{m,B} - \sum_{j=1}^{m} v_{j,B}}{2(v_{1,A} + v_{m,B})}\sum_{i=1}^{n} v_{i,A} -$$
$$- \frac{v_{1,A}\left(\sum_{j=1}^{m} v_{j,B} + (2-m)v_{m,B}\right)\left(2v_{1,A} + mv_{m,B} - \sum_{j=1}^{m} v_{j,B}\right)}{4(v_{1,A} + v_{m,B})^2} \qquad (9.21)$$

$$\sum_{j=1}^{m} U_{j,B} = \frac{\sum_{j=1}^{m} v_{j,B} + (2-m)v_{m,B}}{2(v_{m,B} + v_{1,A})}\sum_{j=1}^{m} v_{j,B} - \frac{v_{1,A}\left(\sum_{j=1}^{m} v_{j,B} + (2-m)v_{m,B}\right)^2}{4(v_{m,B} + v_{1,A})^2}$$

5.3 Agent n Active on the A-Side, Agent m Active with Partial Support on the B-Side

In this section, we go through the equilibrium path for the five stages of the game, presented in section 1, in case neither (9.19) nor (9.18) is satisfied. Then agent n will be active on the A-side and there will be partial support with agent m active on the B-side.

1. The A-side designates agent n as the active agent. The B-side designates agent m as the active agent.

2. On the A-side, the agents $f = 1, ..., n\text{-}1$ offer support to agent n. The support rate from agent f is, from (9.9) and (9.16b):

$$s_{f,A} = \frac{(v_{n,A} + v_{m,B})(v_{f,A} - v_{n,A})}{v_{n,A}\left(\sum_{j=1}^{m} v_{j,B} + (1-m)v_{m,B}\right) + v_{m,B}\left(\sum_{i=1}^{n} v_{i,A} + (1-n)v_{n,A}\right)} \tag{9.22a}$$

The total amount of support is, from (9.8) and (9.16b):

$$\sum_{f=1}^{n-1} s_{f,A} = \frac{(v_{n,A} + v_{m,B})\left(\sum_{i=1}^{n} v_{i,A} - nv_{n,A}\right)}{v_{n,A}\left(\sum_{j=1}^{m} v_{j,B} + (1-m)v_{m,B}\right) + v_{m,B}\left(\sum_{i=1}^{n} v_{i,A} + (1-n)v_{n,A}\right)} \tag{9.23a}$$

On the B-side, the agents $w = 1, ..., m\text{-}1$ offer support to agent m. The support rate from agent w is, from (9.9) and (9.16a):

$$s_{w,B} = \frac{(v_{n,A} + v_{m,B})(v_{w,B} - v_{m,B})}{v_{n,A}\left(\sum_{j=1}^{m} v_{j,B} + (1-m)v_{m,B}\right) + v_{m,B}\left(\sum_{i=1}^{n} v_{i,A} + (1-n)v_{n,A}\right)} \tag{9.22b}$$

The total amount of support is, from (9.8) and (9.16a):

$$\sum_{w=1}^{m-1} s_{w,B} = \frac{(v_{n,A} + v_{m,B})\left(\sum_{j=1}^{m} v_{j,B} - mv_{m,B}\right)}{v_{n,A}\left(\sum_{j=1}^{m} v_{j,B} + (1-m)v_{m,B}\right) + v_{m,B}\left(\sum_{i=1}^{n} v_{i,A} + (1-n)v_{n,A}\right)} \tag{9.23b}$$

This results in the following enlarged stakes for agents n and m respectively:

$$T_A(n,m) = \frac{v_{n,A}\left(\sum_{j=1}^{m} v_{j,B} + (1-m)v_{m,B}\right) + v_{m,B}\left(\sum_{i=1}^{n} v_{i,A} + (1-n)v_{n,A}\right)}{\left(\sum_{j=1}^{m} v_{j,B} + (2-m)v_{m,B}\right) - \left(\sum_{i=1}^{n} v_{i,A} - nv_{n,A}\right)} \tag{9.16a}$$

$$T_B(n,m) = \frac{v_{n,A}\left(\sum_{j=1}^{m} v_{j,B} + (1-m)v_{m,B}\right) + v_{m,B}\left(\sum_{i=1}^{n} v_{i,A} + (1-n)v_{n,A}\right)}{\left(\sum_{i=1}^{n} v_{i,A} + (2-n)v_{n,A}\right) - \left(\sum_{j=1}^{m} v_{j,B} - mv_{m,B}\right)} \tag{9.16b}$$

3. The active agents' efforts are, from (7.8), (9.16a) and (9.16b):

$$x_{n,A} = \left[\left(\sum_{i=1}^{n} v_{i,A} + (2-n)v_{n,A}\right) - \left(\sum_{j=1}^{m} v_{j,B} - mv_{m,B}\right)\right] *$$

$$* \frac{v_{n,A}\left(\sum_{j=1}^{m} v_{j,B} + (1-m)v_{m,B}\right) + v_{m,B}\left(\sum_{i=1}^{n} v_{i,A} + (1-n)v_{n,A}\right)}{4(v_{n,A} + v_{m,B})^2}$$

$$x_{m,B} = \left[\left(\sum_{j=1}^{m} v_{j,B} + (2-m)v_{m,B}\right) - \left(\sum_{i=1}^{n} v_{i,A} - nv_{n,A}\right)\right] *$$

$$* \frac{v_{n,A}\left(\sum_{j=1}^{m} v_{j,B} + (1-m)v_{m,B}\right) + v_{m,B}\left(\sum_{i=1}^{n} v_{i,A} + (1-n)v_{n,A}\right)}{4(v_{n,A} + v_{m,B})^2}$$

4. On the A-side, the agents $f = 1, ..., n-1$ pay the support they promised to agent n. The amount that agent f has to pay is:

$$s_{f,A}x_{n,A} = \frac{(v_{f,A} - v_{n,A})\left[\left(\sum_{i=1}^{n} v_{i,A} + (2-n)v_{n,A}\right) - \left(\sum_{j=1}^{m} v_{j,B} - mv_{m,B}\right)\right]}{4(v_{n,A} + v_{m,B})}$$

On the B-side, the agents $w = 1,..,m-1$ pay the support they promised to agent m. The amount that agent w has to pay is:

$$s_{w,B}x_{m,B} = \frac{(v_{w,B} - v_{m,B})\left[\left(\sum_{j=1}^{m} v_{j,B} + (2-m)v_{m,B}\right) - \left(\sum_{i=1}^{n} v_{i,A} - nv_{n,A}\right)\right]}{4(v_{n,A} + v_{m,B})}$$

5. The success probabilities are, from (7.9), (9.16a) and (9.16b):

$$\rho_A = \frac{\sum_{i=1}^{n} v_{i,A} + (2-n)v_{n,A} - \left(\sum_{j=1}^{m} v_{j,B} - mv_{m,B}\right)}{2(v_{n,A} + v_{m,B})}$$

$$\rho_B = \frac{\sum_{j=1}^{m} v_{j,B} + (2-m)v_{m,B} - \left(\sum_{i=1}^{n} v_{i,A} - nv_{n,A}\right)}{2(v_{n,A} + v_{m,B})}$$

The aggregate payoffs are:

$$\sum_{i=1}^{n} U_{i,A} = \frac{\left(\sum_{i=1}^{n} v_{i,A} + (2-n)v_{n,A}\right) - \left(\sum_{j=1}^{m} v_{j,B} - mv_{m,B}\right)}{2(v_{n,A} + v_{m,B})} *$$

$$* \left[\sum_{i=1}^{n} v_{i,A} - \frac{v_{n,A}\left(\sum_{j=1}^{m} v_{j,B} + (1-m)v_{m,B}\right) + v_{m,B}\left(\sum_{i=1}^{n} v_{i,A} + (1-n)v_{n,A}\right)}{2(v_{n,A} + v_{m,B})}\right] \quad (9.24)$$

$$\sum_{j=1}^{m} U_{j,B} = \frac{\left(\sum_{j=1}^{m} v_{j,B} + (2-m)v_{m,B}\right) - \left(\sum_{i=1}^{n} v_{i,A} - nv_{n,A}\right)}{2(v_{n,A} + v_{m,B})} *$$

$$* \left[\sum_{j=1}^{m} v_{j,B} - \frac{v_{n,A}\left(\sum_{j=1}^{m} v_{j,B} + (1-m)v_{m,B}\right) + v_{m,B}\left(\sum_{i=1}^{n} v_{i,A} + (1-n)v_{n,A}\right)}{2(v_{n,A} + v_{m,B})}\right]$$

5.4 Full Support on the B-Side

In this section, we go through the equilibrium path for the five stages of the game, presented in section 1, in case (9.19) is satisfied and:

- (9.25') and (9.26') are satisfied;
- (9.25') is not satisfied and (9.27') is satisfied.

Then there will be full support with agent $y+1$ active on the B-side. For simplicity, we assume that the induced stake of the active agent on the A-side will be T_{AS}, as defined in (9.10b). Thus, T_A is as high as possible. As a result, there is a unique solution for the individual support rates on the B-side.

1. The A-side designates an agent g, $g = 1, \ldots, n$ as the active agent. The B-side designates agent $y+1$ as the active agent, where y is given by (9.19").
2. On the A-side, the agents $f = 1, \ldots, g-1, g+1, \ldots, n$ offer support to agent g such that the aggregate support rate $\Sigma s_{f,A}$ satisfies:

$$\frac{v_{g,A}}{1 - \sum_{\substack{f=1 \\ f \neq g}}^{n} s_{f,A}} = T_{AS} \equiv \frac{1}{2}\left(\sum_{w=1}^{y} v_{w,B} - yv_{y+1,B}\right)$$

On the B-side, the agents $w = 1, \ldots, y$ offer support to agent $y+1$. The aggregate support rate is one. The support rate from agent w is, from (9.7") and (9.10b):

$$s_{w,B} = \frac{v_{w,B} - v_{y+1,B}}{\sum_{w=1}^{y} v_{w,B} - yv_{y+1,B}}$$

3. Agent g on the A-side spends nothing. Agent $y+1$ on the B-side spends:

$$x_{y+1,B} = T_{AS} \equiv \frac{1}{2}\left(\sum_{w=1}^{y} v_{w,B} - yv_{y+1,B}\right)$$

4. On the B-side, the agents $w = 1, ..., y$ pay the support they promised to agent $y+1$. The amount that agent w has to pay is:

$$s_{w,B}x_{y+1,B} = \frac{1}{2}(v_{w,B} - v_{y+1,B})$$

5. The success probability of the A-side is zero, and so is its aggregate payoff. The success probability of the B-side is one. The aggregate payoff on the B-side is:

$$\sum_{j=1}^{m} U_{j,B} = \sum_{j=1}^{m} v_{j,B} - \frac{1}{2}\left(\sum_{w=1}^{y} v_{w,B} - yv_{y+1,B}\right)$$

5.5 Agent 1 Active on the A-Side, Agent y Active with Partial Support on the B-Side

In this section, we go through the equilibrium path for the five stages of the game, presented in section 1, in case (9.19) and (9.25') are satisfied and (9.26') is not. Then agent 1 is active on the A-side and there will be partial support with agent y active on the B-side.

1. The A-side designates agent 1 as the active agent. The B-sides designates agent y as the active agent, where y is given by (9.19").
2. The agents $w = 1, ..., y-1$ offer support to agent m on the B-side. The support rate from agent w is, from (9.9):

$$s_{w,B} = \frac{(v_{1,A} + v_{y,B})(v_{w,B} - v_{y,B})}{v_{1,A}\left(\sum_{w=1}^{y-1} v_{w,B} + (3-y)v_{y,B}\right)}$$

The total amount of support is, from (9.8):

$$\sum_{w=1}^{y-1} s_{w,B} = \frac{(v_{1,A} + v_{y,B})\left(\sum_{w=1}^{y-1} v_{w,B} + (1-y)v_{y,B}\right)}{v_{1,A}\left(\sum_{w=1}^{y-1} v_{w,B} + (3-y)v_{y,B}\right)}$$

This results in an enlarged stake $T_B(1,y)$ for agent y of:

$$T_B(1,y) = \frac{v_{1,A}\left(\sum_{w=1}^{y-1} v_{w,B} + (3-y)v_{y,B}\right)}{2v_{1,A} + (y-1)v_{y,B} - \sum_{w=1}^{y-1} v_{w,B}} \tag{9.25}$$

3. The agents' efforts are, from (7.8) and (9.25):

$$x_{1,A} = \frac{v_{1,A}\left(2v_{1,A} + (1-y)v_{y,B} - \sum_{w=1}^{y-1} v_{w,B}\right)\left(\sum_{w=1}^{y-1} v_{w,B} + (3-y)v_{y,B}\right)}{4(v_{1,A} + v_{y,B})^2}$$

$$x_{y,B} = \frac{v_{1,A}\left(\sum_{w=1}^{y-1} v_{w,B} + (3-y)v_{y,B}\right)^2}{4(v_{1,A} + v_{y,B})^2}$$

4. On the B-side, the agents $w = 1, ..., y\text{-}1$ pay the support they promised to agent y. The amount that agent w pays is:

$$s_{w,B}x_{y,B} = \frac{(v_{w,B} - v_{m,B})\left(\sum_{w=1}^{y-1} v_{w,B} + (3-y)v_{y,B}\right)}{4(v_{y,B} + v_{1,A})}$$

5. The success probabilities are, from (7.9) and (9.25):

$$\rho_A = \frac{2v_{1,A} + (1-y)v_{y,B} - \sum_{w=1}^{y-1} v_{w,B}}{2(v_{1,A} + v_{y,B})} \qquad \rho_B = \frac{\sum_{w=1}^{y-1} v_{w,B} + (3-y)v_{y,B}}{2(v_{1,A} + v_{y,B})}$$

The aggregate payoffs are:

$$\sum_{i=1}^{n} U_{i,A} = \frac{2v_{1,A} + (1-y)v_{y,B} - \sum_{w=1}^{y-1} v_{w,B}}{2(v_{1,A} + v_{y,B})}\sum_{i=1}^{n} v_{i,A} -$$
$$- \frac{v_{1,A}\left(\sum_{w=1}^{y-1} v_{w,B} + (3-y)v_{y,B}\right)\left(2v_{1,A} + (1-y)v_{y,B} - \sum_{w=1}^{y-1} v_{w,B}\right)}{4(v_{1,A} + v_{y,B})^2} \quad (9.26)$$

$$\sum_{j=1}^{m} U_{j,B} = \frac{\sum_{w=1}^{y-1} v_{w,B} + (3-y)v_{y,B}}{2(v_{y,B} + v_{1,A})}\sum_{j=1}^{m} v_{j,B} - \frac{v_{1,A}\left(\sum_{w=1}^{y-1} v_{w,B} + (3-y)v_{y,B}\right)^2}{4(v_{y,B} + v_{1,A})^2}$$

5.6   Agent *n* Active on the A-Side, Agent *y* with Partial Support Active on the B-Side

In this section, we go through the equilibrium path for the five stages of the game, presented in section1, in case (9.19) is satisfied and (9.25') and (9.27') is not. Then agent *n* will be active on the A-side and agent *y* will be active on the B-side, receiving partial support.

1. The A-side designates agent n as the active agent. The B-sides designates agent y as the active agent, where y is given by (9.19'').
2. On the A-side, the agents $f = 1, ..., n-1$ offer support to agent n. The support rate from agent f is, replacing m by y in (9.22b):

$$S_{f,A} = \frac{(v_{n,A} + v_{y,B})(v_{f,A} - v_{n,A})}{v_{n,A}\left(\sum_{w=1}^{y-1} v_{w,B} + (2-y)v_{y,B}\right) + v_{m,B}\left(\sum_{i=1}^{n} v_{i,A} + (1-n)v_{n,A}\right)}$$

The total amount of support is, replacing m by y in (9.23a):

$$\sum_{f=1}^{n-1} S_{f,A} = \frac{(v_{n,A} + v_{y,B})\left(\sum_{i=1}^{n} v_{i,A} - nv_{n,A}\right)}{v_{n,A}\left(\sum_{w=1}^{y-1} v_{j,B} + (2-y)v_{y,B}\right) + v_{y,B}\left(\sum_{i=1}^{n} v_{i,A} + (1-n)v_{n,A}\right)}$$

On the B-side, the agents $w = 1, ..., y-1$ offer support to agent y. The support rate from agent w is, replacing m by y in (9.22b):

$$S_{w,B} = \frac{(v_{n,A} + v_{y,B})(v_{w,B} - v_{y,B})}{v_{n,A}\left(\sum_{w=1}^{y-1} v_{w,B} + (2-y)v_{y,B}\right) + v_{y,B}\left(\sum_{i=1}^{n} v_{i,A} + (1-n)v_{n,A}\right)}$$

The total amount of support is, replacing m by y in (9.23b):

$$\sum_{w=1}^{y-1} S_{w,B} = \frac{(v_{n,A} + v_{y,B})\left(\sum_{w=1}^{y-1} v_{w,B} + (1-y)v_{m,B}\right)}{v_{n,A}\left(\sum_{w=1}^{y-1} v_{w,B} + (2-y)v_{y,B}\right) + v_{y,B}\left(\sum_{i=1}^{n} v_{i,A} + (1-n)v_{n,A}\right)}$$

This results in the following enlarged stakes for agents n and y, which can be found by replacing m by y in (9.16a) and (9.16b) respectively:

$$T_A(n,y) = \frac{v_{n,A}\left(\sum_{w=1}^{y-1} v_{w,B} + (2-y)v_{y,B}\right) + v_{y,B}\left(\sum_{i=1}^{n} v_{i,A} + (1-n)v_{n,A}\right)}{\left(\sum_{w=1}^{y-1} v_{w,B} + (3-y)v_{y,B}\right) - \left(\sum_{i=1}^{n} v_{i,A} - nv_{n,A}\right)} \quad (9.27a)$$

$$T_B(n,y) = \frac{v_{n,A}\left(\sum_{w=1}^{y-1} v_{w,B} + (2-y)v_{y,B}\right) + v_{y,B}\left(\sum_{i=1}^{n} v_{i,A} + (1-n)v_{n,A}\right)}{\left(\sum_{i=1}^{n} v_{i,A} + (2-n)v_{n,A}\right) - \left(\sum_{w=1}^{y-1} v_{w,B} + (1-y)v_{y,B}\right)} \quad (9.27b)$$

3. The active agents' efforts are, from (7.8), (9.27a) and (9.27b):

$$x_{n,A} = \left[\left(\sum_{i=1}^{n} v_{i,A} + (2-n)v_{n,A} \right) - \left(\sum_{w=1}^{y-1} v_{w,B} + (1-y)v_{y,B} \right) \right] *$$

$$* \frac{v_{n,A} \left(\sum_{w=1}^{y-1} v_{w,B} + (2-y)v_{y,B} \right) + v_{y,B} \left(\sum_{i=1}^{n} v_{i,A} + (1-n)v_{n,A} \right)}{4(v_{n,A} + v_{m,B})^2}$$

$$x_{m,B} = \left[\left(\sum_{j=1}^{m} v_{j,B} + (2-m)v_{m,B} \right) - \left(\sum_{i=1}^{n} v_{i,A} - nv_{n,A} \right) \right] *$$

$$* \frac{v_{n,A} \left(\sum_{j=1}^{m} v_{j,B} + (1-m)v_{m,B} \right) + v_{m,B} \left(\sum_{i=1}^{n} v_{i,A} + (1-n)v_{n,A} \right)}{4(v_{n,A} + v_{m,B})^2}$$

4. On the A-side, the agents $f = 1, ..., n-1$ pay the support they promised to agent n. The amount that agent f has to pay is:

$$s_{f,A} x_{n,A} = \frac{(v_{f,A} - v_{n,A}) \left[\left(\sum_{i=1}^{n} v_{i,A} + (2-n)v_{n,A} \right) - \left(\sum_{w=1}^{y-1} v_{w,B} + (1-y)v_{y,B} \right) \right]}{4(v_{n,A} + v_{y,B})}$$

On the B-side, the agents $w = 1, ..., y-1$ pay the support they promised to agent y. The amount that agent w has to pay is:

$$s_{w,B} x_{m,B} = \frac{(v_{w,B} - v_{y,B}) \left[\left(\sum_{w=1}^{y-1} v_{w,B} + (3-y)v_{y,B} \right) - \left(\sum_{i=1}^{n} v_{i,A} - nv_{n,A} \right) \right]}{4(v_{n,A} + v_{y,B})}$$

5. The success probabilities are, from (7.9), (9.27a) and (9.27b):

$$\rho_A = \frac{\sum_{i=1}^{n} v_{i,A} + (2-n)v_{n,A} - \sum_{w=1}^{y-1} v_{y,B} + (y-1)v_{y,B}}{2(v_{n,A} + v_{y,B})}$$

$$\rho_B = \frac{\sum_{w=1}^{y-1} v_{w,B} + (3-y)v_{y,B} - \sum_{i=1}^{n} v_{i,A} + nv_{n,A}}{2(v_{n,A} + v_{y,B})}$$

The aggregate payoffs are:

$$\sum_{i=1}^{n} U_{i,A} = \frac{\left(\sum_{i=1}^{n} v_{i,A} + (2-n)v_{n,A}\right) - \left(\sum_{w=1}^{y-1} v_{y,B} + (1-y)v_{y,B}\right)}{2(v_{n,A} + v_{y,B})} *$$

$$* \left[\sum_{i=1}^{n} v_{i,A} - \frac{v_{n,A}\left(\sum_{w=1}^{y-1} v_{w,B} + (2-y)v_{y,B}\right) + v_{y,B}\left(\sum_{i=1}^{n} v_{i,A} + (1-n)v_{n,A}\right)}{2(v_{n,A} + v_{y,B})}\right]$$

$$\sum_{j=1}^{m} U_{j,B} = \frac{\left(\sum_{w=1}^{y-1} v_{w,B} + (3-y)v_{y,B}\right) - \left(\sum_{i=1}^{n} v_{i,A} - nv_{n,A}\right)}{2(v_{n,A} + v_{y,B})} *$$

$$* \left[\sum_{j=1}^{m} v_{j,B} - \frac{v_{n,A}\left(\sum_{w=1}^{y-1} v_{w,B} + (2-y)v_{y,B}\right) + v_{y,B}\left(\sum_{i=1}^{n} v_{i,A} + (1-n)v_{n,A}\right)}{2(v_{n,A} + v_{y,B})}\right] \quad (9.28)$$

6. APPLICATION

6.1 Introduction

In this section, we will apply our model of cooperative rent seeking to instrument choice in environmental policy, when the choice is between a market instrument and an instrument of direct regulation. The central question of our application is: 'Can the model explain why the market instrument has a low, or even zero, success probability, although it has the highest aggregate valuation?'

In section 6.2 we will see that the answer to this question is affirmative. We will give the general result and the intuition behind it. In section 6.3 we illustrate the general rule with some numerical simulations. In section 6.4 we turn to instrument choice in environmental policy with the four interest groups of shareholders, workers, environmentalists and the environmental bureaucracy. There we will also go through the whole five-stage game for specific values of the agents' stakes.

6.2 The General Result

With cooperation in the form of support, the side with the highest aggregate stake can be the underdog, i.e. have a success probability below one half. For our present purpose, the key result from our previous analysis is the definition of the underdog in Proposition 9.7. We saw that the A-side is the underdog if and only if:

$$\sum_{i=1}^{n} v_{i,A} + (1-n)v_{n,A} < \sum_{j=1}^{m} v_{j,B} + (1-m)v_{m,B} \tag{9.15}$$

We see that it is possible that the A-side is the underdog even if $\Sigma v_{i,A} > \Sigma v_{j,B}$, i.e. even though the aggregate stake on the A-side exceeds the aggregate stake on the B-side. Given that $\Sigma v_{i,A} > \Sigma v_{j,B}$, there are two factors that can cause the A-side to be the underdog. These two factors are readily derived from inequality (9.15):[6]

1. on the A-side the agent with the lowest stake has a higher stake than on the B-side ($v_{n,A} > v_{m,B}$);
2. on the A-side there are more agents than on the B-side ($n > m$).

Ad 1. The agent with the lowest stake (agent n on the A-side) will be the active agent with support.[7] All other agents $f = 1, ..., n-1$, will support agent n. The agents f move in stage 2 of the rent seeking game, and agent n moves in stage 3 of the rent seeking game. Thus, the agents f move before agent n.

We can say that when $v_{n,A} > v_{m,B}$, the B-side has a relative first mover advantage over the A-side. The aggregate stake $\Sigma v_{j,B} - v_{m,B}$ of the supporting agents, moving in stage 2, is relatively high, and the stake $v_{m,B}$ of the active agent, moving in stage 3, is relatively low. It is advantageous for a side to have a lot of stake concentrated in an earlier stage, in 2 rather than in 3. The agents moving in stage 2 have a larger influence on the outcome of the game than the agents moving in stage 3, because in stage 2 total support is being determined, and in stage 3, total support has already been determined. Thus, the higher the stakes of the supporting agents, who move in stage 2, relative to the stake of the active agent who moves in stage 3, the more influence a side has on the course of the game. If $v_{n,A} = 0$, the A-side would have all its stake in stage 2. Then it would receive the maximum possible payoff from cooperation, given the value of T_B (inequality (9.12) in Lemma 9.3 would become an equality). Then it would not even matter if $n > m$.

Ad 2. When there are more agents on the A-side than on the B-side ($n > m$), there will be more agents supporting agent n on the A-side than supporting agent m on the B-side. Having a lot of supporting agents is a disadvantage, because an agent determines his support, taking the support by other agents as given. Therefore, total support will be lower than optimal (cf. Lemma 9.3). The higher the number of supporting agents (given the aggregate stake), the stronger this deviation will be.

This result of cooperative rent seeking concurs with the general finding of political economy (see Chapter 2, section 4.2), that large groups of agents with small per capita stakes are less effective than small groups of agents with large per capita stake (Olson, 1965). To be more precise, the explanation that this model offers is not that agents with low per capita stakes are hard to identify (or do not even know that they have a stake), nor is the explanation that the agents would rather free ride on others' efforts than do anything themselves. However, one can say that in this model, the agents free ride on each other's support rates. Looking at it from a different angle, the explanation for too little support is that each agent determines his support rate by himself, taking as given the support from others. An agent only takes into account that his support raises his own payoff, and not that it also raises the other agents' payoffs. Therefore he will offer too little support from the point of view of the common cause. The more fragmented the aggregate stake across the agents, the lower will be the aggregate support.

The above analysis highlights the requirement that when analysing support, we must know whether a certain group can be regarded as one agent. Applying the analysis to instrument choice, we must know at which aggregation level we can still speak of one agent. For instance: can high-skilled workers and low-skilled workers from an industry be regarded as one agent? Can shareholders from different firms be regarded as one agent?

6.3   Numerical Simulations

In this section, I will present some numerical findings to illustrate the general result that the side with the highest aggregate stake can have the lowest success probability. We will first elaborate the possibility that the side with the highest aggregate stake is the underdog. Then we will see for which parameter values the side with the highest aggregate stake has zero success probability.

The Figures 9.4 accompany our numerical simulations. In Figure 9.4a, the number of agents on the A-side n is 4, in Figure 9.4b, $n = 8$. The area in which we are interested is the area above the lines AB and BC. We assume $\Sigma v_{j,B} = 200$, so that we shall only look at $\Sigma v_{i,A} > 200$, i.e. the area above the line AB. On the line BC:

$$nv_{n,A} = \sum_{i=1}^{n} v_{i,A}$$

To illustrate inequality (9.15), let us assume that and $v_{m,B} = 0.$[8] From the A-side's point of view, this is the worst case scenario. The lower $v_{m,B}$, the higher the LHS of (9.15) must be in order to be the favourite.

The line AC in Figures 9.4 gives the parameter values for which the A-side has success probability one half. Above and to the left of AC, that is: with a higher $\Sigma v_{i,A}$ or a lower $v_{n,A}$, the A-side is the favourite. Below and to the right of AC, that is: with a lower $\Sigma v_{i,A}$ or a higher $v_{n,A}$, the A-side is the underdog. We also see that for $n = 8$, AC is higher than for $n = 4$. This illustrates the disadvantage of a high number of agents. It means that there are values of $\Sigma v_{i,A}$ and $v_{n,A}$ for which the A-

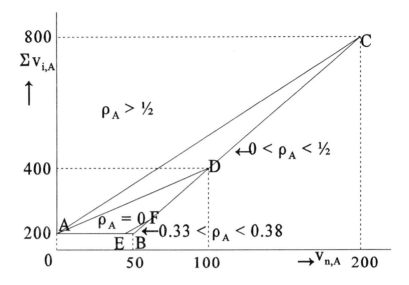

Figure 9.4a   Success probability for n = 4

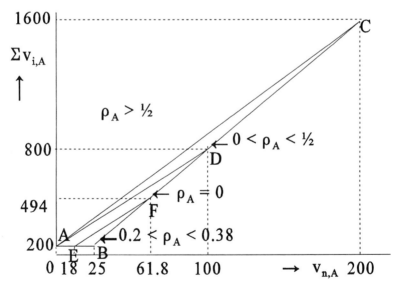

Figure 9.4b   Success probability for n = 8

side is the favourite with $n = 4$ but the underdog with $n = 8$.

The lower $\Sigma v_{i,A}$ and the higher $v_{n,A}$, i.e. the lower and more to the right the A-side is in Figures 9.4, the 'weaker' the A-side is. The weaker the A-side is, the lower is its success probability, at least until the point where the B-side can play full support. At this point, the A-side is so weak that its success probability is zero, even though $\Sigma v_{i,A} > \Sigma v_{j,B}$. We have seen in section 4.3 that the B-side can play full support when:

$$\max \left[\sum_{i=1}^{n} v_{i,A} + (2 - n)v_{n,A}; \, 2v_{1,A} \right] \leq \sum_{j=1}^{m} v_{j,B} - mv_{m,B} \qquad (9.19)$$

Again, let us assume $v_{m,B} = 0$, which is as bad as it can get for the A-side. Then we can infer from (9.19) that a necessary condition for $\rho_A = 0$ is $2v_{1,A} \leq \Sigma v_{j,B}$. Note that this condition cannot be satisfied for $n = 2$ and $\Sigma v_{i,A} > \Sigma v_{j,B}$. Thus, when $n = 2$, the A-side will always have a positive success probability.

For further elaboration, we again take $\Sigma v_{j,B} = 200$. Thus, the right hand side of (9.19) equals 200. Then a necessary condition for $\rho_A = 0$ is $v_{1,A} \leq 100$.

For $n = 3$:

$$2v_{1,A} \geq \sum_{i=1}^{n} v_{i,A} + (2 - n)v_{n,A} = v_{1,A} + v_{2,A}$$

Thus, for $n = 3$, $\rho_A = 0$ is only possible when $v_{1,A} \leq 100$.

For $n > 3$ and $v_{1,A} \leq 100$, we have to check whether:

$$\sum_{i=1}^{n} v_{i,A} + (2 - n)v_{n,A} \leq \sum_{j=1}^{m} v_{j,B} - mv_{m,B} \qquad (9.16)$$

Condition (9.16) is drawn in Figures 9.4 as AD. When we assume $v_{1,A} \leq 100$, the success probability of the A-side is positive above and to the left of AD. Below and to the right of AD, there is an area where the A-side has zero success probability.

However, there can be an area below AD where the success probability of the A-side is positive again. This is due to the other condition for full support on the B-side, namely that the B-side must prefer to play full support. To illustrate this condition, we must specify the alternative to full support on the B-side. Let us assume that there are three agents on the B-side with $v_{1,B} = v_{2,B} = 100$, $v_{3,B} = 0$. Then, when the B-side does not designate agent 3 as the active agent, there will be no support and the stake of the active agent on the B-side will be 100.

Whether the B-side prefers to play full support or no support, depends upon the stake of the active agent on the A-side T_A. When T_A is large, the aggregate payoff on the B-side will be low with no support and the B-side prefers to play full support. When T_A is small, the aggregate payoff on the B-side will be high with no support and the B-side prefers to play no support. We shall now determine the critical value of T_A.

First we determine the aggregate payoff on the B-side with full support. With full support, the aggregate payoff on the B-side is $\Sigma v_{j,B} - T_A$. From (9.10b), agents 1 and 2 on the B-side will still offer full support to agent 3 when T_A is as high as 100. Then the aggregate payoff on the B-side with full support can become as low as $200 - 100 = 100$. And of course, if the A-side can keep the B-side from playing full support by setting $T_A = 100$, it will do just that. Thus, the B-side prefers to play no support instead of full support when the aggregate payoff with no support is above 100.

When the B-side plays no support, its aggregate payoff is, from (A.1):

$$\sum_{j=1}^{m} U_{j,B} = \frac{T_B}{T_A + T_B} \sum_{j=1}^{m} v_{j,B} - \frac{T_A T_B^2}{(T_A + T_B)^2}$$

The B-side prefers to play no support when:

$$\frac{T_B}{T_A + T_B} 200 - \frac{T_A T_B^2}{(T_A + T_B)^2} > 100$$

To keep the analysis general, we have not substituted $T_B = 100$ yet. The critical value of T_A as a function of T_B is:

$$T_{AC} = \frac{-T_B + \sqrt{T_B^4 + 40,000 * T_B^2}}{2}$$

Substituting $T_B = 100$, we find $T_{AC} \approx 61.8$. Thus, when $T_A < 61.8$ against $T_B = 100$, the B-side prefers to play no support. When $T_A > 61.8$ against $T_B = 100$, the B-side prefers to play full support.

As we know from Lemma 9.6, the B-side will only consider no support when it is the favourite with no support. Our finding that $T_{AC} < T_B$ confirms this. On the A-side, either agent 1 or agent n will be active when the B-side plays no support. As we know from Proposition 9.8, the agent with the highest enlarged stake will be active on the A-side. When $v_{1,A} > 61.8$, then $T_A > 61.8$, so that the B-side prefers to play full support. Thus, a necessary condition for the B-side to play no support is $v_{1,A} < 61.8$. For $v_{1,A} < 61.8$, we still have to check whether the enlarged stake of agent n is below 61.8 as well.

For $n = 2$ and $n = 3$, $v_{1,A} > 61.8$, because $v_{1,A} < 61.8$ would imply $\Sigma_{i,A} < 200$. For $n > 3$ and $v_{1,A} < 61.8$, we have to apply (9.12) in order to check whether:

$$\frac{100 \left(\sum_{i=1}^{n} v_{i,A} + (2 - n) v_{n,A} \right)}{200 - n v_{n,A} + \sum_{i=1}^{n} v_{i,A}} > 61.8$$

This inequality can be rewritten as:

$$\sum_{i=1}^{n} v_{i,A} + (1.236 - n)v_{n,A} > 76.4 \qquad (9.29)$$

The critical value of $\Sigma v_{i,A}$ as a function of $v_{n,A}$ is drawn in Figures 9.4 as EF. To find the location of point E in Figures 9.4, we set $\Sigma v_{i,A} = 200$. Then the LHS of (9.29) assumes the value of 76.4 for $n = 4$ when $v_{n,A} \approx 44.7$ and for $n = 8$ when $v_{n,A} \approx 18.3$. Point F is located where $nv_{n,A} = \Sigma v_{i,A}$, in which case the LHS of (9.29) is 76.4 when $v_{n,A} = T_{AC} \approx 61.8$.

Thus, as long as $61.8 < v_{1,A} \leq 100$, the success probability of the A-side is zero in the area ADFE. In the area EFB, the A-side has a positive success probability. Since $T_A < 61.8$ in this area, the success probability is below:

$$\frac{61.8}{61.8 + 100} \approx 0.38$$

The lowest success probability in the area EFB is at point B, where $\Sigma v_{i,A} = nv_{n,A} = 200$. In that case, $T_A = v_{n,A}$, so that for $n = 4$ we find $T_A = 50$ and $\rho_A = 1/3$ and for $n = 8$ we find $T_A = 25$ and $\rho_A = 1/5$.

Finally, we note that the A-side's success probability is not a monotonous function of its 'weakness'. We can say that the A-side is weaker, the lower $\Sigma v_{i,A}$, the higher n and $v_{n,A}$ and (in case the B-side can play full support) the lower $v_{1,A}$. As long as neither side can play full support, the A-side's success probability declines when it becomes weaker. When $v_{1,A} \leq 100$ and below the line AD in Figures 9.4, the A-side is so weak that the B-side can play full support. However, the B-side will only play full support when the A-side is not too weak. When the A-side is very weak, the B-side prefers not to play full support, so that the A-side has a positive success probability again. The reason for this is as follows. When the A-side is so weak that the B-side can play full support, the (minimum) aggregate payoff on the B-side is $\Sigma v_{j,B} - T_{AS}$. The value of T_{AS}, given by (9.10b), does not depend on the weakness of the A-side. Thus, the B-side's aggregate payoff with full support does not depend on the A-side's weakness. On the other hand, the B-side's aggregate payoff under the alternative to full support (either partial or no support) increases, the weaker the A-side becomes. Thus, the weaker the A-side, the more attractive it becomes for the B-side not to play full support. When the A-side is very weak, the B-side chooses not to play full support.

6.4 Instrument Choice in Environmental Policy with Four Interest Groups

We will now look more closely at instrument choice in environmental policy with the four interest groups we identified in Chapter 4, section 6: environmentalists, the environmental bureaucracy, shareholders and workers. The market instrument is instrument A, direct regulation is instrument B, and $\Sigma v_{i,A} > \Sigma v_{j,B}$. Let us first look at the general results for four agents, and then at specific instruments.

With four interest groups, we cannot achieve all too spectacular results. First of all, it is impossible for the success probability of market instruments to be zero. When there is one interest group on the A-side and three on the B-side, the A-side will be the favourite. This can be seen from (9.15) with $n = 1$, $m = 3$, and $\Sigma v_{i,A} > \Sigma v_{j,B}$. In section 6.3 we have already seen that the A-side cannot have zero success probability when there are two agents on the A-side. And when there are three agents on the A-side, there is only one agent on the B-side. This one agent can only enter the rent seeking contest with his own finite stake, so that ρ_A will be positive.

When there are two agents on either side, the condition for the A-side to be the losing side is, from (9.15) with $n = m = 2$:

$$v_{1,A} < v_{1,B} \qquad\qquad (9.30)$$

Note that this is the same condition as in the noncooperative equilibrium, where only the agents 1 on either side will be active (Chapter 8, section 2.1).

When there are three agents on the A-side and one on the B-side, the condition for the A-side to be on the losing side is, from (9.15) with $n = 3$ and $m = 1$:

$$v_{1,A} + v_{2,A} - v_{3,A} < v_{1,B} \qquad\qquad (9.31)$$

What is the implication of these general results for the contest between a market instrument and an instrument of direct regulation? Let us first consider grand-fathering. It is unlikely that the side promoting grandfathering will be the underdog. This is because shareholders will have a large stake in grandfathering. If instrument choice is a contest between shareholders (in favour of grandfathe-ring) and the other three interest groups (in favour of direct regulation), then the shareholders will be the favourite, as we saw above. The environmental organization may also be in favour of grandfathering, as we saw in Chapter 4, section 4. In a contest of two against two, condition (9.30) tells us we should compare the stakes of the agents with the highest stakes on either side. Again, this looks good for grandfathering, because the shareholders will have a large stake in grandfathering.

Financial instruments, on the other hand, may have a low success probability with support. As with noncooperative behaviour studied in Chapter 8, the outcome depends crucially on the distribution of the financial instrument's revenues.

The following example illustrates the workings of cooperation. Suppose the choice is between charges and bubbles. All four interest groups would prefer bubbles if they did not receive anything from the charge revenues. In the terms to be used in Chapter 10, they have a no-revenue stake (NRS) in bubbles. Table 9.4a

Table 9.4a   No-revenue stakes (NRSs) and revenue distributions

	NRS in bubbles	revenue distr. 2/2	revenue distr. 3/1
Environmentalists	20	100	100
Env. bureaucracy	20	90	70
Workers	50	40	60
Shareholders	150	50	50
Total	240	280	280

Table 9.4b   Revenue stakes

	revenue distribution 2/2		revenue distribution 3/1	
	charges	bubbles	charges	bubbles
Environmentalists	80		80	
Env. bureaucracy	70		50	
Workers		10	10	
Shareholders		100		100

gives the interest groups' no-revenue stakes in bubbles. It also gives two possible distributions of the charge revenue, labelled 2/2 and 3/1. Note that the total revenues from charges exceed the sum of the no-revenue stakes in bubbles. This reflects our assumption that the aggregate valuation of the market instrument exceeds the aggregate valuation of direct regulation.

When an interest group's share in the charge revenues exceeds its no-revenue stake in bubbles, we say it has a *revenue stake* in charges. Conversely, when an interest group's share in the charge revenues is below its no-revenue stake in bubbles, it has a revenue stake in bubbles. Table 9.4b gives the interest groups' revenue stakes for the no-revenue stakes and the revenue distributions from Table 9.4a.

Let charges be instrument A and bubbles instrument B. With revenue distribution 2/2, the A-side will be the underdog. This is because, according to inequality (9.30), we should compare the stakes of the agents with the highest stakes on either side. These are the shareholders for bubbles and the environmentalists for charges. Since the shareholders have a larger stake, charges have a success probability below one half. With revenue distribution 3/1, the workers receive 20 more and the environmental bureaucracy receives 20 less than with 2/2. Now the workers will be on the A-side as well. This time, the A-side is the favourite because inequality (9.31) is not satisfied. On the left hand side of (9.31) we have 120, and on the right hand side we have 100.

Thus, in this example ρ_A is higher when there are three instead of two agents on the A-side. The disadvantage of having an extra agent on the A-side is more than compensated by the fact that this extra agent has a small stake. This example impresses upon us that when identifying the underdog, we should not only look at which side has the highest number of agent. The agent with the lowest stake also plays an important role.

Let us now work out the details of the games for both revenue distributions. We begin with revenue distribution 3/1, because this is the easiest case. In fact, it is the numerical elaboration of the equilibrium path presented in section 5.2, but with the labels 'A-side' and 'B-side' interchanged.

1. The shareholders are the only agents on the B-side (in favour of bubbles), so they must enter the contest with their own stake. The A-side is the favourite, so it designates the workers, the interest group with the lowest stake, as the active agent.

2. On the A-side, the environmentalists and the environmental bureaucracy support the workers. The support rate s_{1A} from the environmentalists is, analogous to (9.20):

$$s_{1A} = \frac{(100 + 10)(80 - 10)}{100*(140 - 10)} \approx 0.592$$

The support rate s_{2A} from the environmental bureaucracy is, analogous to (9.20):

$$s_{2A} = \frac{(100 + 10)(50 - 10)}{100*(140 - 10)} \approx 0.338$$

Thus, between them, the environmentalists and the environmental bureaucracy pay for approximately 93% of the workers' efforts. The workers only have to pay 7% themselves. Their enlarged stake is, from (9.17):

$$T_A = \frac{100*(140 - 10)}{2*100 + 3*10 - 140} = 144\frac{4}{9}$$

3. The effort levels $x_{3,A}$ of the workers and $x_{1,B}$ of the shareholders are most easily calculated from their (enlarged) stakes of 144.4 and 100, respectively, and (7.8):

$$x_{3,A} = \frac{144.4^2 * 100}{(144.4 + 100)^2} \approx 34.9 \qquad x_{1,B} = \frac{144.4 * 100^2}{(144.4 + 100)^2} \approx 24.2$$

4. The amounts the environmentalists and the environmental bureaucracy pay to the workers are, respectively:

$$s_{1,A} x_{3,A} \approx 0.592 * 34.9 \approx 20.7 \qquad s_{2,A} x_{3,A} \approx 0.338 * 34.9 \approx 11.8$$

5. The success probabilities are most easily calculated from the active agents' stakes and (7.9):

$$\rho_A = \frac{144.4}{144.4 + 100} = \frac{13}{22} \approx 0.59 \qquad \rho_B = \frac{100}{144.4 + 100} = \frac{9}{22} \approx 0.41$$

The aggregate payoffs are, from the above and (7.10):

$$\Sigma U_{i,A} = \frac{13}{22} * 140 - 34.9 \approx 47.8 \qquad v_{1,B} = \frac{100^3}{(144.4 + 100)^2} \approx 16.7$$

The payoffs for the environmentalists, the environmental bureaucracy and the workers are, respectively:

$$U_{1,A} \approx \frac{13}{22} * 80 - 20.7 \approx 26.6$$

$$U_{2,A} \approx \frac{13}{22} * 50 - 11.8 \approx 17.7$$

$$U_{3,A} \approx \frac{13}{22} * 10 - 0.07 * 34.9 \approx 3.5$$

Now we turn to revenue distribution 2/2. This is a more complicated case than 3/1, because now we have to find out which form of cooperation the A-side will use. We know the B-side will use support, because it is the favourite. But we have to determine whether the A-side will use support or not, i.e. whether it designates agent 2 (the environmental bureaucracy) or agent 1 (the environmentalists) as the active agent.

To this end, we apply Proposition 9.8. We have to calculate $T_A(2,2)$, the equilibrium stake of the environmental bureaucracy in the contest against the workers. From (9.18), agent 2 will be active if:

$$T_A(2,2) = \frac{v_{2,A} v_{1,B} + v_{2,B} v_{1,A}}{v_{1,B} + v_{2,B} - v_{1,A} + v_{2,A}} > v_{1,A} \qquad (9.32)$$

However, substituting the values of the stakes, we find:

$$T_A(2,2) = \frac{70*100 + 10*80}{(100 + 10) - (80 - 70)} = 78 < v_{1,A} = 80$$

Thus, according to Proposition 9.8, the A-side should designate agent 1, the environmentalists, as its active agent. In fact, it can be shown that, with two agents on either side, agent 1 will always be designated as the active agent for the underdog. This is because the condition for agent 2 to be the active agent, i.e. for (9.32) to hold, is $v_{1,A} > v_{1,B}$. But condition (9.30) for the A-side to be the underdog is $v_{1,A} < v_{1,B}$.

Now we can go through the whole game for revenue distribution 2/2. Again, this is a numerical elaboration of the equilibrium path presented in section 5.2, but now the labels 'A-side' and 'B-side' are the same as in section 5.2.

1. The A-side designates the environmentalists as the active agent. The B-side designates the workers as the active agent.
2. On the A-side, the environmental bureaucracy does not offer support to the environmentalists. On the B-side, the shareholders support the workers. Their support rate $s_{1,B}$ is, from (9.20):

$$s_{1,B} = \frac{(80 + 10)(100 - 10)}{80*110} \approx 0.92$$

3. The efforts $x_{1,A}$ of the environmentalists and $x_{2,B}$ of the workers are most easily calculated from their (enlarged) stakes of 80 and 125.7, respectively, and (7.8):

$$x_{1,A} \approx \frac{80^2*125.7}{(80 + 125.7)^2} \approx 19 \qquad x_{2,B} \approx \frac{80*125.7^2}{(80 + 125.7)^2} \approx 29.9$$

4. The shareholders pay the support they promised to the workers. The amount they pay is:

$$s_{1,B}x_{2,B} = 0.92*29.9 = 27.5$$

5. The success probabilities are, from the agents' stakes and (7.9):

$$p_A = \frac{80}{80 + 125.7} = \frac{7}{18} \approx 0.39 \qquad p_B = \frac{125.7}{80 + 125.7} = \frac{11}{18} \approx 0.61$$

From the above and (7.10), the payoffs for the environmentalists and the environmental bureaucracy are, respectively:

$$U_{1,A} \approx \frac{80^3}{(80 + 125.7)^2} \approx 12.1 \qquad U_{2,A} = \frac{7}{18} * 70 \approx 27.2$$

The aggregate payoff on the B-side is:

$$\Sigma U_{j,B} \approx \frac{11}{18} * 110 - 29.9 \approx 37.3$$

The payoffs for the shareholders and the workers are:

$$U_{1,B} = \frac{11}{18} * 100 - 27.5 \approx 33.6$$

$$U_{2,B} \approx \frac{11}{18} * 100 - 0.08 * 29.9 \approx 3.7$$

From this numerical elaboration, two conclusions can be drawn. First, a small change in the distribution of the revenues can have a dramatic impact on the success probabilities of the instruments. Taking 20 units of the revenue away from the environmental bureacracy and giving them to the workers results in an increase of the success probability of charges from 0.39 to 0.59.

Secondly, although the success probability of the charge is higher with revenue distribution 3/1, the aggregate payoff of all agents together is lower: 64.5 versus 76.7. This is because in 3/1 instrument choice is more hotly contested than in 2/2. This implies that, when we are concerned with welfare, we should not simply embrace the revenue distribution that yields the highest success probability for the welfare-maximizing financial instrument. Society as a whole may be better off with a lower success probability for the financial instrument, if this also means lower wasteful rent seeking expenditures. We will come back to this argument at length in Chapter 10.

7.   CONCLUSION

In this chapter, we looked at a rent seeking contest for an impure public good, where two sides are opposed to each other. We introduced and analysed support as a mechanism of cooperation for agents on the same side. With support, one agent is active on behalf of a whole side. The other agents can support this active agent, i.e. pay part of his effort. We have seen that the active agent will receive support from agents with a higher stake.

Whether and how a side makes use of the support mechanism, depends on whether a side is the favourite or the underdog. The favourite side has a success probability above one half, the underdog's success probability is below one half.

When the underdog plays support, the agent with the lowest stake will be active. This agent will be supported by all other agents. However, the underdog may also designate agent 1 as the active agent. Agent 1 will not receive any support. Thus, when agent 1 is designated as the active agent, the underdog is effectively playing the noncooperative equilibrium strategy identified in Chapter 8, section 2.1.

When the equilibrium success probability is less than one, the agent with the lowest stake will be active on the favourite side. This agent will be supported by all other agents. When the agents' stakes on the favourite side are relatively large, the favourite can play full support: the supporting agents pay for all of the active agent's efforts. However, the favourite may not want to make use of this opportunity. The aggregate payoff may be higher when it plays partial support. Partial support can be implemented by designating a different agent (not the one with the lowest stake) as the active agent.

The most interesting finding from the model of support for our application to instrument choice is that the side with the highest aggregate stake can actually be the underdog. There are two reasons for this. First, with support, each agent sets the support rate that maximizes his own payoff. He does not take into account that when he increases his support rate, the payoff of the other agents on his side also increases. Thus, total support will be below the optimum for the side as a whole. As a result, a side with a few agents with large per capita stakes will be more successful than a side with a lot of agents with small per capita stakes.

This result is common to the political economy literature (Olson, 1965). We have already encountered it in Chapter 8, section 2, when we discussed the noncooperative equilibrium of a rent seeking contest for a public good. There we saw that the aggregate effort level of a side is too low, because every agent sets the effort level that maximizes his own payoff. The same mechanism is at work in the model of support, but this time it pertains to the support rates instead of the effort levels.

The second reason why the side with the higher aggregate stake can be the underdog is that with support the own stake of its active agent (the agent with the lowest stake) is higher. Because the supporting agents determine their support to the active agent before the active agent makes his effort, the supporting agents have a larger influence on the course of the game. A side has a relative first mover advantage when its supporting agents have a high aggregate stake and its active agent has a low stake.

Thus, with the model of support we can explain why the side with the highest aggregate stake is the underdog. Its success probability can even be zero. Applying the model to instrument choice in environmental policy, we have seen that it is not very useful in explaining a low success probability for grandfathering. This is because there is an interest group with a large stake in grandfathering, namely the shareholders. The model of support is more successful in explaining the low success probability of financial instruments. However, the outcome of a rent seeking contest involving a financial instrument greatly depends on the distribution of the revenues of financial instruments. This distribution was taken as exogenous in this chapter. In Chapter 10, we will endogenize revenue distribution.

APPENDIX. PROOF OF PROPOSITION 9.2

To prove Proposition 9.2, we will analyse $\Sigma U_{i,A}$, the aggregate payoff on the A-side, as a function of T_A and T_B.

Let us first express $\Sigma U_{i,A}$ as a function of x_A and x_B, i.e. the effort level on the A-side and the B-side respectively, made in stage 3 of the rent seeking game. The aggregate payoff on the A-side is:

$$\sum_{i=1}^{n} U_{i,A} = \left(\frac{x_A}{x_A + x_B} \right) \sum_{i=1}^{n} v_{i,A} - x_A$$

Applying Proposition 9.1, we can see (x_A, x_B) as the Nash equilibrium of a rent seeking contest between two agents with stakes T_A and T_B. With the aid of (7.8) and (7.9), we can then write the aggregate payoff of the A-side as a function of T_A and T_B:

$$\sum_{i=1}^{n} U_{i,A} = \left(\frac{T_A}{T_A + T_B} \right) \sum_{i=1}^{n} v_{i,A} - \frac{T_A^2 T_B}{(T_A + T_B)^2} \tag{A.1}$$

The condition for $\Sigma U_{i,A}$ to be nonnegative is:

$$\sum_{i=1}^{n} v_{i,A}(T_A + T_B) - T_A T_B > 0 \tag{A.2}$$

We can now derive:

Lemma 9.7
a. Given the value of T_B and given that $\Sigma v_{i,A} < 2T_B$, the aggregate payoff on the A-side is rising in T_A for:

$$T_A < T_A^* \equiv \frac{\sum\limits_{i=1}^{n} v_{i,A}}{2 - \sum\limits_{i=1}^{n} v_{i,A}/T_B}$$

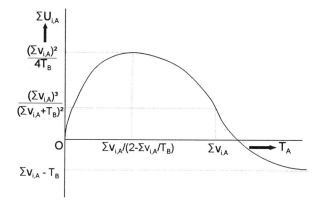

Figure 9.5a   Aggregate payoff as a function of T_A for $\Sigma v_{i,A} < T_B$

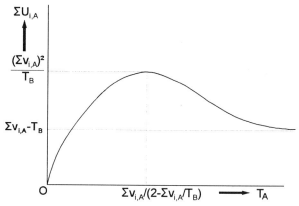

Figure 9.5b   Aggregate payoff as a function of T_A for $T_B < \Sigma v_{i,A} < 2T_B$

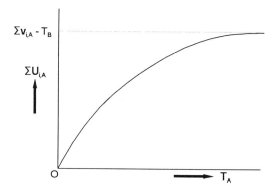

Figure 9.5c   Aggregate payoff as a function of T_A for $\Sigma v_{i,A} > 2T_B$

b. Given the value of T_B and given that $\Sigma v_{i,A} \geq 2T_B$, the aggregate payoff on the A-side is rising monotonically in T_A.

Proof The aggregate payoff on the A-side as a function of T_A and given the value of T_B is drawn in Figures 9.5a to c.

a. Looking at the Figures 9.5a and b, we see that for $\Sigma v_{i,A} < 2T_B$, the A-side's aggregate payoff $\Sigma U_{i,A}$ as a function of T_A has an interior maximum. This can be found as follows:

$$\max_{T_A} \sum_{i=1}^{n} U_{i,A} = \left(\frac{T_A}{T_A + T_B}\right)\sum_{i=1}^{n} v_{i,A} - \frac{T_A^2 T_B}{(T_A + T_B)^2}$$

The first order condition, from which the optimal stake T_A^* can be derived, is:

$$\sum_{i=1}^{n} U_{i,A}' = \left(\frac{T_B}{(T_A^* + T_B)^2}\right)\sum_{i=1}^{n} v_{i,A} - \frac{2T_A^* T_B(T_A^* + T_B) - 2T_A^{*2} T_B}{(T_A^* + T_B)^3} = 0 \quad \text{(A.3)}$$

When $\Sigma v_{i,A} < 2T_B$, the optimal stake of the active agent on the A-side T_A^* is:

$$T_A^* = \frac{\displaystyle\sum_{i=1}^{n} v_{i,A}}{2 - \displaystyle\sum_{i=1}^{n} v_{i,A}/T_B} \quad \text{(9.11)}$$

We see that the optimal stake of the active agent T_A^* is declining in T_B. T_A^* is below (above) $\Sigma v_{i,A}$ when $\Sigma v_{i,A}$ is below (above) T_B.

Differentiating (A.3) with respect to T_A, we find the second derivative:

$$\sum_{i=1}^{n} U_{i,A}'' = \left(\frac{-2T_B}{(T_A + T_B)^3}\right)\sum_{i=1}^{n} v_{i,A} - \frac{2T_B^2(T_A + T_B)^3 - 6T_A T_B(T_A + T_B)^2}{(T_A + T_B)^6} \quad \text{(A.4)}$$

The sign of (A.4) is the sign of:

$$-\sum_{i=1}^{n} v_{i,A}(T_A + T_B) + 2T_A T_B - T_B^2 \quad \text{(A.4')}$$

Substituting $T_A = T_A^*$ from (9.11) into (A.4'), we find:

$$-\sum_{i=1}^{n} v_{i,A}\left(\frac{\displaystyle\sum_{i=1}^{n} v_{i,A}}{2 - \displaystyle\sum_{i=1}^{n} v_{i,A}/T_B} + T_B\right) + 2T_B\left(\frac{\displaystyle\sum_{i=1}^{n} v_{i,A}}{2 - \displaystyle\sum_{i=1}^{n} v_{i,A}/T_B}\right) - T_B^2 = -T_B^2 < 0$$

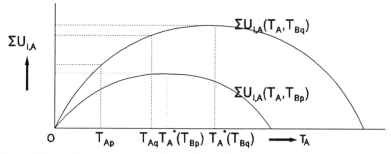

Figure 9.6a   Comparing payoffs for $\Sigma v_{i,A} < T_{Bq}$

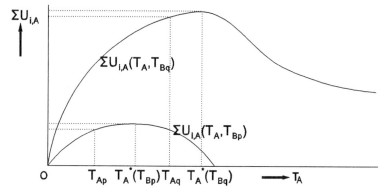

Figure 9.6b   Comparing payoffs for $\frac{1}{2}\Sigma v_{i,A} < T_{Bq} < \Sigma v_{i,A} < T_{Bp}$

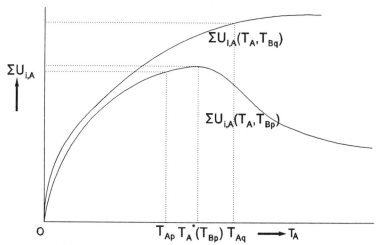

Figure 9.6c   Comparing payoffs for $\Sigma v_{i,A} > T_{Bp} > \frac{1}{2}\Sigma v_{i,A} > T_{Bq}$

Thus, the second order condition is satisfied at $T_A = T_A^*$, so that the aggregate payoff is rising for $T_A < T_A^*$ and there is an interior maximum at $T_A = T_A^*$.

b. For the case $\Sigma v_{i,A} \geq 2T_B$, the aggregate payoff on the A-side is as shown in Figure 9.5c. As can be seen from (A.3), the payoff is rising monotonically in T_A, approaching the value $\Sigma v_{i,A} - T_B$. Whatever the finite value of T_A, the A-side would always like to increase it. This is because the extra payoff (resulting from a higher success probability) always exceeds the extra effort that the active agent will make. It always pays to make the active agent more eager to win. ∎

Let us now examine $\Sigma U_{i,A}$ as a function of T_B, given the value of T_A. It turns out that $\Sigma U_{i,A} \geq 0$ is declining in T_B. This is intuitively clear: the lower the opposition from the B-side, the higher the payoff on the A-side. The formal proof is as follows:

Lemma 9.8 The aggregate payoff on the A-side $\Sigma U_{i,A} \geq 0$ is declining in T_B.

Proof Let us differentiate (A.1) with respect to T_B:

$$\frac{\partial \sum_{i=1}^{n} U_{i,A}}{\partial T_B} = \left(\frac{-T_A}{(T_A + T_B)^2} \right) \sum_{i=1}^{n} v_{i,A} - T_A^2 \left[\frac{(T_A + T_B)^2 - 2(T_A + T_B)T_B}{(T_A + T_B)^4} \right] \quad (A.5)$$

The sign of (A.5) is the sign of:

$$-\sum_{i=1}^{n} v_{i,A}(T_A + T_B) + T_A(T_B - T_A) < 0 \quad (A.5')$$

The inequality follows from (A.2), the condition that $\Sigma U_{i,A} \geq 0$. ∎

In the following, we shall write T_{Ap}, T_{Bp}, T_{Aq} and T_{Bq} instead of $T_A(p,y)$, $T_B(p,y)$, $T_A(q,y)$ and $T_B(q,y)$ respectively, for short. We are now in a position to compare $\Sigma U_{i,A}(T_{Ap}, T_{Bp}) \geq 0$ and $\Sigma U_{i,A}(T_{Aq}, T_{Bq}) \geq 0$, where $T_{Ap} < T_{Aq}$ and $T_{Bp} \geq T_{Bq}$. When we draw the functions $\Sigma U_{i,A}(T_A, T_{Bp}) \geq 0$ and $\Sigma U_{i,A}(T_A, T_{Bq}) \geq 0$ in one figure, then $\Sigma U_{i,A}(T_A, T_{Bp})$ will be below $\Sigma U_{i,A}(T_A, T_{Bq})$ for all T_A, because of Lemma 9.8 and $T_{Bp} > T_{Bq}$.[9] This is shown in Figures 9.6. We are interested in the value of $\Sigma U_{i,A}(T_A, T_{Bp})$ at $T_A = T_{Ap}$, and in the value of $\Sigma U_{i,A}(T_A, T_{Bq})$ at $T_A = T_{Aq}$. We see that, as long as T_{Aq} is on the rising part of $\Sigma U_{i,A}(T_A, T_{Bq})$, then $\Sigma U_{i,A}(T_{Aq}, T_{Bq}) > \Sigma U_{i,A}(T_{Ap}, T_{Bp})$. From Lemma 9.7, we know that when $\Sigma v_{i,A} \geq 2T_{Bq}$, $\Sigma U_{i,A}$ is rising monotonically in T_A. For $\Sigma v_{i,A} < 2T_{Bq}$, $\Sigma U_{i,A}$ is rising in T_A for:

$$T_A < T_A^*(T_{Bq}) \equiv \frac{\sum_{i=1}^{n} v_{i,A}}{2 - \sum_{i=1}^{n} v_{i,A}/T_{Bq}}$$

This completes our proof of Proposition 9.2.

NOTES

1. When the active agent on the other side receives full support, agent 1 may receive support, but he will not make an effort.
2. See Chapter 11, section 2.9, for the concept of ability.
3. Note that when there is no favourite, i.e. when:

$$\sum_{i=1}^{n} v_{i,A} + (1 - n)v_{n,A} = \sum_{j=1}^{m} v_{j,B} + (1 - m)v_{m,B}$$

    inequality (9.15') applies and inequality (9.19) does not hold. In that case, neither side can play full support.
4. Of course, when $y = 1$, the B-side has nothing to choose: it can only play partial support when agent 1 is active.
5. To save space, we do not explicity present the equilibrium with $y = 1$, i.e. where the B-side has to choose between agents 1 and 2 for its active agent, where agent 1 will not receive support and agent 2 will receive full support from agent 1. However, all the expressions used in the conditions in Figure 9.3 and the expressions in sections 5.5 and 5.6 are valid for $y = 1$. Note however, that agent 1 will not receive support.
6. Because $T_A(n,y) < T_A^*[T_B(n,y)]$ according to Lemma 9.3, i.e. the equilibrium stake of the active agent is below the optimal stake of the active agent, the A-side's payoff would be higher if it could achieve a higher success probability. Thus, the two factors that depress the success probability, also depress the aggregate payoff. That is why we can call a high $v_{n,A}$ and a high n disadvantages for the A-side.
7. In our explanation of the two factors, we will assume both sides will play support. In fact, as we know from section 4.2.4, the underdog could also play no support. However, paying attention to this in the explanation would only complicate things, and not add new insight.
8. Of course, $v_{m,B}$ cannot be exactly zero. An agent with stake zero does not have an incentive to make a rent seeking effort, regardless of whether he is partially or fully supported. However, $v_{n,A}$ can be very small.
9. For $T_{Bp} = T_{Bq}$, the functions are identical. The rest of the argument still holds.

10. A Two-Stage Rent Seeking Contest for Instrument Choice and Revenue Division

1. INTRODUCTION

In Chapters 8 and 9 we have only partially taken into account that some instruments of environmental policy, namely the financial instruments (emissions charges and auctioned emission permits), yield government revenue. We have taken into account that the revenues from financial instruments will be distributed amoung the interest groups, but we have taken the distribution itself as given. We assumed that either the interest groups could not influence the distribution, or in case they could influence the distribution, it had already been decided before instrument choice was at stake. Either way, the rent seeking contest for the revenues of financial instruments was not analysed.

Indeed, the reader may suspect we have been 'cooking up' results. In the models of Chapters 8 and 9, the success probability of financial instruments depends critically on how their revenues are distributed. With some distributions, the success probability of financial instruments is one, and with others, it is quite low or even zero. But we have mainly focused on revenue distributions that harm the success probability of financial instruments.

However, one might expect that when we endogenize the revenue distribution, the agents will prefer a procedure by which the revenues are distributed such that all agents prefer the financial instrument. In that case the financial instrument (remember that this is the instrument with the highest aggregate payoff) will be selected without a contest for instrument choice.

But in this chapter we shall see that the above reasoning is only partly correct. It is true that there is a procedure that guarantees the adoption of the financial instrument. But the agents do not necessarily prefer this procedure, because it may entail high rent seeking costs. Thus, the analysis of this chapter gives us another reason why financial instruments are not selected, although aggregate payoff is highest with these instruments.

In this chapter we will analyse the combined contests of instrument choice and revenue distribution. In the analysis, the choice is between two instruments of environmental policy: an instrument of direct regulation and a financial instrument. There are two decisions to be made: which instrument to apply, and in case the financial instrument is chosen, how to distribute its revenue. There are two rent-seeking agents involved, trying to get their favourite instrument chosen, and to obtain as much as possible from the revenues of the financial instrument.

The two political decisions can be taken in two following orders. Thus, the contest can have two different designs:

- IR: first instrument choice, and then, if the financial instrument has been chosen, revenue division;
- RI: first a decision on how to divide the revenue, in case the financial instrument will be chosen, and then instrument choice.

The design RI may seem far-fetched at first sight, but as we saw in Chapter 6, section 2.4, one of the strategies the European Environment Agency recommends to overcome the barriers to implementation of an environmental tax is (EEA, 1996: 7):

> the use of environmental taxes and respective revenues as part of policy packages and green tax reforms.

Thus the EEA recommends the RI design: the government should first work out what to do with the revenues of the charge, and then present the proposal to introduce the charge. The EEA recommendation, based on practice rather than theoretical analysis, is vindicated by the model of this chapter. The success probability of the financial instrument is higher with the design RI than with the design IR. The game RI results in the adoption of instrument A, whereas IR may result in the adoption of B.

However, this does not necessarily imply that the game RI yields a higher aggregate payoff. The aggregate expected payoff may be lower than in IR due to higher rent seeking expenditures. Hence instrument A may not be the welfare-maximizing instrument.

It is possible that both agents have a higher payoff in IR. Then they would like to play the game as IR rather than as RI. As a result, instrument B rather than instrument A will be selected. This is an explanation of the fact that financial instruments are hardly ever applied in practice.

This kind of two-stage game has not been analysed before in the rent seeking literature. Multi-stage rent seeking games have been analysed in the following contexts:

1. A contest for a monopoly, where there is first a contest between firms to obtain the monopoly licence and then the consumers challenge the monopoly (Ellingsen, 1991).[1]
2. The rent is a public good. The agents first work out a scheme for cooperation

and then play the contest (the sharing literature reviewed in Chapter 9, section 2.2), or the agents first try to obtain the rent for their group and then for themselves (Katz and Tokatlidu, 1996).

3. Games with delegation, where an agent manipulates the incentives of another agent, who will be active in the contest. Delegation is closely related to cooperation in a contest for a public good (point 2). Other references, also reviewed in Chapter 9, section 2.3, are Baik and Kim (1997) and Konrad (1997).

4. An infinite repetition of the same game (Rogerson, 1982; Cairns, 1989; Linster, 1994).

5. Games involving the decision maker. The decision maker designs the rent seeking game in a way that maximizes his own income (Michaels, 1988; Glazer, 1993), or agents are involved in a rent seeking game to become the decision maker (Hillman and Katz, 1987).

6. The combination of a rent seeking game and an election campaign (Ursprung, 1990).

Of the above games, the game in this chapter is most akin to Katz and Tokatlidu (1996). In both games, the government decision has two dimensions. In Katz and Tokatlidu, these are the group that receives the rent and the agents within the group that receive the rent. Here, these are the instrument chosen and the allocation of the revenue from the financial instrument. In the model of this chapter, an agent can try to obtain part of the revenue from the financial instrument, even though he is a proponent of direct regulation. In Katz and Tokatlidu (1996), an agent can only try to obtain (part of) the rent for himself, after his group has obtained the rent. Whereas Katz and Tokatlidu consider only one following order for the two-stage game, we will consider two possible following orders.

The rest of this chapter is organized as follows. Section 2 introduces the setting for the game. In section 3, the equilibria for the games IR and RI are given. In section 4, the games IR and RI are compared with respect to the probability that the financial instrument is chosen (section 4.2), expected rent seeking expenditures (section 4.3) and expected payoffs (section 4.4). Section 5 is the application of the model to instrument choice in environmental policy. There we elaborate the idea that the agents may prefer the game to be played as IR, which is to the detriment of the financial instrument. Furthermore, we interpret the early discussion in the Netherlands about regulatory energy charges (Chapter 6, section 3.4.6) in terms of our two-stage game. We argue that industry preferred the IR design, whereas the environmental movement favoured the RI design. Section 6 contains the conclusion.

Table 10.1 The agents' valuations of the instrument, ignoring R

	instrument A	instrument B
agent 1	0	v_1
agent 2	0	v_2

2.   SETTING

In this chapter, we analyse the political choice between two instruments as a rent seeking contest. Instrument A yields government revenue R, instrument B does not yield any government revenue. In the context of environmental policy, instrument A is the financial instrument, and instrument B is direct regulation.

There are two rent-seeking agents, labelled 1 and 2. It will be useful to distinguish between an agent's *revenue stake* and his *no-revenue stake*. An agent's *no-revenue stake* is his stake if he does not receive any part of R. Agent 1 (2)'s no-revenue stake in instrument B is v_1 (v_2). These stakes are the difference between an agent's valuation of the two instruments (without taking R into account), as is shown in Table 10.1.

We assume

$$v_1 + v_2 < R \qquad\qquad (10.1)$$

$$0 \le v_2 < v_1 \qquad\qquad (10.2)$$

Condition (10.1) means that the agents' aggregate valuation of instrument A, including the government revenue that it yields, exceeds the agents' aggregate valuation of instrument B. This reflects the assumption we have maintained throughout the analysis, that market instruments are welfare-maximizing.

Condition (10.2) says that agent 1 would prefer instrument B, if he didn't receive any part of R. Agent 2 would weakly prefer instrument B, if she didn't receive any part of R.[2] But her no-revenue stake in B must be smaller than agent 1's. Condition (10.2) is inspired by our theoretical discussion of the interest groups' preferences in Chapters 3 and 4. There we saw that most interest groups are not interested in financial instruments *per se*. Their only attraction is that they yield government revenue. The only possible exception is that the environmentalist movement prefers an auction of tradable permits to direct regulation.

An agent's *revenue stake*, which is relevant in the instrument choice stage, is her stake taking into account that instrument A also yields the payoff from a rent seeking contest for R. An agent's revenue stake not only depends on the agents' no-revenue stakes and R, but also on the design of the rent seeking contest. We will write agent i's revenue stake in instrument Y as $v_{i,Y}$; $i = 1, 2$; $Y = A, B$. Thus $v_{i,A} \equiv --v_{i,B}$; $i = 1, 2$.

The instrument choice or I-stage is a 'winner takes all' game. We analysed the one-stage 'winner takes all' game in Chapter 7, section 3.5.2. We shall denote rent seeking efforts by agent i ($i = 1, 2$) for instrument Y (Y = A, B) by $x_{i,Y}$. We will use expression (7.2) as our contest success function. Thus, suppose agent 1 is in favour of instrument B and agent 2 is in favour of instrument A. Then the probability that instrument A will be chosen is:

$$\rho_A = \frac{x_{2,A}}{x_{1,B} + x_{2,A}}$$

The revenue division, or R-stage, is a 'division of the pie' game. We analysed the one stage 'division of the pie' game in Chapter 7, section 3.5.3. We shall denote rent seeking efforts by agent i ($i = 1, 2$) for a part of R by x_i. Again, we will use expression (7.2) as our contest success function. Thus, the part of R that goes to agent 1 is:

$$\rho_1 = \frac{x_1}{x_1 + x_2}$$

We will denote total rent seeking expenditures by agent i ($i = 1, 2$) in the whole game by X_i.

In the game under consideration, both agents may have a revenue stake in the same instrument. It is intuitively clear that in that case, this instrument will be chosen without rent seeking expenditures from the agents. But it is somewhat problematic to model this. Here, we will model it by letting the I-stage consist of two rounds. The first round is the enlistment round. The agents can enlist as proponents for instrument A, instrument B or neither instrument (O). The act of enlistment is costless. What happens next, depends upon the enlistments:

- (A, A) and (A, O): instrument A is chosen;
- (B, B) and (B, O): instrument B is chosen;
- (A, B): the agents enter the second round of the I-stage where they make rent seeking expenditures for the instrument they enlisted for;
- (O, O): the decision maker chooses A with probability 0.5 and B with probability 0.5.

We assume that an agent will enlist as a proponent for the instrument in which he has a revenue stake. This is because when the other agent enlists as a proponent for the other instrument, the agents are expected to make a rent seeking effort for the instrument they enlisted for.

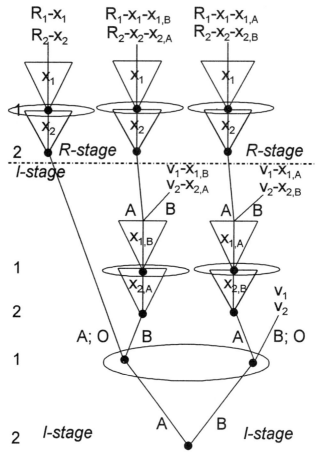

Figure 10.1   The game IR

Table 10.2   The agents' valuations in the I-stage of IR

	Instrument A	Instrument B
Agent 1	$R/4$	v_1
Agent 2	$R/4$	v_2

3. EQUILIBRIA OF THE GAMES

3.1 Introduction

In this section, we analyse the equilibria of the rent seeking game, when played as IR (section 3.2) and when played as RI (section 3.3). We will derive the expressions for the success probabilities of the instruments, the rent seeking expenditures and the agents' payoffs.

3.2 First Instrument Choice, then Revenue Division (IR)

The game tree of IR is drawn in Figure 10.1. The agents begin with the I-stage. First they simultaneously enlist for the I-stage. To keep the figure manageable, the 'do not enlist' (O) strategy is only shown for agent 1. If both agents enlist for instrument A, they immediately move to the R-stage. If both agents enlist for instrument B, B is selected, and the game ends. If the agents enlist for different instruments, there is a rent seeking contest for the instrument. After this contest, the decision maker chooses an instrument, with probabilities determined by the rent seeking efforts. If instrument B is selected, the game ends. If instrument A is selected, the agents enter the R-stage. The R-stage consists of a rent seeking contest for R.

The analysis of this game, as the analysis of any multi-stage game, starts with the final stage. In IR this is the R-stage. This stage is only reached if instrument A is chosen, either because both agents have enlisted for (or not against) A or A is the outcome of the rent seeking contest for the instrument. The equilibrium of the R-stage has been discussed in Chapter 7, section 3.5.3: both players spend $R/4$ ($x_1 = x_2 = R/4$) and receive half of R, so that their payoff from the R-stage is $R/4$. This payoff is added to the agents' valuations of instrument A, so that the agents' valuations in the I-stage of IR are as shown in Table 10.2.

In IR, an agent's revenue stake is the difference between her valuations of the two instruments, as given in Table 10.2:

$$v_{1,B} \equiv -v_{1,A} = v_1 - \frac{R}{4} \qquad v_{2,B} \equiv -v_{2,A} = v_2 - \frac{R}{4} \qquad (10.3)$$

There are three kinds of equilibrium, which we will call IR1, IR2 and IR3. Figure 10.2 shows the equilibria of IR as a function of the variables v_1/R and v_2/R. The diagonal lines depict the bounds of the area under consideration, according to (10.1) and (10.2). Figure 10.2 also shows whether an instrument will be chosen with certainty ('A' or 'B'), or there will be a contest for instrument choice ('A/B'). Now we will discuss the three equilibria.

IR1. $v_2 \geq R/4$

In this case, $v_{1,B} > 0$ and $v_{2,B} \geq 0$, according to (10.2) and (10.3). Even after taking into account the payoff from a rent seeking contest for R, both agents still (weakly) prefer B. Both agents will enlist for instrument B, so that it will be chosen with certainty.

Rent seeking expenditures are zero. An agent's payoff is his valuation of instrument B:

$$U_1(IR1) = v_1 \qquad\qquad U_2(IR1) = v_2$$

IR2. $v_1 \leq R/4$

In this case, $v_{1,A} \geq 0$ and $v_{2,A} > 0$, from (10.2) and (10.3). The payoff from the contest for R has turned both agents into supporters of instrument A. Both agents will enlist for instrument A, so that it will be chosen with certainty. After this enlistment, the rent seeking contest for R takes place.

Rent seeking expenditures in IR2 are only made in the R-stage. Thus, total rent seeking expenditures equal rent seeking expenditures for R. From (7.8'):

$$X_1 = x_1 = \frac{R}{4} \qquad\qquad X_2 = x_2 = \frac{R}{4} \qquad\qquad X_1 + X_2 = \frac{R}{2}$$

An agent's payoff from IR is his equilibrium payoff from the R-stage. From (7.10'):

$$U_1(IR2) = \frac{R}{4} \qquad\qquad U_2(IR2) = \frac{R}{4}$$

IR3. $v_1 > R/4$, $v_2 < R/4$.

In this case $v_{1,B} > 0$ and $v_{2,A} > 0$, from (10.3). Agent 2 enlists for instrument A and agent 1 enlists for instrument B. Then there will be a rent seeking contest with agent 2 promoting instrument A and agent 1 promoting instrument B. Their revenue stakes are given by (10.3). The probability that instrument A will be chosen is, from (7.9) and (10.3):

$$p_A = \frac{v_{2,A}}{v_{2,A} + v_{1,B}} = \frac{R/4 - v_2}{v_1 - v_2} \qquad\qquad (10.4)$$

We must now speak of total *expected* rent seeking expenditures. The agents will spend $x_{1,B}$ and $x_{2,A}$ with certainty, but they will only spend $x_1 = R/4$ and $x_2 = R/4$ if instrument A is chosen. The expressions for expected rent seeking expenditures can be derived from (7.8), (10.3) and (10.4). For agent 1's expected rent seeking expenditure we find:

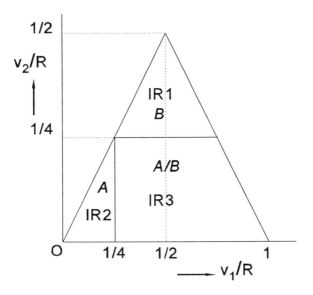

Figure 10.2   Equilibria of IR

$$E(X_1) = x_{1,A} + \rho_A x_1 = \frac{v_{1,B}^2 v_{2,A}}{(v_{1,B} + v_{2,A})^2} + \frac{v_{2,A}}{v_{1,B} + v_{2,A}} \frac{R}{4} =$$

$$= \frac{R/4 - v_2}{v_1 - v_2}\left(\frac{(v_1 - R/4)^2)}{v_1 - v_2} + \frac{R}{4}\right)$$

Agent 2's expected rent seeking expenditure is:

$$E(X_2) = x_{2,A} + \rho_A x_2 = \frac{v_{1,B} v_{2,A}^2}{(v_{1,B} + v_{2,A})^2} + \frac{v_{2,A}}{v_{1,B} + v_{2,A}} \frac{R}{4}$$

$$= \frac{R/4 - v_2}{v_1 - v_2}\left(\frac{(v_1 - R/4)(v_2 - R/4)}{v_1 - v_2} + \frac{R}{4}\right)$$

Total expected rent seeking expenditures are:

$$E(X_1) + E(X_2) = \frac{(R/4 - v_2)(v_1 + R/4)}{v_1 - v_2}$$

Agent 1's expected payoff is the success probability of instrument A times his valuation (in the I-stage) of instrument A, plus the success probability of instrument B times his valuation of instrument B, minus his rent seeking expenditure in the I-stage:

$$U_1(IR3) \;=\; p_A\frac{R}{4} + p_B v_1 - x_{1,B} \;=\; \frac{R}{4} + \frac{x_{1,B}}{x_{1,B} + x_{2,A}} v_{1,B} - x_{1,B} \quad (10.5)$$

When we compare the right hand side of (10.5) to the well-known expression of an agent's payoff in a one-stage game (7.5), we see that the first term is new. This term is agent 1's payoff from the R-stage, i.e. if his least favourite instrument is chosen. In the one-stage game, an agent's payoff of his least favourite outcome is normalized to zero, but here it is not.

Rewriting (10.5) to obtain an expression similar to (7.10), we have, from (7.9) and (10.3):

$$U_1(IR3) \;=\; \frac{R}{4} + \frac{v_{1,B}}{v_{1,B} + v_{2,A}} v_{1,B} - \frac{v_{1,B}^2 v_{2,A}}{(v_{1,B} + v_{2,A})^3}$$

$$=\; \frac{R}{4} + \frac{v_{1,B}^3}{(v_{1,B} + v_{2,A})^2} \;=\; \frac{R}{4} + \frac{(v_1 - R/4)^3}{(v_1 - v_2)^2}$$

Again we see that $U_1(IR3)$ consists of a term derived from (7.10) plus the 'base' level of payoff $R/4$. Analogously, agent 2's payoff is:

$$U_2(IR3) \;=\; v_2 + \frac{v_{2,A}^3}{(v_{1,B} + v_{2,A})^2} \;=\; v_2 + \frac{(R/4 - v_2)^3}{(v_1 - v_2)^2}$$

3.3   First Revenue Division, then Instrument Choice (RI)

The game tree of RI is drawn in Figure 10.3. The agents begin with the R-stage, the rent seeking contest for R. R will be divided according to the outcome of this contest if instrument A is selected in the I-stage following the R-stage. In the I-stage, the agents first enlist for an instrument. To keep the figure manageable, the 'do not enlist' (O) strategy is only shown for agent 1. If both agents enlist for B, instrument B is selected. If they both enlist for A, instrument A is selected and R is divided according to the outcome of the R-stage. If the agents enlist for different instruments, there will be a rent seeking contest for the instrument. After this contest, the decision maker chooses an instrument, with probabilities determined by the rent seeking efforts. If instrument A is chosen, R is divided according to the outcome of the R-stage.

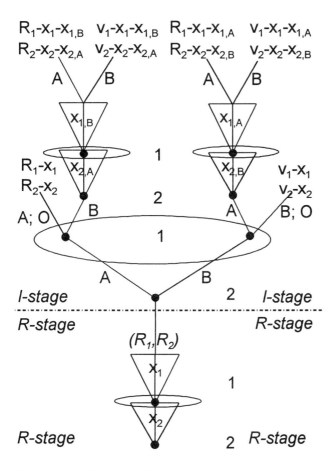

$R_1-x_1-x_{1,B}$ $V_1-x_1-x_{1,B}$ $R_1-x_1-x_{1,A}$ $V_1-x_1-x_{1,A}$
$R_2-x_2-x_{2,A}$ $V_2-x_2-x_{2,A}$ $R_2-x_2-x_{2,B}$ $V_2-x_2-x_{2,B}$

A   B   A   B

$x_{1,B}$ $x_{1,A}$

R_1-x_1 $x_{2,A}$ $x_{2,B}$ v_1-x_1
R_2-x_2 v_2-x_2

A; O   B   A   B; O

A   B

I-stage   *I-stage*

R-stage   *R-stage*

(R_1,R_2)

x_1

x_2

R-stage   *R-stage*

Figure 10.3   The game RI

Table 10.3   The agents' valuations in the I-stage of RI

	Instrument A	Instrument B
Agent 1	$x_1R/(x_1 + x_2)$	v_1
Agent 2	$x_2R/(x_1 + x_2)$	v_2

Again, we start by analysing the second stage, which is now the instrument choice stage. The revenue stakes in stage two depend upon the efforts made in stage one to obtain part of R. Denoting the effort by agent 1 (2) in the R-stage by x_1 (x_2), the agents' valuations of the instruments in the I-stage of RI are as shown in Table 10.3.

In RI, an agent's revenue stake is the difference between his valuations of the two instruments, as shown in Table 10.3:

$$v_{1,A} \equiv -v_{1,B} = \frac{x_1}{x_1 + x_2}R - v_1$$

$$v_{2,A} \equiv -v_{2,B} = \frac{x_2}{x_1 + x_2}R - v_2 \qquad (10.6)$$

We see that it is impossible that instrument B will be chosen with certainty in the I-stage. Since part of R goes to agent 1 and the rest goes to agent 2, condition (10.1) implies that there will always be at least one agent i with $v_{i,A} > 0$, i.e. in favour of instrument A. We will focus here on equilibria in which instrument A is chosen with certainty. These equilibria cover about 97% of the area under consideration.[3]

Thus, the agents' payoffs will be:

$$U_1(RI) = \frac{x_1}{x_1 + x_2}R - x_1 \qquad U_2(RI) = \frac{x_2}{x_1 + x_2}R - x_2 \qquad (10.7)$$

Figure 10.4 shows the equilibria for the game RI, in which instrument A will be chosen with certainty:

RI1. $v_1 \leq R/2$
In this case, the RI game can simply be interpreted as a rent seeking game for R only. Suppose both agents enter the game RI with the expectation that it will only be about the division of R: neither of the agents will want to promote instrument B in the I-stage. Then the game is reduced to a one stage 'division of the pie' game, as analysed in Chapter 7, section 3.5.3. The equilibrium of this game is: $x_1 = x_2 = R/4$, and both agents will acquire half of R. After the R-stage, agent i's ($i = 1, 2$) revenue stake in instrument A is, from (10.6):

$$v_{i,A} = \frac{R}{2} - v_i \geq 0$$

The inequality follows from (10.1) and (10.2). Both agents have a revenue stake in A, so that the game is in fact only about the division of R. Both agents will enlist as proponents for A, so that instrument A will be chosen.

The equilibrium efforts are, from (7.8'):

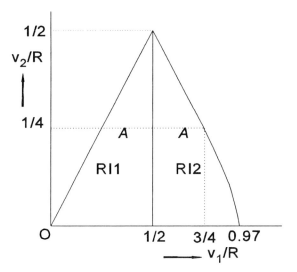

Figure 10.4   Equilibria of RI in which instrument A is chosen with certainty

$$X_1(RI1) = x_1(RI1) = \frac{R}{4} \qquad X_2(RI2) = x_2(RI1) = \frac{R}{4} \qquad X_1(RI1) + X_2(RI1) = \frac{R}{2}$$

The equilibrium payoffs are, from (7.10'):

$$U_1(RI1) = \frac{1}{4}R \qquad\qquad U_2(RI1) = \frac{1}{4}R$$

In Appendix A I will give the formal proof that RI1 is the equilibrium for $v_1 \leq R/2$.

RI2. $R/2 < v_1 \leq V_1$

In this case agent 2 will enlist for instrument A in the I-stage and agent 1 will not enlist. Thus, instrument A will be chosen with certainty. In the R-stage, agent 1 obtains so much from R that his revenue stake in instrument B becomes zero:

$$v_{1,B} = v_1 - \frac{x_1(RI2)}{x_1(RI2) + x_2(RI2)}R = 0 \qquad\qquad (10.8)$$

Furthermore, $x_1(RI2)$ is the optimum effort for agent 1:

$$\frac{x_2(RI2)}{(x_1(RI2) + x_2(RI2))^2}R - 1 = 0 \qquad\qquad (10.9)$$

It can be shown that $x_1(RI2)$ maximizes $U_1(RI)$ for $v_{1,A} \geq 0$ (from (10.7) and (7.6)) as well as U_1 for $v_{1,B} \geq 0$.

Solving (10.8) and (10.9) for the equilibrium efforts $x_1(RI2)$ and $x_2(RI2)$:

$$X_1(RI2) = x_1(RI2) = v_1 - \frac{v_1^2}{R} \qquad X_2(RI2) = x_2(RI2) = \frac{1}{R}(R - v_1)^2 \quad (10.10)$$

In the same way as for RI1, we can show that agent 2 will not spend $x_2 < x_2(RI2)$. Beyond V_1, equilibrium RI2 no longer holds, because when agent 1 spends $x_1(RI2)$, agent 2 will want to spend more than $x_2(RI2)$. In Appendix B we derive V_1 as a function of v_2. For $v_2 = 0$, $V_1/R = 0.929$. The intersection with the line $R = v_1 + v_2$ occurs at $(V_1/R; v_2/R) = (0.8; 0.2)$.

Substituting (10.10) into (10.7), we find the agents' payoffs:

$$U_1(RI2) = v_1 - \left(v_1 + \frac{v_1^2}{R} \right) = \frac{v_1^2}{R}$$

$$(10.11)$$

$$U_2(RI2) = R - v_1 - \frac{1}{R}(R - v_1)^2 = v_1 - \frac{v_1^2}{R}$$

4.   COMPARING IR AND RI

4.1   Introduction

In this section, we compare the games IR and RI with respect to the probability that instrument A is chosen (section 4.2), the expected rent seeking expenditures (section 4.3) and the agents' expected payoffs (section 4.4).

Note that for $v_1 \leq R/4$ the outcome of the games (IR2 and RI1) is identical. This case will be included in the tables, but not in the text and the figures.

4.2   Instrument Choice

In RI1 and RI2, instrument A is always chosen. In IR, it depends on the agents' stakes, whether instrument A will be chosen with certainty (IR2), or there will be a contest for the instrument (IR3) or instrument B will be chosen with certainty (IR1). There are two reasons why RI is more favourable to instrument A:

- cost attribution. In IR, the net payoff from the contest for R is added to the agents' valuations for instrument A. This net payoff is the share of R that they *will* obtain minus the effort they *will* spend on obtaining it. In RI, the rent seeking contest for R has already taken place when the instrument choice is at stake. Thus, only the share of R that the agent has secured, and *will* obtain if instrument A is chosen, is added to the agents' valuations for instrument A. The efforts to obtain part of R *have* already *been made* when the contest for the instrument starts: they are sunk costs. This makes the agents' valuation of instrument A higher in RI than in IR. This can also be seen in Tables 10.2 and 10.3, where the sum of the agents' valuations of instrument A is R in RI and $R/2$ in IR.

– the strategic interest of agent 2. This reason pertains to RI2. In IR, both agents receive half of R when instrument A is chosen. In RI2, agent 2 concedes more than half of R to agent 1 in the R-stage, so that agent 1 will not enlist for instrument B in the I-stage. Conceding more than half of R to agent 1 only makes sense when the R-stage is the first stage of the game. It results in a higher payoff for agent 2 than letting agent 1 promote instrument B in the I-stage, and *en passant* it secures the acceptance of instrument A.

In the introduction to this chapter, we interpreted the EEA recommendation (EEA, 1996) to make the environmental charge and its revenue part of a policy package and green tax reform as an advice to play the game of instrument choice as RI. We see that the model of this chapter offers a theoretical foundation for this advice: RI is more favourable to the financial instrument than IR. Thus, the EEA recommendation is a sound advice for those who want to boost the success probability of the financial instrument. In the following, we shall see whether playing the game as RI is also a good idea from a welfare point of view.

4.3   Rent Seeking Expenditures

Since the beginning of rent seeking analysis with Tullock (1967), the determination of rent seeking expenditures, especially in relation to the value of the rent, has been the primary focus of the literature (see Nitzan's (1994) overview). The so-called dissipation rate shows how wasteful rent seeking is.

Rent seeking expenditures, especially in the form of 'wining and dining', can also be of interest to the decision maker. The decision maker may be able to enhance these expenditures by a suitable design of the contest (Michaels, 1988; Glazer, 1993) or the exclusion of certain agents from the contest (Baye et al., 1993).[4] In the model of this chapter, the decision maker may be able to choose between IR and RI.

The expected rent seeking expenditures for IR and RI are shown in Tables 10.4. They were calculated when the equilibria were discussed. The result of the comparison is shown in Figure 10.5. In the area 'RI > IR = 0', rent seeking expenditures are positive in RI and zero in IR. In the area 'RI > IR', rent seeking expenditures are positive in IR, but still higher in RI. In the area 'IR > RI', rent seeking expenditures are higher in IR.

We now proceed with a detailed comparison of expected rent seeking expenditures (ere). For $v_2 \geq R/4$, comparing IR1 and RI1, re are positive for RI

Table 10.4IR Expected rent seeking expenditures (ere) for IR

	$E(X_1 + X_2)$
IR1. $v_2 \geq R/4$	0
IR2. $v_1 \leq R/4$	$R/2$
IR3. $v_2 < R/4, v_1 > R/4$	$\dfrac{(R/4 - v_2)(v_1 + R/4)}{v_1 - v_2}$

Table 10.4RI Rent seeking expenditures (re) for RI

	$X_1 + X_2$
RI1. $v_1 \leq R/2$	$R/2$
RI2. $R/2 < v_1 < V_1$	$R - v_1$

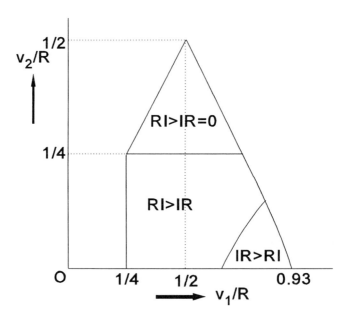

Figure 10.5   Comparing rent seeking expenditures

and zero for IR.

For $R/4 < v_1 \leq R/2$, $v_2 < R/4$, comparing IR3 and RI1, ere are lower for IR. In IR3, ere in the I-stage are rising in v_1, but the probability that the R-stage (with its re of $R/2$) is reached, is declining in v_1. The first effect is dominant: ere are declining in v_1.

For $v_2 < R/4$, $R/2 < v_1 < V_1$, the comparison is between IR3 and RI2. In RI ere are declining in v_1, because the higher v_1, the more of R agent 2 concedes. For low values of v_1, ere are higher in RI2. But eventually, re is declining faster in v_1 for RI than for IR. Ere are lower for IR if:

$$v_1 < \frac{3}{8}R + v_2 + \sqrt{v_2^2 + \frac{5}{64}R^2}$$

The line where ere are equal crosses the bounds of the region at $(v_1/R; v_2/R) = (0.655; 0)$ and $(0.842; 0.150)$.

4.4 Expected Payoffs

The agents' expected payoffs are important for two reasons. First, they indicate an agent's preference for either IR or RI.[5] Secondly, under the assumptions that v_1 and v_2 comprise all effects of instrument choice and interpret rent seeking expenditures as a loss to society,[6] the sum $U_1 + U_2$ is total welfare. Although RI is more favourable to the welfare-maximizing instrument A, total welfare might be higher with IR because of low rent seeking expenditures.

The expected payoffs for IR and RI are shown in Tables 10.5. They were calculated when the equilibria were discussed.

Figure 10.6 shows the regions where U_1, U_2 and $U_1 + U_2$ are higher for IR. In the area marked '1' ('2'), U_1 (U_2) is higher in IR than in RI. In the area marked '1+2', $U_1 + U_2$ is higher in IR than in RI. In the unmarked area, U_1 as well as U_2 are higher in RI than in IR. We will now give the detailed comparisons of the payoffs.

For $R/4 < v_1 \leq R/2$, $v_2 \geq R/4$, comparing IR1 and RI1, U_1 and U_2 are higher for IR. The payoffs in RI are also the payoffs in the R-stage of IR, had instrument A been selected in the I-stage. But for both agents, rent seeking expenditures in the R-stage are so high, that they prefer not to enter the contest for R and agree that instrument B is chosen in the I-stage.

In RI, however, the agents are forced to go through the contest for R first. Only after that can they compare the instruments. Of course they look more favourably upon instrument A now. In fact, they both prefer A to B.

For $v_1 > R/2$, $v_2 \geq R/4$, comparing IR1 and RI2, U_1 and U_2 are higher for IR. In RI, agent 1 is indifferent between instruments A and B, after he has made an effort to acquire part of R. This effort is agent 1's difference in payoff between IR and

Table 10.5IR Expected payoffs for IR

	U_1	U_2
IR1. $v_2 \geq R/4$	v_1	v_2
IR2. $v_1 \leq R/4$	$R/4$	$R/4$
IR3. $v_1 > R/4, v_2 < R/4$	$\dfrac{(v_1 - R/4)^3 + R/4}{(v_1 - v_2)^2}$	$\dfrac{(R/4 - v_2)^3 + v_2}{(v_1 - v_2)^2}$

Table 10.5RI Expected payoffs for RI

	U_1	U_2
RI1. $v_1 \leq R/2$	$R/4$	$R/4$
RI2. $R/2 < v_1 < V_1$	v_1^2/R	$v_1 - v_1^2/R$

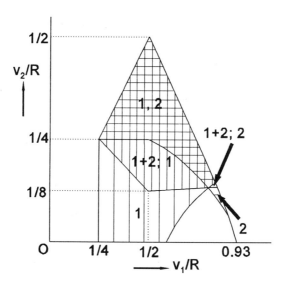

Figure 10.6 Comparing payoffs

RI. We already saw that $U_2(\text{RI1})$ was lower than $U_2(\text{IR1})$. $U_2(\text{RI2})$ is declining in v_1 (because the higher v_1, the less of R is left for agent 2), so that $U_2(\text{RI2})$ is below $U_2(\text{RI1})$ and below $U_2(\text{IR1})$.

For $R/4 < v_1 \le R/2$, $v_2 < R/4$, comparing IR3 and RI1, U_1 is higher for IR and U_2 is higher for RI. This is because in RI, A is chosen with certainty, and in IR, there is a contest between A and B. Thus agent 1's payoff in RI is his base level of payoff in IR. On top of that is a bonus for promoting instrument B. Agent 2's RI payoff is her gross payoff in IR, if instrument A is chosen. From this gross payoff, her effort should be subtracted. If instrument B is chosen, her payoff is even lower. For high v_1 and v_2, U_2 is slightly higher in RI, and U_1 is much higher in IR. Aggregate expected payoff is higher for IR when:

$$v_1 > -2v_2 + \frac{3}{4}R$$

For $R/2 < v_1 < V_1$, $v_2 < R/4$, comparing IR3 and RI2, $\partial U_1 (\text{RI})/\partial v_1$ is higher than $\partial U_1(\text{IR})/\partial v_1$. In IR, an increase in v_1 translates into an equal increase in agent 1's revenue stake and a lower than equal increase in U_1. In RI, however, an increase in v_1 translates into a more than equal increase in U_1. Agent 1's gross payoff is v_1 and his rent seeking expenditures are declining in v_1. Furthermore, $U_1(\text{IR3})$ is rising in v_2, while $U_1(\text{RI2})$ is unaffected by v_2. $U_1(\text{IR3})$ will be higher for:

$$v_2 > v_1 - \frac{\sqrt{4\dfrac{v_1^5}{R} - 3v_1^4 - \dfrac{1}{4}v_1^3R + \dfrac{11}{16}v_1^2R^2 - \dfrac{3}{16}v_1R^3 + \dfrac{1}{64}R^4}}{2\dfrac{v_1^2}{R} - \dfrac{1}{2}R}$$

The line where U_1 is equal for RI and IR crosses the bounds of the region at $(v_1/R, v_2/R) = (0.832;\ 0.164)$ and $(0.616;\ 0)$.

$U_2(\text{RI2})$ is unaffected by v_2, whereas $U_2(\text{IR3})$ is rising in v_2. This is because an increase in v_2 increases the 'base' payoff for agent 2 and decreases the incentive to make an effort for instrument A's higher payoff of $R/4$. Thus, U_2 is lower for IR with low v_2, but U_2 is higher for RI when:

$$v_2 > \frac{\dfrac{3}{16}R^2 - 3v_1^2 + 2\dfrac{v_1^3}{R} + \sqrt{4\dfrac{v_1^5}{R} - 6v_1^4 + \dfrac{15}{4}v_1^3R - \dfrac{19}{16}v_1^2R^2 + \dfrac{3}{16}v_1R^3 - \dfrac{3}{256}R^4}}{\dfrac{3}{2}R + 2\dfrac{v_1^2}{R} - 6v_1}$$

The line where U_2 is equal for IR and RI crosses the bounds of the region at $(v_1/R, v_2/R) = (1/2, 1/4)$ and $(0.868;\ 0.110)$.

For $R/2 < v_1 < V_1$, $v_2 < R/4$, aggregate expected payoff is higher in IR if:

$$v_2 > \frac{8v_1R - 3R^2}{48v_1 - 16R}$$

The line where the aggregate expected payoffs are equal for RI and IR crosses the bounds of the region at $(v_1/R, v_2/R) = (1/2, 1/8)$ and $(0.840; 0.153)$.

5.   APPLICATION

5.1   Introduction

When applying our models of rent seeking contests to instrument choice in environmental policy, our central question has always been: 'Can the model explain why market instruments (among them financial instruments) are not chosen in environmental policy, although they are welfare-maximizing?' The model of this chapter does give an explanation why financial instruments are not chosen. We will give this explanation in section 5.2. In section 5.3, we compare the outcome of our model to Grossman and Helpman's (1994) results. In section 5.4 we apply our model to the discussion about the regulatory energy charge in the Netherlands (Chapter 6, section 3.4).

5.2   The Preference for IR

In this chapter, we analysed the choice between two instruments as a rent seeking contest. The financial instrument yields government revenue. The instrument of direct regulation does not. The financial instrument yields the highest aggregate payoff.

There are two agents involved. We can think of these as e.g. the shareholders and the workers in the polluting industry, or the polluting industry and the environmental movement.

The game can be played in two ways:

– IR: first instrument choice, and then, if the financial instrument has been chosen, revenue division;
– RI: first a decision on how to divide the revenue, in case the financial instrument will be chosen, and then instrument choice.

We saw that RI results in the choice for the financial instrument, whereas IR can also result in the choice for direct regulation. However, rent seeking expenditures are often higher in RI, as can be seen in Figure 10.5. As a result, the agents' payoffs can be higher in IR.

This latter result is essential to our application. As we can see in Figure 10.6, there is a large area in which both agents have a higher payoff in IR than in RI. This means they prefer the game to be played as IR rather than as RI. Strictly speaking, the decision of how to play the game falls outside of our analysis. But we can imagine that when both agents want to play the game as IR, the game will actually be played as IR. As a result, direct regulation will be selected with certainty (if we are in IR1), or with a large probability (if we are in IR3). Thus, the agents' preference to play the game as IR is to the detriment of the financial instrument, that would have been chosen with certainty in RI.

The agents' preference for IR above RI is most dramatically illustrated with the case $R/4 < v_1 < R/2$, $v_2 > R/4$. The comparison is between IR1 and RI1. In IR1, direct regulation is chosen with certainty. In RI1, the financial instrument is chosen with certainty. At first sight, it may look as if the agents would be better off with RI, resulting in the choice for the 'welfare-maximizing' financial instrument. However, in RI1 there will be a rent seeking contest for R, the revenues of the financial instrument. Each agent will spend $R/4$ and receive half of R. Thus, their payoffs in RI are $U_1 = U_2 = R/4$.

By contrast, in IR1 there are no rent seeking expenditures at all. At the beginning of the game, both agents realize that their payoffs will be $R/4$ if the financial instrument is selected. If direct regulation is selected, their payoffs will be v_1 and v_2 respectively. Because v_1 and v_2 both exceed $R/4$, both agents prefer direct regulation.

Both agents have a higher payoff in IR than in RI. We can say that the game IR allows the agents to avoid the wasteful rent seeking contest for R, whereas in RI the agents are forced to go through this contest at the beginning of the game.

Thus, for certain configurations of stakes, the interest groups involved prefer to play the game IR. Applying this analysis to instrument choice in environmental policy, the result is that the instrument chosen is (likely to be) direct regulation instead of the financial instrument.

5.3   Comparison with Grossman and Helpman (1994)

A conclusion similar to ours, concerning the disadvantage of welfare maximizing instruments in politics, is reached in Grossman and Helpman (G&H, 1994), treated in Chapter 2, section 4.3.4. However, there are important differences. In G&H, the level of government intervention is at stake, given the instrument. Here, instrument choice is at stake, given the strictness of the policy. The similarity, which must be stated loosely, is that there may be situations where interest groups prefer inefficient (non-welfare maximizing) instruments because of lower lobbying expenditures.[7] The first difference is that in G&H, the interest groups would like to prohibit the government from considering the use of efficient instruments. In our model, the interest groups prefer the design IR of the game that results in a lower (or zero) probability that the efficient instrument is chosen. The second difference pertains to the reason why a lobby has higher lobbying expenditures with the efficient instrument (G&H) or with the design RI that favours the efficient instrument (our model). In G&H, this is because the welfare level that the government and the other lobbies can reach, is higher with than without the efficient instrument. Thus, a lobby must increase its expenditure, or else it will be ignored by the government. In the rent seeking contest it is because the efficient instrument yields government revenue, for which there will be a contest. In RI, this contest always takes place, but in IR, it only takes place when the efficient instrument has been chosen.

5.4 The Regulatory Energy Charge in the Netherlands

We can apply the analysis of this chapter to the discussion in the Netherlands about the regulatory energy charge (Chapter 6, section 3.4). We saw that the environmental movement was lobbying in favour of the charge and industry was lobbying against the charge. The environmental movement released a number of ideas on how to spend the revenue from the charge. These ideas were meant to enhance the acceptability of the charge, for instance by compensating the energy intensive industry. However, industry refused to discuss alternative ways of redistributing the charge revenue, on the ground that it opposed the charge altogether.

With the model of this chapter, we can interpret the environmental movement's willingness, and industry's refusal, to discuss revenue distribution. Applying our analysis, industry is agent 1, and the environmental movement is agent 2. They are in an area marked '1' in Figure 10.6.

The environmental movement wants to play the game as RI. It wants the charge to be selected. In order to boost the success probability of the charge, they want to reach agreement on the revenue distribution before the instrument of the charge itself is at stake. They know that once industry has secured a large part of the revenue, it will give up its resistance against the charge, and the charge will be selected.[8]

However, industry wants to play the game as IR. They first want to discuss instrument choice: charge or no charge, in which case they will lobby against the charge. If, in spite of their efforts, the charge is chosen, then they want to discuss revenue distribution, but no earlier.[9] In this way, industry hopes to avoid making efforts over revenue distribution. This wish overrides the disadvantages of IR: that industry has to lobby for direct regulation, and that efforts for revenue distribution are lower in RI than in IR (if they are made). Due to industry's refusal to discuss revenue distribution, the discussion in the Netherlands on the regulatory energy charge took place along the lines of IR, resulting in the rejection of the charge for large users.

From this discussion we can also learn something about the choice between IR and RI. In section 5.2 we said that if both agents prefer IR, the game will probably be played as IR. But now we see what can happen if one agent prefers IR and the other prefers RI. Then the former agent can simply refuse to discuss revenue distribution, thereby dictating that the game be played as IR. This can happen when, as in the Netherlands, the decision maker (i.e. the government) does not make the choice between IR and RI.

6. CONCLUSION

In this chapter, we have combined the contest for instrument choice (either a financial instrument or an instrument of direct regulation) with a contest for the revenues of the financial instrument. Since there are two decisions to be made, there are two following orders in which the game can be played: first instrument choice, then revenue division (IR), and first revenue division, then instrument choice (RI).

In section 3 we analysed the equilibria of these games and in section 4 we compared them. We saw that in RI, the financial instrument has a higher success probability than in IR, but RI may also result in higher rent seeking expenditures. Therefore the rent-seeking agents may prefer to play the game as IR, because their payoffs are higher in IR.

As we saw in section 5, this may serve as an explanation of why financial instruments are not applied in environmental policy, although, if one disregards rent seeking expenditures, one can call them welfare maximizing. Financial instruments would be selected in the game RI, but the rent-seeking agents may prefer to play the game as IR, in which the financial instrument has a small, or even zero, success probability.

In section 5.4 we applied our model to the discussion about the regulatory energy charge in the Netherlands (Chapter 6, section 3.4). We interpreted the industry's refusal to discuss the environmental movement's ideas about spending the charge revenues as a preference to play the game as IR, whereas the environmental movement preferred RI.

A final remark is in order, about the welfare-maximizing property of financial instruments. When economists derive the welfare-maximizing property of financial instruments, they always treat the revenues of these instruments as a 100% addition to welfare. But rent seeking analysis shows that interest groups will make an effort to obtain part of these revenues. Subtracting these efforts from welfare, the financial instrument may no longer be welfare maximizing.[10]

With this in mind, there is no need to deplore the choice for direct regulation from a welfare point of view, if the choice is arrived at in the following way. The game is played as IR, because both rent-seeking agents prefer IR to RI. In IR, both agents prefer direct regulation, so direct regulation is chosen. In that case, direct regulation is in fact welfare-maximizing, because the financial instrument results in too much wasteful rent seeking effort for its revenue. Then the choice for direct regulation can only be applauded.

In Chapter 2, section 2, we used the term 'second best' (Lipsey and Lancaster, 1956) for the argument that in an ideal world, market instruments are the best instruments, but in a less ideal world, direct regulation could be more appropriate. The argument of this chapter can also be called 'second best'. In a 'first best' world, the government would not be under pressure from interest groups. It would select the financial instrument, because it maximizes aggregate welfare, and it would determine some distribution of its revenues. However, in the second best world we live in, the government is susceptible to pressure from interest groups. In such a world, society may be better of with the decision making procedure IR which favours direct regulation over the market instrument.

APPENDIX A. RI1

To prove that RI1 is the equilibrium for $v_1 \leq R/2$, we must show that:

(1M)   agent 1 will not spend so much more than $R/4$, that $v_{2,B}$ becomes positive;
(2M)   agent 2 will not spend so much more than $R/4$, that $v_{1,B}$ becomes positive;
(1L)   agent 1 will not spend so much less than $R/4$, that $v_{1,B}$ becomes positive;
(2L)   agent 2 will not spend so much less than $R/4$, that $v_{2,B}$ becomes positive;

I will only prove (2M) and (2L), because the proofs for (1M) and (1L) are analogous. (2M) holds, because even without the complication that agent 1 would promote instrument B in the I-stage, agent 2 would not spend more than $R/4$ in the R-stage. With this complication, spending more than $R/4$ becomes even more unattractive.

To prove that (2L) holds, we calculate the derivative of U_2 with respect to x_2 below x_2^*, where x_2^* is defined by:

$$v_{2,B} = v_2 - \frac{x_2^* R}{x_1 + x_2^*} = 0$$

Remember that the equilibrium x_1 of RI1 is $R/4$. Thus, the value of x_2^* is:

$$x_2^* = \frac{v_2 R}{4(R - v_2)} \tag{A.1}$$

We know that U_2 is rising in x_2 in the interval $[x_2^*; R/4]$, because in that interval the game is identical to a one-stage rent seeking game for R.

For x_2 below x_2^*: $v_{2,B} > 0$. Then there will be a contest in the I-stage of RI. Agent 2 will promote instrument B, and agent 1 will promote instrument A. Agent 2's payoff in the whole game is, from (10.6):

$$U_2(B) = \frac{x_2R}{x_1 + x_2} + \frac{v_{2,B}^3}{(v_{1,A} + v_{2,B})^2} - x_2 = \frac{x_2R}{x_1 + x_2} + \frac{\left(v_2 - \dfrac{x_2R}{x_1 + x_2}\right)^3}{\left(v_2 - v_1 + R - \dfrac{2x_2R}{x_1 + x_2}\right)^2} - x_2$$

The first term is agent 2's 'base' payoff: her valuation of the least favourite instrument A. In a one-stage rent seeking game, this payoff is normalized to zero, but here it is not. The second term is agent 2's bonus for making an effort for instrument B in the I-stage. This term is analogous to $v_i^3/(v_i + v_j)^2$ from (7.10). The last term is agent 2's effort in the R-stage.

Differentiating $U_2(B)$ with respect to x_2 yields:

$$\frac{dU_2(B)}{dx_2} = \frac{x_1R}{(x_1 + x_2)^2} + \frac{x_1Rv_{2,B}^2(v_{2,A} - 3v_{1,B})}{(x_1 + x_2)^2(v_{1,A} + v_{2,B})^3} - 1 \qquad \text{(A.2)}$$

Evaluating this expression at $x_1 = R/4$ and $x_2 = x_2^*$, we see that $v_{2,B} = 0$. The second term on the right hand side of (A.2) vanishes and the expression is reduced to:

$$\frac{x_1R}{x_1 + x_2} - 1 = \frac{R^2/4}{\left(\dfrac{R}{4} + \dfrac{v_2R}{4(R - v_2)}\right)} - 1 = \left(\frac{R/2}{R - v_2}\right)^2 - 1 > 0$$

The inequality follows from $v_2 < R/2$ in (10.1) and (10.2). Thus, U_2 is rising in x_2 for x_2 just below x_2^*. Differentiating (A.2) again with respect to x_2 yields:

$$\frac{d^2U_2(B)}{(dx_2)^2} = -\frac{2x_1R}{(x_1 + x_2)^3} \cdot \frac{v_{1,A}^3 + 3v_{1,A}^3v_{2,B} + 2v_{2,A}^3}{(v_{1,A} + v_{2,B})^3} < 0$$

Thus, U_2 is rising in x_2 for all $x_2 < x_2^*$

The conclusion is that U_2 is rising in x_2 for all $x_2 < R/4$ and declining in x_2 for all $x_2 > R/4$. In the same way, it can be shown that U_1 is rising in x_1 for all $x_1 < R/4$ and declining in x_1 for all $x_1 > R/4$. Thus, the unique maximum occurs at $(x_1, x_2) = (R/4, R/4)$.

APPENDIX B. THE BOUNDARY OF RI2

For high values of v_1, RI2 is no longer an equilibrium. This is because it profitable for agent 2 to spend more than x_2(RI2), the equilibrium effort in the R-stage of RI2. Remember that in RI2, agent 1 did not enlist in the I-stage ($v_{1,B} = 0$) and agent 2 enlisted for instrument A ($v_{2,A} > 0$). Thus, when agent 2 spends more than x_2(RI2), agent 1 will enlist for instrument B ($v_{1,B} > 0$) and agent 2 will still enlist for instrument A ($v_{2,A} > 0$). Then there will be a rent seeking contest in the I-stage. In this case, agent 2's payoff in the whole game can be written as:

$$U_2(B) = v_2 + \frac{v_{2,A}^3}{(v_{1,B} + v_{2,A})^2} - x_2$$

The first term is agent 2's 'base' payoff: her valuation of the least favourite instrument B. In a one-stage rent seeking game, this payoff is normalized to zero, but here it is not. The second term is agent 2's bonus for making an effort for instrument A in the I-stage. This term is analogous to $v_i^3/(v_i + v_j)^2$ from (7.10). The last term is agent 2's effort in the R-stage.

Agent 2 will set x_2 such that $U_2(B)$ is maximized:

$$\max_{x_2} \ U_2(B) = v_2 + \frac{\left(\dfrac{x_2 R}{x_1 + x_2} - v_2 \right)^3}{\left(v_1 - v_2 + \dfrac{(x_2 - x_1)R}{x_1 + x_2} \right)^2} - x_2 \tag{B.1}$$

The first order condition is:

$$\frac{x_1 R}{(x_1 + x_2)^2} \frac{v_{2,A}^2 (3v_{1,B} - v_{2,A})}{(v_{1,B} + v_{2,A})^3} - 1 = 0 \tag{B.2}$$

Agent 2 will compare this maximum U_2 to her equilibrium payoff in RI2. When $U_2(B)$ exceeds this payoff, RI2 is not an equilibrium.

At the boundary of the area where RI2 is an equilibrium, the maximum $U_2(B)$ equals agent 2's equilibrium payoff in RI2. Let V_1 be the boundary value of v_1 as a function of v_2. It can be solved from the condition for equal payoffs and the first order condition, respectively:

$$V_1 + \frac{V_1^2}{R} = v_2 + \frac{v_{2,A}^3}{(V_{1,B} + v_{2,A})^2} - x_2 \tag{B.1'}$$

$$\frac{V_1 R - V_1^2}{(V_1 - V_1^2/R + x_2)^2} \frac{v_{2A}^2(3V_{1,B} - v_{2A})}{(V_{1,B} + v_{2A})^3} - 1 = 0 \qquad (B.2')$$

where:

$$V_{1,B} \equiv V_1 - \frac{V_1 R - V_1^2}{V_1 - V_1^2/R + x_2} \qquad (B.3)$$

$$v_{2A} \equiv \frac{x_2 R}{V_1 - V_1^2/R + x_2} - v_2$$

Condition (B.1') states that agent 2's payoff in the equilibrium of RI2, given by (10.11), should equal her payoff when she decides to spend so much in the R-stage that agent 1 becomes a proponent of instrument B, i.e. to antagonize agent 1. Condition (B.2') gives the optimal x_2 in case agent 2 decides to antagonize agent 1. (B.3) gives the revenue stake for agent 1 in instrument B and for agent 2 in instrument A. In (B.2') and (B.3) we substituted the equilibrium x_1(RI2) from (10.10).

NOTES

1. See also Chapter 7, section 3.2.
2. $v_2 = 0$ indicates that agent 2 is not affected by the instrument choice *per se*, but is 'only in it for the money'.
3. Dijkstra (1998) shows that in the remaining 3%, there is an equilibrium RI3 in which agent 1 promotes instrument B and agent 2 promotes instrument A. Between RI2 and RI 3 there is an area in which there is no equilibrium in pure strategies. According to the existence conditions presently known, there is no equilibrium in mixed strategies either.
4. On the other hand, the decision maker would perhaps also like to decrease certain forms of efforts, so that he does not have to listen to boring arguments.
5. We will come back to this point in section 5.
6. When we assume the decision maker is interested in maximizing rent seeking expenditures, we can no longer interpret these expenditures as a welfare loss. However, they may trigger a wasteful contest for the position of recipient of these expenditures. This possibility was first mentioned in Krueger (1974) and Posner (1975) and modelled by Hillman and Katz (1987). See also Brooks and Heijdra (1988) on the concept of waste in rent seeking contests.
7. In a rent seeking contest, the lobbies make their expenditures before the government makes a decision. In G&H, the lobbies make their expenditures afterwards, as a reward. Both kinds of expenditures are brought under the heading of 'lobbying expenditures'.
8. If industry stands to lose a lot from the tax ($v_1 > R/2$), the environmental movement is willing to leave more of the revenue R to industry than in a one-stage game over R.
9. Although industry is not willing to discuss revenue distribution initially, they are unlikely to be excluded from the revenues after the charge has been chosen. In that case, industry can say: 'Now that this charge, that we were against, is in place, we demand to be compensated.'
10. Migué and Marceau (1993) already identify this and other categories of rent seeking costs associated with charges and subsidies, but they do not make the comparison with direct regulation. Lee (1985) also argues that rent seeking costs for the charge revenue should be subtracted from social welfare. He discusses the consequences of this point for the optimal charge rate. Brooks and Heijdra (1987) extend his analysis.

11. Assessment of Political Economy Models

1. INTRODUCTION

With this penultimate chapter we conclude the treatment of our second research question, about the influence of interest groups on the political decision making process. The treatment of this question started in Chapter 6 with an overview of market instruments in practice around the world, and in Dutch policy discussions. In Chapter 7 we introduced two models of political decision making: the institutional model and the rent seeking model. The rent seeking model was developed further in Chapters 8 to 10.

Now is the time to assess these political decision making or political economy models. We are not directly concerned with the question why the political process results in the choice for direct regulation, but we will assess the models used and developed in this book to address this question. The assessment will take place from two perspectives. Section 2 is a report of the interviews with representatives from interest groups about the influence of interest groups on environmental policy. Thus, in section 2 we confront our models with reality, that is: reality as experienced by the interest groups themselves. Section 3 identifies directions for future research into interest group influence. Thus, in section 3 we confront the models we have developed with what has yet to be done, or what we might have done instead. Section 4 concludes the chapter.

2. INTERVIEWS WITH INTEREST GROUP REPRESENTATIVES

2.1 Introduction

Theoretical research into interest group influence, as we conducted it in Chapters 7 to 10, should be combined with empirical research. Empirical research is necessary to check the validity of the assumptions and results from theoretical research and to inspire new ideas for theoretical research.

Empirical research into interest group influence can take four forms. The first form is the quantitative analysis, where policies are linked to the activities and characteristics of interest groups.[1] The second form is the analysis of government documents, newspaper articles, interest group publications etc., as in Chapter 6, section 3. The third form is the interviewing of persons involved in interest groups' attempts to influence policy: the decision makers and the interest groups. The fourth form is the direct presence of the researcher when attempts to influence the political decision are made or prepared. The researcher can be present at actual attempts, as an observer or an active participant. The researcher can also set up an experiment with participants with or without practical experience. Experiments with 'inexperienced' subjects have frequently been performed of late for rent seeking games.[2]

In this section we take the third approach. Representatives of interest groups were interviewed about their influence on political decisions. Because we feared the respondents might have little experience with instrument choice in environmental policy, which is the subject of our research, we inquired after their influence on environmental policy in general.

We interviewed Van der Veer, head of the Ecology and Economy department of the environmental organization SNM and Klerken and Zijlstra from the Environment and Spatial Planning Bureau of the industry organization VNO-NCW. The subject of interest group influence was also addressed in our interviews with Thomassen of the refinery industry organization OCC and Dekkers of the Department of VROM.

The rest of this section is organized as follows. In section 2.2 we see how the interest groups plan their lobbying activities: to which subjects they direct their attention and how much attention they direct to these subjects. Section 2.3 discusses how the interest groups operate: do they use a confrontational or a conciliatory style? In section 2.4 we see what kind of activities the interest groups engage in. In section 2.5 we look at how VNONCW coordinates industry lobbying and how SNM cooperates with other environmental organizations and with different organizations. In section 2.6, the interest group representatives indicate which factors are important for the success of an attempt to influence environmental policy. One factor, the political importance attached to the environment, is further discussed in section 2.7. We continue our discussion of politics in section 2.8, where we look at the role of the Minister of the Environment and the cabinet. In the concluding section 2.9 we reflect upon the implications of our interviews for the relevance and further modification and expansion of our political economy models.

2.2   Planning of Activities

SNM has had a formal planning process for a number of years. Its sponsors forced SNM to adopt a more formal planning process, but the formalization was also seen as a good idea in its own right.

The planning takes place in a number of steps. The first step is the strategic question how to allocate the employees' time among various fields of interest for the next five years. The fundamental decision to be taken is how much to allocate to the whole breadth of environmental policy, and how much to an in-depth treatment of a selected number of themes. In its most recent strategy plan, SNM has allocated 30% of its resources to the breadth of environmental policy, including maintenance of expertise, reacting to current events and aid in crisis situations. A total of 40% has been allocated to seven specific topics. These are topics for which SNM is willing to go to great lengths, and it is not easily dissuaded from its goals. The remaining 30% has been allocated to miscellaneous themes.

The next step required in the formal planning process takes place when embarking on a new project. A 'force field analysis' must be made, stating which other groups agree or disagree with SNM, the desired goals and their feasibility, and the time to be spent on the project. Of course, the plan should leave room for flexibility to react to unexpected developments in the course of the project.

When the end of a project comes near, it is time to take a position (Van der Veer, 1997):

> Do we want to hold on to all of our demands, risking that we will end up with empty hands? Or do we give up part of our demands, increasing the chance that the rest will be realized?

The last step in the formal planning process is the evaluation of the project. This includes an analysis of why SNM has been successful, or unsuccessful, in the project.

At VNONCW, there is no formal project planning. The activities are allocated in an informal way. More effort is spent on important issues and on issues where the opinions of other groups are fairly evenly divided, so that VNONCW's activities can make the difference. On very important issues, like the energy charge (Chapter 6, section 3.4), VNONCW spends a lot of effort, even though the success probability may initially seem low.

2.3   Style

In this section we look at the interest groups' style: do they rigidly adhere to their own points of view or are they willing to cooperate and to reach a compromise?

SNM presents itself as a serious negotiation partner of government and industry, willing to reach agreements. This is in contrast with other, more radical and action-oriented environmental groups.[3]

However, SNM does adopt different styles. Sometimes they are very flexible, sometimes very rigid. One might think this could cause confusion with the other players, but this is not the case. Research commissioned by SNM has shown that they understand and appreciate the fact that SNM takes these different approaches. It adds to SNM's legitimacy and credibility that it can do both.

Lately, VNONCW has been trying to cooperate with government to reach agreements and solutions, instead of opposing all environmental policy. VNONCW offers technical and strategic comments on proposals.

The technical comments pertain to the policy design, and are needed because the government lacks information on how things work in practice. The technical comments are mostly well-heeded, because the government has no objections of principle against changing the technical details of a proposal.

Lately, the government has been paying increasing attention to industry's strategic comments. These are the more fundamental comments, often involving attempts to relax the stringency and rigidity of the policy proposal. According to Klerken and Zijlstra (VNONCW), the success of covenants has made the government realize that when they make a good agreement with industry, industry will adhere to it. This is so important for the government, that it now seeks industry advice at an early stage.

2.4 Kind of Activities

Klerken and Zijlstra (VNONCW) ordered the list of activities presented to them in the following descending order of importance:

1. contacts with civil servants;
2. contacts with politicians;
3. consultation platforms;
4. publicity;
5. publishing reports;
6. direct contact with the environmental movement.

Thomassen (OCC) finds contact with the environmental movement often easier than contacts with civil servants:

> Civil servants like to speak 'on behalf of environmentalists and action groups'. Civil servants often have a political goal: to do something that suits the plans of the political party in charge.

Klerken and Zijlstra (VNONCW) did not subscribe to this view.

Direct contact with the environmental movement is not very important to VNONCW:

> It is a good thing to listen to each other's arguments, but one does not convince the other in such a meeting.

Van der Veer (SNM) did not order the list of activities presented to him, which also included actions. He stressed the importance of contacts with civil servants and politicians.[4]

SNM's contacts with industry are mainly with individual firms and industry organizations, and less with VNONCW. The contacts with individual firms are increasing. SNM used to focus on legal procedures against 'dirty firms', which is still an important activity. But SNM now also has contacts with the progressive firms, trying to stimulate them and to develop plans together. Furthermore, firms contact the environmental movement when they have a plan that the environmentalists might object to. SNM only issues calls for actions, like consumer boycotts, in cooperation with other environmental organizations.

2.5   Coordination and Cooperation

VNONCW conducts the general industry lobby. It represents the common interests of its members, the industry organizations. The industry organizations have to lobby themselves for their specific interests (Klerken and Zijlstra, 1997):

> If one industry organization has opinions A, B and C, and the other has A, B and D, we only defend A and B.

Thus, when VNONCW makes a statement, one can conclude that this is the view of the whole Dutch industry.

Van der Veer (SNM) stresses the cost of cooperation. Cooperation costs time, because all actions have to be coordinated. When the cooperation partners disagree, they have to get together. Furthermore, an organization may not be able to promote all of its points or only its own points, because all cooperation partners have to agree on a common platform.

Cooperation between environmental organizations did not amount to much in the past, because the organizations had separate working fields. Now that these distinctions are more diffuse, coordination is needed. To that end, the environmental organizations have set up a strategic council.

For SNM it can be worthwhile to act together with two other environmental organizations, especially when it is a diverse partnership, for instance including Greenpeace. It is less worthwhile to find a third and a fourth partner within the environmental movement. This increases cooperation costs more than it increases political leverage.

Cooperation with organizations outside the environmental and nature sphere can sometimes be useful. It is often more effective, because it is more surprising. However, it is also more difficult to organize.

SNM has regular contact with the trade unions. They are a powerful factor that both government and industry have to reckon with.

In Chapter 6, section 3.4.6, we have already seen that SNM participated in a coalition that advocated regulatory energy charges. Together with the Dutch Touring Club and a number of agricultural organizations, SNM took a stand in the debate (in 1996) about the trajectory of the High Speed Train between Amsterdam and Rotterdam. They were against a new track cutting through the so-called Green Core, and in favour of the trajectory across the existing track. However, in the end the government decided for the new track through the Green Core.

2.6 Success

Klerken and Zijlstra (VNONCW) and Van der Veer (SNM) were asked to what extent the following factors are important for the success of an attempt to influence environmental policy:

a. which organization and which interest one represents;
b. access to certain persons (civil servants, politicians) and certain consultation platforms;
c. insight in the decision making process;
d. insight in the 'opponent's' strategy;
e. the quantity of time and resources spent;
f. the force of arguments;
g. luck;
h. other factors.

According to Klerken and Zijlstra (VNONCW), *the force of arguments* is by far the most important factor. Van der Veer's (SNM) first reaction was that all factors mentioned were relevant. He noted that other organizations especially praise SNM's expertise:

We always provide factually correct information.

Thus, for SNM as well, *the force of arguments* is an important factor.

Klerken and Zijlstra as well as Van der Veer recognize that it is important *on behalf of which organization one acts*. They are fortunate in this respect, because both VNONCW and SNM are established and respected organizations.

VNONCW also benefits from the fact that it represents a large group: the whole of Dutch industry. Therefore it has easier access and carries more weight than a small industry organization.

According to Van der Veer, it also matters *which interest one represents*. Thus SNM tries to cooperate with other interest groups to increase its influence, as we saw in section 2.5. Van der Veer found that the political importance attached to the environment is lower now than around 1990.[5]

Insight in the decision making process was also deemed important by both

Klerken and Zijlstra and Van der Veer. Both emphasized the importance of starting one's lobbying activities early in the process, preferably before anything is written down. Thus, *access to certain persons (civil servants, politicians)* is necessary, to find out their plans.

About the factor *insight in the opponent's strategy*, Klerken and Zijlstra remarked:

> That sounds too polarizing, too Stratego-like. The environmental movement may sometimes pull a trick, but not especially on us.

Klerken and Zijlstra did not attach much importance to *chance*. Van der Veer acknowledged that it could play a role:

> The fact that we have no nuclear energy in the Netherlands, is due to three factors: it costs too much, the resistance of the environmental movement and Chernobyl.

The quantity of time and resources spent can be an important factor, according to both Klerken and Zijlstra and Van der Veer. In section 2.2 we already saw how VNONCW and SNM go about planning their activities. Van der Veer remarked:

> Time and resources spent depend very much on the nature and complexity of the subject and the political phase it is in. There is also the danger of saturation. Careful dosage of effort is essential, with respect to persons, organizations and time.

Dekkers (VROM) was asked how industry and the environmental movement influenced him. He replied this was mainly by the force of arguments. The style of argumentation is also important:

> When someone rigidly hangs on to his own point of view, and will not see the other side of the story, he cannot convince me.

Furthermore, Dekkers (VROM) noted that the arguments should be verifiable and that one must always wonder: 'Why does this person want to tell me this?'

Dekkers has experienced a number of occasions where industry overestimated the cost of environmental policy. When asked whether this undermined industry credibility, he replied that this might happen, but:

> On the other hand, one typically speaks to five or six people in the industry, from which one constructs 'the' industry point of view. But perhaps those people are not representative for the industry. Perhaps one has happened to meet a number of people with a particularly bleak view of the costs.

2.7   The Political Importance of the Environment

According to Van der Veer (SNM), the political importance attached to the environment is lower now than it was around 1990, when it was the most important political issue. Thomassen (OCC) and Reijnders (SNM)[6] agree with him.

Van der Veer (SNM) notices that it is more difficult now to get new environmental issues on the agenda. The debate has become more technocratic. He relates this decline in the political importance of the environment to the political life cycle. In the 1980s the goal was to get the environment on the political agenda. Now it is time to implement the policies, which meets with more resistance. As another factor contributing to more influence for the industry and less for the environmental movement, Van den Biggelaar and Van der Veer (SNM) mention the current 'pro-market' fashion in politics.[7]

Klerken and Zijlstra (VNONCW) do not agree that the political importance of the environment has recently declined. Like Blankert (VNONCW) and Wijnolst (MKB: the medium and small firms) before the Climate Committee (Klimaat-commissie, 1996), they argue:

> Firms are paying more attention to the environment than they ever did. The environment has become an accepted part of firm policy.
> We are now in the implementation phase of environmental policy, which is less spectacular than the battle on the barricades that we had before. Some environmental leaders miss this battle, where they had a lot of publicity. Now they think: nothing much is happening, the environment is not so important anymore. But they are wrong.

Accordingly, Klerken and Zijlstra (VNONCW) have a different explanation for the growing influence of industry than Van den Biggelaar and Van der Veer (SNM). As we have seen in section 2.3, Klerken and Zijlstra attribute it to a switch in industry style, from negative to cooperative.

2.8   The Minister and the Cabinet

For easy reference, Table 11.1 presents an overview of the Dutch cabinets and the Ministers of VROM from 1982 to 1998. Table 11.2 gives a short characterization of the political parties mentioned in this section.

Klerken and Zijlstra (VNONCW), Van der Veer (SNM), Dekkers (VROM) and Thomassen (OCC) all agree that it does not matter much for environmental policy which parties are in the government coalition, or which party supplies the Minister for the Environment.

According to Klerken and Zijlstra (VNONCW), environmental policy commands broad support in Parliament. They see only minor differences between the parties with respect to environmental policy, with the VVD on the conservative end and GL on the progressive end.

To support their thesis that the Environmental Minister's party affiliation is not important, Klerken and Zijlstra (VNONCW) note that the VVD Ministers Winsemius and Nijpels were very successful. Van der Veer (SNM) attributes part

Table 11.1   Dutch cabinets and VROM Ministers

Years	Coalition parties	VROM Minister (party)
1982–1986	CDA, VVD	Winsemius (VVD)
1986–1989	CDA, VVD	Nijpels (VVD)
1989–1994	CDA, PvdA	Alders (PvdA)
1994–1998	PvdA, VVD, D66	De Boer (PvdA)

Table 11.2   Dutch political parties

CDA	Christian Democrats
VVD	conservative liberals
PvdA	Social Democrats
D66	progressive liberals
GL	Green Left

of their success to the fact that environmental policy was becoming increasingly important in the 1980s.

Klerken and Zijlstra (VNONCW) and Dekkers (VROM) argue that the personality of the Minister makes a difference. Dekkers emphasizes the differences in style and specific qualities between the Ministers. According to Klerken and Zijlstra, PvdA Minister Alders was more of an ideologue, whereas the current PvdA Minister De Boer operates in a more matter-of-fact and solution-oriented way. The latter approach has Klerken and Zijlstra's sympathy.

Dekkers (VROM) argues that the Minister's position should be seen in the complete social and political context. In that sense, the Minister is only a small wheel in the whole mechanism, and his/her influence should not be overstated.

Dekkers agrees with Van der Veer's (SNM) statement that the Prime Minister's role is very important. Van der Veer points out that environmental problems typically concern other departments as well. When departments have conflicting interests, the Prime Minister has a crucial role in settling the conflict. As with the Minister of the Environment, Van der Veer notes that it is the Prime Minister's personal convictions, and not his party affiliation, that matters:

> Our present Prime Minister Kok (PvdA) does take the environment into account, but it is not his prime concern. The fact that De Boer has suffered a number of defeats in this cabinet, is partly due to lack of support from Kok.

Van der Veer (SNM) also mentions the coalition agreement as important.[8] This agreement is drawn up between the parties that are going to form the new government. According to Van der Veer, it is mainly written by the leaders of the coalition partners. The attention given to the environment in the coalition agreement depends on the personal environmental concern of the party leaders.

2.9   Conclusion

In this conclusion, we will examine the implications of the interviews for the relevance of our institutional model and our rent seeking model. We will also identify the suggestions that the interviews offer for modification and expansion of the models.

In order for our rent seeking model to be applicable, the interest groups should plan their lobbying activities. In section 2.2, we have seen that both SNM and VNONCW do plan their lobbying activities, although SNM does this more formally.

From section 2.4 we can conclude that the quality, as well as the quantity, of lobbying efforts is important. The respondents indicated that lobbying in an early stage is more effective. We can model this with the method of influence factors that we shall describe below. Another modelling strategy is to assume that all agents have sufficient insight into the decision making process and sufficient access to decision makers for their lobbying efforts to be maximally effective.

The respondents name the force of arguments as the most important success factor in lobbying. This seems to support the model we discussed in Chapter 2, section 3, of democracy as a process of mutual persuasion. It seems to conflict with our models of Chapter 7, where arguments do not play an explicit role. For our rent seeking model, it is also worrying that the respondents saw the quantity of time and resources spent as a factor of only minor importance.

However, there are three reasons why the role of arguments could be overstated in our survey. First, the respondents may try to conform to the ideal concept of democracy as mutual persuasion. They do not like to admit that who you are or how much pressure you apply is more important in the political process than what you say. Interest groups may also try to present their interests in the form of 'scientific' arguments. Van Soest (1992) criticizes the Dutch energy-intensive industry for this. They claimed that an energy charge would harm 'the' international competitiveness, 'the' employment situation and 'the' Dutch economy. But in fact, the charge would harm some sectors (mainly the energy-intensive industry, of course), but benefit other sectors.

Secondly, we have mainly asked the opinion of a few interest group representatives. For instance, Van der Veer of the environmental organization SNM was interviewed. Within the Dutch environmental movement, SNM's strategy is to negotiate with government and industry, while other interest groups are more 'action'-oriented (Pleune, 1997). However, no one from these other organizations was interviewed. Furthermore, interest group representatives may ascribe their success to the force of arguments (or to what they present as arguments), but perhaps the motivations of the decision makers themselves are different. Thus, to get a more complete picture, we should also ask the politicians, and perhaps the bureaucrats, making the decisions. Of course, they could also overstate the importance of arguments.[9] Therefore we should also analyse the actual decisions that are made, to try and find out why they were taken in favour of a particular interest. The number of decisions by the Dutch government as described in Chapter 6, section 3, is still too low to make any definite statement about this. However, it will always be difficult to disentangle the importance of arguments, pressure and the nature of the interest.

Thirdly, as we have argued in Chapter 7, section 3.1, arguments can sometimes be seen as an intermediate input, because they are costly. When an interest group wants to make a solid argument about the costs or the benefits of environmental policy, it has to base the argument on research. And research is costly. Thus, the complete chain of causality is costs–research–arguments–influence. Then the short-cut of rent seeking analysis, going directly from costs to influence, is justified. But of course, it is worthwhile to examine how exactly costs produce influence.

The respondents indicate that it makes a difference which organization makes a lobbying effort. This factor is taken into account in our institutional model, but not in our rent seeking model. The fact that one agent is more powerful than another in a rent seeking contest, has already been modelled by a number of authors (e.g. Baik, 1994a). The most simple amendment of the contest success function (csf) is the following.

Suppose there is a contest between industry and the environmental movement. Let x_i (x_e) be the effort by industry (the environmental movement). In Chapters 7 to 10, we employed the following csf, with ρ_i the success probability of industry:

$$\rho_i(x_i, x_e) = \frac{x_i}{x_i + x_e}$$

To take into account differences in influence, we change this csf into:

$$\rho_i(x_i, x_e, a_{it}) = \frac{a_{it} x_i}{a_{it} x_i + x_e}$$

Industry effort is now multiplied by the factor a_{it}. This factor indicates the influence of industry relative to the environmental movement. $a_{it} > 1$ means that industry is more influential than the environmental movement. When $a_{it} > 1$, and industry effort is equal to the effort of the environmental movement, industry has a success probability of more than one half. Likewise, $a_{it} < 1$ means that the environmental movement is more influential than industry.

The influence of an interest group can also vary in time. This is denoted by the subscript t in a_{it}. For instance, according to Van der Veer, a_{it} is higher now than it was around 1990.

While it is straightforward to introduce influence in this way into a rent seeking model for a private good with noncooperative behaviour, it is more difficult with cooperative behaviour and a public good. Take, for instance, the rent seeking contest for an impure public good, discussed in Chapter 8, section 2, and Chapter 9. When one agent i is active on the A-side, can he claim that he also acts on behalf of the other agents on the A-side, even though the other agents do not contribute to his effort? And what does 'speaking on behalf of others as well', or an effort by agent i that is paid for by several agents, mean for the influence factor a_i of agent i's effort?

The fact that cooperation itself is costly, as emphasized by Van der Veer, may seem to have been neglected in our analysis of cooperation in Chapter 9. It looks like we have assumed costless cooperation, so that the agents' costs only consist of rent seeking effort. However, the distinction between the cost of cooperation and the cost of rent seeking effort becomes less strict when we look at the model of asymmetric information, reviewed in Chapter 2, section 4.2. In this model, that is closely linked to the rent seeking model, the interest group knows its own stake, but the decision maker does not know the interest group's stake. Thus, the interest group has to undertake a costly action to convince the decision maker that it has a high stake, in which case the decision maker will take more notice of the interest group's wishes. When cooperation is costly and the interest group's stake is high, it can choose to cooperate. Then the decision maker will think: 'The interest group must have a high stake, because it goes through the trouble of cooperating with other groups.' Then he will take more notice of the interest group's wishes. When we interpret cooperation in this manner, the costs of organizing cooperation are actually costs of rent seeking effort.

In section 2.8 we saw that according to the respondents, the partisan composition of the government coalition and the party affiliation of the Minister of the Environment was not important for environmental policy. The respondents found that the personality of the Minister of the Environment and of the Prime Minister were more important. This undermines our institutional model, in which we assume that instrument choice depends on the partisan composition of the government coalition and the party affiliation of the Minister of the Environment. However, the applicability of this model may increase in the future. According to this reasoning, the differences between parties had a small or negligible impact on environmental policy compared to the secular development of the environmental policy field in the past (from recognizing the problem to writing laws to implementing laws). But environmental policy will increasingly become an established area of government policy. When it becomes an established area, the differences between parties will become more important relative to the secular development.

3.   DIRECTIONS FOR FUTURE RESEARCH

3.1   Introduction

In this section we will identify directions for future research into models of political economy. Besides being of interest in itself, looking ahead to what there is to be done also allows us to assess the contribution of this book.

Because theoretical developments should be based on and tested with empirical research, we begin with the subjects that are in need of further empirical research in section 3.2. In section 3.3 we discuss potential extensions to the rent seeking model beyond what has been achieved in Chapters 8 to 10. Finally, in section 3.4, we indicate some directions in which other models of interest group influence could be expanded.

3.2   Empirical research

We will address three issues in need of empirical research:

1. the relation between interest groups in practice and rent-seeking agents;
2. the interest groups' stakes;
3. the success of interest groups' attempts to influence political decisions.

Ad 1. Empirical research is required into the question to which extent we can see an interest group, for example the shareholders of different firms or different industries, as one agent. This question is relevant for a rent seeking contest for an impure public good, as we modelled it in Chapters 8 and 9. The more agents there are on one side in these models, the lower their aggregate payoff from the contest.

The likely outcome of the empirical research is that we cannot see the broad interest groups of shareholders, workers and environmentalists as one agent, but there is substantial cooperation between the agents in the same field. It is also interesting to find out how cooperation takes place. We would like to know what kind of agreements interest groups make about joint efforts and sharing the cost of efforts. In Chapter 9 we modelled cooperation in the form of support, but we can think of many other forms of cooperation. Empirical research can provide evidence about which forms of cooperation are actually used and for that reason deserve modelling.

Ad 2. In the conclusion to Chapter 7 we said that one of the advantages of the rent seeking model over the institutional model is that it takes into account the preference intensities, or the size of the stakes, of the interest groups. However, we do not know much about the size of the stakes. Our research in Chapters 3 and 4 into the interest groups' preferences was qualitative rather than quantitative. We know shareholders prefer grandfathering to standards, but we do not know by how much. Thus, the rent seeking model is more sophisticated than the institutional model, but it is actually too sophisticated. As a result, the applications of our models to instrument choice in Chapters 8 to 10 strongly had the character of illustrations: 'If these are the agents' stakes, this will be the outcome of the contest.'

To make the application more concrete, we should empirically quantify the agents' stakes. Ideally, we should investigate the effects of instruments on criteria that interest groups find important, rather than what we think they are interested in.

The difference between the empirical and theoretical approach to criteria, as well as the difficulty with the empirical approach, can be illustrated with our survey of Dutch interest groups. In our theoretical approach, we assumed shareholders were only interested in profits. But in Chapter 5, section 3.2.4, we saw that Zijlstra from the Dutch general industry organization placed profits fifth in his list of criteria. Thus it seems profits are not that important for industry. But we should also look at the motivation Zijlstra gave for putting profits fifth. He wanted to indicate that profits should not be made at the expense of the environment. This calls our attention to the problem of getting an accurate picture of an interest group's criteria from the interest group itself.

Another problem is the quantification of effects and their commensurability. Suppose a trade union is interested in employment and in innovation. How do we quantify the favourable effect that market instruments have on innovation, compared to direct regulation? And how does the trade union trade this off against the negative effect of market instruments on employment?

As a first step, we should look at the quantifiable effects of instruments, for example profits and employment. These can be estimated in an empirical industry model, or even a general equilibrium model. This will also give us an indication of the possible importance of other effects. For instance, when there is a large difference in employment effects between the instruments, the trade union is not interested in other effects anymore.[10] But when the difference is small, the trade union will also look at other effects, for example on innovation.

Ad 3. We have seen in section 2.6 that the interviewees from the interest groups and the civil service attach great importance to the force of arguments. But as we said in section 2.9, we would also like to hear what the decision makers, especially politicians, have to say about how interest groups affect their decisions. As a complement, research into actual decisions is necessary.

However, it will be difficult to uncover a contest success function. We may be able to find out what interest groups did to influence a certain decision. But we only observe the outcome of the decision itself, and not the probability that the outcome might have been different. This is a problem with a decision between discrete alternatives: either A or B. It will be easier to assess an interest group's success in influencing a decision from a wide (or even continuous) range of alternatives. Then we can see how close the outcome is to the interest group's most preferred outcome.

3.3   The Rent Seeking Model

In Chapters 8 to 10, we have made considerable progress in expanding rent seeking theory into the areas of the impure public good, cooperation and a combined contest for instrument choice and revenue distribution.[11] But in our treatment of cooperation, we only looked at one particular form of cooperation and we limited the number of alternatives to two. And in our treatment of the combined contest, we limited the number of agents to two. Thus, we have stopped short of a complete treatment of instrument choice as a rent seeking contest, featuring the combined contest with and without cooperation and without exogenous restrictions on the number of agents and on the number of alternatives.

Three remarks should be made in order to put this failure to give a complete treatment in the right perspective. First, analysing a contest with a minimum of exogenously given restrictions and structure is quite painstaking. There is a bewildering variety of potential equilibria for the researcher (not to mention the agents themselves) to examine. In the end, we are bound to be left with multiple equilibria (of which we had a foretaste in Chapter 8, section 3.1) or the non-existence of pure strategy equilibria (of which Appendix C to Chapter 10 of Dijkstra (1998) offers a foretaste).

Secondly, in reality there is some structure to the rent seeking game. The number of agents, as well as the number of alternatives, will be limited. For instance, the government will not introduce tradable permits without having thoroughly examined the design and the effects of this instrument. As long as the government has not done this, it is no use lobbying for the introduction of tradable permits at short notice. One can lobby for a serious investigation of tradable permits, but not for its introduction at short notice.

Thirdly, the generalization considered is a generalization in one particular direction: what is to be decided, and who try to influence that decision. It may be more fruitful to consider generalization in another direction: the contest success function (csf) or how the decision is made. Let us now turn to the potential of generalizing the csf. In our analysis we have used the following csf:

$$\rho_i(x_1,...,x_n) \; = \; \frac{x_i}{x_i + \sum_{\substack{j=1 \\ j \neq i}}^{n} x_j}$$

As we have seen in Chapter 7, this is the Constant Returns to Scale (CRS) version of Tullock's csf for the imperfectly discriminating rent seeking contest. But we could also use the Decreasing Returns to Scale (DRS) or the Increasing Returns to Scale (IRS) version.[12] Next to that, we could also use other specifications of the csf, like the csf for the perfectly discriminating contest.[13]

It is particularly interesting to use a general csf, encompassing many, or even all, different specifications (Baik, 1993). In this general csf, we could perhaps also include the difference in influence between agents, a subject we discussed in section 2.9.

Furthermore, it will be fruitful to analyse different forms of cooperation in a rent seeking contest for an impure public good. From the overview in Chapter 9, section 2, the schemes of reward (analysed by Baik and Kim, 1997 and Konrad, 1997) and matching (analysed by Guttman, 1987, 1991) seem to be especially interesting.

Another possible extension is in the direction of multiple decision makers, e.g. political parties. With the exceptions of Congleton (1984) and Van Cayseele et al. (1993), this subject has hardly been addressed in the rent seeking literature. Keohane et al. (1998) propose a model in which interest groups try to influence the effective support, instead of just the vote, of a politician for a particular instrument. One politician may be more efficient than the other in transforming his effort into effective support. Thus, Keohane et al. (1998) also envisage a rent-seeking contest at the level of the political decision makers.

We have modelled instrument choice as if there were only one decision maker. This assumption is not only valid when there is literally only one decision maker. It also holds when there are multiple decision makers, but:

- the rent-seeking agents cannot aim their efforts at one particular decision maker;
- it is more cost-effective to aim efforts at all decision makers in general than at one decision maker in particular;
- the effect of the effort is independent of which decision maker it is aimed at.

If, on the other hand, there are multiple decision makers and the rent-seeking agents are willing and able to aim their efforts at a particular decision maker, then we should model the contest as a multiple decision maker contest.

We can also differentiate the influence of particular rent-seeking agents on particular decision makers, expanding the influence factor approach we discussed in section 2.9. For instance, a political party on the left is more sensitive to workers' efforts than to shareholders' efforts. And workers' efforts have a larger influence on a left wing party than on a right wing party.

In this framework, we can also try to do more justice to the role of the (environmental) bureaucracy. The bureaucracy has an intermediate role. On the one hand, interest groups try to influence the bureaucracy, but on the other hand, the bureaucracy has its own motives to influence the political decision. In the institutional model, we tried to take this intermediate role of the bureaucracy into account. In the rent seeking model, we just assumed the bureaucracy was an interest group like any other.

One way to incorporate the bureaucracy in the model is to make it one of the multiple decision makers. The bureaucracy will be biased in favour of instruments that do well on the criteria it finds important, like control and slack (see Chapter 4, section 3).[14] In fact, politicians could also be biased: toward the instrument that is best for the general electorate or their own voters or toward an instrument for which they can make a good argumentative case (see Chapter 2, section 3).

However, there are two major difficulties in modelling instrument choice, and in fact any political choice, as a multiple decision maker rent seeking contest. First, Congleton (1984) and Van Cayseele et al. (1993) assume that the rent-seeking agents will direct their efforts separately at the decision makers. But in general, the agents have a choice between aiming their efforts at the political parties in general (e.g. by way of publicity) and aiming efforts at one party (e.g. in bilateral meetings). As we have noted above, 'general' efforts should be more costly than 'targeted' efforts to make targeted efforts worthwhile. But what will happen when targeted efforts are worthwhile? Perhaps we will find that there is no cost ratio at which targeted and general efforts coexist. This may seem to be unrealistic. But if we are able to construct a model where targeted and general efforts coexist, the model becomes more complicated and may become intractable.

Secondly, we must know the procedure by which the decision makers reach a decision. If one decision maker favours instrument A and another favours instrument B, what will happen? Congleton (1984) and Van Cayseele et al. (1993) assume there will be majority voting. This looks appropriate for countries like the US, with a weak link between administration and Congress. But in Western European countries there is an overriding tendency for the coalition parties to vote for government proposals.[15] Thus, most differences between coalition parties are resolved within the government or in consultation between the government and the coalition parties in Parliament. It is difficult for the outside observer, and perhaps for the interest groups as well, to find out how exactly these differences are resolved. But the interest groups should have some idea of the decision rule within the coalition,[16] to determine how much effort they should spend on a particular coalition party.

We can conclude that the analysis of other forms of cooperation is an interesting, and probably the least problematic, way of expanding the analysis from Chapters 8 to 10. The generalization of the csf to other functional forms, and a more general form including differential influence, is also worthwhile. However, the analysis and presentation of all possible variants may become quite involved. Finally, the analysis of multiple decision makers is an intriguing area of research.

It has not received much attention yet and a lot of modelling issues are still unresolved. Thus, one cannot expect to quickly obtain definite results.

3.4   Other Interest Group Models

In this section we will look at some promising directions for future research involving other models than the rent seeking model.

It would be interesting to further develop the model of asymmetric information we discussed in Chapter 2, section 4.2. As we have seen, this model does not yet enable us to study what happens when two interest groups have opposing interests. This is of course possible in the rent seeking model, but the model of asymmetric information is a 'richer' model in that it explains why interest group activities influence the decision maker. Once we have incorporated agents with opposing interests into the model of asymmetric information, we can compare the model with the rent seeking model, and we can give a stronger foundation to the contest success function used in rent seeking analysis.

Another aspect that deserves modelling is the importance of arguments, as expressed by the interviewees in section 2.6. In section 2.9, we have made a case against overstating the importance of arguments, but arguments are still likely to be an important factor in their own right.

We can link this factor to the question why rent seeking expenditures are so low, relative to the political issues at stake (Tullock, 1997). One possible explanation is that interest groups first try to reach an agreement among themselves, possibly with a politician or a political party as a broker. Institutions like the Dutch SER (Socio-Economic Council), in which employers' organizations and trade unions are represented, can facilitate contacts between interest groups. The interest groups will incur relatively low costs in this negotiation process, in which there is also room for trying to convince the other with arguments. However, if the negotiations fail, there will be an adversarial rent seeking contest, and the interest groups have to incur high rent seeking costs. Because of the high costs of rent seeking, the interest groups have an incentive to try and negotiate an agreement.[17]

Another explanation for low rent seeking costs and the importance of arguments is that interest groups and the government repeatedly have contacts with each other. When interest groups repeatedly have to fight a rent seeking contest against each other, they can come to an agreement to drastically cut back their rent seeking expenditures (Linster, 1994; Aidt, 1997). In the model of asymmetric information, an interest group can build up credibility.[18] This means that an interest group can simply tell the government, using arguments, that it is against a certain policy. The interest group does not have to undertake costly actions to convince the government that it is really against the policy, because the government takes the interest group's word for it.

4. CONCLUSION

In this chapter we have assessed the institutional model and the model of the rent seeking contest, both introduced in Chapter 7. In section 2, we have seen what representatives from interest groups, mainly from the environmental organization SNM and the industry organization VNONCW, had to say about their influence on environmental policy. In section 3 we identified directions for future research.

The most conspicuous difference between our rent seeking model and the experience of the interest group representatives is that the interest group representatives see environmental policy more as a process of mutual persuasion than as the outcome of a contest. In section 2.9 we argued that the interest group representatives may overstate the importance of arguments and that the production of arguments is costly. However, arguments and negotiations may also play a role in their own right. As suggested in section 3.4, agents with opposed interest are interested in negotiations in order to avoid an adversarial and costly rent seeking contest. However, even if environmental policy is the result of negotiations between interest groups that have managed to avoid a contest, the outcome of the contest is important in analysing environmental policy. The reason is that when an interest group evaluates a proposal that looks unfavourable, it must compare the options of accepting the proposal and (running the risk of) breaking off the negotiations, which will result in a contest.

NOTES

1. Potters and Sloof (1996) review the literature.
2. For example Millner and Pratt (1991), Shogren and Baik (1991), Loehman et al. (1996) and Potters et al. (1997).
3. See also Pleune (1997) on the subject of strategies followed by Dutch environmental organizations.
4. See also section 2.6 on this subject.
5. In section 2.7 we will elaborate on this subject.
6. Testimony before the Parliamentary Committee on Climate Change (Klimaatcommissie, 1996).
7. See also Chapter 5, section 3.3.6.
8. Chapter 6, section 3.4.8, shows the importance of the coalition agreement for the introduction of regulatory energy charges in the Netherlands.
9. As we have seen, Dekkers (VROM) stated he was mainly influenced by the interest groups' arguments.
10. Of course, we need a yardstick to determine whether a certain difference in employment is large or small.
11. In the following, we will refer to this latter item as 'the combined contest', for short.
12. IRS is perhaps less attractive, because it may not have a pure strategy equilibrium for the private good case, and the mixed strategy equilibrium is not known, although Baye et al. (1994) have made some progress.
13. See Chapter 7, section 3.2.

14. The concept of bias should be distinguished from the concept of differential influence we discussed before. Differential influence means that a decision maker is more inclined to listen to one rent-seeking agent than to another, irrespective of which instruments the agents promote. Bias means that a decision maker is more inclined to choose a particular instrument, abstracting from the actions of the rent-seeking agents.

15. See Chapter 7, section 2, for a discussion of the Western European political system.

16. The interest groups can also see the decision rule as probabilistic: if one party favours instrument A, and two parties favour instrument B, there is a probability of 1/3 (2/3) that instrument A (B) will be selected.

17. There is an analogy with a legal dispute, where parties have an incentive to reach a pretrial settlement in order to avoid a costly trial (Cooter and Rubinfeld, 1989; Hay, 1995; Hughes and Snyder, 1995).

18. Note the difference between the idea presented here and the model by Sloof and Van Winden (1996). Sloof and Van Winden examine the interest group's choice between lobbying and pressure, where pressure is more costly and also harms the decision maker. They conclude that pressure is typically used to build up a reputation and lobbying to maintain a reputation. I argue that the reputation of an interest group may be so high, that it does not even have to undertake lobbying expenditures, but can simply tell the decision maker that it is in favour of or against a proposal. This may be modelled as an extension to Sloof and Van Winden's model.

12. Conclusion

Why are market instruments not more widely applied in environmental policy, although economists believe they are efficient? This is the question with which we started the book. It was decided to take the efficiency, or welfare-maximizing property, of market instruments for granted. This allowed us to rephrase the question as: why are market instruments not more widely applied in environmental policy, although they are efficient?

We have taken the political economy approach to this question. The political economy argument is that apparently there are powerful interest groups that prefer direct regulation to market instruments. These interest groups have so much influence on the political decision, that they can block the introduction of market instruments. Taking the political economy approach, we have split the original question into two research questions:

1. What are the preferences of the relevant interest groups for environmental policy instruments?
2. Given the preferences of everyone affected by instrument choice and given that market instruments are efficient, why does the political process so often result in the choice of direct regulation?

We can now look back to see what we have learned about these questions. Here we shall discuss a more specific version of the first research question, namely: why would interest groups be against market instruments?

From the industry model of Chapter 3, it is clear that the shareholders in the polluting industry are against the market instruments of emissions charges and an auction of tradable permits (also called the financial instruments), because these instruments are worst for profits. Workers in the polluting industry are against all market instruments, because they are worst for employment. In contrast to our theory, however, the Dutch trade unions are willing to let the environment take precedence over employment. The trade unions were part of the coalition for regulatory energy charges.

Part of the attraction of a charge to trade unions lies in the idea to reduce labour taxes with the government revenues from the charge. Thus, leaping ahead to our second research question, we cannot simply attribute the lack of financial instruments in environmental policy to the resistance from the shareholders and the workers. Although these interest groups rank financial instruments as such lowest, they would rank them higher if they were to receive part of the government revenues from financial instruments. And when the shareholders and the workers do not receive all of the revenues, other groups will receive part of the revenues, and they will lobby for financial instruments. This illustrates the general point that what one interest group sees as a disadvantage of market instruments can be an advantage for another group. However, as we know from Chapter 10, it is not a perfect illustration of this point, because interest groups may have to make costly lobbying expenditures to acquire part of the government revenues from financial instruments.

The environmental bureaucracy might be against market instruments, because with market instruments they have less control over industry emissions than with direct regulation. We saw that opinions in the Dutch environmental bureacracy about grandfathering of tradable permits are divided. Within the Department of VROM, there is a group that wants to give industry more responsibility for reaching environmental targets and another group that argues that industry cannot handle this responsibility. The proponents of grandfathering can be found in the first group. Although the regional environmental bureaucracy is also divided, they are on balance more in favour of grandfathering. This is clear from the fact that just when VROM had discarded the idea of tradable permits, the regional environmental agencies initiated another round of discussion and research about it. This project, which has not been concluded yet, might lead to the introduction of some kind of tradability of emission permits in the Netherlands.

In our theoretical treatment, we ascribed the criteria of certainty of emission reduction and the generation of government revenue to the environmental movement. Because emission reduction is certain with tradable permits, the environmental movement would prefer this instrument to emissions charges. Because the financial instruments yield government revenue, the environmental movement would prefer these to grandfathering and to direct regulation.

The fact that market instruments can be seen as giving a 'licence to pollute' and putting a price tag to the environment gives rise to objections of principle against market instruments, especially in the environmental movement. However, we should realize that industry may see these aspects as a positive feature of market instruments, because they imply a neutral instead of a stigmatizing attitude toward the act of polluting.

The existence of objections of principle against market instruments is an empirical matter. We saw that although the importance of these objections has diminished in the course of time,[1] they still exist in the Dutch environmental movement. We also saw that the Dutch environmental movement is more enthusiastic about emissions charges than about tradable emission permits.

A number of barriers to the introduction of tradable permits emerged from our survey among Dutch interest groups (Chapter 5). When the permits are initially grandfathered, there is the problem of how to distribute the permits. When present emissions are chosen as a basis for distributing the permits, firms that have already done a lot about reducing their emissions are punished, because they only receive a small amount of permits. Firms that have not done much about reducing emissions are rewarded, because they receive a lot of permits. Of course one can think of other benchmarks on which to base the initial distribution of permits, but the respondents to our survey agree that it will be difficult to find an acceptable benchmark.[2]

Another problem is that tradable permits imply a 'hard' ceiling on industry emissions. Regardless of how much an industry grows, it is not allowed to emit more than the total amount of tradable emission permits, stated in tons of emissions. Industry is more comfortable with a 'soft' ceiling, where total emissions are allowed to increase when the industry grows. As we saw above, however, the hard ceiling on total emissions is an attractive feature of tradable permits in the eyes of the environmentalists. Thus, once more, there are two sides to this story.

The extent to which existing direct regulation will be maintained when tradability is introduced is a source of uncertainty. The Department of VROM emphasizes the problem that tradability is not compatible with existing principles of environmental legislation. Thus, introducing tradability would require a time-consuming revision of environmental legislation. One may wonder whether this is really a problem or VROM 'blows it up' because they are against tradability for other reasons. Anyway, restrictions upon trade will reduce the efficiency gains of tradable permits.[3] Trades that would otherwise have taken place will be ruled out by the restrictions. Furthermore, a firm will be wary to propose a trade that may be rejected by the environmental agency or contested in court by the environmental movement. By reducing the number of trades, the restrictions may also prevent the permit market from functioning well, further reducing the efficiency gains. The more efficiency gains are reduced, the less enthusiastic industry will be about tradable permits.

Finally, we mention an element that may constitute a barrier to the introduction of tradable permits only at first sight. This is the emergence of covenants. With covenants, industry can already achieve great gains in flexibility and efficiency compared to the current form of direct regulation. The flexibility gain on the level of the firm is probably smaller than with tradable permits, because firms do not explicitly trade permits. However, there are offsetting advantages to covenants. One is that covenants, unlike tradable permits, can be combined with a 'soft' ceiling on industry emissions. Compared with tradable permits, covenants thus offer less flexibility on the firm level, but more flexibility on the level of the target group. With covenants, industry will also have a larger say in other design matters than with tradable permits. Furthermore, it appears that covenants can be implemented more quickly and cheaply. There is no need for a rewriting of environmental legislation or an institute to organize trade. It also seems that the environmental bureaucracy, at least the Dutch Department of VROM, will be more cooperative when industry asks for covenants than when it asks for tradable permits. The reaction of the environmental movement is difficult to assess. On the one hand, the environmental movement may have objections of principle against tradable permits, but not against covenants. On the other hand, the design of a tradable permit system is more transparent for outsiders, including a 'hard' ceiling on total emissions.

Covenants are meant to increase flexibility in emission abatement, not only by letting firms decide how to abate, but also by letting industry decide how to allocate the available emission room across firms. The way in which this allocation takes place under covenants is obscure, due to the general obscurity of covenants to outsiders. But one can imagine that an allocation method similar to tradable permits is in place or develops. More generally, it may be easier to switch from current direct regulation to covenants first and then to tradable permits than to switch from current direct regulation to tradable permits directly. In that sense, covenants are more properly seen as a stepping stone than as a barrier to the introduction of tradable permits.

To sum up the contribution of this book to answering our first research question, the theoretical contribution consists mainly of the derivation of shareholders' and workers' preferences from a basic industry model. Furthermore, we have examined the preferences of interest groups and instrument choice in the Netherlands. Of course, it remains to be seen whether our empirical findings generalize to other countries and other periods, but at least the future researcher can find some clues about what to look and ask for.

We now turn to our second research question, which asks how the political process can result in the choice for direct regulation, when market instruments are welfare-maximizing. In our institutional model we saw that the chances of market instruments were bleak. But this was a rudimentary and behaviourally poor model. We decided to further develop another model of interest group influence, namely the model of the rent seeking contest.

In a rent seeking contest, the interest groups (called rent-seeking agents) do their best to increase the success probability of their favourite instrument, i.e. the probability that the decision maker will select this instrument. Rent seeking analysis commonly assumes that the interests of the rent-seeking agents are completely opposed to each other. But with respect to instrument choice, agents' interests can run (partly) parallel. For instance, two interest groups both prefer instrument A to instrument B. This means that a rent seeking contest for instrument choice is a rent seeking contest for an impure public good.

In Chapter 8 we studied noncooperative behaviour in rent seeking contests for impure public goods. We first studied the contest with two policy alternatives (i.e. instruments), where either alternative has more than one proponent. We saw that in the noncooperative equilibrium only the agent with the highest stake on either side is active. Thus, if there is one interest group with a large stake in direct regulation versus many interest groups with a small per capita stake in the market instrument, direct regulation will have a large success probability. This can occur even when the aggregate stake in the market instrument exceeds the aggregate stake in direct regulation, i.e. when the market instrument is welfare-maximizing. We also examined the three-agent, three-alternative case. There we saw that when the choice is between two instruments of direct regulation and one market instrument, the market instrument can even have zero success probability, even when it has the highest aggregate stake. The market instrument will have zero success probability when the proponent of instrument X of direct regulation is strongly opposed to instrument Y of direct regulation and vice versa.

In Chapter 9 we studied cooperative behaviour in a rent seeking contest for an impure public good. We examined cooperation in the form of support, which has not been analysed in a rent seeking contest before. With support, one agent pays a fraction of the other agent's rent seeking efforts. Again we studied the contest with two policy alternatives, where either alternative has more than one proponent. We found that with cooperation as well, the alternative with the highest aggregate valuation can have a success probability below one half and even zero. The more proponents an alternative has (given its aggregate stake) and the higher the stake of the agent with the lowest stake, the lower will be the success probability of the alternative.

Thus, in a rent seeking contest there are circumstances under which the instrument with the highest aggregate valuation has a low or even zero success probability. But do these circumstances apply to instrument choice in environmental policy? We have seen that an important condition for an instrument to have a high success probability is the existence of one agent with a large stake. In our theoretical analysis of interest group preferences we saw that shareholders will have a large stake in tradable permits with grandfathering. Thus, when we regard shareholders as one group, the rent seeking model predicts a high instead of a low success probability for the market instrument of grandfathering. However, there can be many agents with small per capita stakes in a financial instrument. Whether or not this occurs depends upon the distribution of the government revenues from financial instruments. This distribution was taken as exogenously given in Chapters 8 and 9.

In Chapter 10, the distribution of the government revenues from financial instruments is endogenized. When the government considers the application of a financial instrument, it has to make two decisions: whether to apply the financial instrument or direct regulation, and how to distribute the revenues from the financial instrument. In Chapter 10, both decisions are the subject of a rent seeking contest between two agents. There are two following orders of decision making. The following order RI (first revenue distribution and then instrument choice) results in a higher success probability of the financial instrument.

However, the rent-seeking agents may have a higher payoff with the following order IR (first instrument choice and then revenue division), because their rent seeking expenditures are much higher in RI. When both agents prefer IR to RI, they may agree to play the game as IR, resulting in a low or even zero success probability for the financial instrument. Thus, endogenizing the division of the revenue from the financial instrument gives us another explanation for the low success probability of financial instruments. The financial instruments are welfare-maximizing if one does not take rent seeking expenditures into account. Subtracting rent seeking expenditures from welfare, direct regulation may actually be welfare-maximizing.

Thus, the main contribution of this book to answering the second research question lies in the extensions of rent seeking analysis to make it more applicable to instrument choice in environmental policy. The analysis of the rent seeking contest for an impure public good has been extended, and the combined contest for instrument choice and revenue division was studied for the first time. In all our extensions, we found that the alternative with the highest aggregate valuation could have a low, and sometimes even zero, success probability.

After this review of the results (what we have found), let us now consider the method (how we found it). Our major theoretical contribution to interest groups' preferences for instruments was the derivation of shareholders' and workers' preferences from an industry model in Chapter 3. The industry model was the partial equilibrium model of a perfectly competitive industry. One may feel that since this is quite an unrealistic model, the value of the preference orderings derived from it is questionable. However, two points are in order here.

First, this derivation from 'fundamentals', which has not been performed before, is important as a benchmark. The effects of instruments on profits and employment in more realistic models, for instance with imperfect competition or in a general equilibrium setup, can analytically be split into the effect in the benchmark model of partial equilibrium with perfect competition and an effect that is due to the difference between the model studied and the benchmark model. Thus, before instruments can be compared in more realistic models, which has hardly been done yet, the elaboration of the benchmark model, as performed in Chapter 3, is necessary.

Secondly, we have also derived industry preferences from other sources. In Chapter 4, we have looked at the more verbal literature. In our survey (Chapter 5) we asked representatives of Dutch industry organizations and trade unions about their preferences for environmental policy instruments.

For our second research question we have mainly used the rent seeking model. In Chapter 2 we saw that this is but one of many political economy models with, as we may assume for instrument choice in environmental policy, a minimal electoral influence. The choice of the rent seeking model does not imply that we feel this is the most appropriate model for instrument choice in environmental policy. Indeed, the fact that we have had to expand the model and that it can still be expanded considerably to make it more appropriate,[4] could lead one to wonder whether the rent seeking model was an adequate choice in the first place. We have chosen the rent seeking model because there were some interesting extensions to be made with which we could shed more light on some aspects of instrument choice in environmental policy. Furthermore, it is hoped these extensions will also be valuable for other applications of rent seeking analysis.

We will now take up one particular argument against the use of rent seeking analysis for instrument choice in environmental policy. From the report of our interviews in Chapter 11, section 2, one does not get the impression that the representatives of Dutch interest groups see environmental policy as a contest, with lots of efforts being spent by the interest groups. It is more a process of consultation, negotiation and persuasion, which seems less costly than a rent seeking contest. One can try to find an explanation for this apparent difference in the size of costs within the rent seeking model. For instance, one may argue that the contest success function is such that there are relatively low rent seeking expenditures in equilbrium.[5] Or it could be that there is a large group of agents with a small per capita stake, who fail to cooperate. Another explanation, which may be more appropriate, goes beyond the rent seeking model. This explanation is that the rent-seeking agents with opposed interests first get together to try and work out a compromise between themselves. Only if they fail to reach an agreement, there will be a costly rent seeking contest. However, if the explanation for the low costs of influencing a political decision is that the rent-seeking agents manage to avoid a costly rent seeking contest, it is still important to analyse this contest. An agent needs to know his payoff from a contest in order to decide whether to accept an offer that looks unfavourable or to break off the negotiations and have the contest. To repeat a term we have used above in a different context, we can say that the model of the rent seeking contest offers a 'benchmark' for other models of interest group influence.

Finally, we note that unlike e.g. Grossman and Helpman (1994), we have not formally connected the models of interest group preferences with the models of interest group influence. We theoretically derived preference orderings for environmentalists, the environmental bureaucracy and the shareholders and workers in the polluting industry. The preferences of the latter two interest groups were even derived from a formal model. However, we did not give formal expressions for the size of an interest group's stake in an instrument, which we could subsequently plug into our rent seeking model.[6] Three reasons can be given for this choice. First, we derived the preferences of interest groups from a variety of sources: the literature, theoretical analysis, a survey and the actual political choice of instruments. Summarizing all this material into a single preference ordering for an interest group, possibly even with expressions for the intensity of their preferences, would not do justice to the richness of the information.

Secondly, a lot of variables would have to be determined exogenously to link the information about interest group preferences to the rent seeking model. To name but a few: how does a trade union trade off short-run employment against long-run employment? Which value does the environmental movement attach to the certainty that the environmental target will be reached? When a lot of exogenous variables have to be added in order to link two models, it may be better not to link them at all. This brings us to the third reason for not linking the models. The political economy component of our analysis is more versatile, because we have decided to use the self-contained model of the rent seeking contest. Everyone can plug in the interest groups and the stakes which they think are appropriate, and our extensions to the rent seeking model can also be used for other applications.

Thus, our elaboration of the political economy approach to the question 'Why are market instruments not more widely applied in environmental policy, although they are efficient?' is certainly not the only possible elaboration, nor do our results constitute the definitive answer from political economy to our question. We have made considerable progress in the theoretical analysis of shareholders' and workers' preferences, in the empirical analysis of interest group preferences and instrument choice in the Netherlands and in expanding rent seeking theory. But even within our self-imposed constraints upon the approach to the question 'Why are market instruments not more widely applied in environmental policy, although economists believe they are efficient?', we have not been able to be comprehensive. We hardly touched upon the questions whether market instruments are really efficient and how the political economy explanation for their absence compares to other explanations. With the application of instruments in actual environmental policy far from settled and the analysis of this application far from complete, instrument choice in environmental policy remains an interesting area of research.

NOTES

1. The conclusion that the importance of objections of principle against market instruments has diminished in the course of time, can be drawn for the Dutch environmental movement from our Chapter 6. For the US and the Danish environmental movement, the same conclusion can be drawn from Kelman (1981, 1983) and Svendsen (1998).
2. See the responses to statement 8 of our second round questionnaire in Chapter 5, section 4.5.
3. Of course, restrictions upon trade in order to maintain local environmental quality are necessary.
4. See Chapter 11.
5. In the contest success function for the imperfectly discriminating rent seeking contest, discussed in the Appendix to Chapter 7, equilibrium rent seeking expenditures are decreasing in r, given the number of active agents.
6. We did use the preference orderings from Chapter 4, section 6, for the institutional model in Chapter 7, section 2. However, this was mainly meant as an illustration.

Interviews

References

Aarden, Marieke (1987), 'Minister Nijpels van Milieu heeft droeve boodschap: "Het gaat met verzuring de verkeerde kant op" [Minister Nijpels of Environment has sad message: "Acidification is going the wrong way"]', *Volkskrant* **24/12**.

Aarden, Marieke (1997), 'Chemie gaat de hoge appels plukken [Chemical sector is going to pick the high apples]', *Volkskrant* **27/09**.

Aarden, Marieke and Harko van den Hende (1992), '"Regulerende energieheffing is politiek gesproken dood en begraven" ["Politically speaking, regulatory energy charge is dead and buried"]', *Volkskrant* **18/02**.

Ackerman, Bruce A. and William T. Hassler (1981), *Clean Coal/Dirty Air: Or how the Clean Air Act Became a Multibillion-Dollar Bail-Out for High-Sulphur Coal Producers and What Should be Done About it*, Yale University Press, New Haven.

AER [General Energy Council] (1992), *Regulerende Energieheffingen [Regulatory Energy Charges]*, The Hague.

Aidt, Toke S. (1997), 'Cooperative lobbying and endogenous trade policy', *Public Choice* **93**: 455–475.

Aidt, Toke S. (1998), 'Political internalization of economic externalities and environmental policy', *Journal of Public Economics* **69**: 1–16.

Andersen, Mikael S. (1996), *Governance by Green Taxes, Making Pollution Prevention Pay*, Manchester University Press, Manchester/New York.

Anderson, Frederick R., Allen V. Kneese, Phillip D. Reed, Russell B. Stevenson and Serge Taylor (1977), *Environmental Improvement Through Economic Incentives*, Johns Hopkins University Press, Baltimore.

Andeweg, Rudy B. and Susan Bakema (1994), 'The Netherlands: Ministers and cabinet policy', in: M. Laver and K. Shepsle (eds), *Cabinet Ministers and Parliamentary Government*, Cambridge University Press, Cambridge, 56–72.

Andeweg, R.B. and H.W. Nijzink (1992), 'De verhouding tussen parlement en regering [The relation between parliament and government]', in: J.J.A. Thomassen, M.P.C.M. van Schendelen and M.L. Zielonka-Goei (eds), 158–194.

Anonymous (1988a), 'Bedrijfsleven gelooft niet in milieubiljettenspel [Industry does not believe in environmental coupon game]', *Het Financieele Dagblad* **14/07**.

Anonymous (1988b), 'Goed voor rariteitenkabinet. Anti-verzuringsfonds: idee uit de studeerkamer [Good for collection of curiosities. Anti-acidification fund: armchair proposal]', *De Werkgever* **14**: 9.

Anonymous (1992), 'Meerderheid Kamer voelt weinig voor Nederlandse ecotax [Chamber majority opposed to Dutch ecotax]', *Volkskrant* **19/05**.

Anonymous (1993a), 'SER bereikt compromis over energieheffing [SER reaches compromise on energy charge]', *Het Financieele Dagblad* **20/01**.

Anonymous (1993b), 'Achterban fluit werkgevers terug bij energieheffing [Constituency calls back employers on energy charge]', *Het Financieele Dagblad* **12/02**.

Baik, Kyung Hwan (1993), 'Effort levels in contests: The public-good prize case', *Economics Letters* **41**: 363–367.

Baik, Kyung Hwan (1994a), 'Effort levels in contests with two asymmetric players', *Southern Economic Journal* **61**: 367–378.

Baik, Kyung Hwan (1994b), 'Winner-help-loser group formation in rent-seeking contests', *Economics and Politics* **6**: 147–162.

Baik, Kyung Hwan and In-Gyu Kim (1997), 'Delegation in contests', *European Journal of Political Economy* **13**: 281–298.

Baik, Kyung Hwan and Sanghack Lee (1997), 'Collective rent seeking with endogenous group sizes', *European Journal of Political Economy* **13**: 121–130.

Baik, Kyung Hwan and Jason F. Shogren (1995), 'Competitive-share group formation in rent-seeking contests', *Public Choice* **83**: 113–126.

Barde, Jean-Philippe (1996), 'Implementing environmental taxes: Lessons from OECD countries and perspectives', paper presented at the conference of the European Society for Ecological Economics, Université de Versailles Saint-Quentin-en-Yvelines, May 23–25.

Baumol, William J. and Wallace E. Oates (1971), 'The use of standards and prices for protection of the environment', *Swedish Journal of Economics* **73**: 42–54.

Baumol, William J. and Wallace E. Oates (1988), *The theory of environmental policy*, Cambridge University Press, Cambridge.

Baye, Michael R., Dan Kovenock and Casper G. de Vries (1993), 'Rigging the lobbying process: An application of the all-pay auction', *American Economic Review* **83**: 289–294.

Baye, Michael R., Dan Kovenock and Casper G. de Vries (1994), 'The solution to the Tullock rent-seeking game when $R > 2$: Mixed-strategy equilibria and mean dissipation rates', *Public Choice* **81**: 363–380.

Becker, Gary S. (1983), 'A theory of competition among pressure groups for political influence', *Quarterly Journal of Economics* **98**: 371–400.

Becker, Gary S. (1985), 'Public policies, pressure groups, and dead weight costs', *Journal of Public Economics* **28**: 329–347.

Beder, Sharon (1996), 'Charging the earth: The promotion of price-based measures for pollution control', *Ecological Economics* **16**: 51–63.

Besanko, David (1987), 'Performance versus design standards in the regulation of pollution', *Journal of Public Economics* **34**: 19–44.

Blok, Kornelis, Detlef van Vuuren, Ad van Wijk and Lars Hein (1996), *WWF Climate Change Campaign, Policies and Measures to reduce CO$_2$ Emissions by Efficiency and Renewables. A Preliminary Survey for the Period to 2005*, Department of Science, Technology and Society, Utrecht University, The Netherlands.

Bohm, Peter, and Clifford S. Russell (1985), 'Comparative analysis of alternative policy instruments', in: A.V. Kneese and J.L. Sweeney (eds), *Handbook of Natural Resource and Energy Economics*, North-Holland, Amsterdam, 395–460.

Boorsma, P.B, P.C. Gilhuis, J.B. Opschoor and B.M.S van Praag (1988), *Een anti-verzuringsfonds [An anti-pollution fund]*, Department of VROM: Air 77, The Hague.

Bovenberg, A.L., M.E.T van den Broek and R.J. Mulder (1991), *Instrumentkeuze in het Milieubeleid [Instrument Choice in Environmental Policy]*, Discussion Paper 9102, Department of Economic Affairs, General Economic Policy Department.

Bovenberg, A. Lans and Sybrand Cnossen (1991), 'Fiscaal fata morgana [Fiscal mirage]', *Economisch Statistische Berichten* **04/12**: 1200–1203.

Bressers, Hans Th. A. (1983), *Beleidseffectiviteit en waterkwaliteitsbeleid, Een bestuurskundig onderzoek [Policy Effectiveness and Water Quality Policy, An Administrative Science Research]* , PhD thesis, Twente University, Enschede.

Brooks, Michael A. and Ben J. Heijdra (1987), 'Rent-seeking and pollution taxation: An extension', *Southern Economic Journal* **54**: 335–342.

Brooks, Michael A. and Ben J. Heijdra (1988), 'In Search of Rent-Seeking', in: C.K. Rowley, R.D. Tollison and G. Tullock (eds), *The Political Economy of Rent Seeking*, Kluwer, Boston/Dordrecht/London, 27–50.

Buchanan, James M. (1969), 'External diseconomies, corrective taxes, and market structure', *American Economic Review* **59**: 174–177.

Buchanan, James M. and Gordon Tullock (1975), 'Polluters' profits and political response: Direct controls versus taxes', *American Economic Review* **65**: 139–147.

Buchanan, James M. and Gordon Tullock (1976), 'Polluters' profits and political response: Direct controls versus taxes: Reply', *American Economic Review* **66**: 983–985.

Budge, Ian and Hans Keman (1990), *Parties and Democracy, Coalition Formation and Government Functioning in Twenty States*, Oxford University Press, New York.

Burtraw, Dallas (1996), 'The SO$_2$ emissions trading program: Cost savings without allowance trades', *Contemporary Economic Policy* **14**: 79–94.

Buys, Anton (1994), 'Milieu [Environment]', *Essoscope:* 4–7.

Cairns, Robert D. (1989), 'Dynamic rent seeking', *Journal of Public Economics* **39**: 315–334.

Campos, Jose E.L. (1989), 'Legislative institutions, lobbying, and the endogenous choice of regulatory instruments: A political economy approach to instrument choice', *Journal of Law, Economics, and Organization* **5**: 333–353.

Cansier, Dieter and Raimund Krumm (1997), 'Air pollutant taxation: an empirical survey', *Ecological Economics* **23**: 59–70.

Carlton, Dennis W. and Glenn C. Loury (1980), 'The limitations of Pigouvian taxes as a long-run remedy for externalities', *Quarterly Journal of Economics* **95**: 559–566.

Carlton, Dennis W. and Glenn C. Loury (1986), 'The limitations of Pigouvian taxes as a long-run remedy for externalities: An extension of results', *Quarterly Journal of Economics* **101**: 631–634.

Carter, John R. and Michael D. Irons (1991), 'Are economists different, and if so, why?', *Journal of Economic Perspectives* **5** (2): 171–177.

Coelho, Philip R.P. (1976), 'Comment on Polluters' profits and political response', *American Economic Review* **66**: 976–978.

Congleton, Roger (1984), 'Committees and rent-seeking efforts', *Journal of Public Economics* **25**: 197–209.

Consumentenbond, FNV, CNV, Sectie sociale vragen Raad van Kerken, Stichting Natuur en Milieu, Vereniging Milieudefensie, Bezinningsgroep Energiebeleid, Stichting MilieuEducatie, Organisatie voor Duurzame Energie, Centrum voor energiebesparing en schone technologie and Waddenvereniging (1992), *Pleidooi voor een Nederlandse energieheffing [Plea for a Dutch Energy Charge]*.

Cooter, Robert D. and Daniel L. Rubinfeld (1989), 'Economic analysis of legal disputes and their resolution', *Journal of Economic Literature* **27**: 1067–1097.

CPB [Central Planning Bureau] (1992a), *Economische Gevolgen op Lange Termijn van Heffingen op Energie [Long-Term Economic Results of Energy Charges]*, Working Paper 43, The Hague.

CPB [Central Planning Bureau] (1992b), *Nederlandse Industrie en Regulerende Energieheffing [Dutch Industry and Regulatory Energy Charge]*, Research Memorandum 90, The Hague.

CPB [Central Planning Bureau] (1996), *Economie en Milieu: Op Zoek naar Duurzaamheid [Economy and Environment: In Search of Sustainability]*, Sdu, The Hague.

Crandall, Robert W. (1983), 'Air pollution, environmentalists, and the coal lobby', in: R.G. Noll and B.M. Owen (eds), *The Political Economy of Deregulation*, American Enterprise Institute for Public Policy Research, Washington, 84–96.

Daalder, Hans (1987), 'The Dutch party system: From segmentation to polarization – and then?', in: H. Daalder (ed.), *Party Systems in Denmark, Austria, Switzerland, the Netherlands, and Belgium*, Frances Pinter, London, 193–284.

Dales, John H. (1968), *Pollution, Property, and Prices*, University Press, Toronto.

Daly, George and Thomas Mayor (1986), 'Equity, efficiency, and environmental quality', *Public Choice* **51**: 139–159.

Davidson, Marc D. and Gerrit de Wit (1995a), *Verhandelbare Emissierechten voor SO₂ en NOₓ in Nederland [Tradable Emission Permits for SO₂ and NOₓ in the Netherlands]*, Centrum voor Energiebesparing en schone technologie, Delft.

Davidson, Marc D. and Gerrit de Wit (1995b), *Workshop Verhandelbare Emissierechten voor SO₂ en NOₓ in Nederland [Workshop Tradable Emission Permits for SO₂ and NOₓ in the Netherlands]*, Centrum voor Energiebesparing en schone technologie, Delft.

De Bruin, Willem (1988), 'De privatisering van het milieubeleid. Commissie-Boorsma komt met opmerkelijk plan voor anti-verzuringsfonds [The privatization of environmental policy. Boorsma committee presents remarkable plan for anti-acidification fund]', *MilieuDefensie* **17**: 26–28.

De Clercq, M. (1996), 'The political economy of green taxes: The Belgian experience', *Environmental and Resource Economics* **8**: 273–291.

De Goede, B., J.H.M. Kienhuis, H. van der Linden and J.G. Steenbeek (1982), *Het Waterschap, Recht en Werking [The Water Board, Law and Functioning]*, Kluwer, Deventer.

Department of EZ (1990), *Nota Energiebesparing [Energy Saving Memorandum]*, **21 570: 1–2**.

Department of VROM (1989), *Nationaal Milieubeleidsplan [National Environmental Policy Plan]*, **21 137: 1–2**.

Department of VROM (1990), *Nationaal Milieubeleidsplan Plus [National Environmental Policy Plan Plus]*, **21 137: 20–21**.

Department of VROM (1993), *Nationaal Milieubeleidsplan 2 [National Environmental Policy Plan 2]*, **23 560: 1–2**.

Department of VROM (1996), 'Verhandelbare Emissierechten [Tradable Emission Permits]', Letter from Minister De Boer to the Second Chamber.

Department of VROM (1998), *Nationaal Milieubeleidsplan 3 [National Environmental Policy Plan 3]*.

De Savornin Lohman, Alex (1994a), 'Incentive charges in environmental policy: Why are they white ravens?', in: M. Faure, J. Vervaele, A. Weale (eds): *Environmental Standards in the European Union in an interdisciplinary Framework*, Maklu, Antwerpen, 117–133.

De Savornin Lohman, Lex (1994b), 'Economic incentives in environmental policy: Why are they white ravens?', in: J.B. Opschoor and R.K. Turner (eds), *Economic Incentives and Environmental Policies: Principles and Practice*, Kluwer Academic Publishers, Boston/Dordrecht/London, 55–67.

De Swaan, Abram (1973), *Coalition Theories and Cabinet Formation*, Elsevier, Amsterdam.

Dewees, Donald N. (1983), 'Instrument choice in environmental policy', *Economic Inquiry* **21**: 53–71.

DHV (1988), *De Hoofdlijnen van een Egaliserend Verzuringsfonds [Outlining an Equalizing Acidification Fund]*, Department of VROM, The Hague.

Dijkstra, Bouwe R. (1994), 'Polluters' profits: Direct controls vs. taxes vs. tradeable permits. Buchanan & Tullock revisited', Research Memorandum nr. 12, Department of Economics and Public Finance, Faculty of Law, University of Groningen.

Dijkstra, Bouwe R. (1997a), 'Voorkeuren van belangengroepen voor instrumenten van milieubeleid. De Nederlandse enquête [Interest group preferences for environmental policy instruments. The Dutch survey]', Research Memorandum nr. 16, Department of Economics and Public Finance, Faculty of Law, University of Groningen.

Dijkstra, Bouwe R. (1997b), 'Interest group preferences for environmental policy instruments. The Dutch survey', Research Memorandum nr. 16', Department of Economics and Public Finance, Faculty of Law, University of Groningen.

Dijkstra, Bouwe R. (1998), *The Political Economy of Instrument Choice in Environmental Policy*, PhD thesis, University of Groningen.

Dijkstra, Bouwe R. and A. Nentjes (1998), 'Income distribution and environmental policy instruments', forthcoming in: J.T.J.M. van der Linden and A.J.C. Manders (eds), *Heterodox Economics and Income Distribution*, Edward Elgar, Cheltenham.

Dixit, Avinash, Gene Grossman and Elhanan Helpman (1997), 'Common agency and coordination: General theory and application to government policy making', *Journal of Political Economy* **105**: 752–769.

DNPP (1994), *Verkiezingsprogramma's 1994 [Election Programmes 1994]*, Sdu, The Hague.

Dudek, Daniel J. and John Palmisano (1988), 'Emissions trading: Why is this thoroughbred hobbled?' *Columbia Journal of Environmental Law* **13**: 217–233.

Duizendstraal, Anton and Andries Nentjes (1994a), 'Migué and Bélanger on managerial discretion: A note', *Public Choice* **81**: 191–193.

Duizendstraal, Anton and Andries Nentjes (1994b), 'Organizational slack in subsidized nonprofit institutions', *Public Choice* **81**: 297–321.

EEA [European Environment Agency] (1996), *Environmental Taxes: Implementation and Environmental Effectiveness*, Environmental Issues Series 1, EEA, Copenhagen.

Eichenberger, Reiner and Angel Serna (1996), 'Random errors, dirty information, and politics', *Public Choice* **86**: 137–156.

Ellingsen, Tore (1991), 'Strategic buyers and the social cost of monopoly',

American Economic Review **81**: 648–657.

Emeny, Matthew, Per G. Fredriksson and Noel Gaston (1997), 'Politics and the environment in federal systems: Big brother or local czars?', paper presented at the EAERE Conference, 26–28 June, Tilburg, the Netherlands.

Ermoliev, Yuri, Ger Klaassen and Andries Nentjes (1996), 'Adaptive cost-effective ambient charges under incomplete information', *Journal of Environmental Economics and Management* **31**: 37–48.

Fiorina, Morris P. (1982), 'Legislative control, and the delegation of legislative power', *Public Choice* **39**: 33–66.

FNV [Federation of Dutch trade unions] (1993), *Veelkleurige Vooruitzichten voor een Samenleving, waarin Mensen Zelf Kiezen en Samen Delen [Multi-coloured Prospects for a Society, in which People Themselves Choose and Share with Each Other]*, Amsterdam.

Frank, Robert, Thomas Gilovich and Dennis Regan (1993), 'Does studying economics inhibit cooperation?', *Journal of Economic Perspectives* **7** (2): 159–171.

Fransen, Jan T.J. (1987), *Zure Regen: Een Nieuw Beleid [Acid Rain: A New Policy]*, Stichting Natuur en Milieu, Utrecht.

Fredriksson, Per G. (1997), 'The political economy of pollution taxes in a small open economy', *Journal of Environmental Economics and Management* **33**: 44–58.

Freeman III, A. Myrick, Robert H. Haveman and Allen V. Kneese (1973), *The Economics of Environmental Policy*, John Wiley & Sons, New York.

Frey, Bruno S. (1992), 'Pricing and regulating affect environmental ethics', *Environmental and Resource Economics* **2**: 399–414.

Fromm, Oliver and Bernd Hansjürgens (1996), 'Emission trading in theory and practice: An analysis of RECLAIM in Southern California', *Environment and Planning C* **14**: 367–384.

Glazer, Amihai (1993), 'On the incentives to establish and play political rent-seeking games', *Public Choice* **75**: 139–148.

Goulder, Lawrence H. (1995), 'Environmental taxation and the double dividend: A reader's guide', *International Tax and Public Finance* **2**: 157–183.

Goulder, Lawrence H., Ian W.H. Parry, Roberton C. Williams III and Dallas Burtraw (1998), 'The cost-effectiveness of alternative instruments for environmental protection in a second-best setting', paper presented at the World Congress of Environmental and Resource Economists, Venice, 25–27 June.

Greenhut, Melvin L., George Norman and Chao-Shun Hung (1987), *The Economics of Imperfect Competition: A Spatial Approach*, Cambridge University Press, Cambridge.

Grofman, Bernard (1982), 'A dynamic model of protocoalition formation in ideological n-space', *Behavioral Science* **27**: 77–90.

Grossman, Gene M. and Elhanan Helpman (1994), 'Protection for sale', *American Economic Review* **84**: 833–850.

Guttman, Joel M. (1987), 'A non-Cournot model of voluntary collective action', *Economica* **54**: 1–19.

Guttman, Joel M. (1991), 'Voluntary collective action', in: A. Hillman (ed.), *Markets and Politicians, Politicized Economic Choice*, Kluwer Academic Publishers, Boston/Dordrecht/London, 27–41.

Hahn, Robert W. (1984), 'Market power and transferable property rights', *Quarterly Journal of Economics* **99**: 753–765.

Hahn, Robert W. (1988), 'Jobs and environmental quality: some implications for instrument choice', *Policy Sciences* **20**: 289–306.

Hahn, Robert W. (1990), 'The political economy of environmental regulation: Towards a unifying framework', *Public Choice* **65**: 21–47.

Hahn, Robert W. and Gordon L. Hester (1989a), 'Marketable permits: Lessons for theory and practice', *Ecology Law Quarterly* **16**: 361–406.

Hahn, Robert W. and Gordon L. Hester (1989b), 'Where did all the markets go? An analysis of EPA's emissions trading program', *Yale Journal on Regulation* **6**: 109–140.

Hahn, Robert W. and Roger G. Noll (1990), 'Environmental markets in the year 2000', *Journal of Risk and Uncertainty* **3**: 351–367.

Hamilton, James T. (1997), 'Taxes, torts, and the toxic release inventory: Congressional voting on instruments to control pollution', *Economic Inquiry* **35**: 745–732.

Harberger, Arnold C. (1954), 'Monopoly and resource allocation', *American Economic Review* **44**: 77–87.

Harford, Jon D. (1989), 'Efficient scale of the pollution-abating firm: Comment', *Land Economics* **65**: 413–416.

Harford, Jon D. and Gordon Karp (1983), 'The effects and efficiencies of different pollution standards', *Eastern Economic Journal* **9**: 79–89.

Hay, Bruce L. (1995), 'Effort, information, settlement, trial', *Journal of Legal Studies* **24**: 29–62.

Helfand, Gloria (1991), 'Standards versus standards: the effects of different pollution restrictions', *American Economic Review* **81**: 622–634.

Helfand, Gloria (1993), 'The relative efficiency of different standards when firms vary', *Natural Resource Modeling* **7**: 203–217.

Henderson, James M. and Richard E. Quandt (1958), *Microeconomic Theory: A Mathematical Approach*, McGraw-Hill, New York.

Heyes, Anthony G. (1997), 'Environmental regulation by private contest', *Journal of Public Economics* **63**: 407–428.

Hillebrand, R. and J. Meulman (1992), 'Afstand en nabijheid: verhoudingen in de Tweede Kamer [Distance and closeness: relations in the Second Chamber]', in: J.J.A. Thomassen, M.P.C.M. van Schendelen and M.L. Zielonka-Goei (eds),

98–128.

Hillman, Arye L. (1989), *The Political Economy of Protection*, Harwood Academic Publishers, London.

Hillman, Arye L. and Eliakim Katz (1984), 'Risk-averse rent seekers and the soical cost of monopoly power', *Economic Journal* **94**: 104–110.

Hillman, Arye L. and Eliakim Katz (1987), 'Hierarchical structure and the social costs of bribes and transfers', *Journal of Public Economics* **34**: 129–142.

Hillman, Arye L. and John G. Riley (1989), 'Politically contestable rents and transfers', *Economics and Politics* **1**: 17–37.

Hillman, Arye L. and D. Samet (1987), 'Dissipation of rents and revenues in small number contests', *Public Choice* **54**: 63–82.

Hirshleifer, Jack (1989), 'Conflict and rent-seeking success functions: Ratio vs. difference models of relative success', *Public Choice* **63**: 101–112.

Hochman, Eithan and David Zilberman (1978), 'Examination of environmental policies using production and pollution microparameter distributions', *Econometrica* **46**: 739–760.

Hughes, James W. and Edward A. Snyder (1995), 'Litigation and settlement under the English and American rules: Theory and evidence', *Journal of Law and Economics* **38**: 225–250.

Hung, Nguyen M. and Eftichios S. Sartzetakis (1997), 'Cross-industry emission permits trading', *Journal of Regulatory Economics* **13**: 121–137.

Hurley, Terrance M. and Jason F. Shogren (1997), 'Environmental conflicts and the SLAPP', *Journal of Environmental Economics and Management* **33**: 253–273.

Isaac, R. Mark, Kenneth McCue and Charles Plott (1985), 'Public goods provision in an experimental environment', *Journal of Public Economics* **26**: 51–74.

Jaarsma, Esther (1993), *Reconstructie van het Beleidsproces rond Regulerende Energieheffingen [Reconstruction of the Policy Process Concerning Regulatory Energy Charges]*, Wageningen Agricultural University.

Jaarsma, Esther and Tuur Mol (1994), 'De rol van onderzoek in het beleidsproces rond regulerende energieheffingen [The role of research in the policy process concerning regulatory energy charges]', *Tijdschrift voor Milieukunde* **3**: 120–128.

Jehae, Michel (1997), 'Draagvlak voor verhandelbare emissierechten groeit [Growing support for tradable emission permits]', *Natuur en Milieu* **21** (10): 20–21.

Katz, Eliakim, Schmuel Nitzan and Jacob Rosenberg (1990), 'Rent seeking for pure public goods', *Public Choice* **45**: 73–87.

Katz, Eliakim, and Julia Tokatlidu (1996), 'Group competition for rents', *European Journal of Political Economy* **12**: 599–607.

Kelman, Steven (1981), *What Price Incentives? Economists and the Environ-*

ment, Auburn House, Boston (Mass.).

Kelman, Steven (1983), 'Economic incentives and environmental policy: Politics, ideology, and philosophy', in: T.C. Schelling (ed.), *Economic Incentives for Environmental Protection*, MIT Press, Cambridge (Mass.), 291–331.

Keohane, Nathaniel O., Richard L. Revesz and Robert N. Stavins (1998), 'The positive political economy of instrument choice in environmental policy', in: P. Portney and L. Schwab (eds), *Environmental Economics and Public Policy*, Edward Elgar, Cheltenham.

Kete, Nancy (1992), 'The US acid rain control allowance system', in: *Climate Change: Designing a Tradeable Permit System*, OECD, Paris, 78–108.

Klaassen, Ger (ed.) (1985), *Werk maken van zure regen*, Landelijk Milieu Overleg, Utrecht.

Klaassen, Ger (1996), *Acid Rain and Environmental Degradation: the Economics of Emission Trading,* Edward Elgar, Cheltenham.

Klaassen, Ger and Andries Nentjes (1997), 'Sulfur trading under the 1990 CAAA in the US: An assessment of first experiences', *Journal of Institutional and Theoretical Economics* **153**: 384–410.

Klabbers, J., P. Vellinga, R. Swart, A. van Ulden and R. Janssen (1993), *Policy Options Addressing the Greenhouse Effect*, NRP, Bilthoven.

Klimaatcommissie [Climate Committee] (1996), 'Kamercommissie Klimaatverandering: Gesprekken [Parliamentary Committee on Climate Change: Interviews]', **24 695: 4**.

Klok, Pieter J. (1991), *Een instrumententheorie voor milieubeleid [A Theory of Instruments for Environmental Policy*, PhD thesis, Twente University, Enschede.

Kneese, Alan V. and Charles L. Schultze (1975), *Pollution, Prices, and Public Policy*, Brookings Institution, Washington DC.

Kohn, Robert E. (1998), *Pollution and the Firm*, Edward Elgar, Cheltenham.

Konrad, Kai A. (1997), 'Trade contests', paper presented at the Contest Conference, 22–23 August, Rotterdam.

Körber, Achim and Martin Kolmar (1996), 'To fight or not to fight? An analysis of submission, struggle, and the design of contests', *Public Choice* **88**: 381–392.

Koster, J. M. Mirjam (1996), *Market Failures and Tradeable Emission Permits – A Survey*, Research Memorandum nr. 13, Department of Economics and Public Finance, Faculty of Law, University of Groningen.

Koutstaal, Paul R. (1992), 'Verhandelbare emissierechten en convenanten [Tradable Emission Permits and Covenants]', *Economisch Statistische Berichten* **22/04**: 388-391.

Koutstaal, Paul R. (1997), *Economic Policy and Climate Change: Tradable Permits for Reducing Carbon Emissions*, Edward Elgar, Cheltenham.

Krueger, Anne O. (1974), 'The political economy of the rent-seeking society',

American Economic Review **64**: 291–303.

Laver, Michael and Norman Schofield (1990), *Multiparty Government: The Politics of Coalition in Europe*, Oxford University Press, New York.

Laver, Michael and Kenneth A. Shepsle (1994a), 'Cabinet ministers and government formation in parliamentary democracies', in: M. Laver and K. Shepsle (eds), *Cabinet Ministers and Parliamentary Government*, Cambridge University Press, Cambridge, 3–12.

Laver, Michael and Kenneth A. Shepsle (1994b), 'Cabinet government in theoretical perspective', in: M. Laver and K. Shepsle (eds), *Cabinet Ministers and Parliamentary Government*, Cambridge University Press, Cambridge, 285–310.

Lee, Dwight (1985), 'Rent-seeking and its implications for pollution taxation', *Southern Economic Journal* **51**: 731–744.

Lee, Sanghack (1995), 'Endogenous sharing rules in collective-group rent-seeking', *Public Choice* **85**: 31–44.

Leidy, Michael P. and Bernard M. Hoekman (1994), '"Cleaning up" while cleaning up? Pollution abatement, interest groups and contingent trade policies', *Public Choice* **78**: 241–258.

Leidy, Michael P. and Bernard M. Hoekman (1996), 'Pollution abatement, interest groups, and contingent trade policies', in: R. Congleton (ed.), *The Political Economy of Environmental Protection. Analysis and Evidence*, University of Michigan Press, Ann Arbor, 43–68.

Linster, Bruce G. (1993a), 'Stackelberg rent-seeking', *Public Choice* **77**: 307–321.

Linster, Bruce G. (1993b), 'A generalized model of rentseeking behavior', *Public Choice* **77**: 421–436.

Linster, Bruce G. (1994), 'Cooperative rent-seeking', *Public Choice* **81**: 23–34.

Lipsey, R.G. and Kevin Lancaster (1956), 'The general theory of second best', *Review of Economic Studies* **24**: 11–32.

Liroff, Richard A. (1986), *Reforming Air Pollution Regulation: The Toil and Trouble of EPA's Bubble*, The Conservation Foundation, Washington, DC.

Loehman, Edna, Fabrice N. Quesnel and Emerson M. Babb (1996), 'Free-rider effects in rent-seeking groups competing for public goods', *Public Choice* **86**: 35–61.

Lövgren, Kerstin (1994), 'Economic instruments for air pollution control in Sweden', in: G. Klaassen and F.R. Førsund (eds), *Economic Instruments for Air Pollution Control*, Kluwer, Boston/Dordrecht/London, 107–121.

Majone, Giandomenico (1989), *Evidence, Arguments, and Persuasion in the Policy Process*, Yale University Press, New Haven.

Maloney, Michael T. and Robert E. McCormick (1982), 'A positive theory of environmental quality regulation', *Journal of Law and Economics* **25**: 99–124.

Marwell, Gerald and Ruth E. Ames (1981), 'Economists free ride, does anyone else? Experiments on the provision of public goods, IV', *Journal of Public Economics* **15**: 215–235.

McCubbins, Mathew D. and Talbot Page (1986), 'The congressional foundations of agency performance', *Public Choice* **51**: 173–190.

Michaels, Robert (1988), 'The design of rent-seeking competitions', *Public Choice* **56**: 17–29.

Migué, Jean L. and Gérard Bélanger (1974), 'Toward a general theory of managerial discretion', *Public Choice* **17**: 27–43.

Migué, Jean L. and Richard Marceau (1993), 'Pollution taxes, subsidies, and rent seeking', *Canadian Journal of Economics* **26**: 355–365.

Millner, Edward L. and Michael D. Pratt (1991), 'Risk aversion and rent-seeking', *Public Choice* **69**: 81–92.

Misiolek, Walter S. and Harold W. Elder (1989), 'Exclusionary manipulation of markets for pollution rights', *Journal of Environmental Economics and Management* **16**: 156–166.

Nentjes, Andries (1988), 'Marktconform milieubeleid [Market-oriented environmental policy]', *Economisch Statistische Berichten* **27/4**: 401–408.

Nentjes, Andries (1991), 'Environmental taxes as an instrument of environmental policy: When are they appropriate?', *Documentatieblad Studie- en Documentatiedienst Ministerie van Financiën* **8**: 265–282.

Nentjes, Andries and Bouwe Dijkstra (1994), 'The political economy of instrument choice in environmental policy', in: M. Faure, J. Vervaele and A. Weale (eds): *Environmental Standards in the European Union in an interdisciplinary Framework*, Maklu, Antwerpen, 197–219.

Nitzan, Shmuel (1991a), 'Collective rent dissipation', *Economic Journal* **101**: 1522–1534.

Nitzan, Shmuel (1991b), 'Rent seeking with non-identical sharing rules', *Public Choice* **71**: 43–50.

Nitzan, Shmuel (1994), 'Modelling rent-seeking contests', *European Journal of Political Economy* **10**: 41–60.

OCC [Oil Contact Committee], Belgian Petroleum Federation and Europia (European petroleum industry organization) (n.d.), *Voor een Zuiverdere Lucht, Wat de Petroleumindustrie Doet om Autoverkeer en Luchtkwaliteit te Verzoenen: Het Auto-Oil Programma [For Cleaner Air, What the Petroleum Industry Does to Reconcile Car Traffic and Air Quality: The Auto-Oil Programme]*.

OECD (1993), *Taxation and the Environment: Complementary Policies,* OECD, Paris.

OECD (1994), *The Distributive Effects of Economic Instruments for Environmental Policy,* OECD, Paris.

OECD (1995), *Environmental Performance Reviews, Netherlands*, OECD, Paris.

OECD (1997), *Evaluating Economic Instruments for Environmental Policy,*

OECD, Paris.

Olson, Mancur (1965), *The Logic of Collective Action*, Harvard University Press, Cambrige (Mass.).

Opschoor, Hans, Lex de Savornin Lohman and Hans Vos (1994), *Managing the Environment: The Role of Economic Instruments*, OECD, Paris.

Peeters, Marjan (1992), *Marktconform Milieurecht? Een Rechtsvergelijkende Studie naar de Verhandelbaarheid van Vervuilingsrechten [Market-oriented Environmental Law? A Comparative Law Study into the Tradability of Pollution Permits]*, Tjeenk Willink, Zwolle.

Peltzman, Sam (1976), 'Toward a more general theory of regulation', *Journal of Law and Economics* **19**: 211–240.

Pérez-Castrillo, J. David and Thierry Verdier (1992), 'A general analysis of rent-seeking games', *Public Choice* **73**: 335–350.

Pigou, Arthur C. (1920), *The Economics of Welfare*, MacMillan, London.

Pleune, Ruud (1997), *Strategies of Dutch Environmental Organizations: Ozone Depletion, Acidification and Climate Change*, PhD thesis, University of Utrecht.

Posner, Richard A. (1974), 'Theories of economic regulation', *Bell Journal of Economics and Management Science* **5**: 335–358.

Posner, Richard A. (1975), 'The social costs of monopoly and regulation', *Journal of Political Economy* **83**: 807–827.

Potters, Jan and Randolph Sloof (1996), 'Interest groups: A survey of empirical models that try to assess their influence', *European Journal of Political Economy* **12**: 403–442.

Potters, Jan, Casper G. de Vries and Frans van Winden (1997), 'Are laboratories conducive to rational rent-seeking?', paper presented at the Contest Conference, 22–23 August, Rotterdam.

Potters, Jan and Frans van Winden (1996), 'Models of interest groups: Four different approaches', in: N. Schofield (ed.), *Collective Decision-Making: Social Choice and Political Economy*, Kluwer Academic Publishers, Boston/Dordrecht/London, 337–362.

Riaz, Khalid, Jason F. Shogren and Stanley R. Johnson (1995), 'A general model of rent seeking for public goods', *Public Choice* **82**: 243–257.

Rico, Renee (1995), 'The U.S. allowance trading system for sulfur dioxide: An update on market experience', *Environmental and Resource Economics* **5**: 115–129.

Rogerson, William P. (1982), 'The social costs of monopoly and regulation: A game-theoretic analysis', *Bell Journal of Economics* **13**: 391–401.

Rolph, Elizabeth (1983), 'Government allocation of property rights: Who gets what?', *Journal of Policy Analysis and Management* **3**: 45–61.

Russell, Clifford S. (1979), 'What can we get from effluent charges?', in: R.H. Haveman and B.B. Zellner (eds), *Policy Studies Review Annual* **3**, Sage

Publications, Beverly Hills, 251–276.

Sartzetakis, Eftichios S. (1993), 'Cost-efficiency and welfare comparison of tradeable emissions permits to command and control', Working Paper, Cahier 93–21, GREEN, Département d'économique, Université Laval, Quebec.

Sartzetakis, Eftichios S. (1997), 'Tradeable emission permits regulations in the presence of imperfectly competitive product markets: Welfare implications', *Environmental and Resource Economics* **9**: 65–81.

Schuurman, Jacob (1988), *De Prijs van Water [The Price of Water]*, Gouda Quint, Arnhem.

SEP [Cooperating Electricity Producers] (1988), *Jaarverslag [Annual Report]*, Arnhem.

SEP [Cooperating Electricity Producers] (1990), *Jaarverslag [Annual Report]*, Arnhem.

SEP [Cooperating Electricity Producers] (1993), *Toelichting bij het Elektriciteits-plan 1993-2002 [Explanation to the Electricity Plan]*, Arnhem.

SER [Socio-Economic Council] (1989), *Advies Nationaal Milieubeleidsplan [Advice National Environmental Policy Plan]*, 89/17.

SER [Socio-Economic Council] (1993), *Advies over de Invoering van Reguleren-de Energieheffingen [Advice on the Introduction of Regulatory Energy Charges]*, 93/01.

Shogren, Jason F. and Kyung-Hwan Baik (1991), 'Reexamining efficient rent-seeking in laboratory markets', *Public Choice* **69**: 69–79.

Skjærseth, Jon B. (1994), 'The climate policy of the EU: Too hot to handle?', *Journal of Common Market Studies* **32**: 25–45.

Sloof, Randolph and Frans van Winden (1996), 'Show them your teeth first! A game-theoretic analysis of lobbying and pressure', paper presented at the European Public Choice conference, Israel, March 10–13.

Snels, Bart (1992), *De Economie van de Energieheffing [The Economics of the Energy Charge]*, Scientific Bureau Groen Links, Amsterdam.

SNM [Nature and Environment Foundation] (1996), *Strategisch Plan 1996–2000 [Strategic Plan 1996–2000]*, Utrecht.

Spiller, Pablo T. (1990), 'Politicians, interest groups, and regulators: a multiple principals–agency theory of regulation, or "Let Them be Bribed"', *Journal of Law and Economics* **33**: 65–101.

Spulber, Daniel F. (1985), 'Effluent regulation and long-run optimality', *Journal of Environmental Economics and Management* **12**: 103–116.

Spulber, Daniel F. (1989), *Regulation and Markets*, The MIT Press, Cambridge, London.

Stavins, Robert N. (1995), 'Transaction costs and tradeable permits', *Journal of Environmental Economics and Management* **29**: 133–148.

Stavins, Robert N. (1997), 'What can we learn from the grand policy experiment? Positive and normative lessons from SO_2 allowance trading', *Journal of*

Economic Perspectives (forthcoming).

Stigler, George J. (1971), 'The theory of economic regulation', *Bell Journal of Economics and Management Science* 2: 3–21.

Stuurgroep [Steering Group] (1992), *Eindrapportage Stuurgroep Regulerende Energieheffingen [Final Report Steering Group Regulatory Energy Charges]*, The Hague.

Svendsen, Gert T. (1998), *Public Choice and Environmental Regulation: Tradable Permit Systems in the United States and CO_2 Taxation in Europe*, Edward Elgar, Cheltenham.

Tabak, Lin (1997), 'Handel in vuile lucht [Trade in dirty air]', in: K. Waagmeester (ed.), *Houdbare Economie, Kroniek van Duurzaam Nederland [Sustainable Economy, Chronicle of the Sustainable Netherlands]*, NCDO/Kok Agora, Amsterdam, 118–134.

Tellegen, Egbert (1981), 'The environmental movement in the Netherlands', in: T. O'Riordan and R. K. Turner (eds), *Progress in Resource Management and Environmental Planning* 3, John Wiley and Sons, London, 1–32.

Thomassen, J.J.A and M.L. Zielonka-Goei (1992), 'Het parlement als volksvertegenwoordiging [Parliament as representative of the people]', in: J.J.A. Thomassen, M.P.C.M. van Schendelen and M.L. Zielonka-Goei (eds), 195–224.

J.J.A. Thomassen, M.P.C.M. van Schendelen and M.L. Zielonka-Goei (eds) (1992), *De Geachte Afgevaardigde...: Hoe Kamerleden Denken over het Nederlandse Parlement [The Honourable Member...: How MPs View the Dutch Parliament]*, Dick Coutinho, Muiderberg.

Tietenberg, Tom (1985), *Emission Trading: An Exercise in Reforming Pollution Policy*, Resources for the Future, Washington, DC.

TME, Tebodin, Grontmij and RuG (1997), *Milieu-Emissies: Kiezen voor Winst! Marktwerking in het Milieubeleid: De Potentiële Kostenvoordelen van een Systeem van Verhandelbare EmissieRechten (VER) [Environmental Emissions: Choosing to Gain! Market Functioning in Environmental Policy: The Potential Cost Advantages of a Tradable Emission Permit (TEP) System]*, IPO–publication number 105, The Hague.

Tullock, Gordon (1967), 'The welfare cost of tariffs, monopolies and theft', *Western Economic Journal* 5: 224–232.

Tullock, Gordon (1980), 'Efficient rent seeking', in: J.M. Buchanan, R. Tollison and G. Tullock (eds), *Toward a Theory of the Rent-Seeking Society*, Texas A&M Press, College Station, 269–282.

Tullock, Gordon (1997), 'Where is the rectangle?', *Public Choice* 91: 149–159.

Turner, R. Kerry and Hans Opschoor (1994), 'Environmental economics and environmental policy instruments: Introduction and overview', in: J.B. Opschoor and R.K. Turner (eds), *Economic Incentives and Environmental Policies: Principles and Practice*, Kluwer Academic Publishers, Boston/Dordrecht/London, 1–38.

Ursprung, Heinrich W. (1990), 'Public goods, rent dissipation, and candidate competition', *Economics and Politics* **2**: 115–131.

Van Cayseele, Patrick J., Raymond J. Deneckere, and Casper G. de Vries (1993), 'A nontrivial multidimensional all-pay tournament', Working paper, Tinbergen Institute.

Van den Biggelaar, Ad (1995), 'Naar een nieuwe collectieve ambitie [Toward a new collective ambition]', in: H. Tieleman (ed.), *Uitgegroeid, Economie tussen Wetmatigheid en Utopie [Finished Growing, Economy between Inevitability and Utopia]*, Thomas More Academie, Gooi en Sticht, Baarn, 102–118.

Van den Biggelaar, Ad and Peter van der Veer (1992), 'Het speelveld van Wolfson [Wolfson's playing field]', *Economisch Statistische Berichten* **25/03**: 302–305.

Van den Biggelaar, Ad and Peter van der Veer (1995), ' Structureel herstel vergt actief milieubeleid [Structural recovery requires active environmental policy]', *Economisch Statistische Berichten* **18/01**: 69.

Van den Biggelaar, Ad and Teo Wams (1991), 'Protest tegen hogere energieheffing is kortzichtig [Protest against higher energy charges is myopic]', *Volkskrant* **20/09**.

Van den Biggelaar, Ad, Lucas Reijnders and Peter van der Veer (1994a), 'Belemmeringen voor een duurzame ontwikkeling [Impediments to sustainable development]', *Economisch Statistische Berichten* **05/01**: 9–13.

Van den Biggelaar, Ad, Lucas Reijnders and Peter van der Veer (1994b), 'Naschrift [Rejoinder]', *Economisch Statistische Berichten* **23/02**: 182–184.

Van den Burg, Tsjalle, Mildi Rouw and Jan L. de Vries (1993), *Regulerende Energieheffingen in Nederland: Analyse van Effecten en Suggesties voor Vormgeving [Regulatory Energy Charges in the Netherlands: Analysis of Effects and Suggestions for Design]*, Landelijk Milieu-overleg, Utrecht.

Van de Peppel, Robert A. (1995), *Naleving van Milieurecht: Toepassing van Beleidsinstrumenten op de Nederlandse Verfindustrie [Compliance with Enviornmental Law: Application of Policy Instruments to the Dutch Paint Industry]*, Kluwer, Deventer.

Van der Schot, Jos (1992), 'Politiek kapt discussie energieheffing voortijdig af [Discussion on energy charge cut short by politicians]', *MilieuMagazine* **3** (4): 12–15.

Van der Straaten, Jan (1990), *Zure Regen, Economische Theorie en Nederlands Beleid [Acid Rain, Economic Theory and Dutch Policy]*, Jan van Arkel, Utrecht.

Van Roozendaal, Peter (1992), *Cabinets in Multi-Party Democracies: The Effect of Dominant and Central Parties on Cabinet Composition and Durability*, Thesis Publishers, Amsterdam.

Van Schendelen, M.P.C.M (1992a), 'Fracties en kamercommissies [Parliamentary parties and Chamber committees]', in: J.J.A. Thomassen, M.P.C.M. van Schendelen and M.L. Zielonka-Goei (eds), 75–97.

Van Schendelen, M.P.C.M (1992b), 'Parlement, pressiegroepen en lobby's [Parliament, pressure groups and lobbies]', in: J.J.A. Thomassen, M.P.C.M. van Schendelen and M.L. Zielonka-Goei (eds), 225–248.

Van Soest, Jan P. (1992), 'Dubieuze claims in discussie over energieheffing. Over belang en argument [Dubious claims in discussion on energy charge. About interest and argument]', *MilieuMagazine* **3** (1): 15.

Van Venetië, Erik (1992), 'Bemiddelaar Andriessen werd onverstoorbaar buitenbeentje [Mediator Andriessen became imperturbable outsider]', *Volkskrant* **01/02**.

Verbruggen, Harmen (1992), 'De regulerende energieheffing is geen toverbal [The regulatory energy charge is not a magic ball]', *Economisch Statistische Berichten* **04/03**: 230–233.

Versteege, H.M.J. and J.B. Vos (DHV) (1995), *Verhandelbare Emissierechten in het Nederlandse Verzuringsbeleid [Tradable Emission Permits in Dutch Acidification Policy]*, Air and Energy Publication Series nr. 116, Department of VROM.

VMD, Werkgroep Water [Environmental Defense, Working Group Water] (1976), *Milieheffing: Betalen of niet? [Environmental Charge: To Pay or not to Pay?]*, Vereniging MilieuDefensie, Amsterdam.

VMD, Werkgroep Water [Environmental Defense, Working Group Water] (1979), *Schoonwaterboek [Clean Water Book]*, Vereniging MilieuDefensie, Amsterdam.

VNO and NCW [Confederation of Netherlands Industry and Employers] (1992), 'Commentaar rapport Wolfson [Comment on the Wolfson report]', Letter to the Minister of EZ, 14/05/92.

Wallart, Nicolas and Beat Bürgenmeier (1996), 'L'acceptabilité des taxes incitatives en Suisse [The acceptability of incentive charges in Switzerland]', *Swiss Journal of Economics and Statistics* **132**: 3–30.

Welch, W.P. (1983), 'The political feasibility of full ownership property rights: The case of pollution and fisheries', *Policy Sciences* **16**: 165–180.

White, Lawrence J. (1976), 'Effluent charges as a faster means of achieving pollution abatement', *Public Policy* **24**: 111–125.

Williamson, Oliver E. (1963), 'A model of rational managerial behavior', in: R.M. Cyert and J.G. March (eds), *A Behavioral Theory of the Firm*, Prentice Hall, Englewood Cliffs, 237–252.

Williamson, Oliver E. (1964), *The Economics of Discretionary Behavior: Managerial Objectives in the Theory of the Firm*, Prentice Hall, Englewood Cliffs.

Wirtz, Wim (1992), '"Ik sta dus ook achter minister Andriessen" ["So I support Minister Andriessen"]', *Volkskrant* **11/02**.

Wittman, Donald (1995), *The Myth of Democratic Failure: Why Political Institutions Are Efficient,* University of Chicago Press, Chicago.

WRR [Scientific Council for Government Policy] (1992), *Milieubeleid: Strategie, Instrumenten en Handhaafbaarheid [Environmental Policy: Strategy, Instruments and Enforceability],* Sdu, The Hague.

Yohe, Gary W. (1976), 'Comment on polluters' profits and political response', *American Economic Review* **66**: 981–982.

Zeckhauser, Richard (1981), 'Preferred policies when there is concern for probability of adoption', *Journal of Environmental Economics and Management* **8**: 215–238.

Index